The Global Political Economy

The Global Political Economy

Perspectives, Problems, and Policies

Stephen Gill and David Law

The Johns Hopkins University Press
Baltimore

The Johns Hopkins University Press
2715 North Charles Street
Baltimore, Maryland 21218-4319

Library of Congress Cataloging-in-Publication Data

Gill, Stephen, 1950–
  The global political economy.

  Bibliography: p.
  Includes index.
  1. International economic relations. 2. International
trade. 3. International finance. 4. International
business enterprises. 5. East-West trade (1945–   )
6. Commercial policy. 7. Economic policy. I. Law,
David, 1946–   . II. Title.
HF1359.G55 1988   337   88-45409
ISBN 0–8018–3763–4
ISBN 0–8018–3764–2 (pbk.)

A catalog record for this book is available from the British Library.

To our parents

Contents

List of Tables

List of Figures

Acknowledgements

The nature of this book is such that we owe an intellectual debt to many writers. We hope that we have done justice to their ideas and insights, and of course, we are responsible for any errors in this respect. In particular, we have been stimulated by the writings of Robert Cox and the late Fred Hirsch. We would also like to express our special appreciation to Dr Neil Malcolm, Professor Susan Strange and an anonymous American reviewer for valuable comments on drafts of this book. In his inimitable and sometimes indirect way, Dr Steve Smith has been a consistent ally and supporter of our efforts, and we would like to thank him for this. We are also grateful for the consistent and kind support given by Wheatsheaf Books. Although Stephen Gill bore the burden of most of the typing, we would like to thank Jill Kirby for typing and support whilst this book has been written.

Preface

We have written this book as a contribution to the understanding and development of the study of international political economy. The book is a response to our dissatisfaction with the textbooks which have sought to define the field of study for students. Our dissatisfaction stems from two major sources: their inadequate theoretical exposition and the limited range of their substantive analysis.

One text, *The Politics of Global Economic Relations* by David Blake and Robert Walters introduced rival perspectives (liberal and 'radical') in a stimulating way.[1] However, the authors did not take this approach further in subsequent editions, thereby neglecting significant theoretical developments. In the late 1970s and the first half of the 1980s, the best-selling text in this field was *The Politics of International Economic Relations* by Joan Spero.[2] She consciously restricted her approach to the way in which politics shapes international economic relations. In so doing she often neglected the ways in which economic changes and structures shape political forces. Her book was written from a single, 'managerial' perspective, organised around 'issue areas'. In contrast, our approach is based upon a range of competing liberal, realist and Marxist perspectives. These include recent developments in the public choice literature and game theory, as well as in Gramscian historical materialism.[3] In this respect we go well beyond Robert Gilpin's well-argued realist approach in *The Political Economy of International Relations*.[4] In addition, our analysis stresses the ways in which perspectives are themselves one of the interacting social forces in the political economy, as well as a basis for theories which seek to explain it (see our chapter 2 on the nature and evaluation of perspectives).

Apart from their inadequate treatment of perspectives, another shortcoming of the main texts (and much of the literature in the academic journals) is a lack of attention, not only to the links between *military* developments and those in the economic and political structures, but also to the nature and international orientations of communist states. Whereas military rivalry is largely the province of students of strategic studies and international politics, political economists tend to avoid integrating strategic rivalries into their analysis of the global political economy. At most, theorists usually discuss military questions with reference to East-West and superpower relations.[5] We seek to begin to redress this tendency in our book, especially in chapter 8, on military-industrial rivalry, and chapter 15 on communist states. Given the economic and military weight of the Soviet Union and China, we think that a detailed examination of the place of these states within the global system is essential. This point has taken on added significance because of the economic reforms within these and other communist states during the 1970s and 1980s. Neglect of communist states and the military-industrial question is a major source of disappointment with previous texts. Another limitation of all of the texts so far mentioned is their failure to discuss long-term questions concerning the interaction between the ecological and the military, political and economic structures. Whilst being unable, at least in this edition, comprehensively to deal with this issue, we none the less discuss it, especially in our concluding chapter.

1. POLITICS AND ECONOMICS: A CONTESTED RELATIONSHIP

We see political economy as an integrated field that encompasses the specialised disciplines of politics, economics and international relations. In conventional terms, political economy requires analysis of both the way in which politics shapes the economy, and of the way in which the economy shapes politics. More fundamentally, political economy requires analysis of the way in which ideas about what constitutes the *political* and the *economic* have emerged historically. Indeed, the notion of the 'economy' as something autonomous is a contestable abstraction. The social grounding of the concept of an autonomous economy is bound up with a particular set of theoretical ideas, economic and political institutions, and historical forces. It was not until the rise of capitalism in Europe during the eighteenth century that such a concept arose. Hence this liberal concept of the economy is historically specific, and is related to the rise of certain ideological, economic and political forces which began to assert themselves at this time.

Often the conception of the economy is identified with the working of markets, while politics is associated with the state and authoritative action. Whilst it is frequently acknowledged that the state (consisting of the institutions of government) is a socially created institution, forged by the application of human intention and collective consciousness, this idea is more controversial when applied to the market. Is the market such a social institution?

Liberal advocates of capitalism, such as von Hayek, like to stress the spontaneous, orderly and efficient character of markets.[6] Sometimes this is contrasted with the inefficient, self-seeking and exploitative character of state institutions. By contrast, various critics of unregulated capitalism (be they Keynesians, Marxists or ecologists) highlight the dangers, social inefficiency and even injustices of allowing too much freedom to markets. Such critics often place considerable faith in the state's potential for rational and benevolent planning of the economy. At issue, of course, are not simply technical questions concerning management of the economy but rather the questions of which is the most desirable social order, and for whose benefit? Thus the issue of state and market is necessarily linked to questions of political philosophy.

Political philosophers, in their attempts to suggest the contours of the good society inevitably make assumptions concerning human nature, particularly the degree to which this is fixed, or can change under different social conditions. Liberals, in the tradition of Hobbes, Locke and von Hayek, hold an essentialist view of human nature as relatively fixed. Hence the range of possible social institutions is conditioned and limited. In this view, human beings act as rational individualists who enter into social relationships primarily for reasons of self interest. Economic institutions are formed by the spontaneous aggregation of these individual actions, whereas the state is the conscious product of a collective human will, for example in Hobbes' concept of the *Leviathan*. The state acts in a negative way, that is as a protector of individual freedoms and ensures social order. This permits, in Adam Smith's phrase, a society where people will be able follow their natural 'propensity to barter, truck and trade'. By contrast, some recent advocates of capitalism see the state as playing a more positive, though perhaps temporary role in fostering a market-orientated 'enterprise culture'.

Other traditions, notably Marxism, see human nature as protean and historically conditioned: social circumstances, rather than innate possessive individualism is the key force which creates a given outlook and set of social predispositions or propensities. The structure and scope of markets is an important aspect of such conditions, especially as it affects the balance of power between capital and labour (see our chapter 7 on the structural power of capital). In this tradition, the state can be used creatively to reconstruct the social conditions of existence and allow for the emergence of a more collective and internationalist outlook, one which does not rest upon, to use Hobbes' phrase, an endless struggle of 'all against all'. Marxists argue that the unfettered market inevitably allows the fittest to dominate and to exploit others: in a market society individuals cannot therefore all freely pursue their natural propensity to trade and exchange.

Each of these positions, when discussing the nature and desirability of markets and reliance on state institutions, is, therefore, implicitly advocating a set of social and political objectives, as well as making assumptions concerning the limits to change in basic motivations and social attitudes. What this implies is that beneath the contestability of the concepts of the 'economic' and the 'political' lies a philosophical debate, a debate which has had world-historical consequences during the last four hundred years. Each of the positions on economy, state and the malleability of human nature implies a different kind of society. Each seeks, either implicitly or explicitly, to either substantially change the social world, or to effectively preserve its established, inherent or spontaneous features.

2. THE NEED FOR AN INTEGRATED APPROACH

The case for an integrated political economy approach can be made with reference to issues and policies, as well as to political philosophies and competing ideologies. We use the examples of the growth of United States military expenditures in the 1980s and of the foreign economic relations of South Africa to show why the conventional divisions of *domestic* and *international* politics and economics need to be overcome for purposes of analysis and policy-making. Our brief examination of these examples also reveals the limitations of analysis which focuses narrowly on 'issue-areas'.

The post-war period has witnessed a relentless rise in military expenditures which, whilst not immediately obvious, can be partly linked in recent years to the debt crisis. The United States' military build-up of the 1980s (the largest ever in peacetime), was a response to a perceived relative increase in Soviet military power during the previous decade. Despite the East–West security concerns which appear to have motivated this build-up, some of its major effects were structural and can only be understood in the context of increasingly integrated global capital markets. Many of its indirect victims were people in debt-ridden developing nations. Of these, the worst hit were the poorest sections of their populations. One major reason for the debt crisis was because the American military build-up led to a rising government budget deficit, which was partly financed by a large inflow of foreign capital to the United States, diverting capital away from developing countries. This led to much higher real interest rates than had prevailed in the 1970s, on a world-wide basis. In response to this situation, the governments of many developing nations implemented domestic austerity programmes, cutting living standards. A major reason for this was that their debt-servicing costs rose considerably, as capital inflows declined. The International Monetary Fund was often instrumental in pressing for such programmes.

The size of United States budget deficits reflected not just high military spending but an unwillingness to raise taxes and cut other types of expenditure. Thus whilst many American consumers – already very wealthy by world standards – enjoyed a spending-spree partly financed by the savings of other countries, the poor of many parts of the Third World were forced to suffer ever greater privations and malnutrition, and their countries' development programmes were undermined through lack of finance. This perverse situation was bound up with the increased global integration of the world's capital and exchange markets, as well as America's apparently ceaseless appetite for consumption and arms. It also reflected the fact that the United States was a safe haven for capital, particularly flight capital removed from countries which were perceived as particularly unstable and their policies unsustainable. Notable instances of such policies were high government spending on strategic industries. Third World governments hoped that these policies would help to create national military and industrial strength.

The above example illustrates how the domestic politics of the world's leading economic and military power can have wide-ranging effects on the domestic political economies of other nations. In Brazil, the debt crisis led to political uncertainty, reflected in the successive resignations of finance ministers. In the case of the Philippines, the end of the Marcos regime, which, for many years, had been supported by the United States, was hastened by its mounting burden of debt. However, sometimes the 'domestic politics' of countries much less powerful than the United States can have global repercussions. A controversial example of this is South Africa.

The ongoing debate over the future of apartheid and white supremacy in South Africa has gone far beyond the 'domestic' politics of one strife-torn country. It has spilled over into debates at the United Nations and into arguments between members of the British Commonwealth. Whilst not all domestic political issues have an international aspect, the range of such interrelated domestic-international issues would appear to have grown since 1945. This growth has been made possible by the spread of communications, as well as closer economic and sometimes military linkages on an international scale. For example, in the United States, the anti-apartheid lobby (a wide coalition of political groups) helped to put sanctions against South Africa onto the domestic political agenda. Even some Western conservative politicians came to see the need for major reforms in South Africa. This was partly in order to avoid chaos, further bloodshed and the potential for a communist-led revolution. For most Western politicians the apartheid debate was not just about justice and civil rights, but about the East–West balance of power, and the long-term security of, and scope for, foreign investment by transnational corporations in Southern Africa.

The debate over sanctions involved reference to first, the internal workings of South African politics. Secondly, it involved the place of South Africa in the inter-state system, and thirdly, the links between the world economy and that of South Africa. The first category included questions about the response to sanctions of various groups, parties and political movements in South Africa. The second related to questions about the geopolitical importance of South Africa, in terms of East–West rivalry and Southern African political stability. It also included the issue of the political legitimacy of the West in the eyes of many Third World countries, who wished to see sanctions imposed effectively, and who might take measures against Western firms. The economic weakness, and often the political instability of most Black African countries, meant, however, that the West generally had little to fear on this score. The third category included questions about the impact of sanctions on output, employment and the balance of payments, both of South Africa, of neighbouring countries (whose economies were highly dependent on South Africa), and of those countries which actually impose and enforce sanctions. Central to such questions was the trade in strategic minerals exported by South Africa to the West and Japan, and for which, in many cases, the main alternative supplier was the Soviet Union. Knowledge of the economic impact of sanctions is a prerequisite for understanding political responses within South Africa.

Thus the two examples discussed above would seem to cut across the conventional divide between 'domestic' and 'international' politics, and also the divide between 'international politics' and 'international economics'. Further, the South African issue affects non-governmental organisations such as foreign manufacturing and mining companies (should they continue to invest and operate there), foreign banks (should they go on lending to South Africa), and churches (should they use such banks and hold shares in companies with South African connections). In the case of churches there was a considerable controversy over whether they should give financial support to black organisations opposed to apartheid.

Thus a political economy analysis should not be narrowly limited to relations between nation-states and their governments. It needs to be global as well as international in character. Hence our preference for the term *global political economy* rather than the more commonly-used term *international political economy*. This preference does not imply, however, that we consider to be unimportant the wide variety of national political traditions and institutions. Such national structures can be major obstacles to international cooperation, as with disputes over agricultural trade. Further, the structure of state institutions must always be taken into account when considering the determinants of policy-making.[7] Our approach should not be confused, therefore, with the tendency in some of the literature to undervalue the importance of the state in national and global political economy.

As we have noted, there is a case for considering an integrated political economy as the object of analysis. Here our examples illustrate the need to take a conception of the *global* political economy as the key ontological entity, that is as the object to be theorised and explained. This case for a global perspective is reinforced by examination of some ethical aspects of the contemporary global system. In the past, philosophers such as Kant attempted to theorise the conditions under which a perpetual peace between nations might be possible. Kant's conception was, however, a limited one, applied to the conditions of his epoch: he was concerned with the prevention of war, so that peaceful commerce and interaction between peoples might take place, whilst each retained its national institutions and identity. The problem which Kant addressed, is, of course, still with us. The world, however, has changed, necessitating a more far-reaching concept of the good society at the international level. This conception, from a political point of view, must be more positive and global in nature. In a world where nuclear weapons, integrated capital markets, and global ecological threats have scant regard for national boundaries, a global concept is more and more needed to make sense of world society, and purposefully to act to shape it.[8] Even the primarily national questions of politics (which formed the basis for Kant's conception of the perpetual peace) have now taken on a global aspect, as our South African example illustrates. In the context of global mass communications, people cannot help but be more aware of the circumstances of others.

3. TWO THEMES OF THIS BOOK

It is easy to state that a global system of political economy has come into being. It is quite another problem to theorise and understand it. In this book, our efforts to do so focus on the elaboration of two major themes. These are partly reflected in the examples we have discussed above. In such examples, we see systematic and, to a certain extent, contradictory forces at work. Our first theme relates to social forces which are primarily economic in nature, our second to such forces which are bound up with security. The themes are:

(a) The Transnationalisation of the Economy.

This involves the globalisation of production, capital and technology flows, and the growth in the world trade, often through the operations of transnational companies. It can also be related to a tendency towards a globalisation of certain aspects of culture, involving the question of which values and ideologies would be most likely to promote the spread of transnational firms. Other key questions concern the effect on governments and the world economy of huge flows of short-term capital; the structural power and influence of transnational corporations, and the consequences of transnationalisation on the rise and fall of countries in the inter-state system. This later issue is also related to the question of hegemony and order in the global political economy, seen not only in terms of the dominance of one state in an inter-state system, but also in terms of the rising power and hegemony of internationally-mobile, transnational capital.

In addition, we would argue that some aspects of the structure in the post-1945 period are different, in certain qualitative and quantitative respects, from earlier stages in the evolution of the global political economy. These correspond to what we call the emerging 'transnational stage' in the development of capitalism.

(b) Military-Industrial Rivalry

This is bound up with what is conventionally referred to as the security structure. It is also linked to production, knowledge/technology and exchange structures, as well as to threats to the ecosystem and to the survival of the species. A peculiarity of the post-war system has been the development and spread of nuclear weapons, as well as of certain types of chemical and biological weapons which threaten the survival of massive numbers of people, and possibly of *homo sapiens*. More generally there has been an immense diffusion of the technologies of mass destruction. We examine the limits to militarisation as well as the forces behind its spread. Further, we relate military-industrial rivalry to the existence and orientation of state structures which can sometimes serve to limit the power of capital.

In addition, we consider there is a third theme of mounting importance to which we would have liked to have paid more attention in this book, not least since it is crucial in the appraisal of future prospects. Whilst ecological aspects have always been potentially global, the processes associated with those which predominate in our two major themes have served to accelerate the global ecological changes we have in mind. These include the use and threat of nuclear power, both military and civilian, resource depletion and pollution of the ecosphere.

4. THE ORGANISATION AND USE OF THIS BOOK

Whilst the themes are intended to give continuity and coherence to this book, it has also been organised in a way which places the question of theory and method at the outset, followed by applied analysis. It has also been constructed so as to facilitate selected use according to the varying backgrounds and interests of different readers.

Its basic structure is as follows. Part I builds a theoretical and conceptual apparatus. Part II elaborates aspects of our two main themes. Part III applies this apparatus in more detail to the post-1945 period. Part IV discusses prospects and problems. The sequence of chapters in Part III generally corresponds to the structural aspects of the global political economy, and our view of their relative importance. For example, we see the question of international oil supplies (which tended to preoccupy writers in the 1970s) as of less importance than the general tendency for transnational corporations to spread and for monetary interdependence to grow.

Given that the themes of this book concern changes which are global in character, we see our volume as potentially useful, in whole or in part, for a wide range of students of the social and human sciences, notably politics, economics, international studies and sociology. It is also useful for students of international business, international organisations, and the growing number of those with a specific focus on international political economy itself. For business people and trade unionists, the conventional academic distinction between politics and economics is of limited value. For practical purposes they have to be constantly interested in trends in the global political economy and variations in the 'business climate' (which is, of course, also a political concept: we discuss this at length in chapter 7).

In consequence, our book is intended to be useful for students of varied levels and disciplinary backgrounds. Upper-level undergraduates, pursuing, say, a one-semester length theory course in international political economy might make full use of Parts I and II, whilst a more applied course might focus on Parts III and IV. A full-length post-graduate course should use all of the book. A course concerned primarily with the advanced capitalist countries could leave out chapters 14 and 15. A course oriented towards less-developed countries could use parts of chapters 5 to 8, and chapters 13 to 15. Courses on socialist states in the world system would find chapter 15 particularly useful, as well as chapters 5 and 9. Courses in international business would benefit from using chapters 6, 7 and 10 to 12.

The Global Political Economy

NOTES

1. D. H. Blake and R. S. Walters, *The Politics of Global Economic Relations* (Englewood Cliffs NJ, Prentice-Hall, 1976).
2. J. E. Spero, *The Politics of International Economic Relations* (London, Allen and Unwin, 1985) 3rd edition.
3. R. W. Cox, *Production, Power, and World Order: Social Forces in the Making of History* (New York, Columbia University Press, 1987).
4. R. Gilpin, *The Political Economy of International Relations* (Princeton NJ, Princeton University Press, 1987).
5. An exception to this is: G. Sen, *The Military Origins of Industrialisation and International Trade Rivalry* (London, Frances Pinter, 1984).
6. See for example, F. A. von Hayek, *Knowledge, Evolution and Society* (London, Adam Smith Institute, 1983).
7. P. B. Evans, D. Rueschemeyer and T. Skocpol (eds), *Bringing the State Back In* (Cambridge, Cambridge University Press, 1985).
8. See for example, J. W. Burton, *World Society* (London and New York, Cambridge University Press, 1972).

PART I
PERSPECTIVES AND CONCEPTS

1 Towards an Integrated Global Political Economy

1. INTRODUCTION

In this chapter we examine the way in which the 'political' and the 'economic' have been separated and integrated by political economists in different historical periods. In so doing, we examine some of the origins of various attempts at political economy analysis in international studies, as well as approaches which are current at the time of writing. The major purpose of this is to point towards certain issues and problems of integrating 'politics' and 'economics'. A further purpose is to explain why there has been a surge of new work in this field since the early 1970s, particularly in the USA.

2. ECONOMICS, POLITICS AND INTERNATIONAL STUDIES

While the emergence of international political economy as a self-conscious field of study took place in the 1970s, the roots of a political economy approach go back centuries. Furthermore, some of the earliest attempts at integrating politics and economics, namely by the Mercantilists, took a particular interest in analysing international economic relations. The belated 'birth' of international political economy is all the more ironic in that, in the nineteenth century, another attempt at such analysis had been begun by Marx and his associates. This Marxist tradition was expanded in the early twentieth century by Social Democrats and other Marxist thinkers in their analysis of (capitalist) imperialism. Such an irony should also alert the reader to the fact that there has been, until recently, a consistent lack of dialogue between different traditions in this field of study.

The historical gap between early efforts to develop international political economy and those of the 1970s and 1980s is especially marked

3

for writers from the Anglo-Saxon countries, notably the USA. In these countries (and others) there was increasing specialisation in social science from the early nineteenth to the middle of the twentieth centuries. This encompassed a growing separation within the field of political economy into 'political science' and 'economics', and also between 'domestic' and 'international' studies. Even within international studies, a distinction was made between 'high' and 'low' politics, with the former focusing on questions of diplomacy and security, and the latter on certain economic questions relating to trade, money and foreign investment.

This trend towards specialisation in the Anglo-Saxon world (which extended to the European continent) was partly reversed in the 1970s when a number of political scientists and economists collaborated in writings which provided a new stimulus towards a more integrated political economy approach. One example was the whole issue of the leading American journal in the field of international political economy, *International Organisation* in Volume 29 (1975). Another was the collection of articles, edited by Leon Lindberg, called *Stress and Contradiction in Modern Capitalism.*[1] This book brought together Marxists, Liberals and Conservatives in a consideration of the comparative problems of advanced capitalist societies. Given the traditional lack of dialogue between these viewpoints this suggested the possibility of a revival of a broad-based political economy such as existed at the time of Adam Smith, when economics was not so clearly separated from politics (and moral philosophy) as it is today. Smith saw such fields as complementary in his two main works, *The Wealth of Nations* and his earlier *The Theory of Moral Sentiments*.

One of the purposes of Smith's new method and approach to political economy was to challenge the dominance of mercantilist thought, which, he argued, helped to undermine the potential for widespread economic growth. For Smith, the mercantilists exaggerated the importance of the national power of a given country relative to others, rather than the general economic conditions and institutions which could be of general benefit to all. Mercantilists placed 'uneconomic' stress on the importance of national security, so that the wealth of the nation (and implicitly of all nations practising such policies) would be curtailed in the long term. In Smith's view, the potential gains to be made from interdependence and specialisation were considerable.

None the less, Smith was willing to concede that, ultimately, defence was of much more importance than 'opulence'. Thus even this early in the evolution of political economy as a field of study, there were signs of an awareness of the tension between the two themes mentioned in the preface: militarisation and transnationalisation. The former can be related to a mercantilist stress on the importance of strong defence and national security, the latter to the importance of liberal international economic conditions and the economic gains from interdependence.

In mercantilism, integration of the political and the economic was based upon the primacy of politics. The supreme goal of politics was national security and external autonomy. As a consequence, the central objective of state policy was the building-up of national power. On the other hand, Smith opened the way towards a separation of 'politics' and 'economics' by highlighting the apparently spontaneous coordination of economic activity which might be achieved through the market mechanism, as if by an 'invisible hand'. This stress on the market suggested the conditions for the relative autonomy of economic forces. If governments were willing, then markets could become self-regulating. This would be achieved through the balancing of supply and demand by means of market signals such as prices, queues and order books. Smith saw, in ideal terms, a specialised role for the state as a 'nightwatchman', namely providing the conditions under which markets could be allowed to operate as freely as possible. Thus a state would need to provide law and order, defence, property rights and a stable currency. In the terminology of modern economics, these are seen as 'public goods' which are jointly supplied to all within a country.

Moreover, in contrast to the Mercantilists, Smith's approach laid emphasis on the individual as the primary unit in the analysis of political economy. This individualism is seen in his definition of the market as an institution which consisted of the aggregation of the separate and differentiated actions of countless individuals, responding as rationally as possible to economic choices. Such choices, as in decisions to buy or to sell, when taken together, formed the market. Seen as a whole, however, the market forms a pattern of incentives and signals which structure the behaviour of individual buyers and sellers. In this way, there was a systematic tendency for apparently self-seeking individual actions (based on the pursuit of material gain) to produce socially beneficial outcomes. Thus the individualistic method was accompanied by a recognition of the importance of (market) structures.

Basic to the analysis of Smith was a new method in political economy. For Smith, this consisted of theorising a set of relationships which were not self-evident in contemporary practices in order to highlight the structures latent in existing conditions. As has been noted, Smith hoped that this might lead to the modification of policies in more economically beneficial ways. This method contrasts with that of mercantilist thinkers who were being implicitly criticised by Smith for concentrating too much on the surface of things and for not pursuing the implications of the distinction between appearance and essence in social analysis. This was necessary to identify more fully the key structures of the political economy.

After Smith, David Ricardo further developed this method of abstract theorising in a way that separated the 'economy' and the 'polity'. Karl Marx was impressed by Ricardo's analysis of the economic order amidst the apparent anarchy of the market. Marx saw this as a 'scientific' advance. Part of the reason why Marx was so impressed by Ricardo was the latter's division of the economy into categories of land, labour and capital, each with its associated classes whose interests were seen to be in conflict. Ricardo's advocacy of free trade involved an attack on the vested interests of the landlord class, who maintained high food prices through protectionist policies. However, Marx criticised Ricardo's class analysis as incomplete, since it failed to examine fully the more fundamental conflict between capital and labour.

Marx thought Ricardo's analysis went too far in its abstraction since the social and political framework of production relations was generally neglected. More fundamentally, Ricardo (and Smith) had neglected the social relations of production. Smith and Ricardo had not completely neglected the political framework of exchange (the latter became a Member of Parliament) since they had allowed for the notion of vested interests. However, Ricardo tended to see economic conflicts as taking place at the level of exchange, e.g. through the terms of trade between landlord and tenant, or agriculture and the rest of the economy. Thus what was missing from Ricardo's writing was a theorisation of the social relations of production:

In money relationships in the developed exchange system ... individuals appear to be ... independent, that is to collide with one another freely and to barter within the limits of this freedom. They appear so, however, only to someone who abstracts from the conditions of existence in which these individuals come into contact ... close investigation of these external circumstances or conditions shows, however, how impossible it is for the individuals forming part of a class etc., to surmount them *en masse* without abolishing them.[2]

Beyond the notion of market structure, Marx was seeking to establish one of a wider social structure. In Marx's approach, it is, in the last analysis, impossible to separate politics, economics and society. For example, capitalist society was divided up into conflicting classes, formed by their relationship with the social relations and forces of production. These forces and relations shaped, and were themselves shaped by the political order. To understand the nature of society, integrated analysis was necessary. Thus for Marx, the concept of the 'economic' was different from that of Smith and Ricardo. Whereas the economic substructure for Marx involved the social relations of production, with the exertion of power by one class over another, for the followers of Smith and Ricardo (those who Marx called the 'vulgar economists'), the 'economy' tended to be equated with the sphere of the market, which was treated as something relatively autonomous.

In consequence, according to Marx, to portray the 'economic world' as one of free choice and equal rights of participation was misleading, especially when the pressures of competition resulted in 'laws' of demand and supply. At any given moment in time, market forces seemed to appear eternal, and thus to operate as if there were no alternative to existing economic institutions. This was because the nature of the politico-economic structure was lost in the process of constructing liberal economic abstractions. Marx suggested that the work of the vulgar economists, and its representation of these ideas in newspapers and everyday life, served to make workers less aware of their collective potential, and thus to subordinate the working class to the rule of capital. Thus the very individualistic and market-oriented tendency which flourished in economics after the 'Marginal Revolution' of the late nineteenth century implicitly served to limit the growth of (revolutionary) class consciousness. Hence for Marxists, this was an *ideological* gain for the capitalist class.

Within Marxism, however, the integration of politics and economics has varied in character. On the one hand, there are those writers such as Engels and Lenin whose analysis of capitalist societies laid heavy emphasis on the determination of politics by economic forces (the latter paradoxically stressing the relative autonomy of political forces in the revolutionary situation in Russia). On the other hand, Marxists, such as Perry Anderson and Antonio Gramsci, have stressed the crucial importance of politics and ideology in the development of capitalism.[3]

In each of the three traditions under consideration, the nature of, and limits to, the integration between politics and economics has been intimately bound up with the basic abstractions and main units of analysis and interaction. While the Mercantilists focused on the nation and the interactions between states, the Liberal economists focused on the individual in the market-place, and Marxists on production and class conflict.

3. RECENT DEVELOPMENTS IN THE FIELD

As we have noted, there was an upsurge in the literature in the field during the 1970s, and this has continued. Much of this was American. There are two types of reason for this. The first was bound up with changes in the world economy, and the related perceptions of the implications of this for the USA. The second was related to the changes in the academic community which occurred partly as a response to the 'real' changes in economic conditions. Some changes, for example in development studies had, of course, preceded the 1970s.

The first reason was that growing economic interdependence was beginning to have significant effects on US policy, as well as that of other nations. This development was reflected in Richard Cooper's influential book, *The Economics of Interdependence*.[4] American theorists sought to analyse the implications of the so-called 'breakdown' of the Bretton Woods international economic order, and the costs of the rise in oil prices after 1973. What had been seen as 'low politics' moved up the political agenda. Such concerns were amplified since the 1970s also witnessed economic stagnation and recession, rising inflation and unemployment, and an apparent end to the long post-war boom. These changes in economic conditions (as well as other changes), in the context of a declining US share of world gross national product (GNP), were interpreted as providing evidence for the view that US economic and political leadership was being eroded. Thus, amongst some American leaders there was a perception of the need to promote a 'smooth management of interdependence', in order to sustain US control over significant international economic outcomes. The perceived loss of US ascendancy was also reflected in the creation of the international private forum, the Trilateral Commission. This institution was composed of leading elements from international business, politics, the media and academia, drawn from North America, Western Europe and Japan.

The Commission claimed that its rationale involved treating the Europeans and the Japanese as 'equal partners' with the North Americans. This was because the balance of international economic power appeared to have shifted away from the USA towards Western Europe and Japan, at the same time as each of the three major poles of developed capitalism were becoming increasingly interdependent. This interdependence was economic, political, cultural and, to an extent, military in nature. In an interdependent global political economy, a growing economic crisis would necessarily have collective repercussions for these wealthy states, as well as for others within the system.

The more academic sources of the resurgence of international political economy were varied in character. We do not intend to cover all of these here, but none the less they included: (i) the emergence of neo-classical political economy analysis; (ii) the revival of Marxist analysis; (iii) the emergence of 'development studies' and concern over 'North–South' relations; (iv) increasing awareness and analysis of international constraints on national policies, expressed in the growing literature which emerged in the 1970s on international interdependence, as well as in dependency theory which developed during the 1960s; and (v) the comparative socio-historical approach, drawing its inspiration from the work of writers such as Barrington Moore.[5] We shall now review some of these approaches and indicate some of their key concepts.

Let us begin our review of developments in the literature by examining some of the developments in mainstream liberal economic analysis. In recent years orthodox economic analysis, grounded in the marginalist tradition of Alfred Marshall and Leon Walras, has been in a state of flux, particularly in macroeconomics. Conflict has raged between Keynesians, monetarists and the new classical economists over the role and limits to macroeconomic policy, and the best instruments to achieve policy objectives. However, for a considerable period mainstream debate did little to question the assumption that the state was external to the basic workings of the economy. Thus 'economics' was separated from 'politics', at least in their analysis. The state was effectively viewed as the mechanism through which policy objectives were resolved. These objectives were then assumed to be implemented by a technocratic cadre of experts who were viewed as being politically neutral. The Keynesian concern was with 'fine-tuning' the economy, whereas monetarists began to question the scope for, and desirability of, discretionary use of monetary and fiscal policy.

The monetarism versus Keynesianism debate was not principally concerned with the analysis of production relations. The debate tended to assume that an intrinsic conflict between, for example, capital and labour either did not exist or had been resolved, although it was allowed that a struggle over the distribution of income (in the form of wages and profits) in the economy was an ongoing issue. Much of the problem was seen in terms of the way rival groups of workers, through their trades unions, tended to push for increased wages for their members, such that there was a tendency for wages to rise ahead of productivity, as one group sought to maintain its wage position relative to others. Thus economic conflict was seen primarily in group terms. Monetarists like Milton Friedman saw such 'wage-inflation' pressures as of minor importance, arguing that they could not be sustained without a continuing monetary expansion. Friedman even went so far as to propose a 'monetary constitution' which would involve a statute specifying the rate of increase of the money supply.[6] This proposal implied the need for a political economy approach to the problem of inflation. The debate on the sources of inflationary pressure in the 1970s came to be related to other work on the 'economics of' democracy, bureaucracy and constitutions.[7] This was strikingly evident in the influential article by Samuel Brittan, 'The Economic Contradictions of Democracy'.[8] Brittan examined the demand for and supply of economic policies, and claimed that there was a tendency towards excess demand. This tendency was amplified by the processes of liberal democratic politics, which generated increasing expectations on the part of voters about what governments could and should do to increase voters' material and social rewards. These pressures help to generate budget deficits, excessive monetary growth and persistent inflation.

More recent developments in macroeconomics, notably in the debate over the 'new classical' rational expectations hypothesis, have highlighted the interdependent role of public expectations, and the potential economic policies of governments. The behaviour of financial markets (which involves estimates concerning future risks and potential profit yields) is crucially influenced by expectations of which policies governments are likely to pursue. This involves not just the general question of what type of 'investment climate' will be promoted, but also the more specific questions related to which party will be in government and the economic policies it will pursue. Thus the workings of the political process are important in analysing the political economy at two levels: first, in explaining the adoption of particular policies, and secondly, through the influence of the ideas that people (notably wealth-holders) have concerning the effects of the political process on economic conditions. The rational expectations hypothesis assumes that such individuals develop a model explaining policy formation and implementation, enabling them to forecast political and economic developments.

The New Classical theorists assume that people's forecasts are quite successful, errors being random in character. This assumption implies the existence of, and general popular access to a 'basically correct' model of politico-economic behaviour of expectations about governments, firms and households. In practice, economists and governments disagree over what this model is! Since much investment is international in nature and capital markets are linked, such models need to encompass the behaviour of foreign governments, especially those where capital is to be invested, and more generally those whose economies are the largest and most important in the global political economy. Thus any adequate theory of expectations has to encompass both the 'national' and 'international' level. Rational expectations theorists have so far done little to construct an economic policy model. However, analysis of the political process has been a feature of the work of public choice theorists, most of whom have been economists. None the less, public choice theory has increasingly engaged the interest of people from a politics and international relations background. This literature has highlighted the concepts of international 'public goods' (such as collective defence systems among nations) and the attendant 'free rider' problem (e.g. some states[s] gaining security without paying its fair share of the cost of provision). Indeed, these liberal concepts have been used by neo-realist writers in their discussion of the problem of international order, particularly in the Theory of Hegemonic Stability and the ensuing debate. Theoretical dialogue and exchange between politics, economics and international relations has been facilitated by the growing understanding and use of game theory.

While recent writers within the realist tradition of international studies have drawn on liberal international economics, others have stayed closer to the traditional mercantilist aspects of realism, for example writers such as Robert Gilpin and David Calleo. They have attempted to analyse the implications of the operations of transnational corporations and of the US state for US domestic economic strength and for its international power.[9] Indeed, some American writers in the 1970s, such as Stephen Krasner, wondered whether there was not too much international economic interdependence.[10] From Europe, the work of Susan Strange on international monetary relations, and Wolfgang Hager on trade and protectionism, are examples of this tradition, especially as it involves a distrust of unrestrained market forces. However, in their case this may reflect more of a concern with social welfare than with national security as it is conventionally defined by Realists.[11]

The Marxist tradition has always used an integrated political economy approach and in the last twenty years has helped to generate new insights in the field. The post-war economic success of the capitalist countries and the often glaring shortcomings of the Soviet state were a challenge to Marxian theorists. Particular attention has been paid to the analysis of the capitalist state (whose size and scope had clearly grown since the 1940s) and the global 'logic' of the evolving capitalist system. The new forms of Marxism had to account for the rise and impact of the transnational corporations and the position of the new Asian and African states in the global political economy. Journals were started in which new ideas and critical debate could flourish.[12] Thus, when in the 1970s the growth of the capitalist countries faltered, inflation rates soared, unemployment rose and the rate of profit fell, there was a growing body of Marxist analysis for other social scientists to examine. It should be noted that Marxist ideas have themselves influenced developments in the Third World, for example, the Chinese Revolution of 1949, and more generally the appeal of planned industrialisation across a range of countries. This illustrates why what we call perspectives are not merely explanations of the global political economy, but are part of it. This point is developed in the following chapter.

A growing number of Marxists have paid attention to the role of ideas and culture, not just at the national, but also at the international and transnational levels. Some writers have found inspiration in the ideas and theories of Gramsci. In particular, Gramsci's theory of hegemony and the political mobilisation of nations and classes have been applied and extended by some contemporary writers, notably Robert Cox in his analysis of international relations.[13] Gramsci theory has become influential in helping to explain the apparent political and ideological resilience of capitalism despite an extended period of slow growth, high unemployment and rampant inflation.

The process of decolonisation after World War II resulted in a large number of new states which, along with Latin America, came to be seen as making up the 'Third World'. Not only Marxist but mainstream social scientists took an interest in 'development studies'. New multidisciplinary journals were established.[14] Some theorists, especially from Latin America, analysed the position of 'less-developed' countries using a global political economy perspective known as *dependencia* or dependency theory. Others were led to raise political economy questions because of their concern over the unequal distribution of the gains from economic growth within less developed countries (LDCs). More recently, questions have been raised about the causes and effects of the growth of military expenditure in the Third World. Writers are either implicitly or explicitly asking the question, who benefits from these policies and why?

The ideas of dependency writers have been taken up and extended by sociologists such as Immanuel Wallerstein, who has been at the forefront of the development of world systems theory. World systems theorists in effect synthesised the realist approach to inter-state rivalry with the structural analysis of the dependency writers, and argued that a single 'world system' had come into existence during what they call the 'long sixteenth century'. This system was articulated through an integrated world market (or capitalist world-economy). This holistic approach again helped to lower disciplinary barriers.

One theme in the *dependencia* literature is that less-developed countries are tightly constrained by international forces. This theme has been taken up by social scientists with reference to developed countries (reflected, for example, in the liberal concept of 'economic interdependence') thus casting doubt on the special 'Third World' claims of dependency theorists. In international economics much attention was paid, in the 1960s, to 'balance of payments problems', international capital mobility and to the special position of the US dollar in the international monetary system. Examination of such problems led on to political economy questions about the global structure of power and wealth. Writers such as Richard Cooper have highlighted how the monetary policy and interest rates of one country will be influenced by those of leading capitalist countries, and more generally by global economic conditions. Higher interest rates in other countries will result in a capital outflow from the country with relatively low interest rates, other things being equal. Similarly, an expansionary fiscal policy in a state with a large economy will have spillover effects on other countries which may be unintended. Economic integration and interdependence thus create constraints for even the most powerful countries.

The concept of interdependence, however, is sometimes taken to imply a relatively symmetrical set of interrelationships amongst states. However, this may only rarely be the case, with respect to certain relationships given that the size of national economies varies considerably. In this respect it is important to introduce a distinction, made by J. D. B. Miller, between economic dominance and economic domination.[15] Economic dominance refers to the way one state can consistently coerce others using economic means: for example the USA's relationship to most other capitalist states is one of 'asymmetrical interdependence' (to use the term of Robert Keohane and Joseph Nye).[16] This is because of the sheer size and importance of the US economy which creates a large market for the goods of other countries. Because other states need access to this market the USA can deny access to its vast market for their exports if they fail to cooperate or to make concessions to the USA. The potential threat of such withdrawal of access will generally be sufficient to make other states (especially those highly dependent on the US market and with little reciprocal leverage over US exports) more cooperative.

On the other hand, US monetary and fiscal policies may not be designed to punish other countries yet may have punitive effects on them, as in the 1930s and the early 1980s, because of the structural dominance of the American economy in the world economy. In both cases severe US recession spread to the rest of the world and the prices of primary products slumped so that LDCs were especially hard-hit. The case of the early 1980s is a matter of some debate: some US writers have seen it as an American-led exercise of 'market power'. This distinction between the direct and indirect forms of power and their relationship to structures in the global political economy is at the heart of conceptual debates within the field of study. Such concepts are discussed at length in chapters 6 and 7.

In common with writers like Wallerstein and Perry Anderson,[17] a number of theorists have sought to develop what can be called a comparative historical method to the study of political economy. One contemporary writer who has developed this method, involving a brilliant synthesis of Marxist and mercantilist approaches is Theda Skocpol, in her analysis of social revolutions. She lays particular emphasis upon the domestic and international determinants of social revolution in 'relatively backward' countries. Those states which failed to adapt successfully to the internal dynamics of class struggle, and the external threats from military challenges and international economic competition were most likely to undergo social revolutions. Examples of such states are Manchu China and Romanov Russia in the late nineteenth and early twentieth centuries.[18] Her work is an example of how international pressures can affect the internal politics and even the political institutions of countries. This contrasts with the more conventional perspective in international studies which sees international relations as being shaped mainly by domestic political forces in a given structure of an anarchic inter-state system. In parallel with Skocpol, Peter Gourevitch has generalised from a range of historical cases, and has shown how the pressures of the inter-state system have significant impact upon domestic political structures and outcomes.[19] For example, the absence of strong external pressures may permit a more open and democratic state structure, such as that of the USA after the American Revolution, and Britain for much of its contemporary history. On the other hand, a state which is subjected to significant external pressures and threats may become more authoritarian in its structures, and may subsequently undergo a social revolution if the state is unable to cope with the challenges from abroad, for example Russia in World War I.

Above and beyond this diversity of approaches to and sources of political economy, a striking feature of much of the recent literature in the field has been its concentration on the problem of international economic order and the related issue of the place of the United States in the system. In discussions of the US position there is a tendency to view US hegemony, or its internationally dominant position, as not only benevolent but also in decline. The problem then becomes how to keep the international 'public goods' such as liberal trade and monetary order (made possible by American leadership) in consistent and continued supply. In particular, there has been a great concern in the American literature over the possibility that trade may become more restricted; that monetary instability may lead to a financial collapse; that regional economic blocs may emerge; and that, in consequence of these possibilities, new forms and methods of cooperation must be developed. In most of the literature there is an uncritical presumption in favour of a liberal international economic order, albeit with some dissenting (usually mercantilist) voices.

4. SUMMARY AND CONCLUSIONS

As will be evident from the preceding section, there is a wide range of approaches and issues to be addressed in the field. Indeed, the very definition of the field is a matter of contestation and debate. This variety is apparent if one reads the contents page of David Whynes' edited book, *What is Political Economy?*.[20] Whynes himself tends to identify loosely 'international' political economy with writers who stress dependency and imperialism, so excluding liberal and mercantilist perspectives. Some writers have reviewed the field seeing international political economy as a branch of international relations, whereas others have suggested that international relations is part of political economy. As we argued in the preface, the very term *international political economy* is unfortunate in so far as it may tend to detract attention from those issues which are more global in nature, such as the degradation of the environment and the militarisation of space.

Given this lack of agreement as to what constitutes the boundary of the field, as well as the different theoretical approaches within it, there is a need for increased communication between, and debate amongst, the contending positions. This is difficult given the rival theoretical frameworks and conceptual disagreements which exist between the various approaches. Each approach may define what constitutes the 'political' and the 'economic', and their integration into a particular 'political economy' in different ways. There are significant contrasts in basic units of analysis and also in research priorities and techniques of appraisal. Moreover, while the rise of international (global) political economy has led to some interdisciplinary exchanges and joint research (this book is an example of the latter), as yet the persistence of conventional discipline boundaries merely adds to the already formidable obstacles to theoretical development and communication.

These conclusions, however, should not be taken to suggest that such obstacles are entirely insurmountable – the work of writers such as Skocpol provides encouragement here. Indeed, an aim of this book is to help enhance the prospects for both theoretical development and communication in the field.

NOTES

1. Leon Lindberg et al. (eds), *Stress and Contradiction in Modern Capitalism: Public Policy and the Theory of the State* (Lexington, Mass., Lexington Books, 1975).
2. David McClellan (ed.), *Marx's 'Grundrisse'* (Harmondsworth, Penguin, 1971), pp. 83–4.
3. Perry Anderson, *Passages from Antiquity to Feudalism* (London, New Left Books, 1974); and *The Lineages of the Absolutist State* (London, New Left Books, 1974); Antonio Gramsci, *Selections from the Prison Notebooks of Antonio Gramsci*, translated and edited Quentin Hoare and Geoffrey Nowell Smith (London, Lawrence and Wishart/New York, International Publishers, 1971).
4. Richard Cooper, *The Economics of Interdependence: Economic Policy in the Atlantic Community* (New York, McGraw-Hill/Council on Foreign Relations, 1968).
5. Barrington Moore Jr, *Social Origins of Dictatorship and Democracy: Lord and Peasant in the Making of the Modern World* (Boston, Mass., Beacon Press/Harmondsworth, Penguin, 1966).
6. This is an argument made consistently over the years by Milton Friedman. See for example, Milton and Rose Friedman, *The Tyranny of the Status Quo* (Harmondsworth, Penguin Books, 1983), chapter 3, pp. 40–70.
7. Anthony Downs, *An Economic Theory of Democracy* (New York, Harper and Row, 1957); Albert Breton, *An Economic Theory of Representative*

Government (Chicago, Aldine, 1974); Peter Jackson, *The Political Economy of Bureaucracy* (London, Philip Allan, 1982).

8. Samuel Brittan, 'The Economic Contradictions of Democracy', *British Journal of Political Science* (1975) Vol. 5, pp. 129–59.

9. Robert Gilpin, *US Power and the Multinational Corporation: The Political Economy of Foreign Direct Investment* (New York, Basic Books, 1975); *War and Change in World Politics* (Princeton NJ, Princeton University Press, 1981); and *The Political Economy of International Relations* (Princeton NJ, Princeton University Press, 1987); David P. Calleo, *The Imperious Economy* (Cambridge, Mass., Harvard University Press, 1982); and *Beyond American Hegemony: The Future of the Western Alliance* (New York, Basic Books/Brighton, Wheatsheaf Books, 1987).

10. Wolfgang Hager, 'Political Implications of US-EC economic conflicts: Atlantic Trade Problems and Prospects' *Government and Opposition* (1986), Vol. 22, pp. 49–63; Susan Strange, *Casino Capitalism* (Oxford, Basil Blackwell, 1986).

11. Stephen Krasner, 'State Power and the Structure of Foreign Trade', *World Politics* (1976), Vol. 28, pp. 317–43. For Krasner's more recent thinking see his *Structural Conflict: The Third World Against Global Liberalism* (Berkeley, Cal./London, University of California Press, 1985).

12. For example the *Review of Radical Political Economy, Capital and Class*, and *Cambridge Journal of Economics*.

13. Robert W. Cox, *Production, Power and World Order: Social Forces in the Making of History* (New York, Columbia University Press, 1987). This is the first in a four-volume set, *Power and Production*, co-written with Jeffrey Harrod. Harrod's first volume *Power, Production, and the Unprotected Worker* was published simultaneously by Columbia with that of Cox.

14. For example, *Development and Change, World Development* and *Journal of Developing Areas*.

15. J. D. B. Miller, *The World of States: Connected Essays* (London, Croom Helm, 1981), chapter 6.

16. Robert O. Keohane and Joseph S. Nye, *Power and Interdependence* (Boston, Mass., Little, Brown, 1977).

17. Anderson, op. cit.; Immanuel Wallerstein, *The Capitalist World Economy* (Cambridge, Cambridge University Press, 1979); and his *The Modern World System: Capitalist Agriculture and the Origins of the European World-Economy in the Sixteenth Century* (New York, Academic Press, 1974).

18. Theda Skocpol, *States and Social Revolutions: A Comparative Analysis of France, Russia, and China* (Cambridge, Cambridge University Press, 1979).

19. See Peter A. Gourevitch, 'The Second Image Reversed: The International Sources of Domestic Politics', *International Organisation* (1978), Vol. 32, pp. 929–52.

20. D. Whynes (ed.), *What is Political Economy?: Eight Perspectives* (Oxford, Basil Blackwell, 1984).

2 On Perspectives and their Appraisal

In this chapter we define the term 'perspective', and introduce criteria for the evaluation of the rival perspectives in political economy which are elaborated in chapters 3, 4 and 5, and discussed throughout this book. These criteria include scope, consistency and reflexivity. These criteria are discussed with respect to the quest for parsimonious explanation, and with reference to the debate in social theory concerning structure and agency.

1. ON PERSPECTIVES

The notion of 'perspective' used in this book is akin to the way the word 'paradigm' is often used in that it refers to the basic concepts and assumptions which underpin theoretical explanation. These concepts and assumptions shape, and to some extent limit, the types of question that are posed, and the types of answer that can be given. However, even rival perspectives may share a wider framework of thought which contains some fundamental assumptions about the universe, and the place of humankind within it. Each may be underpinned by a concept of human nature, and the limits of human possibility and progress. In particular, they may share certain notions of secular (scientific) rationality. Secular and materialist assumptions can be said to underpin the three major perspectives in the field of global political economy: realist-mercantilism, liberalism and Marxism.

Secularism implies a particular type of rationalism in which humankind is assumed to be autonomous and self-reliant, and is further assumed to be able to control, or at least regulate its relationship with, the natural world. In contrast, many religions stress divine revelation and such goals as being at one with God and establishing the Kingdom of God on earth. Human rationality is seen as imperfect and insufficient at best, dangerous at worst. Further, in so far as God's way is clearly defined (as in holy books) then an open-ended process of questioning based upon science's endless thirst for knowledge and human mastery has led, at least in the past, to religious condemnation or even damnation as in the myth of Doctor Faustus.

A perspective is like a paradigm in that it contains a range of specific theories, and facilitates the creation of more such theories: for example, the 'domestic' quantity theory of money in neo-classical economics. More complex 'monetarist' theories of inflation have developed since World War II, theories which allow for interest rate effects and international economic interdependence. Criticism of a specific theory can take two forms: one is from within the perspective, on the basis of shared assumptions, some of which may be methodological. The other is from outside, where criticism of basic assumptions is often prominent: here a critique of a particular theory may in effect take the form of a critique of the wider paradigm within which it was developed.[1]

In addition, our view of a perspective is similar to Kuhn's analysis of scientific paradigms in that we see them as having a social character. Each perspective emerges in a given historical and institutional context, which it may outlive. Within the framework of a paradigm, Kuhn suggests that there is some scope for differences of opinion and the development of new, specific theories. However, the nature and extent of this scope can vary with the particular institutional features of the academic community, and also with the relationship of that community to wider political forces. In any academic community, those who lead tend to develop vested interests in their definition of a subject, and its disciplinary boundaries. Moreover, to gain an authoritative voice, initiates into the community must communicate their ideas according to the formal methods adopted by the community. They must carry out their research in a manner which is regarded as 'exemplary'. Initiates must thus behave according to the custom and practice of the community if they are to be influential and achieve positions of authority. These social processes tend to discourage challenges to the basic assumptions of the paradigm or perspective. One problem for the development of global political economy is that it cuts across and transcends established subjects or disciplines, some of which have become especially associated with a particular perspective: for example economics which is dominated by the neo-classical approach, and international relations, where the realist perspective is preponderant.

An ironic example of this form of closure, with a particular perspective becoming extensively dominant, and subsequently stagnant, is the rigid Marxist–Leninism of the Stalinist period, especially, though not only, in the Soviet Union. Even when Marxist theoretical debate and innovation revived from the mid-1950s through to the 1970s, it was principally a Western phenomenon. In the West, the hold of the Soviet Communist Party on left-wing intellectuals was less complete than in the Soviet bloc, and challenges to dogma and orthodoxy were allowed to go unpunished.

2. CRITERIA FOR EVALUATION

As we have seen in the previous chapter, there are contending approaches and perspectives in the field of study. Because of this it is important to develop criteria for their evaluation: not all theories are equally valid in secular 'scientific' terms. At this stage in the development of the field, and given the tremendous complexity of the global political economy itself, it is unlikely that a single general theory will emerge which can systematically identify and explain all the key structures and dynamics of the system. Indeed progress in this theoretical task may lead to significant changes in the political economy as people come to modify their views about how the world works, and may, as a result, change the way that they act within it.

One might suggest that the ultimate criterion for evaluating a perspective is whether it contributes to the survival of the human race. From an academic viewpoint, less wide-ranging criteria are usually stressed, such as understanding, explanatory power, predictive success and intellectual coherence. At the methodological level this involves the criteria of scope, consistency and reflexivity.

Usually, scientific criteria are seen as related to the goal of improving the analysis of the way the (material) world works, and by implication better diagnosis of problems and improved methods of, for example, production, distribution and participation. At the more academic level, there are rival philosophies of science. These differ over the relative importance they attach to ontology and epistemology. Ontology refers to the nature of reality and its underlying units, which form the starting point for theoretical explanation. For example, liberals take the individual, realists take the state, and world systems and Marxists theorists take a global capitalist system as the basic unit of analysis. As has been noted, each defines the reality to be analysed in material terms.

Epistemology is the theoretical view of the nature of, and conditions for, the growth of knowledge. Different epistemologies are associated with different philosophies of science, such as empiricism, rationalism and scientific realism.[2] Different epistemologies give rise to different criteria of appraisal. Whereas some have stressed the scope and general consistency of explanation, others (positivists and instrumentalists) have narrowed their focus and given greater priority to prediction and testing of empirical hypotheses. While most writers would accept that explanation and prediction are linked, the nature of their connection is a matter of dispute.

In political economy, given its complexity, there has been a tendency for some writers to stress parsimonious (that is, economical) forms of explanation in order to generate hypotheses which are amenable to testing. By parsimonious is meant a theory which explains (and predicts) 'a lot from a little': thus it should contain the fewest possible variables which can be used to explain interactions within the political economy. Sometimes such an interest in parsimony is bound up with a wish to identify specific policy options. An example of parsimonious theory with policy implications is that concerning comparative advantage developed by David Ricardo which we discussed in the previous chapter. According to this theory, a country will export goods in which it has a comparative advantage, and will import those in which it has a comparative disadvantage. Such a pattern of international specialisation will raise economic welfare. Therefore, freer trade will result in a rise in the wealth and economic welfare of all nations. Ricardo's theory was parsimonious because it assumed full employment (so ignoring adjustment costs), complete immobility of factors between countries, and constant costs (that is, no economies of scale would develop). These assumptions therefore severely limited the scope of application of the theory. However, a strong policy orientation need not always go with parsimony. For example, some large macroeconomic forecasting models contain hundreds of equations.

Parsimony is often associated with simplification and abstraction, as is evident in Ricardo's theory. Ricardo was obviously aware of international flows of capital and labour but excluded them from his theory of trade (presuming them to be too small to be significant for policy purposes). Much writing in international relations, especially in the neo-realist tradition has often abstracted from domestic political forces in order to concentrate on the structure of inter-state relations. By assuming that states can and do pursue a given 'national interest', the more international aspects of political economy are brought into relief. However, this method brings with it the cost of eliminating from consideration a series of crucial issues, for example those concerning the aggregation and definition of 'national' interests, the relationship between domestic and international forces, and sometimes the question of time-horizons.

In addition, in so far as 'economics' and 'politics' are separated in explanation, the scope of theory is likely to be severely circumscribed. In this context it is worth recalling how there is evidence that the global political economy is becoming increasingly integrated in a complex and interdependent way. The density of the linkages which have developed carries with it the implication that the pursuit of parsimony may now carry greater costs in terms of foregone explanatory power than was the case in the days of Ricardo. More generally, a specific theory within a perspective may have more validity and usefulness for one historical period than another. Hence, the constant need for historical appraisal and the development of new, specific theories. An example of this was early Marxist theories of imperialism, which were developed in order to analyse a particular historical conjuncture. Proponents of dependency theory and what we call transnational historical materialism often see themselves as developing a new theory to explain the new stage in the post-1945 development of capitalism. However, if specific theories need continually to be developed to analyse what in effect is the same type of system (e.g. capitalism) there is a danger of superficial *ad hoc* explanations, which may be designed to protect or immunise the perspective. For practical purposes, a specific theory which has validity over a long period of time is to be preferred. While the scope of a theory may be limited by historical change, it can also be more or less circumscribed in the range of phenomena which it explains, and/or predicts.

One criterion, therefore, is the relative scope or extensiveness of a theory or perspective. A second is the question of explanatory power: some theories sacrifice some explanatory power and comprehensiveness in the search for parsimony, sometimes because of the desire to generate clear-cut predictions. Parsimonious theories may generate simplified, but powerful, explanations of international relations. This may, as a result, add to their persuasiveness.

An example of parsimony is the neo-realist refusal, for example by writers like Kenneth Waltz, to open up and theorise the 'black box' of the state.[3] In effect, Waltz ignores the effects of domestic politics and takes 'national interests' as already aggregated and stable, so that the state, as it were, is free to act at the international level, unhindered by domestic constraint. What constrains the state is the structure of the inter-state system. This system is, in turn, conceived in individualist terms, that is as deriving from the interaction of autonomous individual units. By contrast, much writing by structural Marxists suggests that the global capitalist structure determines 'in the last instance' the nature of, and relations between, both classes and states.[4] Both types of structural analysis run the risks of oversimplification, and even determinism.

The danger with the latter approach is that actors, or agents, will be reduced to the status of 'bearers' of systemic features. Thus the problem of free will versus determination in social life is collapsed into one of the pervasiveness, or overdetermination, of structure. The danger with Waltz's structuralism is that global systemic forces and features will be reduced to 'taken-as-given' level, relative to the inter-state system which is the object of his analysis. In effect, such systemic forces are indirectly embodied in the policy preferences (utility functions) of nation-states. By contrast to these forms of structural determinism (that is, Waltzian, Althusserian), part of the project of this book is to develop a form of structural analysis which allows for the role of agency, action, consciousness and choice. Even if we assume that actors are constrained by their structural locations (however defined), they still make decisions, usually from within a range of alternatives. In our analysis, the formation of expectations and perceptions about the range and costs and benefits of alternatives is crucial. The ultimate problem in resolving the structure-agency divide is a practical, rather than a meta-theoretical one, in that it inherently requires historical analysis. Such historical analysis implies two major limitations for theorising in political economy. The first is that parsimonious theories may be of very limited explanatory power (even if they 'predict well', at least for a while). However, they may be useful as a starting point for investigation. The second, and more fundamental, limitation is that changing historical circumstances (including the consciousness and understanding of human beings) limit the scope for the law-like generalisations favoured by empiricists and historicists.

Since political economy is a field of study which, in part, is meant to generate 'practical' or policy applications, a further criterion is the degree to which a perspective is able to meet certain practical requirements, that is whether it is useful as a guide to action beyond the academic community. Political economy is concerned with the way people live, and how, and under what conditions, their circumstances can be changed, or, indeed, how and when changes can be resisted. Thus it is important to know whose practical requirements are best served by different theories and perspectives.

It might be thought that those theories which are internally logical and consistent with available data and evidence would tend to be the most useful guides to action. However, where persuasiveness is sought, a comparatively parsimonious and even oversimplified theory may be advantageous, particularly if it can be linked to a 'commonsense' view of the world. An example of this was the particular brand of monetarism (stressing monetary targets) adopted by the British government under Prime Minister Thatcher in the early 1980s. Allied to this was an emphasis on reducing the public sector budget deficit and getting better value for public money, even at the expense of drastically reducing capital expenditures with possible long-term payoffs. She represented this strategy to the public as 'good housekeeping'.

3. PERSPECTIVES AND THEIR PRACTICAL IMPLICATIONS

The previous paragraph leads to the question, who is guided, and in what ways, by a given perspective? In so far as different perspectives are geared, either consciously or unconsciously, to different practical purposes, appraisal of their relative merits will be, to a certain extent, value-laden and contentious. Because of this problem it can be argued that a further criterion is the degree to which a given perspective is conscious or unconscious of its practical implications, and thus, in this respect, can be said to 'understand' itself. Let us now consider examples of such practical orientations among the perspectives.

A well-known example of an explicit 'policy engineering' orientation is that of macroeconomists, especially those of the Keynesian persuasion, who seek to identify and quantify the effects of specific policy changes such as the impact of a cut in income tax on the level of aggregate demand. Such an orientation towards policy is one in which the technocratic macroeconomist does not claim to lay down policy objectives or priorities, but instead to provide a 'menu' of policy options for the politicians. Such macroeconomists have often claimed to be apolitical and disinterested, with their personal 'values' (seen as something political) separated from the 'facts' they analyse. They claim to take the 'real world' as given as separate from the task of theorising. However, this positivist perspective on the role of the policy technocrat begs the question: what are the sources and assumptions of the approach which is being applied?

That economic and social ideas can influence and constrain the thinking of politicians was recognised by Keynes, long before some of his ideas became operationalised in post-war economic management: in the *General Theory* he referred to the way in which politicians (or 'madmen in authority') were themselves prisoners of the 'academic scribblers' of a bygone era.[5] We suggest that this implies that although a theory in political economy may have no direct or obvious policy application, its impact at the practical level may be potentially vast. By this we mean not merely policy, narrowly defined, but the way in which individuals and groups think about the world they live in, and how they attempt to understand it. Keynes, though well aware of the deficiencies of capitalism, was attempting to get better management of the system so that it might survive in an improved and modified form.

The example of Keynes and the Keynesian technocrats suggests a final criterion for the evaluation of perspectives and the theories that each helps to generate. This is the criterion of reflexivity. By this we mean the capacity of a perspective to reflect on its own origins and conditions of existence. This also involves an awareness of how the perspective, or theory, may itself enter into, and be part of, the global political economy. For this to be possible, reflexivity entails some understanding of contending perspectives.

Our argument here is not to suggest that all perspectives should be viewed in relativist terms: some are likely to be more successful than others in explaining the changing character of the global political economy. In order to do this, they should be able to account for the way that perspectives are a part of the political economy, and the way that theoretical innovation actually changes or sustains it.

NOTES

1. This distinction is associated with Imré Lakatos, as well as Thomas Kuhn. Lakatos refers to research programmes which have a 'hard core' of basic concepts and assumptions, and a 'protective belt' of specific theories. See I. Lakatos and Alan Musgrave (eds), *Criticism and the Growth of Knowledge* (Cambridge, Cambridge University Press, 1974); Thomas S. Kuhn, *The Structure of Scientific Revolutions* (Chicago, University of Chicago Press, 1970).
2. On these different epistemological traditions see A. F. Chalmers, *What is This Thing Called Science?* (Milton Keynes, Open University Press, 1982) 2nd edition; Russell Keat and John Urry, *Social Theory as Science* (London, Routledge and Kegan Paul, 1982).
3. Kenneth Waltz, *Theory of International Politics* (Reading, Mass., Addison-Wesley, 1979).
4. Louis Althusser, *For Marx*, translated by Ben Brewster (London, Allen Lane, Penguin, 1969).
5. John Maynard Keynes, *The General Theory of Employment, Interest and Money* (New York, Harcourt Brace, 1936).

3   Realism, Mercantilism and International Dominance

The oldest political economy approach is realist-mercantilism. Mercantilism can, for the purposes of this book, be taken as the economic variant of realism. In this chapter we discuss realist assumptions and units of analysis, the relationship between realist ideas and strategies of foreign economic policy, and some implications of the realist perspective. We then discuss recent attempts from within this perspective to theorise the conditions under which cooperation between states and international actors is rational. In this latter context we discuss the use of game theory, and the concept of international regimes.

1.   REALIST ASSUMPTIONS

Realist-mercantilism starts from the assumption that international life is inherently conflictual, with anarchy the rule, order, stability and justice the exceptions. In this world of conflict, power is the ultimate arbiter of politics, and the distribution of national power resources determines the pattern of relations between rival states in the inter-state system. By anarchy is meant the absence of a global force, such as that which would be provided by a world state, which can impose order on nation-states.

The state, which is the primary unit of analysis in the realist study of international relations, is assumed to aggregate and reflect the sum of the interests of the members of civil society. The interests of each individual are founded in the primary human impulses of survival, the search for security and the quest for power. Human nature is sometimes taken as relatively fixed, unchanging, egotistical and self-interested. Underpinning this conception of human nature is an image of society without the state which approximates a Hobbesian 'state of nature', or of anarchy, where there is potentially a 'war of all against all'. On the other hand, a realist conception of international anarchy may be compatible with a limited concept of human community, at the local level, as in the ancient Greek city-states, or present-day Swiss cantons, and also at the national level. Such concepts of community are expressed, for example, in Rousseau's ideas concerning the general will and the social contract. These ideas can be seen to relate to the means through which a coherent concept of national interests can be forged. The German political economist, Friedrich List, took this idea one step further in his ideas concerning the cultural and socio-economic potency of the nation, relative to others: at this level, List argued, the highest level of human community, consciousness and development was possible.

In international relations, Hobbes' notion of egotistic individuals (rationally) pursuing their own self-interest is modified to encompass the state, aggregating the general interests of a greater tribe or nation. This general interest is assumed to be the consolidation (or even extension) of the territory of the nation, and with maximising its relative power and wealth. Achievement of the latter goal is seen as helping to generate more auspicious domestic conditions which might mitigate some of the undesirable social consequences of individual selfishness.

Hobbesian individualism can thus be contrasted with the more holistic and organic conceptions of the community and nation of writers such as Rousseau and List. Indeed, not all liberal writers are as individualistic in their perspective as was Hobbes: for example Locke. Thus realism is a ground in which a range of philosophical traditions can meet.[1]

Perhaps the most common and crucial assumption is that the interests of nations must be in conflict. This is either because states value power for its own sake, and/or value security and status. Because one nation's security can normally only be enhanced by measures, such as an arms build-up, which reduce the security of some other states, the apparently rational pursuit of national interests can potentially produce a collectively irrational outcome. If all states pursue an arms build-up, their efforts may cancel each other out, and fail to achieve increases in security, either individually, or for the world as a whole. This paradoxical outcome is usually related in the literature to the concept of a *zero-sum game*; where any redistribution of a relatively fixed amount of power resources in the favour of one state will necessarily be at the expense of others.

Under these conditions, the key question for this perspective is how is order possible in international relations? The answers to this question have varied, but in essence the most stable international system would be one where a world state or global *Leviathan* were to impose order. A second-best solution would be a global empire, or hegemony, where one nation was so overwhelmingly powerful that it was able to discipline others and maintain the peace. Intermediate solutions would involve a carefully constructed, and rationally maintained balance of power (or terror), where it would not be in any state's interest to upset the *status quo*.

Let us now pursue some of the implications of these assumptions and examine realist-mercantilist foreign economic policies.

2. REALISM AND FOREIGN ECONOMIC POLICY

We shall first examine the concept of the 'national interest'. In its focus on the nation-state, writers from this perspective assume that such an interest exists and can be clearly defined. At the core of such an interest is the overriding imperative of the survival of the state. The latter gives rise to a concept of national security, a concept which is central to the construction of a state's foreign economic policy. While national security is usually related to external relations, it can also have an internal aspect with regard to domestic order and social cohesion. Where the state is internally fragmented, and where there is little social cohesion, the realisation of the concepts of national interest and national security will be difficult, or even impossible, as in many black African states.

Even assuming there is a domestic consensus on the national interest in a given state, and assuming that leaders are able to pursue it rationally, the national interests of different states are usually seen as being at odds, or even in fundamental conflict with each other. Measures to increase the security of one state (such as building up a bigger army) are often seen by other states as reducing their security. Measures to increase the economic wealth of one nation (for example, by getting a trade surplus) are often seen as being at the expense of other nations (one nation's surplus is another's deficit). From this perspective, the national interest is usually seen to imply the need for increasing the dependence of other states on the home state's economy. The other side of the same coin is reducing the home state's dependence on others. By definition, since dependence is relative, when one country succeeds in doing this it must be at the expense of others. From this viewpoint, the game of international economic interdependence is hazardous. The ideal condition for a country's economic security would be complete self-sufficiency.

Given that self-sufficiency is largely unobtainable for most states, the second-best condition would be one of asymmetrical interdependence, balanced in favour of the home state. Such an imbalance can be understood in terms of the distinction between 'sensitivity' and 'vulnerability' interdependence. For Keohane and Nye, sensitivity interdependence involves taking a set of policies as given. It concerns how quickly changes in one country (such as changes in monetary and fiscal policy) bring costly changes in another (for example, transmitted inflation). It also concerns the scale of the costly effects. 'The vulnerability dimension of interdependence rests on the relative availability and costliness of the alternatives that various actors face.'[2] Thus vulnerability relates to policy options which may be more or less costly (an example being deflationary policies to offset imported inflation). These opportunity costs may be both political and economic, and may vary over time. In practice these two dimensions of interdependence always go together and both may be seen as a matter of degree. From a realist-mercantilist perspective, the point is to construct policies which will minimise such sensitivity and reduce adjustment costs when policy changes are necessary. For example, South Africa remains sensitive to changes in the gold price, but its sensitivity was less in the 1980s, after decades of import-substitution and some diversification of exports, than it was before 1945. In terms of the second dimension of interdependence, South Africa reduced its vulnerability through increasing its policy options, notably through the stockpiling of one of its major imports, oil, and increasing its foreign exchange reserves. However, one option – loans from foreign banks – was substantially curtailed in the mid-1980s because of external political pressures partly generated by anti-apartheid movements.

At the heart of the practical aspect of this perspective is the concept of 'strategic industries', which is derived from the concern with national security and self-sufficiency in vital sectors. By this concept is meant that constellation of industries which can create the optimum conditions for a high degree of national autonomy and economic sovereignty in the short and long term. This also entails the ability to exert power within the inter-state system. The actual mix of such industries will vary between nations, depending on their factor endowments (including natural resources and skill levels) and level of industrialisation. Such strategic industries might therefore include arms and related industries, capital goods more generally, and sometimes agriculture.

Let us now discuss more specifically the policy implications of this perspective for industrial policy, international trade, and capital and labour flows. Since this perspective emphasises the political determination of economic policy, these different aspects of policy should be seen as interrelated parts of an overall strategy of attaining the maximum possible national power.

With regard to industrial policy, the principal criterion which is normally applied is national control. This can take the form of state or private ownership within the strategic industries, that is those deemed crucial for national security and substantive, as opposed to formal, economic sovereignty. Foreign takeovers of national firms in such industries are likely to be discouraged or even proscribed. High-technology industries, especially when linked to defence needs and arms production, are likely either to be subsidised and/or aided through national preference in purchases by the state. Education and training policies may be oriented to the needs of such industries. The same may apply to research and development more generally. The configuration of these industrial policies helps to set the context for what can be called 'optimal' trade policies from this perspective.

Dependence on imports for non-essential items need not be a source of concern, whereas reliance on imports for arms, capital goods, crucial raw materials and basic food supplies implies major vulnerability, unless there are varied and plentiful supplies of these items in the world market. Thus in trade policy, more protection will be afforded to those industries and sectors which are of strategic value but as yet uncompetitive. For agricultural less-developed countries (LDCs) this is likely to mean protection for manufacturing industry since LDCs will wish to reduce their dependence on imports of manufactures from developed countries. For highly industrialised countries which are not self-sufficient in food, protection for agriculture is much more likely than it is for agrarian LDCs. As regards manufacturing industry, arms production will tend to be more highly protected than most, whether by subsidies and/or tariffs. This is the trade side to the 'strategic industries' argument. Such protection for military production is likely to be greatest for those countries which feel most vulnerable, for two main reasons. One is their leaders' perception of the intensity of external threats; another is the availability and reliability of arms imports. Where there is concern over the reliability of supply of strategic imports, stockpiling is more likely as we saw in the case of oil in the South African example. The import pattern of countries, especially those not in the forefront of technology, is likely to be dominated by capital goods and licensed technology. By contrast, technology leaders will have an incentive to restrict the export of high-technology and the goods which embody it. This point is now increasingly crucial for military questions, particularly since the range of technologies required for modern warfare is expanding.

A state interested in building up its national power will see the import of capital as a rational policy so long as it does not become too dependent on foreign funding, or else become weighed down with foreign debts. On the other hand, it will be reluctant to export capital which might otherwise be usefully invested at home. To this end, the means to restrict capital outflows are vital. The expectation is, therefore, that restrictions on international capital flows will be common in a realist-mercantilist world, both for portfolio and direct investment, as well as short-term capital flows. One way of trying to control capital flows is by having national ownership of banks. In the case of foreign direct investments in a country, it will be rational to regulate and restrict the activities of foreign companies, so as to make them serve the 'national interest'. This may be achieved by imposing performance requirements (such as the training of local labour) and laws requiring some shares in a subsidiary to be in local hands. On the other hand, it will be tempting for a state to make use of those of its home-based companies with direct investments abroad, as an arm of its foreign policy, for example in restricting the outflow of technology.

In the case of labour outflows it is essential to distinguish between scarce, highly-educated, skilled labour and relatively more abundant semi- and unskilled labour. The former category can be seen as crucial to research activities and the strategic industries, so that it is rational to restrict emigration by such workers. This is known as preventing a 'brain drain'. Immigration by such workers, will, however, often be welcomed. For low-skilled labour, emigration may be seen as undesirable if the country is close to, or at, full employment, since this will create a labour shortage and drive wages and costs of production upwards. When there is a sustained glut of labour, such emigration entails few domestic costs, and may provide a useful source of foreign income if the migrants send money back to their parent country. Such income can also be obtained from (temporarily) migrant workers (such as Turkish guestworkers in West Germany; Pakistanis working in the Middle East). Immigration of unskilled labour may be welcomed when there is a shortage of such labour but much may depend on the scale and cultural character of the immigrants, since social cohesion (a value held to be crucial to mercantilists) may be reduced because of racial and religious tensions.

3.   SOME IMPLICATIONS OF THE REALIST PERSPECTIVE

What are the international implications of the pursuit of realist policies for international economic order? And how do writers from within this perspective predict the likely evolution of the current international system?

A way to suggest some of these international implications is to assume the system is a fully realist-mercantilist one. Realist-mercantilists see domestic and international aspects of the global political economy as linked in that they view 'national capital' operating internationally. Of central concern to the state is the ability to control the movement of goods, technology and capital and to channel such economic power resources for rational purposes. This capacity will be at its greatest when there is a national consensus (based upon a strong nationalism) in favour of such policies, and where the state has a large market which can be used to gain concessions from foreign companies and acts as an incentive for domestic producers not to export the best of their managerial and technological prowess. If all states were to pursue such policies effectively, it would mean that international economic liberalism would cease to be a possibility. Thus in this perspective, politics largely determines the shape of the economy, both nationally and internationally.

In typical interpretations of the post-1945 order, the re-emergence of economic liberalism is principally explained as resulting from the power and foreign policy objectives of the dominant (or hegemonic) capitalist state, the USA. Put simply, the construction of the post-war order along liberal principles is seen as being in US national interests at the time, since America had the strongest and biggest economy in the world, her corporations were the most technologically advanced, were the most competitive, and had the largest cash reserves. US national interests have now changed, however, since Realists argue that many of the USA's transnational corporations were not always wise in their export of the package of management, technology and finance. Thus, in the long term, they helped contribute to the recovery and development of other nations, who were also assiduously building up their national power, using mercantilist policies. This served, in turn, to undercut the primacy of the United States. As US dominance was undermined, the central political and strategic pillar of the liberal order was weakened, and the USA's foreign economic policies became more overtly mercantilist, and thus more similar to those of other powers in the system. The USA began to abandon its custodial role in international economic management and the Bretton Woods system broke down. The puzzles from this viewpoint are, first, why the United States was so myopic and so 'liberal' in the first place, and secondly, why this liberalism was still very much alive during the 1980s. Nevertheless some realist-mercantilist writers of the late 1970s suggested that the decline of US hegemony might mean the re-emergence of economic blocs, similar to those seen in the 1930s. As US relative power declined nationalist sentiments rose once again to represent the 'normal politics' of the inter-state system.[3]

What are the long-term implications of this perspective? In the final analysis, realist-mercantilism is a deeply pessimistic perspective, at least with respect to the possibilities for the eradication of conflict in international relations. By its anthropological stress on competing tribes and rival nationalisms, it suggests a world of perpetual conflict, only partly stabilised through the balance of power. This perspective is, however, widely adhered to, particularly in the national security complexes of most states, as well as in most less-developed countries which are concerned with nation-building. Indeed, many less-developed countries are actually ruled by military governments, who often pursue policies of state-led industrialisation in an attempt to 'catch up' with the developed capitalist and state socialist nations.

In conclusion, the realist perspective has long been associated with policy advice to rulers of city-states, princes and national governments. Its exponents see such a 'practical realism' as transcending political ideologies. The mercantilist aspect of realism was historically associated with the rise of capitalism in Europe. However, mercantilist policies of non-capitalist states (such as the USSR and the People's Republic of China) and the wars which have taken place between communist states are seen as evidence, by Realists, that their perspective is not inevitably linked to the capitalist system. Realism, in this sense, is not viewed by its advocates as simply a legitimation of national capitalism and capitalist imperialism. The priority accorded to national security by Realists has made their ideas a natural component of nationalism, with a special appeal to the military. The concept of strategic industries also implies a wider appeal which cements the interests of parts of the state, the military elite, and some industrial interests.

However, some writers, notably Richard Ashley, have suggested that an 'emancipatory realism' with universal moral concerns that transcend the nation-state, is a possibility.[4] John Herz, whilst sharing Ashley's hopes of more global cooperation (as in ecological matters), is closer to traditional realism in that such cooperation is seen as possible only because it is grounded in the long term, enlightened self-interest of states. There is a trend in recent realist writing towards the analysis of the conditions for greater cooperation and the creation of a more stable international order. For American writers in particular, part of this has been motivated by a perception that something is needed to replace the loss of international order which has accompanied the relative decline in American hegemony, or international dominance. For all Realists, however, there is a growing realisation that, in a nuclear age, the costs of international conflict are potentially catastrophic for all states.

4. GAME THEORY, COOPERATION AND INSTITUTIONS

Recent writers whose work is partly inspired by the realist tradition, have attempted to extend the perspective by making use of game theory, notably concerning those games which are not zero-sum in character.[5] One advantage of game theory for realist political economy is that it offers a common theoretical approach to the analysis of security and economic issues. The approach assumes that international 'games' are played by rational actors, pursuing self-interest, and facing a given pay-off structure (or environment) which creates different costs and benefits for different courses of action.

Starting from basic realist assumptions concerning the conflictual character of international relations, theorists such as Robert Keohane and

Robert Axelrod use a range of different games, notably the Prisoners' Dilemma, to analyse the conditions under which cooperation may become impossible 'under anarchy'.[6] The Prisoners' Dilemma starts from conditions which may be said to mirror the conflictual and uncertain character of much of international relations. At its simplest, the game assumes two players (the prisoners), in a one-off single-play situation (involving whether they are to be imprisoned or freed for a specific crime), and where no communication is possible between the players (the prisoners, A and B, are held in separate cells). In addition, the evidence available to the authorities about the crime is weak. The alternatives are that if each refuses to inform, they will both get a light sentence. If both inform, each will each receive a heavier sentence. Finally, if A informs, and B does not, the informant, A, will go free, and B is severely punished. Thus the the payoff structure (the pattern of potential costs and benefits to each player) is such that the players do better (that is they receive lighter sentences) if they both cooperate by keeping silent [CC], than if they both defect, owning up to the crime [DD].

However, one player, A, can do even better (obtaining freedom) by defecting to the authorities and owning up, provided that the other, B, fails to cooperate [DC]. On the other hand, the worst possible outcome for A is if he cooperates and keeps silent, whilst B defects [CD], since this will result in severe punishment for A. Since the prisoners cannot communicate, distrust is likely to prevail, and the incentive for each to inform or defect is very high. This is despite the potential gains to each from cooperation. This is a case of a variable sum game, since two light sentences will be preferred to two heavy sentences, or one severe sentence. Indeed, formally, for each player, the rational ordering of preferences is:

$$[DC] > [CC] > [DD] > [CD]$$

Many situations of inter-state rivalry and conflict are seen as akin to that depicted in the Prisoners' Dilemma game. Two good examples are arms races and 'trade wars'. In each of these situations the rational ordering of preferences for the two rival states is the same as for the two prisoners. Even if, in the case of inter-state relations, some communication is possible, distrust may arise since promises to cooperate (for example through non-aggression pacts and treaties) may be broken in the hope of gaining a unilateral advantage. One political theorist, Jon Elster, has even gone as far as to say that politics can be defined as 'the study of ways to transcend the Prisoners' Dilemma'.[7]

In this context, neo-realist and other writers are paying increasing attention to the features of international games which facilitate cooperation.[8] The environmental context of the game is seen as crucial, and key questions are: Is the game repetitive? How easy is communication between the players? What scope, if any, is there for monitoring and enforcement of agreements (for example, by an international institution like the IMF, or else by a hegemonic state)?

Repeat games lend themselves to a 'tit-for-tat' strategy in which one player (or state) retaliates, next time round, if the other does not cooperate. So long as the 'time discount' (that is, the preference for immediate gains) is not too great, players will find it in their interest not to defect, provided that the payoff structure offers longer-term gains for mutual cooperation. Thus changes in the context (as with improved communication and possibilities of monitoring mutual behaviour) and/or in pay-off structure of costs and benefits (as when cooperation offers greater long-term benefits) may make cooperation more attractive and thus more likely, and vice versa.

Further, an improved knowledge of the existing environment may, on its own, be sufficient to raise the level of cooperation, simply by reducing the element of risk and unpredictability. For example, technological developments have made monitoring easier and more reliable, thus giving a more credible basis to certain types of agreements (such as improvements in satellites, aerial photography and information processing in the verification of arms control agreements, improved seismic devices in the monitoring of nuclear test-ban treaties). Improvement in communication, such as the upgrading of 'hot lines' also help in this respect, and supplement improvements in communication which may arise by the institutionalisation of regular inter-state consultations between both allies and rivals.

The advent of nuclear, biological and chemical weapons has altered the pay-off structure of inter-state conflict. Large-scale wars are now more costly and risky than in the past (although this is less the case for smaller-scale, more localised wars). Indeed, in the 'nuclear desert' which would follow the massive use of nuclear weapons there are no 'winners'. On the other hand, other forms of inter-state violence, such as state-sponsored terrorism, and various forms of subversion are both cheaper, and since they are often hard to prove, more 'deniable'. In the economic sphere, it has been frequently suggested that the growing condition of international interdependence changes the economic payoff structure for all nations, such that unilateral economic policies, even for the United States, are more costly than in the past.[9] Again, increased knowledge of the environment (or conditions) may affect the payoff structure, particularly if the players had previously held erroneous beliefs. An example of this was the common view, held especially by Germany in 1914, that offensive wars could lead to swift decisive victory. In fact the technological changes in the nature of weapons prior to the Great War of 1914–18 meant that defensive strategies involving trench warfare were more likely to be effective.

In so far as it is possible to group such theorists within the 'realist' tradition (Keohane in fact rejects the label), it can be argued that a more subtle realism is developing. These developments have strong links to liberal economic ideas on the logic of collective action, which we discuss in the next chapter.[10] The implications for inter-state conflict from the 'new neo-realism' (if we may be allowed to call it such), depend on the nature of the 'game' the nations are playing. The pessimism of the traditional realist position is upheld if international actors are 'status maximisers' (that is where status equals power), where states are striving to achieve the highest possible position in the international hierarchy. Status games have a zero-sum character, such that gains for one actor, or group of actors, involve losses for others. Gains equal losses (net gains are therefore zero). This contrasts with the variable and potentially positive-sum quality of the Prisoners' Dilemma. If desire for absolute (rather than relative) gains and/or fear of absolute losses is strong enough, then cooperation is more likely. International relations involve a mixture of various games: states might cooperate to avoid nuclear war while competing for status through sporting and economic achievements.

In practice, states have usually been more cooperative on economic matters than in the sphere of security. Why should this be so? The nature of economic activity is such that economic interaction takes on a regular, low-cost character which lacks the all-or-nothing quality of wars, where often 'the winner takes all'. The 'shadow of the future', is substantial in many economic relationships since retaliation may be used in the future by any state in response to unacceptable actions by another (as in the case of the use of trade barriers). Security relations may also be more affected by questions of history and national identity with the result that distrust of, and antagonism towards, another nation or people may be deeply embedded in a given political culture. This makes security cooperation more difficult. Here, the 'shadow of the past' may outweigh that of the future. If such conditions prevail, then the game may be less one of Prisoners' Dilemma than one of 'Deadlock'. The conflicts between Israel and several Arab nations in the Middle East may be said to have taken on this character, at least since the Suez crisis of 1956. By contrast, economic issues may often be seen in more instrumental terms with economic welfare rather than national (or ethnic) identity and status coming more to the fore (for example, Israeli trade with South Africa, arms excepted).

Realists have traditionally viewed both international politico-economic and military/security issues as involving 'games' between states. This has been based on a separate 'level of analysis', one which effectively abstracts away the 'level' of domestic politics. However, domestic politics frequently is crucial in the determination of international negotiations and outcomes.

For example, the US Senate rejected the Treaty of Versailles in 1919 on the basis of 'non-entanglement' in Europe, and later, in 1979, despite protests from all of the USA's allies in Western Europe, and after seven years' careful negotiations with the Soviet Union, the Senate rejected ratification of the SALT II Treaty limiting the growth of stategic nuclear arsenals. Another way of looking at this is to see governments as playing both international and domestic games simultaneously, often on several issues at the same time.

Multi-level games may make cooperation more difficult. More generally, different games may be more or less compatible with each other. However, the linkage of different issues may sometimes make an agreement more attainable (such as the granting of US food aid to Egypt in exchange for military facilities, and general support for US policy in the Middle East). On the other hand, one country may demand so much of the other(s) in a range of issue-areas that cooperation fails to occur. Also, a reputation for unreliability in one area may spill over into other areas. One bleak scenario for international cooperation is where players are very concerned to establish a reputation for firmness in that it gives them an incentive to avoid cooperation in the short run (an extreme case of this is the game of 'Chicken'). A more optimistic scenario is where players who have worked together successfully in the past (such as Britain and the United States during World War II) come to value cooperation , and seek to maintain their reputation for effective cooperation in the future (as in the game 'Stag Hunt'). Most case studies suggest that (international) cooperation is more likely the smaller the number of actors, the greater are potential mutual interests, and the greater the 'shadow of the future'. This aspect of collective action is discussed more fully in the next chapter.

5. COOPERATION AND INTERNATIONAL REGIMES

One theme in much of the recent literature is the importance of expectations about cooperation by others, and the possibility for retaliation against defectors. If effective retaliation is more certain, and cheating easily detected, then cooperation is more likely. International institutions may facilitate cooperation by changing such expectations, improving knowledge and human contacts, and by regularising retaliation. An example of the latter is the safeguards clause of the General Agreement on Tariffs and Trade, or GATT (see chapter 12, on trade). Game theory has also provided a rationale for international procedures which build in an element of reciprocity, or a rough but incomplete equivalent of concessions (such as in the GATT). Robert Axelrod has shown, through computer analysis of the iterated two-player Prisoners' Dilemma, that a strategy based on reciprocity (such as tit-for-tat) can be effective in promoting cooperation.[11]

One lesson from the game theory literature is that behaviour can be sufficiently affected by contextual factors such as the ease of communication, the availability of information, the density and regularity of interactions, the length of time-horizons, the existence of centralised enforcement agencies and the ability to practise exclusion. Such factors have been prominent in the neo-realist literature on international regimes which flourished from the 1970s. By that time, fears had grown in the US academic and policy-making community that the relative decline of the United States, and its reduced willingness to provide responsible leadership would lead to a weakening, and even a breakdown, of the international economic order.

In this context, theorists like Robert Keohane and Stephen Krasner looked to international organisations, and also to international habits of interaction, norms and conventions as a means to help sustain the international economic order. How could existing 'regimes' be strengthened, extended and made more effective? How could new regimes be developed? For example, how could the General Agreement on Trade and Tariffs be extended and made more effective? The implication of much of this literature was that 'regimes' served to institutionalise inter-state relations in ways which went beyond specific deals between two or more countries. Regimes were seen as a mediating influence in negotiations between governments, and as such a constraining element on national policies. But were they?

International regimes have been defined as:

sets of implicit or explicit principles, norms, rules, and decision-making procedures around which actors expectations converge in a given area of international relations. Principles are beliefs of fact, causation, and rectitude. Norms are standards of behaviour defined in terms of rights and obligations. Rules are specific prescriptions or proscriptions for action. Decision-making procedures are prevailing practices for making and implementing collective choice.[12]

Perhaps the key word in this definition is 'expectations', that is about what other states will and should do, and also concerning their expectations of your own state's behaviour.

These expectations concern not only policies (actions), but also procedures (processes). Such expectations may be linked to the way in which states are concerned for their reputation (for example, as dependable negotiators). The implication is that states do not wish to be too isolated or excluded from organisations and networks which may affect their pursuit of policy goals. The greater the number, range and intensity of interactions between states, the more reason states have for being concerned with international reputation. Thus, it is argued, whilst growing economic interdependence may place strains on the post-war (liberal) international economic order, it may also make states more wary of turning their backs on, or repudiating, this order. However, it should be remembered that international regimes have been primarily configured by the more powerful states, and also that they vary in the benefits they offer. They also vary in their ability to detect and deter cheating and in their capacity to generate significant 'reputation effects' which constrain deviant behaviour. Game theory offers clues as to which differences between regimes are likely to be significant and which changes to existing regimes might strengthen them. For example, increased contacts and inspection opportunities between the superpowers might make arms treaties and conventions more effective and serve to build trust between the antagonists. This would then help to strengthen the security regime.

Sceptics, such as Susan Strange, argue that this focus on procedures, habits, communication and reputation tends to divert attention away from the inequalities in power resources which underpin the creation and maintenance of regimes. Such power resources are the traditional realist 'key' to understanding the fundamental aspects of international relations. For Strange, regimes have been defined too loosely and are too vague and epiphenomenal: now you see them, now you don't.[13] In an attempt to generate precision and theoretical integration of the concept of 'regime' Oran Young has argued that the concept needs to be 'nested' within a wider theory of social institutions which clearly distinguishes between negotiation, imposition and spontaneous processes. Such a theory must have the ability to analyse cultural dynamics whereby ethical and moral sensibilities change. Young cites the way changing attitudes helped delegitimise colonialism, in the metropolitan powers as well as in the colonies. Since decolonisation, the sanctity of even the smallest nation-state has become embedded in both the national societies and the charters of international organisations, notably the United Nations.[14] However, none of the above should be taken to imply that states, large or small, adhere systematically to the UN Charter's strictures concerning non-intervention and the primacy of national sovereignty: many direct military interventions and wars have occurred since 1945, mainly in small or weak Third World countries, as well as myriad forms of covert intervention in a wide range of countries.

Another criticism of regime analysis is that its view of the state is inadequate and too narrow: the state tends to be viewed as a unitary actor, often with little reference to the importance of domestic politics. Domestic political forces – such as churches, trades unions, corporations and peace movements – all have an interest in the nature of the international regimes which directly or indirectly affect their interests.[15] Such conflicting domestic forces may mean that the concept of 'national interest' is highly problematic. As in much realist writing, there is also a tendency to overlook transnational social forces, and the role of non-state actors. Conflicts often arise since various actors may stand to gain or lose from the prevailing order and the international arrangements it contains. Just as some writers like Susan Strange wonder whether a particular regime favours one country disproportionately (usually the United States), it can also be argued that certain types of non-state actors (such as transnational corporations, banks) have a strong interest in a particular type of international economic order. Thus a key issue, often neglected by regime theorists, is 'order for whom?'.

Finally, some aspects of the global political economy may go beyond the confines of any game-theoretical model. Thus, if they are viewed as having a holistic character (the 'whole' shaping the 'parts'), game theory is unable to explain these aspects. This is because game theory in political economy operates with an 'individualistic' concept of structure, that is, as the aggregation of the actions and perceptions of individual persons, firms or states.[16] This limits the usefulness of both game theory and realism.

NOTES

1, On the contested varieties of realism, see Richard K. Ashley, 'Political Realism and Human Interests', *International Studies Quarterly* (1981), Vol. 25, pp. 204–36; R. B. J. Walker, 'Realism, Change, and International Political Theory', *International Studies Quarterly* (1987), Vol. 31, pp. 65–86.

2. Robert O. Keohane and Joseph S. Nye, *Power and Interdependence* (Boston, Mass., Little, Brown, 1977), p. 13.

3. Stephen Krasner, 'State Power and the Structure of International Trade', *World Politics* (1976), Vol. 26, pp. 317–43; Robert Gilpin, *US Power and the Multinational Corporation: the Political Economy of Foreign Direct Investment* (New York, Basic Books, 1975).

4. Ashley, op. cit. See John H. Herz, *Political Realism and Political Idealism* (Chicago, University of Chicago Press, 1951).

5. See, for example the whole issue of *World Politics* (1985), Vol. 38, No. 1.

6. Robert Axelrod and Robert O. Keohane, 'Cooperation under Anarchy: Strategies and Institutions; *World Politics* (1985), Vol. 38, pp. 226–54.

7. Jon Elster, 'Some Conceptual Problems in Political Theory', in Brian Barry (ed.), *Power and Political Theory* (London, John Wiley, 1976), p. 249.

8. Robert O. Keohane, *After Hegemony: Cooperation and Discord in the World Political Economy* (Princeton NJ, Princeton University Press, 1984); Kenneth Oye (ed.), *Cooperation Under Anarchy* (Princeton NJ, Princeton University Press, 1986).

9. Keohane and Nye, op. cit.

10. Mancur Olson, *The Logic of Collective Action* (Cambridge, Mass., Harvard University Press, 1982; first published 1965).

11. Robert O. Keohane, 'Reciprocity in International Relations', *International Organisation* (1986), Vol. 40, pp. 1–27.
12. Stephen Krasner (ed.), *International Regimes* (Ithaca NY, Cornell University Press, 1983), p. 3. This was a special edition of *International Organisation* (1982), Vol. 36, p. 3.
13. Susan Strange, '*Cave hic dragones!* A critique of regime analysis', *International Organisation* (1982), Vol. 36, pp. 479–96.
14. Oran R. Young, 'International Regimes: Toward a New Theory of Institutions', *World Politics* (1986), Vol. 39, pp. 104–22.
15. Stephan Haggard and Beth A Simmons, 'Theories of International Regimes', *International Organisation* (1987), Vol. 41, pp. 491–517; James N. Rosenau, 'Before Cooperation: Hegemons, Regimes, and Habit-Driven Actors in World Politics; *International Organisation* (1986), Vol. 40, pp. 853–94.
16. Ashley, op. cit.

FURTHER READING

Thucydides, *History of the Peloponnesian Wars*, translated by R. Warner, introduction and notes by M. I. Finley (Harmondsworth, Penguin Books, 1972).
Niccolo Machiavelli, *The Prince and the Discourses*, translated by L. Ricci and C. E. Detmold (New York, Modern Library, 1958).
Thomas Hobbes, *Leviathan*, ed. C. B. Macpherson (Harmondsworth, Penguin Books, 1968).
Jean Jacques Rousseau, *The Social Contract*, translated by G. D. H. Cole (New York and London, Everyman Library, 1950).
Friedrich List, *The National System of Political Economy* (New York, Kelley, 1966).
Edward Hallett Carr, *The Twenty Years' Crisis 1919–1939*, 2nd edition (London, Macmillan, 1946).
Hans Morgenthau, *Politics Among Nations: The Struggle for Power and Peace*, 5th edition (New York, Knopf, 1978).
Hedley B, *The Anarchical Society: A Study of Order in World Politics* (London, Macmillan, 1977).
Kenneth Waltz, *Theory of World Politics* (Reading, Mass., Addison-Wesley, 1979).
Robert Gilpin, *War and Change in World Politics* (Cambridge, Cambridge University Press, 1981).
Robert Gilpin, *The Political Economy of International Relations* (Princeton NJ, Princeton University Press, 1987).

4 Economic Liberalism and Public Choice

1. INTRODUCTION

In this chapter we introduce the liberal perspective, by examining liberal economics and some of the increasingly influential ideas and concepts of the public choice school. We also discuss which interests are associated with, and promoted by, the spread and acceptance of liberal economic ideas.

At this point it is important to stress two things: first, liberalism is theoretically wide-ranging, like realism and Marxism; and second, economic liberalism may go, in practice, with political authoritarianism (as in Chile after the 1973 *coup d'état*), just as realism may go with political liberalism. However, economic liberalism has generally been associated with capitalism, despite certain writings on 'market socialism'. As has been noted, the liberal economic perspective originates in the writings of Smith, Ricardo (and also the utilitarian philosopher Jeremy Bentham), and, to an extent, John Stuart Mill, in the eighteenth and nineteenth centuries. Economic liberalism was born, in part, as a response to, and critique of, mercantilism.

Our usage of the term 'liberal' differs, therefore, from that which prevails in North America, where political liberalism is often associated with what, in European terms, would be regarded as Social Democracy, and the case for state intervention in, and regulation of markets, for purposes of social welfare. Our use of the term economic liberalism might approximate the term 'free market conservatism', which consciously opposes most forms of state intervention in the economy.

2. LIBERAL ASSUMPTIONS AND UNITS OF ANALYSIS

Whereas the realist approach focuses on the nation-state, liberal thinking has tended to see the individual as the basic unit of analysis. The primary motivating force in the economy is the competitive interaction between individuals, who are assumed to maximise their satisfaction, or utility, especially through the social institution of the market. The market aggregates these individual preferences and utilities (on the demand side), and (on the supply side) the actions of profit-seeking firms. Some modern liberal thinkers, notably von Hayek, have argued that the market is, in fact, a spontaneous social institution, rather than an institution which is a product of human design.[1]

Where realism has focused on competition between states, economic liberalism has focused on competition between firms. Economic outcomes will be affected by market structure. To explain the nature of market structure, liberal economists use ideal-typical cases. At one extreme, so-called 'perfect' competition, with its infinite number of buyers and sellers, full information and perfect foresight, implies that individual buyers and sellers are 'price-takers' and the consumer is 'sovereign'. In this context, the 'power of the market' to constrain all producers is absolute. At the other extreme is monopoly (one supplier) and/or monopsony (one buyer). If both apply, there is a situation of bilateral monopoly, in which the power of one countervails that of the other. If there are many buyers, but only one supplier, then the monopolist has market power over the consumers. If there are many suppliers, but only one buyer, then the monopsonist has market power over the sellers. Of course, almost all markets and industries lie between these two extremes. In the case of oligopoly (when there are relatively few firms), firms will have some degree of market power, which will be increased if they are able to collude and thus impose their collective power over the market. An extreme case of collusion is when firms form a cartel which sets prices and production quotas for the member firms.

Each of these market structures are also examples of different degrees of interdependence or dependence. In the extreme case of perfect competition, there is complete and symmetrical interdependence between buyers and sellers. In the case of oligopoly there is some interdependence between producers. This may be symmetrical or asymmetrical, depending on whether there is a dominant firm, or 'price leader' in a market, such as De Beers in the diamond trade, and IBM in mainframe computers for much of the post-war period. In general, the greater degree of market concentration on the supply side, the more asymmetrical the interdependence between producers and consumers, to the disadvantage of the latter. The main characteristic of oligopolistic competition is that the behaviour of one firm will be affected by its anticipation of the behaviour of rival firms. This characteristic can be also seen in the context of the foreign economic policies of governments. For example, one government may not raise a trade barrier for fear of retaliation. A case of total dependence of consumers on producers would require there to be a firm which had a monopoly in all industries, such that there was no scope for substitution between products. This would close all escape routes from dependence on the super-monopolist. Such a case is virtually inconceivable under capitalism, but has been approximated in some forms of state socialism, as in the Soviet Union from the era of Stalin to Chernenko. The current Soviet leader, Gorbachev, instituted reforms in the 1980s partly designed to break down this monopolistic situation.

Neo-classical economics has an individualist concept of structure that has influenced, and been paralleled in much neo-realist writing. For example, Kenneth Waltz, has drawn on microeconomic market analysis in order to build conceptions of inter-state structure: the world political system after 1945 is likened to duopoly, the inter-war period likened to oligopoly.[2] Balance of power considerations are cast in the framework of market equilibrium analysis, taken from liberal neo-classical economics. For Waltz, a stable international political equilibrium is most likely when there is a high degree of concentration of material power, for example when the two superpowers had consolidated their power blocs, and were relatively equally balanced, as in the 1960s and 1970s: this would lead to 'peaceful coexistence'. In this situation, the question of international political communication is simplified, since only two sets of leaders are involved, whereas any dispersion of power amongst states raises communications requirements in a disproportionate way, so that miscalculations become more likely. As international power becomes more equally distributed across ever-larger numbers of states, the likelihood of conflict will tend to grow, unless leaders are willing and able to collude (through alliances and agreements). Collusion becomes less and less likely as the number of states increases.

Thus an international oligarchy is relatively less stable than a system dominated by two superpowers, but is potentially more stable than one of many competing powers. In contrast, in liberal economics, for the market to efficiently allocate resources, substantial competition is required. For economic liberals, a large number of firms is economically desirable, whereas, for realists, a large number of relatively equal states is undesirable, if primary value is placed on order.

Liberal economists do accept that there may be a case for some state intervention to correct market imperfections, but only if the state has sufficient knowledge to do this, and if administrative costs are not too high. The market mechanism may fail because of externalities in production and consumption which are not captured in the system of property rights, for example in the case of pollution. Here a firm imposes costs on the national society (and perhaps other societies and the global ecosystem) in excess of the costs it incurs itself in the process of production. Monopoly itself is seen as an imperfection requiring either the break-up of the monopoly, or state regulation of the private enterprise.

The above points relate to the microeconomic aspects of liberal economics. At the macroeconomic level intervention, Keynesian economics, with its stress on macroeconomic intervention, is based on assumptions about market failures which cause unemployment due to a lack of aggregate demand. Keynesians therefore argue for active discretionary use of fiscal and monetary policy to offset demand shortfalls, or to cool off the economy if demand is too high. By contrast, monetarists have greater faith in the stability and self-regulating capacity of markets, so long as there is a low and steady growth rate of the money supply.

In recent work on market failures economists have tended to see the economy as a complex mixture of markets, some of which 'clear' (adjust) quickly, have price flexibility, and are highly competitive in structure. Financial and foreign exchange markets are often seen as coming into this category, since they operate internationally, have many buyers and sellers, and use technology which enables price signals to be transmitted very rapidly indeed. Other markets exhibit varying degrees of oligopoly and price inflexibility and disequilibrium. In the latter case, adjustments are much slower, as, for example, in the markets for many goods, and especially for labour. In labour markets, long-term contracts are common, and are often produced through bargaining between employers and unions. These contracts involve not just wages and conditions, but also job security for workers. For flexible labour markets to exist, such job protection would need to be abolished. The ultimate extreme in this case would be the hiring of workers on a day-by-day basis. Wage rates would be set by means of an auction. This practice is widespread in agricultural work in the Third World, and was a common practice in many countries until comparatively recently.

3. PUBLIC GOODS AND FREE-RIDERS

While liberal economics provides theoretical support for possessive individualism and the market mechanism, this is qualified in various ways, notably in the case of the concept of 'public goods'. Public goods are those goods and services which are jointly supplied and are characterised by an inability to exclude beneficiaries on a selective basis. In this sense, such goods cannot be simply limited to those who are willing and able to pay for them. This implies that left to private enterprise these goods will be undersupplied. As a result they are often supplied by the state, and/or through state subsidies given to the private sector.

In the case of the public good of national security, this is supplied by the government to all the population, in part through the commitment of resources to the armed forces. Each individual receives a supply of this public good, regardless of whether he or she has made a contribution to the resources needed to finance the military capacity. The supply of resources normally occurs through taxation (and/or borrowing) and some individuals may not pay such taxes, or indeed may avoid taxes through a variety of means. This gives rise to the so-called 'free-rider' problem. The supply of security takes a form whereby it is impossible, or difficult to exclude a non-contributor from the benefits. Other examples of public goods which are discussed by liberal theorists include monetary stability, and more obviously political goods such as law and order.

Liberal political economists have also sought to apply the concept of public goods at the international level, where the supply of public goods is seen as more problematic since there is no world state which can extract taxation (or contributions) from those who benefit from the supply of goods such as international security. International security, monetary stability and an open international economy, with relatively free and predictable ability to move goods, services and capital are all seen as desirable public goods from this perspective. More generally, international economic order is to be preferred to disorder – with the 1930s as a prime example of the latter.

The desirability of such goods, which are effectively the politico-economic conditions for, and aspects of, a liberal international economy, rests on the argument that economic relations through the market have the character of a positive-sum game. In such a game, there will be potential for increased global economic welfare, although any increase may be very unequally distributed. In addition, liberals argue that such positive-sum interactions generate a rationale for international economic cooperation amongst states. Whether this is subsequently translated into a reduction in international conflict is more problematic, since this will rest upon the nature of the inter-state system, and the degree of international security which prevails therein. Further, conflict, in the sense of friction, normally takes place over the terms of cooperation. This needs to be distinguished from more fundamental conflicts, or antagonisms, about ideology and world order. Most of the squabbles between the partners in the European Economic Community come into the first category of conflicts, whereas the conflict between Western capitalism and Soviet communism, particularly during the height of the Cold War, comes into second.

As was noted in the previous chapter, realist-mercantilists often tend to see international security in zero-sum terms. They also see security as having the first priority, since it provides the precondition for the pursuit of other goals such as economic welfare. It has been argued in the theory of hegemonic stability (which is a fusion of liberal and realist ideas) that in so far as a hegemonic power solves the problem of international security by exercising its international dominance, a liberal economy, which might maximise global economic welfare may be more attainable. A hegemonic state possesses the power and wealth to supply international public goods, even if it is unable to exclude other states from gaining some of the benefit. In practice, its dominance may enable it to get other states to contribute to the supply of international public goods, either through threats and/or inducements. This case of the 'coercive hegemon' may be contrasted with that of the 'benevolent hegemon' which supplies public goods freely.[3] The 'benevolent' hegemon's share in the absolute benefits from supplying public goods is sufficient to make the exercise worthwhile.

The distinction between private (in this context, meaning goods which accrue to a single country, or limited number of countries) and public (that is available to all states) is normally a matter of degree. A good example of this is a military alliance in which members gain more security than non-members, even though the latter may gain to some extent. Thus although neither Sweden nor Yugoslavia are members of NATO, each gains security from its existence, but feels it necessary to spend substantial amounts on defence, mainly to protect itself against the threats from the Warsaw Pact forces. On the other hand, neither Sweden nor Yugoslavia can be certain that NATO forces will help to protect them if a Warsaw Pact attack took place, whereas NATO members benefit from a collective commitment to defend any member which may be attacked by a non-NATO country. Within an alliance, however, some countries may bear a disproportionate burden in terms of the provision or supply of security goods and services. In the case of NATO, in the 1980s, the USA supplied over half the Allied contributions, and in the case of the Warsaw Pact the USSR supplied more than three-quarters of the overall costs of maintaining its alliance. This has led members of the security establishment in the USA to accuse several of its allies (particularly Japan which is outside NATO) of taking a free ride at the USA's expense.

4. THE THEORY OF HEGEMONIC STABILITY

In the application of these public choice ideas in international relations, it is also suggested that if the power of the hegemon decreases, so will the supply of public goods such as security or a stable monetary system, since other states will be relatively less willing to increase their contributions to alliance or system maintenance costs, to match the shortfall caused by a declining hegemonic capacity. Indeed, the 'free-rider' problem is likely to be more severe at the international level, not least because a sense of shared identity and loyalty, which often holds within a country (because of patriotism) is often lacking at the international level.

The Theory of Hegemonic Stability was initially developed by the economist and historian Charles Kindleberger as a means of explaining why the international monetary disorder of the 1930s occurred and continued. Kindleberger's basic argument was that although Britain was willing to supply the public good of international monetary stability, it simply did not have the economic strength to do so. Whilst Britain was willing but unable, the USA, which had massive economic strength and gold reserves, was able but unwilling to take on the mantle of economic leadership from Britain and become the new hegemon.[4] International economic instability and crisis in the 1930s was interpreted as of the first importance in generating the uncertainty which contributed to the outbreak of World War II. This case has been generalised in support of the argument that the maintenance of the stability of the post-1945 international economic order depends crucially on the continued dominance and leadership of the USA within the world economy. For a liberal order to be created and maintained, hegemonic leadership is seen as a necessary but not sufficient condition of its existence, since the hegemon must of course be committed to a liberal approach. In so far as liberal conditions are viewed as contributing to the erosion of the primacy of the hegemon in the post-war system, some theorists, liberal and others, have suggested that liberal orders tend to self-destruct.[5]

Recent appraisals of the Theory of Hegemonic Stability have used game theory of the sort discussed in the previous chapter. For example, Duncan Snidal has shown how this theory ignores the impact of bargaining, negotiation, strategic rationality and cooperation through collective action.[6] As the hegemon (state A) declines, states B and C rise in relative and absolute importance, and are likely to have an increasing incentive to cooperate in the provision of public goods, at least if state A can convince them that it will will not supply the goods if they engage in 'free-riding'. If the size and share of states B and C in the world economy is such as for each of them to obtain sufficient benefits from the provision of a public good, then the top three states (A, B and C) might collectively behave like a 'benevolent hegemon'. This group of countries is so central and large within the world economy that its members will provide public goods, even if other states free ride. Alternatively, these three states may act as a 'coercive hegemon', pressurising other states to adhere to rules and make contributions which help to maintain the supply of international public goods. In the 1980s, such 'collective coercion' has been used by the leading states (such as the USA, Britain, West Germany and France) and their central banks (and large commercial banks) to manage the debt crisis.

More generally, it can be argued the Theory of Hegemonic Stability is too loosely specified with regard to such factors as the exact size and number of states which are involved, the nature and linkage (if any) between issue-areas (such as between security, money and trade), the possibility of reputation effects and the time-horizons of actors. This means that collective action in the provision of international public goods can be extremely difficult and complex to analyse and to achieve. In this sense, the Theory of Hegemonic Stability is an example of a theory which is excessively parsimonious, especially when ideas about how to sustain the supply of public goods are sought.

Snidal contrasts, as polar cases, the single-play Prisoners's Dilemma and that of the 'Coordination Game'. In the former, communication and bargaining between two states, A and B, does not take place. In consequence, the costs to state B which are imposed by the policy choices of state A, are inflicted independently of the choices of State B. In the 'Coordination Game', which may involve more than two players, communication and bargaining take place freely, and each state is able to impose costs or confer benefits on other states, contingent on the policy choices these other states make. An example of the 'Coordination Game' is the repeated attempts made by the major capitalist states in the 1970s and 1980s, to cooperate over the making of their macroeconomic policies, since each state's policies had significant repercussions for the economic welfare of the others. In situations akin to those portrayed in the Coordination Game, the Theory of Hegemonic Stability has little validity. What Snidal does not do is to consider the influence of domestic political 'games' on international cooperation: the area where public choice theory has a contribution to make.

5. PUBLIC CHOICE AND POLICY-MAKING

Public choice writers see the determination of national policies in terms of supply and demand. The demand for policies comes from individuals whose 'voice' may be expressed through collective organisation and action as in industrial lobbies.[7] Usually the demand for policies is related to the economic self-interest of the parties concerned. For example, workers and national capitalists ('home producers') in an industry have a common interest in protection against imports which are more competitive than their own production. On the other hand, consumers will have an interest in access to such products, and therefore in lobbying against the imposition of tariffs. Home producers whose goods are competitive internationally may also share this interest with consumers since they might fear retaliation abroad if tariffs are imposed by their home country against foreign goods. The same applies to home producers who may be using the cheaper imported items as an input for their production.

Despite its apparent rationality, collective action may not always be achieved. This is because those with the interest may be large in number and thus difficult to organise effectively. Geographical dispersion reinforces this point, though perhaps less so as the technology of communications improves. Moreover, the effects of, for example, tariff changes, are distributed differently across various interests. While cheaper foreign goods may increase consumer welfare, they may directly threaten the existence of an entire domestic industry, and the livelihood of workers and capitalists in that industry. Thus the incentive to lobby for protection will tend to be much greater for producer groups, than for the more diffuse groups of consumers. Similar 'demand' considerations will apply to other types of policies, such as taxation, government expenditures and environmental regulations. In these policy areas, many different types of group will be involved, although they can be categorised together as producers and consumers in the 'political market-place' for each policy. One sector that is often easy to organise, and is well placed to exert influence, is banking and finance. Here political channels for interest groups may become institutionalised – for example, the central bank may represent the interests of financial capital, whilst elsewhere the agriculture ministry may identify with the interests of farmers. Thus the demand side is partly linked to the supply side of policy formation through such institutionalisation.

On the supply side of the public choice equation the main actors are governments and bureaucracies. In the case of liberal democracies, politicians are seen as motivated by the need to to win sufficient electoral support, and to remain in office. In order to do this, they will rationally seek to deliver a set of policies which reflects the scale and intensity of some, though not necessarily all, organised demands. In meeting such demands, politicians are likely to deliberately shift resources and other advantages away from some groups towards others. In this view, the civil society is determinative of behaviour of democratically elected political leaders. However, the response to electoral demands may be affected by the organisation, influence and interests of bureaucrats, who are less constrained by electoral considerations. Bureaucrats are usually assumed to have an interest in job security and improving their working conditions and job prospects, and, as a result, in enlarging the size and scale of their jurisdiction. An instance of this, referred to in some of the public choice literature, is the goal of budget maximisation by bureaucrats.

The implication is that an 'equilibrium' set of policies, in the political market-place, will change according to the shifts in industrial structure, the organisation and strength of various group interests, and the characteristics and values of the electorate. The demand for some policies will also be affected by changes in economic conditions. For example, in a recession, certain industries with surplus capacity may be more likely to demand protection than when there is a boom, when they will be nearer to full capacity. The second implication is that foreign economic policies are primarily determined by the balance of domestic forces in national political economies. This means that the policies which might help sustain an open international economy are most likely to be pursued when an 'internationalist' coalition of interests gains sufficient control over foreign economic policy in the major capitalist states, especially in the USA. In addition, in an interdependent world economy, additional pressures which constrain national autonomy and the tendency to pursue protectionist and other policies of economic closure, are generated by the integration of international capital and exchange markets, and the capital flows which take place within this context. Thus political and economic forces, may, under certain conditions, allow for the further deepening of international economic interdependence. However, this may not always be the case, so that the liberal analysis of politics can predict an 'illiberal' outcome for economic policies. This is, of course, in contrast to what liberal economic theory would suggest is desirable from the viewpoint of efficiency and consumer welfare.

6. ECONOMIC LIBERALISM AND POLITICAL INTERESTS

Liberal economic theory claims to be advancing propositions which are in the interests of consumers. As suggested earlier, the consumer interest might be opposed to that of certain producer groups. However, many of the policy recommendations favoured by liberal economists (free trade, freedom of capital flows) can be seen as in the interests of capital (rather than less mobile labour), especially transnational capital. This interest is strengthened if various groups and classes come to define the political economy in liberal terms, reinforcing an individualistic culture. In addition, economic liberalism can be seen as a general critique of various forms of state economic planning, as well as of detailed forms of state intervention. These are criticised on the grounds that they are inefficient, and are often associated with vested interests (e.g. bureaucratic), which are usually seen as curtailing individual freedom, and even threatening the survival of liberal democracy. Let us now review some substantive arguments made by economic liberals.

The liberal critique of monopoly might be seen as even-handed, in that such tendencies are condemned for both capital and labour. At the same time, the liberal focus on the market and on exchange eliminates from consideration the relations of production, which are usually weighted in favour of capital relative to labour. In capitalism, capital has control over strategic decisions, has much more knowledge of the firm's operations and options, and usually has the support of various state agencies in its relations with workers. Thus by largely ignoring relations of production in its theoretical system, liberal economic theory obscures the normally unequal relation of capital to labour. A related point is that liberal theory tends to stress that utility, or satisfaction in economic life, is gained through consumption, rather than through the labour process. It pays less attention to the the quality of work and job satisfaction, although such factors are sometimes considered with regard to the supply of labour for different occupations. The focus on exchange relations thus directs attention away from the question of who controls the production process, and the struggle for such control.[8]

A key concept in liberal economics is efficiency, both in its allocative and productive senses. Productive efficiency concerns output within a firm and whether it is carried out in the most cost-effective way. Allocative efficiency concerns how far the distribution of capital and labour between different industries and products meets consumer demands.[9] Trade unions are often seen as reducing productive efficiency, by raising wages above the competitive equilibrium level and through inhibiting innovations which raise productivity. Thus liberal concepts of efficiency cast doubt on the desirability of the collective organisation of workers. On the other hand, some liberal economic writers have suggested that oligopoly (despite the reduction in competition which may be involved) is acceptable, provided that it generates gains in productive efficiency. Such gains may result from economies of scale and perhaps from vertical integration of the firm, as in many transnational corporations. In this last case, it is suggested that the vertically-integrated firm may coordinate different stages of production more effectively than the market mechanism (which coordinates separate firms at each stage of production). Indeed, such gains have been suggested as a major reason, and justification, for the rise of transnational corporations.

An implication of the above is that internationally mobile transnational capital is well served by the diffusion and acceptance of liberal economic ideas, and their embodiment in policies, especially in the major capitalist states and in significant international organisations. Conversely, the adoption of such policies is likely to undermine the material interests of less competitive 'national' capital, as well as associated (organised) labour.

NOTES

1. F. A. Hayek, *Knowledge, Evolution and Society* (London, Adam Smith Institute, 1983).
2. Kenneth Waltz, *Theory of World Politics* (Reading, Mass., Addison-Wesley, 1979).

3. Duncan Snidal, 'The Limits of Hegemonic Stability Theory', *International Organisation* (1985), Vol. 39, pp. 579–614.
4. Charles Kindleberger, *The World in Depression 1929–1939* (Berkeley, Cal., University of California Press, 1973).
5. These arguments are reviewed in David Sylvan, 'The Newest Mercantilism', *International Organisation* (1981), Vol. 35, pp. 375–9.
6. Ibid. See also, Duncan Snidal, 'Coordination versus Prisoners' Dilemma: Implications for International Cooperation and Regimes', *American Political Science Review* (1985), Vol. 79, pp. 923–42; Duncan Snidal, 'Public Goods, Property Rights, and Political Organisations', *International Studies Quarterly* (1979), Vol. 23, pp. 532–66.
7. A. O. Hirschman, 'Exit, Voice and Loyalty', in *Essays in Trespassing* (Princeton NJ, Princeton University Press, 1981).
8. However, economists have paid attention to the possible conflict of interest between shareholders and managers in so-called managerial theories of the firm. Such theories also relate to the debate in the sociology of organisations over the distinction between ownership and control of capitalist enterprises. A more recent development, the theory of 'principal and agent', may offer some scope for examining issues of control within production relations. See Norman Strong and Michael Waterson, 'Principals, Agents and Information', in Roger Clarke and Tony McGuinness, (eds), *The Economics of the Firm* (Oxford, Basil Blackwell, 1987), pp. 18–41.
9. Optimum allocative efficiency theoretically requires the mix of products coming onto the market to be such as to attain the highest level of consumer satisfaction given the distribution of income, stable tastes, and the stock of the factors of production. (Allocative efficiency as well as productive efficiency is one of the requirements for achieving 'Pareto optimality.') Liberal economists argue that the centrally planned economy is unable to allocate resources efficiently, due to lack of information on consumer demand, since no price signals are transmitted to producers. The latter thus have little incentive to avoid overproduction of some items, or to ensure optimal quality.

FURTHER READING: LIBERALISM

(i) Public Choice
Bruno S. Frey, *International Political Economics* (Oxford, Basil Blackwell, 1984).
Ian McLean, *Public Choice: An Introduction* (Oxford, Basil Blackwell, 1987).
James Alt and Alex Chrystal, *Political Economics* (Brighton, Wheatsheaf Books, 1983).
Robert T. Kudrle, 'The Several Faces of The Multinational Corporation: Political Reaction and Policy Response', in W. Ladd Hollis and F. LaMond Tullis (eds), *An International Political Economy* (Boulder, Col., Westview Press, 1985), pp. 175–97.

(ii) Theorists of Interdependence
Richard Cooper, *The Economics of Interdependence: Economic Policy in the Atlantic Community* (New York, McGraw-Hill/Council on Foreign Relations, 1968).
R. O. Keohane and J. S. Nye, *Power and Interdependence* (Boston, Mass., Little, Brown, 1977).

(iii) Economic Liberals

Adam Smith, *An Enquiry into the Nature and Causes of the Wealth of Nations* (Oxford, Clarendon Press, 1976, first published 1776).

Milton Friedman, *Capitalism and Freedom* (Chicago, University of Chicago Press, 1962).

Friedrich A. von Hayek, *The Road to Serfdom* (Chicago, University of Chicago Press, 1944).

5   Marxism and the World System

1. INTRODUCTION

The Marxist tradition is a rich and varied one. In this chapter, therefore, we focus selectively on certain ideas about the capitalist world economy, and relations between different types of capitalist states. The relations between the capitalist and state socialist systems are analysed later, in chapter 15.

We distinguish between the classical Marxist writing on imperialism of Lenin, Bukharin, Hilferding and Luxemburg prior to the consolidation of the Russian Revolution of 1917; the dependency and world systems schools which have emerged since the 1950s; and the more recent transnational historical materialism of writers like Stephen Hymer and Robert Cox.[1] It should be noted the dependency and world systems theory are not wholly Marxist, especially since they have a strong tendency to prioritise exchange relations when discussing exploitation and inequality. Some would argue that such theorists are not Marxist at all. Dependency and world system theories contrast with the mainstream Marxist tradition which prioritises class conflict in terms of the relations of production. However, these different schools of thought do share an interest in the way the global system of capitalism shapes and influences the nature as well as the behaviour of states, classes, firms and individuals. In this respect their notions of structure are similar, and they contrast with the individualist concepts of structure which are used in liberalism and realism.

In practice, some writers do not fit neatly into one school: for example, Robert Cox often uses the terms 'core and periphery', but is not a world systems theorist, since his starting point is the relations of production. With this in mind, the following exposition of the three schools is constructed in terms of ideal-types.

2. MODES OF PRODUCTION

A central characteristic of the Marxist tradition is that the political economy is viewed as of historically specific nature, with successive and possibly overlapping epochs of development. These epochs – primitive communism, feudalism, capitalism and communism – are defined in terms of modes of production, and the class relations which are typical of each. Different modes of production go with different systems of property rights: for example, in the feudal mode property was parcelled out to, and controlled by, the lord in his fiefdom. This means that the scope for independent capitalist accumulation was severely circumscribed. This was also because labour was not free to move, being attached to the lord's landholding. In the towns, guilds (trade associations) regulated and restricted entry into the production of a range of manufactures. With the withering of feudalism in the countryside, private enterprise, especially in the production of manufactures, could develop beyond the control of guilds. For this to occur, the system of property rights, based upon tradition and conquest, had to change to a new, legal form.

Why does the transition from one mode to another take place? The class relations of one mode of production may become an obstacle to the further development of the 'forces of production', so that the replacement of one mode by another is made possible by its productive superiority. The new mode grows within the old, but ultimately this growth requires a change in social and political institutions to develop to its fullest potential. Thus for capitalism to become the dominant mode, and to supplant feudalism, the factory system replaced the guild system, which had in turn been undermined by the putting-out system of merchant capitalism. In order for the factory system to operate effectively, labour markets had to be created, which implied significant changes in social institutions. Of these, notable changes were the removal of the feudal bonds of duty and obligation which bound the peasant to his land and to his lord, and vice versa. This transition took place first in Europe. The emerging capitalist mode of production had several key characteristics. The first of these was a legally guaranteed system of property rights, which enables individuals or corporations freely to buy, sell or accumulate land and capital. This created a market for land and capital, which operated alongside a market for the newly-freed wage labour which flooded into the new industrial centres. The new system was motivated by the acquisition of capital, itself obtained by making profits from the exploitation of labour by capitalists, and from the earning of rents from the leasing of land.

Within the capitalist epoch, Marxists have attempted to distinguish several stages. A typical periodisation might be as follows: merchant capitalism from the sixteenth to the eighteenth centuries, early industrial capitalism from the late eighteenth to the middle of the nineteenth century, the monopoly or imperialist stage from the late nineteenth into the twentieth century, and 'late' capitalism or the 'super-imperialist' stage since 1945. For all these stages, capitalism is understood as a world, as opposed to a national or regional system.

A mode of production is an abstraction which refers to the main social forces (especially classes) which organise and control the generation and distribution of the economic surplus in a given society or group of societies. For example, in the capitalist mode, the surplus takes the form of interest, dividends and profits for capitalists. By contrast, those who make up the class of labour are wholly or at least mainly dependent on income from their labour-power. Workers have to sell this labour-power as a commodity to capitalists in the labour market, in order to survive. The widespread payment of wages is a defining characteristic of capitalism, as opposed to feudalism, where the peasant had to provide labour services to his lord, and also some payments in kind, such as foodstuffs grown on the land which the lord allowed the peasants to cultivate on their own behalf.

In the capitalist mode, therefore, two basic classes emerge, the capitalists and the workers. Each class has interests which are, ultimately, fundamentally opposed. The capitalist wishes to raise the level of surplus at the expense of wages; workers wish to raise wages relative to profits. In addition, workers seek to gain more autonomy in the labour process at the expense of managers who attempt to impose their prerogatives. For Marxists, the very existence of profits as a category is seen as evidence of capitalist exploitation, since, at least for the mainstream Marxist tradition, all value is traced, directly or indirectly, to labour. This use of the concept of exploitation contrasts to that of the liberal economists discussed in the previous chapter: here the term is confined to the use of market power to exploit consumers by monopolists or sellers by monopsonists.

3. THE STATE AND IMPERIALISM

The traditional Marxist view has been that the state acts, directly or indirectly, in the interests of the ruling class. For Lenin, following Marx and Engels' rhetorical declaration in the *Communist Manifesto*, the capitalist state was seen in instrumental terms: as a committee for managing the affairs of the ruling class or bourgeoisie. However, some later writers have suggested that elements of a previous ruling class may sometimes hold some state power, and also that concessions are necessarily made to subordinate classes in order more smoothly to maintain the class dominance of the bourgeoisie. Such writers allow the state significant relative autonomy. One reason for such relative autonomy relates to divisions within the capitalist class. These are normally referred to as class fractions, for example between industrial and money capital, and their possible fusion into finance capital. Thus the state serves a coordinating, arbitrating and sometimes leading role in the reconciliation of these potentially conflicting capitalist interests. Indeed, the state may arbitrate between different classes, as well as the fractions within them. Such an approach has some similiarities to the interest group analysis of public choice theorists, in that the state, and indeed politics, are seen in instrumental terms. Politics and the state are the terrain where the material interests of groups or classes are advanced. Such interests are aggregated in political parties which seek to capture state power. In the Leninist view, this meant that only one party, the Communist Party, could represent the 'real' or 'objective' interests of the workers against capital. This party should be led by a disciplined elite or vanguard of intellectuals, who, through their mastery of scientific Marxism, had grasped the nature of these 'real' interests, and could articulate the strategies for advancing them. By identifying the inherent contradictions of capitalism, and by developing the class consciousness of workers, the revolutionary leaders would prepare the ground for the inevitable transition to socialism. One substantive issue addressed by these early Marxist intellectuals was the nature of such contradictions on a world scale, and how and why these would lead to the collapse of capitalism. This was developed in the theory of imperialism, which embraces a view of the international role of the capitalist state.

In this context, one function of the capitalist state was to support its national capitalists in the struggle for market shares, access to secure supplies of raw materials and foreign investment opportunities. The classical Marxist writing on imperialism laid particular stress on the necessity of increasing capital exports to avoid the tendency for the rate of profit to fall. This tendency, sometimes called a 'law of motion' of capitalism, was associated by Marx with technological changes which led to increasingly large-scale and capital-intensive methods of production. In turn, such methods would, according to Lenin, result in the concentration of capital in fewer hands, and the emergence of a stage of 'monopoly capitalism'. In this stage, the class divide widened between a small and privileged capitalist class and a huge working class, itself increasingly organised and conscious of its political potential (e.g. through trade unions and workers' parties). For Lenin, imperialist policies such as empire-building and 'gunboat diplomacy' served not merely to maintain the rate of profit (by facilitating foreign investment): they also enabled the capitalist class to use some of the imperial gains to buy off the more privileged members of the workers. This class fraction was termed the 'labour aristocracy'. In this way, a wider domestic political coalition of forces in favour of imperialist policies was created in each of the leading capitalist states. Bukharin noted that such policies went with nationalism and jingoism, which also served to reinforce the identification of workers with national capitalists and their imperialist policies. In this sense, imperialism was an ideology, as well as a policy.[2] Lenin used the term imperialism as a label for a specific, and for him, the 'highest stage of capitalism', after which would come the transition to socialism.

One of the major contradictions of capitalism was embodied in the law of the falling rate of profit. A second was that between the drive of capitalists to exploit workers and their need for workers to be able, as consumers, to buy their products. Marx expected capitalism's fantastic ability to increase productive capacity to run ahead of the growth in the labour force and to outstrip consumer demand. Slower economic growth and increasingly severe recessions were inevitable so that unemployment, and more generally the gulf between the two classes, would grow. The labour-saving bias of technological change would contribute to this outcome, while applying downward pressure on the rate of profit. Exports and foreign investment, and also labour migration (for example, the 'American safety-valve' for Europe), were ways of avoiding a shortfall of demand, a glut of capital, and rising unemployment in the domestic economy. In this sense, the domestic stability of capitalism in the leading states began to increasingly rest upon the operation of capital on a world-wide basis.

On the international level, the classical Marxists saw imperialism as a stage which could only temporarily contain the above contradictions. Once the leading national capitalist states had carved up the world into empires and spheres of influence (that is by creating informal empires, such as the USA had in Central and parts of Latin America in the late nineteenth and early twentieth centuries), then further imperialist expansion could only be achieved at the expense of other imperialists. This would be most likely to be resolved through war between the imperialist powers, as in World War I 1914–18. However, given the race for colonies in the late nineteenth century, a war in the periphery (rather than in the core) over the control of colonies might have been the expected outcome.

Classical Marxist writers explain the dynamics of inter-imperialist rivalry, and its lethal consequences, by reference to a combination of economic, socio-political and strategic forces. For Lenin, inter-imperialist wars would inevitably follow the wars of imperialist expansion (that is to capture colonies), since while national capitalists could usually cooperate within a country, such cooperation was difficult between the capitalists of different countries. For example, while international cartels sometimes occurred, they usually broke down due to significant differences in costs of production. Further, the 'uneven development' (that is the growth rates) of the capitalist states tended to destabilise the balance of power between them. One aspect of this uneven development, for Lenin (following the analysis of the radical liberal J. A. Hobson), was that capitalism had a tendency towards stagnation, a tendency which was most pronounced in Britain, the first country to industrialise. Thus the dynamism of the leading country tended to decline relative to others, as it exported a higher proportion of its capital than did its rivals.

The possibility of a peaceful compromise between the leading capitalist states, in which some reallocation of colonies and/or investment opportunities might take place, was suggested by Karl Kautsky, the German Social Democrat.[3] Lenin fiercely disagreed with 'the renegade' Kautsky, partly since Kautsky's theory of 'ultra-imperialism' denied the imminent possibility of socialist revolution. Lenin's arguments were reinforced by the work of Bukharin, who stressed the ideological aspect and the 'mercantilist-militarist' character of imperialism. The very ideology which cut across the class divide within a country made capitalist cooperation between countries more politically difficult. In addition, each of the leading capitalist states sought to protect its security through military build-ups, provoking the widespread militarisation of 'monopoly capitalism'.

While wars and inter-state rivalry were seen by these writers as inevitable under capitalism, they were seen as unlikely in a world of socialism. Thus, whilst the capitalists of the world were bound to exist in a contradictory world of competition and conflict, the workers of the world were seen as, at least theoretically, able to unite. The red flag would be the international banner for the peaceful alliance of the proletariat.

4. THE CORE–PERIPHERY DIVIDE

Lenin had expected the revolution to occur somewhere in Europe, and in this respect typified the Euro-centrism of classical Marxism. However, after the failure of the Russian Revolution to spread to the rest of Europe, he turned his revolutionary hopes towards India and China, even though the proletariat in these countries was even smaller than that of Tsarist Russia. Imperialism went with the super-exploitation of labour in the colonial areas, whereas in the European countries there was a labour aristocracy, which divided the working class and weakened its collective political potential.

As the twentieth century advanced, Western workers became increasingly affluent, and there was a growing appreciation of the enormity of the gap in living standards between them and workers in Asia, Africa and Latin America. Classical theories of imperialism did not predict such a steadily widening gap. On the contrary, Lenin expected industrialisation of the less-developed regions to proceed, whilst at the same time there would be industrial decline in the metropolitan countries. Lenin thought there would be a tendency towards the equalisation of the economic condition of what the later dependency writers called the 'core' and 'periphery'. Paul Baran, an American Marxist, tried to account for the apparent post-war success of metropolitan capitalism by suggesting that the core countries were able to extract an ever-growing 'economic tribute', in various forms, from the periphery. He stressed the role of transnational corporations in the draining of capital (surplus) from the periphery (underdeveloped countries) to the core.[4] Core states are defined as those with more advanced technologies and a favourable position in the international division of labour.

Radical Third World writers took up and extended Baran's stress on economic dependence, seeing it in increasingly systemic terms.[5] Such writers were oppressively conscious that political independence would not be enough to overcome the core–periphery divide (today sometimes referred to as the North–South gap) unless economic sovereignty was also achieved. The dependence of the periphery on the core, was not seen as temporary or accidental, but as a structural feature of world capitalism. This was reproduced through a process which concentrated capital accumulation and technological innovation in the core. Nearly all research and development activity, and the bulk of the capital goods industries were in the core countries. These financial, technological and trade advantages were sources of the periphery's dependence on the core. Such advantages enabled the core states to exploit the peripheral countries. In so far as this involved draining resources from the less-developed countries, the core–periphery divide was maintained or even increased.

Such an extraction of surplus contrasts with the classical Marxist view that there is a net export of capital to the periphery. Also, the concept of exploitation used by dependency writers differs in that it focuses on exchange processes between (groups of) states, rather than production relations between social classes. The exact mechanisms of exploitation are seen as varying historically and are the subject of debate. One fashionable view in the 1970s was that trade took place at prices which involved an 'unequal exchange'.[6]

Variations can also be noted in the assessment of the severity of the systemic impact of structural dependency on the periphery. Some writers have a very pessimistic view, notably the early work of A. G. Frank. In his view, the development of the core implied a process of underdevelopment of the periphery. As such, peripheral states have very limited external autonomy. Others, notably Henrique Cardoso, suggest that some 'dependent development' may occur in the periphery, with a complex relationship emerging between the state, foreign and local capital. However, the structural condition of dependency still persists, and the insertion of the peripheral political economy into the wider world capitalist economy works to the advantage of foreign (core) capital, although in Cardoso's view rather more external autonomy is possible for the peripheral country than is allowed by Frank.[7] The world systems writers specifically allow for some upward and downward mobility within the world system, and use the term semi-periphery to cover intermediate states which are relatively more developed, and have more external autonomy than their counterparts in the periphery.

The structural condition of dependency can also be seen in cultural terms, whereby Western ideas, languages and tastes are implanted in less-developed countries. One effect of this is to raise the demand for core products and cultural artifacts, such as for French films in West Africa, Disney comics in Latin America, and Coca-Cola world-wide. A related effect is that social aspirations of many groups in the periphery come to be based on the goal of emulating the core countries' lifestyle and consumption patterns.

In addition, the concept of imperialism used by three writers is also different from that of classical Marxism:

For Frank and Wallerstein, imperialism is a term that covers any use by core states of their political strength to impose price structures that they find favourable on the world-economy. Sometimes this takes the form of conquest and political overrule; at other times it takes the form of 'informal imperialism', called by others 'neocolonialism'.[8]

Whereas classical Marxists focused on conflicts between the core states, dependency and world systems writers tend to assume a significant degree of cooperation between these states, particularly when one core state is able to assert its dominance over others, as did Britain in the nineteenth century. World systems writers assume that the level of conflict between core states varies over time, and when power is more dispersed within the core, conflict is more likely. Moreover, in this latter case more direct forms of political control over the periphery tend to predominate, whereas in the case of a hegemonic order, informal imperialism, open trade and even decolonisation are more likely.

The processes of control of the periphery are seen in the wider context of the structural dominance of the core over the periphery. Within this wider context, certain social processes are seen as vital, notably the relationship between the domestic class forces in the periphery and those of core capital. This relationship has been associated with the emergence of a transnational class alliance. A material example of this would be joint ventures between local and foreign capital, and even common membership of an employers' association. Dependency writers note that such transnational tendencies are reinforced by some of the links of cultural dependence which may mean that some Third World elites may identify their interests and outlook more with the western bourgeoisie, than with their peripheral compatriots. Many Third World leaders have been educated in the West, and have adopted the life-styles of their college peer groups. Some keep a substantial amount of their capital in the west, partly as an insurance against political upheaval.

World systems writers have drawn on realist ideas in their analysis of what they call the 'international state-system'. In their historical analysis of the rise of the 'capitalist world-system' they pay much attention to mercantilist policies of competing states which aim at improving their own terms of trade at the expense of other states. In a way which is parallel to recent realist writing, world systems theorists have analysed the rise and decline of hegemonic (dominant) powers, coming to similar conclusions concerning their historical dynamics and effects. In both cases, the rise and fall of hegemonies are seen in cyclical terms, and hegemony is seen as having implications for order and stability in international economic relations.

Thus what distinguishes the world systems writers from their dependency counterparts is a concern with historical dynamics, and a wider set of categories which make possible a more nuanced explanation of the patterns and processes of change. Both approaches are, however, rather deterministic in so far as they identify a relatively fixed set of historical structures, whose foundations were laid in place during what they call the 'long sixteenth century'. From this period onward, the core-periphery divide became the key structural characteristic of the world system.

In so far as radical change was seen as possible, the hopes of dependency writers were often focused on socialist revolutions in the Third World. They argued that the national capitalist route to economic development followed by Japan in the nineteenth century was no longer feasible, so that socialism was the only path to 'auto-centric' (or independent) development. For socialism to be achieved, substantial 'delinking' from the capitalist world-economy was seen as necessary. At the same time, revolutionary states should cooperate to offset the power of the core. Many dependency writers, however, had doubts about the socialist character of the USSR, and, as such, the links between the peripheral states were held to be those which should be cemented. Indeed, some world systems writers have seen the USSR as participating in, and substantially benefiting from, the system of unequal exchange in world trade. However, the Soviet Union exports mainly primary products which gives it an economic interest in common with some less-developed countries, and also with South Africa.

5. TRANSNATIONAL HISTORICAL MATERIALISM

In contrast to the instrumentalism of the classical Marxists, some contemporary Marxism takes its inspiration from the work of the former leader of the Italian Communist Party, Antonio Gramsci.[9] Gramsci's ideas on culture and hegemony are difficult, but we think that the potential contained within them makes the effort of comprehension worthwhile. Indeed, they are essential to understanding the pioneering work of Robert Cox on the changing world order. Gramscian Marxism is, as yet, somewhat underdeveloped in the global political economy literature, but is gaining increasing attention, even among influential non-Marxists like Robert Keohane.[10] The Marxism of the classical theorists of imperialism is now widely seen as neglecting (or ignoring) the role of culture and ideas, while focusing too heavily and narrowly on economic aspects of order and change. In this context, Gramsci's ideas are a useful corrective to what is called the 'economism' and 'determinism' of the classical Marxists, and also of much writing in the dependency and world systems schools.

Whilst motivated by the same political aims as Lenin, Gramsci adopted a quite different method and philosophy. For example, Gramsci developed the concept of the 'ethical state', which he saw as playing an educative role, in which each individual could develop his powers of rationality. This concept of the state was related to the notion of a 'disinterested culture', whereby the concept of culture and personal development was not rendered subservient to political doctrine or expediency. For this to occur, education would necessarily have to encourage debate between different perspectives and viewpoints, on the basis of toleration and an acceptance of the positive virtues of pluralism. Gramsci was in favour of the non-intervention of political power in scientific matters, in contrast to the view implied by Leninism, namely one of total politicisation, and the subordination of science to political power. In this sense, Gramsci was a rationalist, rather than an instrumentalist and a relativist.

Whereas Lenin's concept of strategy was to capture state power and then shape the state and society from above, Gramsci's concept was based upon the widespread development of a collective potential, and the building of socialism from below. This stress on debate, education and ethics is linked to Gramsci's view that revolutionary possibilities are shaped in unique ways by historical conditions. Such conditions provided not only the material circumstances of society, but also their characteristic modes of thought. For example, the consciousness of Italians in the twentieth century was not simply shaped by the emergence of industrial capitalism, and the class forces within it, but also by the long and deep influence of cultural transformations, such as in the Renaissance, and by crucial social institutions such as the Catholic Church.

Indeed, in a similar way to Keynes, Gramsci went as far as to suggest that certain types of ideas can become akin to material forces, in that they can incorporate themselves into the way reality is perceived and understood by the mass of society and/or its leaders, as well as into the way the major social institutions were configured. Any revolutionary party would need to shape its strategy and tactics in order to take these forces into account, and to channel their development in a progressive way. Thus the path to socialism might be long and tortuous, and might never be achieved by an 'insurrectionary' approach to social revolution. For example socialism could only be achieved in Italy through the development of an alternative, ethical conception of society. This conception would need to spread convincingly through the civil society, as well as be at the heart of the workers' party. It would not be enough to say that the alternative could work, the workers' party would need to show that it would. Gramsci termed this process the building of a counter-hegemony, one which could compete with, and eventually supplant, the bourgeois hegemony which prevailed in his time. Given the entrenched nature of dominant ideas and institutions in Italian society, for the counter-hegemony to work, it would imply a change in the way the masses conceived of the limits of the possible in their own lives, as well as seeing the potential for a new type of society. Hence education was crucial.

Moreover, any counter-hegemony implied an alliance with other potentially progressive forces, which might come together and form what Gramsci termed an 'historical bloc'. This concept implies a unity between objective and subjective forces in a given historical situation. By this is meant a congruence or fit between prevailing ideas and conceptions of the society and the forces of production, embodied in political parties, trade unions and associations. The historic bloc is given cohesion by a hegemonic ideology, or a framework of thought which gives it identity and consciousness. Such an historic bloc is the product of conscious political activity, and is not simply accidental, since it implies the resolution of potential or actual conflicts between the forces of production and the relations of production. The scope for the formation of an historic bloc is delimited by the mode of production and the specific historical ideas which prevail in a given country, or across a range of countries.

Gramsci's ideas about social change focused mainly on the nation state (what he called the 'people-nation'). He saw capitalism primarily in national terms. However, some of the most recent Marxist writers have suggested that capitalism is entering into, or is now in, what might be termed a 'transnational stage', which differs from the 'national capitalist', imperialist stage of the Classical Marxists. Applying Gramsci's ideas internationally, and to this particular stage, it is thus possible, at least theoretically, to conceive of hegemony, and the formation of historical blocs on a world scale. Robert Cox is one of the few writers to have suggested this possibility.[11] Cox has noted that in an age of the growing internationalisation of production and exchange, there may be an emerging transnational historic bloc. In this bloc, the key institutions are the biggest transnational corporations, including banks, as well as internationalist elements in the major capitalist states and international organisations such as the IMF. These institutions have a shared ideology, a shared interest in a particular type of world order, and are interlinked by a range of transnational forces. If such a development occurs, there is a radically different implication for the degree to which 'inter-imperialist' cooperation is likely. A major Marxist contribution to the analysis of international economic relations is to highlight the role of socio-economic conditions which are taken as a given by the realist writers who prefer to focus on structural features of the inter-state system. However, in the case of the classical theorists of imperalism, their conception of capitalism in national terms led them to conclusions about conflict and cooperation between states that were largely similar to those of realists. Cox's approach (and its applications to post-war capitalism) implies different conclusions. The possibilities of cooperation between capitalist states may become significantly greater than in the past, not simply because of the 'super-imperialism' of the USA, but more fundamentally because of the growing interpenetration of their economies, and the emergence of an internationalised policy process which enables them to accommodate each other's interests in a collective framework.

Central to this substantive claim is the analysis of the rise of the transnational corporation and its implications for social relations at the domestic and international levels. Whereas Lenin had stressed that the export of capital proceeded from individual 'core' states to their own spheres of influence, recent writers have stressed the cross-cutting, and interpenetrating character of foreign direct investment since World War II. This has involved both the 'core' countries investing in each other (which, in fact, comprises the vast majority of such investment), and firms from many such countries investing in less-developed countries. Significantly, however, such investment in any single peripheral country may come from a range of core states, such as US, West German and Japanese automobile manufacturers in Brazil. Stephen Hymer saw these processes as leading to a world economy increasingly organised in a hierarchical way, centring on the headquarters of the world's biggest transnational corporations (the *Fortune 500*). A second implication was that the question of class formations should now be addressed on a world scale. In addition, Robert Cox, who is the main exponent of what we call transnational historical materialism, has also stressed the rise of institutional linkages of a transnational nature, in the form of 'policy networks'.

In contrast to the dependency and world systems writers, Cox and Hymer give priority to class relations in production. Unlike the classical Marxists, these relations are not seen mainly in terms of national capital and national labour. Rather, Cox and Hymer pay special attention to transnational capital relative to national capital, and thus suggest that a transnational capitalist class may be in the process of formation: something which Lenin said was impossible. Whereas Lenin thought that the workers of the world could unite, these writers argue that the power and mobility of transnational corporations (which can shift the geographical location of their production from one country to another) puts national labour movements on the defensive. Transnational capital is able to play these national labour movements (as well as governments wishing to attract foreign capital) off against each other, in a strategy of divide and rule. Such labour movements, to be successful, must therefore organise on a world-wide basis. However, such forms of organisation are much easier for capital than for labour. Thus the process of transnationalisation places certain sections or fractions of capital at a bigger structural advantage than was the case under a system of relatively separate, 'national' capitals.

It is also important to note that 'national' capital is also placed at a disadvantage, in so far as it is in competition with transnational capital. National capital, like labour, will have an interest in protection against cheap imports. However, Cox argues, there is a segment of labour which is relatively secure (that is managerial and highly skilled workers, for example in research and development) and/or is privileged in terms of wages (for example well-paid auto workers in less-developed countries) which is employed by transnational corporations. This broad group of workers may see its material interests as compatible with, and incorporated by, those of transnational capital. This is Cox's equivalent of Lenin's 'labour aristocracy'. This new labour aristocracy is to be found not only in the core, but also in some peripheral countries. Its existence also contributes to a transnational historic bloc of forces. By this is meant an alliance of material and political interests which cuts across classes, and operates in a range of countries. At the apex of this bloc are the capitalists and managers of the transnational corporations, and those in the state apparatuses of the core states and in the periphery who identify their interests with the internationalisation of production and exchange, and with the liberalisation of the conditions under which transnational corporations are able to operate.

Helping to cement the historic bloc is a hegemonic ideology which serves as the framework of thought for this class alliance. This ideology is associated with some of the liberal writers we have discussed in the previous chapter, namely ideas which suggest that a world of capital mobility contributes to efficiency, consumer welfare and the wealth of nations. Acceptance of this ideology, suggests Cox, is one basis for distinguishing between transnational and national capitalists and their counterparts in state bureaucracies. Indeed, the implication of this line of argument is that some less privileged and secure workers, so long as their outlook is imbued with liberal ideology, are also part of the historic bloc. In this respect Gramscian ideas go beyond the materialism of Lenin's concept of labour aristocracy. However, even Third World workers who appear harshly exploited by transnational corporations (for example, those working in mines or on electronics assembly-lines) often earn above-average incomes for their occupations in their own countries. These workers may, in fact, appear to be relatively affluent in countries where the masses live in rural poverty, with malnutrition rife. In such countries, these workers, as well as what dependency writers have termed the 'comprador bourgeoisie' (those who have close and dependent links with foreign firms) may become part of a transnational historic bloc. Thus a transnational historic bloc may be varied and wide-ranging, and can incorporate a range of class interests.

In addition, Cox advances a novel conception of international order which draws on Gramsci's theory of hegemony.[12] Cox sees three sets of social forces – ideas (theories and ideologies), institutions (organisations, state apparatuses) and material capabilities (the means of production and destruction) – which interact at the level of production, at the level of state-civil society relations, and at the level of world orders. Although Cox usually starts from (domestic) production relations (the mode of production), he sees the three levels as interlinked. He accepts that analysis might start out from any of the three social forces, at each or all of the three levels, since no one-way determinism exists between them. The social forces interact in a dynamic and dialectical way.

At the level of a particular, historically specific world order, Cox argues that the interaction between the three sets of social forces will produce different types, and degrees of global stability or instability. At particular historical conjunctures, there will be a consistency, or fit between the social forces, so that a hegemonic order exists. At other times, there will be a lack of congruence, so that the world order manifests a non-hegemonic condition. Cox sees the post-war *pax americana*, which lasted until the 1960s, as an example of a hegemonic world order. Hymer saw this order as breaking down in the 1960s, and potentially leading to a Hobbesian war of all against all at the world level.[13]

However, it might be observed that the 1945–65 period was one where the transnationalisation of production was only beginning to emerge, and as such a transnational historic bloc could only have been in its infancy at this time. At the time of the so-called *pax americana*, there was an international alliance of some fractions of labour and capital in which transnational capital was not yet as preponderant as it was to become by the 1980s. By the 1980s, the balance of material and political forces had shifted in the favour of internationally mobile capital, weakening the position of labour, and some sections of national capital. In Gramscian terms, this can be described as a crisis (or transformation) of the post-war hegemonic order.

6. REFORM OR REVOLUTION?

All radical writers share concerns which go beyond simply explaining the global political economy: they in various ways seek to change it. Where radicals differ is in which changes they see as most desirable and likely, when they might occur, and what repercussions such changes might have, and how workers' movements and parties can influence such changes. Of central concern has been the question of the longevity of capitalism, and the potential for it to be superseded by socialism, and eventually communism. Classical imperialism expected revolution in the core capitalist states in the near future. Other Marxists, such as Ernest Mandel, despite the continuing vitality of capitalism, are also sanguine concerning the prospects for its early demise.[14] Yet others, despite the end of the post-war boom, see capitalism as still retaining considerable vitality, and changing in character, becoming more transnational and institutionally flexible. Dependency writers have seen revolutionary change as likely only in the periphery.

Radical writing has as its aim the emancipation of workers and peasants on a world scale, and much of it has been produced by intellectuals associated with communist and socialist parties in a range of different countries. However, given the range of different perspectives and assessments referred to above, there is considerable scope for disagreement, as well as for internecine, doctrinal splits which have characterised much left-wing politics in the twentieth century. Moreover, some of their work has often been used by nationalist politicians in less-developed countries, particularly when seeking to place the blame for their failures on the evils of international capitalism. In this context, it is not always easy to trace a simple relationship between radical perspectives and specific sets of material and political interests, or between radical theory and programmes for change.

What this implies is that any transition to socialism will be problematic: is socialism in one country a possibility (for example by a country 'delinking' from the capitalist world-economy, as has been suggested by dependency writers)? If large communist states such as China and the Soviet Union are now attempting to relink with the capitalist system, what hope is there for the smaller communist and socialist states? Or, following a more classical Marxist approach, can revolution occur only in the long run after the transnational corporations and international finance have spread capitalism ever more globally, and in so doing created a world-wide proletariat? Finally, from a Gramscian viewpoint how can a socialist form of international consciousness be realised by workers of different nations, races and religions, thus serving to develop a global counter-hegemony?

NOTES

1. For an excellent review of these theories, see A. Brewer, *Marxist Theories of Imperialism* (London, Routledge and Kegan Paul, 1980). Brewer provides a vast bibliography of Marxist literature, including a comprehensive list of publications by Marx himself. For this reason we have not appended 'further readings' to this chapter. See, in particular, Vladimir Illyich Lenin, *Imperialism: The Highest Stage of Capitalism* (New York International Publishers, 1939; first published 1917); Nikolai I. Bukharin, *Imperialism and World Economy* (London, Merlin Press, 1976; first published 1915). The doyen of world systems theorists is Immanuel Wallerstein, *The Capitalist World Economy* (Cambridge, Cambridge University Press, 1979). More recent transnational historical materialists include Robert W. Cox, *Production, Power and World Order: Social Forces in the Making of History* (New York, Columbia University Press, 1987); Stephen Hymer, 'International Politics and International Economics: A Radical Approach', in Jeffrey A. Frieden and David A. Lake, *International Political Economy: Perspectives on Global Power and Wealth* (New York, St Martin's Press 1987), pp. 31–46.
2. Bukharin, *Imperialism and World Economy*, op. cit.
3. Karl Kautsky, 'Ultra-Imperialism', *New Left Review* ([1914], 1970), No. 59, pp. 41–6.
4. Paul A. Baran, *The Political Economy of Growth* (Harmondsworth, Penguin Books, 1973; first published 1957).
5. See, for example, Andre Gunder Frank, *Capitalism and Underdevelopment in Latin America* (London, Modern Reader Paperbacks, revised edn 1969; first published 1967); Samir Amin, *Imperialism and Unequal Development* (Brighton, Harvester Press, 1977).
6. Arghiri Emmanuel, *Unequal Exchange: A Study of the Imperialism of Trade* (London, New Left Books, 1972; first published 1969).
7. Frank, op. cit.; Henrique Cardoso and Enzo Falletto, *Dependency and Development in Latin America* (Berkeley, Cal., University of California Press, 1979; first published 1971).
8. Samir Amin, Giovanni Arrighi, Andre Gunder Frank and Immanuel Wallerstein, *Dynamics of Global Crisis* (London, Macmillan, 1982), p. 235.
9. Antonio Gramsci, *Selections from The Prison Notebooks of Antonio Gramsci* (New York, International Publishers/London, Lawrence and Wishart, 1971) edited and translated by Quentin Hoare and Geoffrey Nowell Smith.
10. Robert Keohane, *After Hegemony: Cooperation and Discord in the World Political Economy* (Princeton NJ, Princeton University Press, 1984), pp. 44–6.

11. Cox, *Production, Power and World Order*, op. cit.
12. Robert Cox, 'Social Forces, States and World Orders: Beyond International Relations Theory', *Millenium* (1981), Vol. 10, pp. 127–55.
13. Hymer, in Frieden and Lake, op. cit., p. 44.
14. Ernest Mandel, *Late Capitalism* (London, New Left Books, 1975); *The Second Slump: A Marxist Analysis of Recession in the Seventies* (London, New Left Books, 1978).

6 Key Concepts: Power, Structure and Hegemony

1. INTRODUCTION

In this chapter we discuss power resources and their mobilisation; three dimensions of power, including structural power; and related concepts such as dominance and dependence. These concepts provide a basis for examining realist and Gramscian concepts of hegemony, as well as for the following chapter on the power of capital, which we see as central to the analysis of the current global political economy.

A comprehensive concept of power requires specification in terms of: (i) for whom; (ii) in relation to which, if any, others; (iii) the type of power resources involved; (iv) the ends/intentions involved, with some reference to time-horizons; (v) the orientation towards action, either overt or covert; (vi) which structures and associated incentives and constraints are important. These can be both normative and material, actual or potential, anticipated or unanticipated.

2. POWER AND POWER RESOURCES

We can distinguish between power resources and 'power over'. An extreme example of 'power over' was the US military intervention in Grenada in 1983, which led to a change in the island's political system. The use of force is an extreme example because active power (in this case, the coercive use of power resources by the state) can take a variety of forms, as through the use of negative or positive sanctions. Such sanctions imply coercion, manipulation or deterrence. This is in contrast to pure persuasion, which relies on the unconstrained acceptance of (reasoned) argument. Pure persuasion is not contingent on an inequality between those engaged in a power relation. Of course, 'pure' persuasion is very rare, since normally the access to knowledge and funds is unequal. In this respect, large and wealthy states are usually at an advantage relative to small ones, and also, big business is at an advantage relative to its smaller counterparts, to trade unions, and especially to consumers.

The above example raises the questions: what are the most important international power resources, and how are they created? Military might is associated with the size, sophistication and morale of a country's armed forces. Morale is important, as the examples of the US war in Vietnam, and the USSR's war in Afghanistan have revealed: in each case the military superpower with highly sophisticated armaments was thus unable to prevail over the indigenous forces. Also important is the geographical aspect of military power. Some countries may be easier to defend than others: the Pacific and Atlantic Oceans have traditionally enhanced the security of the US, whereas Poland, wedged between a number of hostile powers, has a history of invasion and occupation.

In addition, a comparatively strong economy is necessary for military strength to be sustained in the long term. The wealth of a nation is usually related to its factors of production: land (natural resources), labour and capital. Today, it is usual to single out the category of human capital (skilled labour) as particularly important, since certain types of knowledge are crucial for a range of productive activities. Skilled labour is, of course, of various types, and has different forms and levels of knowledge.

Other types of 'capital' are the stock of physical capital equipment, including infrastructure (ports, roads, etc.), and the net international financial position of a country. The build-up of Japanese foreign investment, especially during the 1980s, led to Japan being the largest net creditor country. By contrast, in terms of indigenous natural resources, Japan was and is in a very poor and indeed vulnerable position. The USSR, on the other hand, with its vast land-mass, is in an unrivalled position with respect to natural resources. However, natural resources have to be located, extracted and transported to productive centres. The case of Siberian development illustrates the difficulties faced by the USSR in this respect. The USSR has tried to obtain Western and Japanese finance and technology to try and overcome some of these problems.

The USA is currently the strongest country as regards human and physical capital. It also possesses vast natural resources, and has by far the world's largest gross national product (GNP) (which we can 'guestimate' at about twice as big as that of its nearest rival, the USSR, and three times the size of that of Japan in the mid-1980s.[1] However, there are great difficulties in making precise comparisons of this type.) None the less, the larger size of America's GNP may not fully account for the magnitude of its lead in internationally usable power resources. The US has privileged access to the power resources of other countries, especially as regards financial capital. The key reason for this is the unique post-war status of the dollar as the primary world reserve currency, and because of the role of New York City as the world's biggest financial centre. For example, in order to finance the US military build-up which took place during the Reagan administration, the US government was able to borrow vast amounts of capital from abroad, much of it from Japan. The USA also has an unsurpassed ability to attract highly-skilled labour from other countries (as well as huge inflows of cheap unskilled labour, most of which is Hispanic).

The potential (military) power of the leading states is almost never fully realised, except perhaps in wartime. One reason for this is the reluctance of the population to forego consumption. This can give rise to binding domestic political constraints. Another reason for this is that devoting too high a proportion of a nation's resources to military expenditures may act as a drag on the growth of productive capacity. If this is the case, it will undermine the country's military strength in the long term. This point relates to a distinction between wealth-creating and wealth-distributing activities. The former refers to investment of various types, such as that in human capital, plant, equipment, and research and development. Wealth-distributing activity includes income redistribution through welfare programmes, subsidies and tariffs for particular industries, and, some would argue, military expenditure. However, it should be noted that military strength may sometimes augment the power resources of a nation, as in the case of colonial conquest and plunder.

3. THREE DIMENSIONS OF POWER: OVERT, COVERT AND STRUCTURAL

Let us now differentiate between three dimensions of power. Our discussion seeks to go beyond the identification of these dimensions first attempted by Steven Lukes.[2] The first dimension is that of active, overt 'power over', that is where an actor or agent (A) makes another (B) alter his behaviour in ways desired by A. The second dimension is that of covert power, so that A has power over B. This may be achieved, for example, through agenda-setting processes, and what Peter Bachrach and Morton Baratz call 'nondecisions'.[3] This dimension is sometimes less obviously active, and more organisational in character. The third dimension is that of structural power, which may involve material and normative aspects, such that patterns of incentives and constraints are systematically created. These condition the relationship between A and B.

We have discussed aspects of the first dimension of power, that of active, overt 'power over' in the previous section. However, such active power over may not be highly visible or measurable. An important example which illustrates this aspect of power, which has been called the second dimension, concerns agenda-setting processes. Such processes help set priorities for policy-making, and do so partly by excluding some items from consideration. In setting the agenda for the 1944 Bretton Woods conference, the USA and Britain, the key participants, agreed to prioritise the establishment of institutions and norms which would promote exchange rate stability and trade liberalisation. The regulation and promotion of foreign direct investment by transnational corporations received little attention. An issue on which the USA and Britain were less in agreement was that of the need for decolonisation. The US stressed the desirability of decolonisation as a question of principle, emphasising the right of nations to self-determination. Britain, with many colonies, had a lot to lose, whilst the US, with few colonies, had little to lose.

However, it has been argued that the US position on this issue involved a 'hidden' agenda in that the USA sought improved access in trade and investment for its firms to major parts of the British and French empires, for example, oil in the Middle East, rubber and tin in South-East Asia. The notion of a less visible 'hidden agenda' has been associated with the idea of covert rather than overt power. One can also distinguish between covert ends and covert means. Improved American access in the previous example can be seen as an important (covert) end. However, covert means were employed by the US and Britain in 1953 to replace the Mossadeq government (which had nationalised foreign oil property) by the pro-Western regime of the Shah of Iran which lasted until 1978. The covert intervention installed the Shah's regime, which remained largely sympathetic to Western interests, and particularly American interests. American oil firms gained a stake in Iran, whose exports were previously controlled by British Petroleum, BP.

The perspective which gives most attention to the third, structural dimension of power is Marxism. In Lukes' formulation of the third dimension, the power of ideas is stressed, particularly as a structural constraint on the outlook of subordinate groups and classes. It may be possible to generalise this concept, as does Robert Cox, to encompass wider 'frameworks of thought', which condition the way individuals and groups are able to understand their social situation, and the possibilities of social change.[4] However, the normative aspects of structural power need to be linked to more material aspects, aspects which are normally stressed in classical Marxist accounts of the relations between labour and capital.

Let us now look at some of the ways that a concept of structural power can be applied in international relations. At the international level, structures of economic dependence are stressed by radical writers of various schools. In the context of North–South relations, less-developed countries are seen as being so deficient in skills, knowledge and financial capital, as to be placed at a systematic disadvantage, compared with the wealthy, core countries. Just as workers have to supply their labour to capitalists in order to survive, so the poorer developing countries have to supply primary products to the industrialised states. The key reason for this is that they need to obtain foreign exchange in order to pay for essential imports. In so far as developing nations become dependent on imported food supplies, the structural imbalance is reinforced.

Why is this structural power, and not simply the exercise of international dominance, or 'power over' by the 'core states'? The answer lies in the fact that the developed countries, today, do not need to exert major military and diplomatic pressure on these developing countries to ensure that they will supply primary products. Market discipline and market necessity mean that they have very little or no alternative. Developing countries have to sell their products in international markets, and normally this involves competition between themselves, and also with some developed countries. These market pressures may lead some countries to increase, rather than reduce their supply of certain primary products, even when their price falls (in contrast to the predictions of conventional supply and demand analysis). For example, in the 1980s, Mexico's desperate need for foreign exchange drove it to increase its oil production – to the disadvantage of the Organisation of Petroleum Exporting Countries (OPEC). This latter instance of a producer cartel is a partial exception to the above generalisation about the structural dependence of less-developed countries. However, such cartels are rare.

While the developed countries may not need directly to exert 'power over' the poorer states today, they did so consistently in the nineteenth and early twentieth centuries, at which time the peripheral regions were forcibly incorporated within the world capitalist system, and certain trade-oriented investments in infrastructure took place. The colonial powers sought, before conceding political independence, to establish social and political structures that would maintain the external orientation of these countries. Central to this was the creation of a Westernised elite. (In parts of black Africa this elite are called the 'Wabenzi', meaning they who drive Mercedes Benz automobiles.) Thus what was a system of direct domination became gradually transformed into a structural condition, in which the indirect nature of market power became more important.

The example of the tastes and cultural preferences of ruling elites in less-developed countries points to the other, more normative aspect of the structure of dependence. This operates at two levels: that of the elite, which seeks to emulate its counterparts in the developed states, and that of the mass, who are gradually incorporated into the aspirations associated with a Westernised consumption culture. Such structures of cultural dependence may ultimately make it difficult for people to envisage a simpler, more self-reliant and egalitarian form development.

4. TWO CONCEPTS OF HEGEMONY: REALIST AND GRAMSCIAN

In the literature, there are three types of explanation of international order. The first, realist explanation requires there to be a carefully managed, balance of power. This should be underpinned by a relatively stable distribution of international power resources between states, with duopoly being seen as more stable than situations with a larger number of powerful states. In a world of many states, a duopoly of power can only be approximated through the existence of two hegemonic powers able to dominate and lead large blocs of countries. Seen from this perspective, the post-war international order combined aspects of duopoly and hegemony: the two superpowers confronted each other in a relatively stable 'balance of terror', whilst simultaneously establishing their dominance in their own spheres of influence.[5]

The second explanation has been developed in order to explain the nature and possibility of order in the capitalist world 'after hegemony'.[6] Here the central assumption is that post-war US hegemony in the capitalist world has been substantially eroded, and the world political economy therefore lacks a credible leader which can discipline deviant behaviour and induce cooperation from other states. Order is possible, however, after hegemony because of the rational self-interest of states and other actors which arises in the context of complex interdependence. Thus cooperation becomes necessary and rational, since the patterns of interdependence may transform the structure of opportunity costs for a given nation such that non-cooperation becomes much more burdensome and risky. In addition, the awareness of such opportunity costs must be backed by forms of domestic political mobilisation which ensure support for prevailing international arrangements. The second concept can be seen as a hybrid between the realist concept of order, and the liberal and public choice approaches which stress that cooperation is founded in an interdependent division of labour and in the rational, self-interested action of interest groups and states.

The third type of explanation of order partially overlaps with that of the second, but stresses interlocking and, sometimes, transnational class interests, particularly for the major capitalist states. It is associated with dependency theory and some types of Marxism, such as that of Robert Cox, who uses the Gramscian concept of hegemony to explain varying degrees of global, as well as domestic stability. The contrast between the realist concept of hegemony and the Gramscian concept can be better appreciated if each is related to the three dimensions of power.

The first dimension of power is associated with the realist explanation of order, notably with the theory of hegemonic stability. The theory is based upon the distribution and mobilisation of material power resources. If these are so unequally distributed, such that the hegemon has predominance, especially in military power, it can exert 'power over' other actors (states). The exertion of power over may not need to be overt. Both realists and liberals, particularly those who stress rational action, assume that states make a 'rational calculus' of the costs and benefits of alternative policies. In this context, subordinate states may effectively avoid actions which might antagonise the hegemon. In this sense, the hegemon often will not need openly to exert its power over other states. The anticipations of subordinate states of what the hegemon might do will cause them to modify their behaviour. An analogy can be made with the case of oligopoly when there is a price-leader, or dominant firm. The subordinate firms will not break ranks on prices since they will fear the consequences of such action: retaliatory price cuts by the leading firm. Hegemony in this sense can be understood as a combination of dominance and, when needed, active domination. An example which would appear to fit this realist concept of hegemony, is that of the relationship between the USSR and the East European members of the Warsaw Pact. After World War II, the Soviet Union installed communist regimes, led by politicians who would follow the 'Soviet line' on policy. Any substantial deviation from this line (which can be understood as the legitimate agenda for policy as defined by the leaders of the Soviet Communist Party, and their counterparts in the other Warsaw Pact states) was usually punished by the Soviet military forces, as occurred in Hungary in 1956, and in Czechoslovakia in 1968. However, for the most part, the leaders and populations of these states did not challenge Soviet hegemony (in the realist sense), and in fact actively ensured their compliance with Soviet preferences. Soviet hegemony in Eastern Europe can thus be seen as combining dominance with active domination. Instances of the latter may have been necessary to ensure the former, since they established the credibility of Soviet interventionary capacity. Soviet hegemony has constrained the autonomy of other East European countries, and thus has undermined their real, as opposed to formal, sovereignty.

The Gramscian concept of hegemony can only be understood in terms of an analysis of structural as well as behavioural power. In particular, Gramscian analysis highlights the role of ideas and culture, in that they serve to shape preferences and constrain perceptions of what is possible.[7] The latter aspect is not the same as the idea of anticipated reactions constraining behaviour: in the Gramscian sense, such constraints are so internalised that they appear both natural and inevitable. As such, they do not necessarily imply any type of rational calculus. Unlike the narrowly-defined realist application of the concept of hegemony, which sees states as the main actors and units of analysis, Cox's application of the Gramscian concept gives weight to transnational social forces. Also, in this formulation, hegemony is not just that of one nation (or group or nations in the 'core') relative to others, but also of one class or class fraction relative to others.

Power, for Gramsci, was like a centaur: half-man and half-beast. In the example of North–South relations discussed with respect to structural power, the direct, and coercive face of colonial power gave way to an indirect, and perhaps more consensual face, in that market constraints, as well as a set of aspirations on the part of the elite and mass in developing countries come together to both motivate their productive arrangements, as well as to constrain their potential for economic, as well as cultural development. This is particularly the case in a cultural sense, if the masses of less-developed countries really do come to believe that 'things go better with Coke'. In terms of the question, 'hegemony for whom?', the classes which benefit most from this situation are those associated with transnational capital and their allies in the Third World.

On the other hand, as Cox has noted, capitalist hegemony is more consistent and embedded in the core countries, than it is in the periphery. In the core, democratic institutions and personal political freedoms are more widely available, the legitimacy of such arrangements is widely held, the right to property is upheld, and the use of coercive power by the state for purposes of domestic order is less frequent, and less draconian. Acceptance of the market system, and of the presence of transnational corporations is more widespread than in many less-developed countries, where pre-capitalist modes of thought and production exist alongside capitalism. Thus, for foreign capital to be guaranteed the political stability it requires, in these states, coercive forms of military rule are often necessary. In this case, naked 'power over', or dominance, rather than hegemony, prevails.

From a Gramscian perspective, the most skilful use of direct, coercive power requires a vision of a self-reproducing structural power, both economic and ideological. Such use of direct power implies a hegemonic, long-term strategy. With time, the coercive use of power may become less necessary and also less obvious as consensus builds up on the basis of shared values, ideas and material interests on the part of both ruling and subordinate classes. What is important in this process is that such ideas and institutions come to be seen as natural and legitimate, and that they become embedded in the frameworks of thought of the politically and economically significant parts of the population. In this way, a hegemonic structure of thought and action emerges, one which militates against the raising, or even conception of alternative types of political, economic and social arrangements.

While the Gramscian approach is able to shed light on the class dimension of international relations, its emphasis on ideas and culture enables it to better explain certain aspects of inter-state relations, the major province of realist theory. It can help to explain why some things happen, and others do not. For example, in the 1950s, the UK gave priority to its relations with the USA and the British Commonwealth, at a time when it had an historic opportunity to become the most influential state in an emerging European Community. That this opportunity was passed over is difficult to explain in terms of a rational calculus of long-term costs and benefits for the UK. However, a Gramscian analysis of the nature of consciousness of the British leadership helps to explain this apparently irrational choice of policy.

The world-view of the British ruling classes had been shaped by its long history of imperialism and empire, and the more immediate experience of a close alliance with the USA during World War II. This outlook was also shared by many members of the British Labour Party. Winston Churchill, Britain's wartime leader and Prime Minister during the early 1950s, was an archetype of the Anglo-Saxon cultural chauvinism at the heart of this world-view. An ex-public schoolboy (Harrow), who had seen military service on the frontiers of empire, and who was married to an American, epitomised this outlook in his *History of the English-Speaking Peoples*.[8] A 'special relationship', born of war, came to be seen as natural in a way that was not possible with France and particularly Germany, who have been traditionally viewed with great distrust, often enmity, by the British. In addition, what informed much of this attitude was the pattern of British trade and foreign investment which had grown up since the nineteenth century. Only a small proportion of this was with continental Europe, and most of it was in the USA, the dominions (Canada, Australia, New Zealand), South Africa and Rhodesia (now Zimbabwe), and in other former colonies. Thus there was a congruence between the hegemonic ideas, and dominant material forces shaping British foreign policy at the time.

Some writers have suggested that the establishment and development of the post-war international economic order in the capitalist part of the world resembled a Gramscian, hegemonic congruence of social forces. Indeed, one writer, who is in fact a neo-realist, John Ruggie, has described the system as one of 'embedded liberalism' in which there was a 'fusion' of power, interests, and 'legitimate social purpose' in the major capitalist states. This system gained widening degrees of acceptance, and came to embrace more and more countries, as the post-war period developed. In addition, as a result of the establishment of certain international institutions (such as the IMF, World Bank and GATT), and the corresponding international regimes for money and trade, Ruggie argues that the system was also premissed on the internationalisation of authority in a non-state form.[9] The class aspect of this settlement was that the material interests of both labour and capital appeared to be in some sort of balance, with the hegemonic ideology of the mixed economy legitimising the new post-war Keynesian welfare states. The strategic framework for this was the USA's world-wide system of alliances, rationalised by a cold war ideology and the USA's policy of global containment of communism. The major political parties in the post-war Western consensus, the social democratic, liberal, and conservative parties, all subscribed to the anti-communism which this strategic posture entailed. The settlement reflected a particular conjuncture and balance between material, institutional and ideological forces in post-war capitalism.

NOTES

1. The estimate for the relative size of the US and Japanese economies is from Alan Cafruny, 'Economic Conflicts and the Transformation of the Atlantic Order: The United States, Europe, and the Liberalisation of Agriculture and Services', in Stephen Gill (ed.) *Atlantic Relations: Beyond the Reagan Era* (Brighton, Wheatsheaf Books, 1988). Japan has been closing the gap on the USSR for much of the post-war period. The size of the gap between these two countries (if any) is rather speculative.

2. Our discussion of the three dimensions of power draws on, but goes beyond the work of Steven Lukes. See his, *Power: A Radical View* (London, Macmillan, 1974). See also Dennis Wrong, *Power: its forms, bases and uses* (Oxford, Basil Blackwell, 1979). On the contestability of the concept of power, and also of the concept of interests, see William Connolly, *The Terms of Political Discourse* (London, Macmillan, 1983, second edition). On structural power see Hugh Ward, 'Structural Power – a Contradiction in Terms?' *Essex Papers in Politics and Government* (Colchester, Essex University Department of Government, 1986); Charles Lindblom, *Politics and Markets* (New York, Basic Books, 1977).

3. Peter Bachrach and Morton S. Baratz, 'The Two Faces of Power', *American Political Science Review* (1962), Vol. 56, pp. 947–952; and their 'Decisions and Non-Decisions: an Analytical Framework', *American Political Science Review* (1963) Vol. 57, pp. 631–642.

4. Robert W. Cox, 'Social Forces, States and World Orders', *Millennium* (1981), Vol. 10, pp. 126–155.

5. Kenneth N. Waltz, *Theory of International Politics* (Reading, Mass., Addison-Wesley, 1979).

6. Robert O. Keohane, *After Hegemony: Cooperation and Discord in the World Political Economy* (Princeton NJ, Princeton University Press, 1984).

7. A. Gramsci, *The Prison Notebooks* (London, Lawrence and Wishart, 1971). Selected, edited and translated by Quentin Hoare and Geoffrey Nowell Smith.

8. Winston S. Churchill, *A History of the English-Speaking Peoples* (London, Cassell, 1958, 4 vols.).

9. J. G. Ruggie, 'International Regimes, Transactions and Change – Embedded Liberalism in the Post-War Order,' *International Organisation* (1982), Vol. 36, pp. 379–415.

PART II
THEMES

7   The Power of Capital

In this chapter we examine the varied and complex nature of the power of capital, relative to both labour and state apparatuses. In particular we highlight the material and normative aspects of structural power. We consider this aspect of the power of capital to be fundamental. Indeed, we see this as central to understanding the rise of transnational firms, relative to their 'national' counterparts. In this context, we theorise the conditions for, and limits to a transnational hegemony of internationally mobile capital.

1. THE CONCEPT OF CAPITAL

Capital is an abstraction which is variously defined and interpreted. In neo-classical economics, capital is normally referred to as one of the factors of production, as if its main form were physical, so that capital in financial terms is usually seen as reflecting, and giving valuation to, productive capital (which might include not only plant and machinery, but also intangible assets such as knowledge and goodwill). For example, the price and value of shares (equities) for a firm on the stock market is often seen as reflecting the potential worth of its assets, and its likely profitability. Neo-classical economists often treat the three factors of production as similar, that is as productive inputs which are equally necessary. In contrast, Marxist economic theory, whilst acknowledging the productive character of capital equipment, also focuses on capital as a social relation. In this relationship, capital exploits labour by extracting surplus. Thus in the Marxist formulation, capital and labour are social and political concepts, as well as purely technical, economic ones. For Marxists, capital takes various forms in the process of exchange and capital accumulation, including fixed capital equipment, knowledge, raw materials, components, and money. Above and beyond these specific aspects of capital is a socio-psychological dimension: the urge to consistently accumulate takes on the force of necessity in order to survive in the competitive jungle. Thus the market exerts structural power over capitalists as well as workers and the state.

2. STATE AND CAPITAL

States are essential for economies, in that they provide the legal conditions for the establishment and maintenance of property rights, which are defined in private terms within capitalism. States also provide a range of what public choice theorists call public goods. In the modern world, these systems of property rights are further defined in the context of the widespread acceptance of national sovereignty and territorial jurisdiction. In the inter-state system, each state has the right to control economic activity within its borders. The right to control implies that states should possess potential direct 'power over' capital. Indeed, the gaining of such a right was a central objective of the anti-colonial movements of the late nineteenth and twentieth centuries. The separation of the world into nation-states however, creates a central condition for the power of internationally mobile forms of capital.

The existence of the state, although it may, within capitalism, act in the general or fractional interests of capital, also creates the possibility for a range of limits to the power of capital. This is partly because of the political goods and services which it supplies to the capitalist economic system, and because of the institutional autonomy it possesses. The precise relationship of the state to capital in general, and the position of the state *vis-à-vis* the market system, is at the heart of this issue. Indeed, the relationship between the state and markets is also central to debates about market socialism, such as found in Yugoslavia, as well as debates about the changing political economies of China and the USSR.

3. THE POWER OF CAPITAL

3.1 The Power of Capital: Domestic Applications

Let us now discuss the power of capital at the domestic level, initially with reference to direct (or behavioural) forms of 'power over', and then with respect to forms of indirect, structural power. It should be noted, however, that these forms of power are often difficult to separate in practice. Our application will be to the case of post-war capitalism, and to the institutions and practices which are prominent in the largest capitalist countries.

3.1.1. Forms of Direct Power: market power, lobbying and networks of influence. In neo-classical economies, 'market power' arises when firms are able to exert influence over the price of their products, and/or over the price of some of their inputs, including labour. (See chapter 4 on monopoly, monopsony, and oligopoly.) In the goods market it is a case of the power of firms over consumers, whereas in the labour market it is the power of firms over labour. In contrast to the neo-classical focus on exchange relations, Marxists see capital as exerting a direct power over labour in the production process, through hiring and firing, and control of the working procedures and conditions. This direct form of power rests, however, on the social structure of capitalism, which creates a subordinate class position for labour.

Both Marxists and neo-classical writers have reasons for claiming that the political influence of capital on the state is likely to be paramount. Public choice theory, using the neo-classical perspective, hypothesises that oligopolistic industries will be better equipped to organise for political ends, and to gain leverage over state policies. In so far as labour is well organised it will be able to exert some countervailing power over capital, and have influence over state policy. At a deeper level, the state's support for capital is grounded in the assumption that property rights are a necessary condition for efficiency in production and exchange, and hence for the prosperity of workers as well as capitalists. Since neo-classical economic theory prioritises consumption in its definition of economic welfare, it is seen as desirable that the state should provide the conditions within which capitalism can flourish. Therefore, on both counts, it is in the interests of politicians and bureaucrats in so far as they are concerned to promote economic growth, to ascertain which conditions are appropriate, by consulting first with capitalists (and under certain conditions, also with organised labour). In return, individual capitalists, business executives and investment houses demand incentives to induce them, or their companies, to invest. They also demand political guarantees to protect their holding, and substantial autonomy in the conduct of business. As a result, capitalists usually have a unique prerogative relative to labour in the making of state policy.

Charles Lindblom has taken up and refined the idea of the 'privileged position' of business in capitalist societies.[1] The very organisation of business for economic purposes means that it is spared many of the costs of collective action for political purposes. Other groups, by contrast, must form, organise and mobilise in ways which business is, in effect, already doing in order to survive in the marketplace. Business has funds at its disposal to pay for lobbyists, and to subsidise the political activity of parties which act directly or indirectly in their interests.

The privileged position of business may be consolidated through the establishment of procedures and channels which regularise and institutionalise state–business consultation and cooperation. In some cases, the state may parcel out its authority to business groups, so that the latter actually create the regulatory framework for their own activities. As such, the power of capital (business) is extended into a form of state authority. This is reinforced by the way that many state bureaucrats and politicians take up positions in business, and the way business people often take up important political and government positions. Such interactions become part of the wider network of relationships which bind business and government together. Top business people and senior officials often have a shared social and educational background, and often, a similar social outlook. Public officials rely on the expertise of business, in their day-to-day activities. Thus both business people and officials know who to contact and how, in a way that other groups and classes usually do not (although organised labour may also have institutionalised its relationship with government in certain countries). The interaction of these elites within capitalism helps to make the sharing of state power between capital and the government seem normal, with property rights and the power relations which stem from them taken as natural, right and inevitable, and thus never on the 'official' agenda.[2]

At the level of consensus-building, governments, accepting the privileged position of business, tend to use mass communications in sustaining support for the current social arrangements. This is reinforced by the patterns of ownership and control of, and access to, the media. The result is that 'every general medium of mass communication carries a heavy freight of business ideology'.[3] Much of the media is privately-owned, and is thus configured by the need to compete in the market-place. In this sense, there is an element of the circular reproduction of certain forms of socialisation which operate to justify and sustain a climate of ideas conducive to the interests of business. This process varies in nature, and in its weight in different societies, and appears to be at its most developed and pervasive in the USA, followed closely by Japan amongst the leading capitalist states.

3.1.2.   Forms of Structural Power: business climate, power of markets and 'limits of the possible'   The more direct forms of the power of capital referred to in the above paragraph can be related, further, to a more indirect, structural aspect, which stems from the place of the private sector within capitalist societies.[4] When business people are lobbying government for concessions they are often able to claim a status akin to that of 'public officials'. Here, Lindblom means that they are performing essential functions, which, in a planned economic system, would be carried out by state-appointed managers. Business people can thus claim an expertise which is of general public value. In a market-oriented liberal democracy (what he calls a 'polyarchy'), this advantage is reinforced by the widespread public acceptance of the view that economic growth and prosperity are fundamentally dependent on investment and innovation by private enterprise. This means that politicians have to be concerned with the cultivation of an appropriate 'business climate', or else investment might be postponed, and a recession might be precipitated. An elected Socialist Party, with a radical programme, would therefore be constrained in its policy choices by the nature of the 'business climate', not least because it would need tax revenue (and/or loans) to finance its ambitious spending plans. The assumption behind these arguments is that there is a market for capital, enterprise and inventiveness, and the supply of these will be reduced by higher taxation. Indeed, such arguments are the essence of so-called 'supply-side' economics which became influential in the USA in the 1980s.

There is a striking contrast between the ability of capital and labour to shape policy in the long term under capitalist conditions. Whereas an 'investment strike' by business may occur spontaneously if the business climate deteriorates, labour, in order to exert corresponding influence, would have to organise directly a wide-ranging or even general strike. The latter form of action would be very difficult to bring about, and, as Lindblom notes, even if it were, almost inevitably it would be opposed, or crushed by the state, as occurred in Britain in 1926. A general strike would probably be perceived as a direct and conscious threat to the state itself, whereas an investment strike would have an almost natural quality, and would be based upon one of the very principles that the capitalist state is committed to uphold: the right of individuals to dispose of their property as they see fit.

The example of an 'investment strike' is a case of structural power, uniquely available to business, and is one which works primarily through the market mechanism in capitalist economies. Whereas a reduced willingness to invest for productive purposes usually comes about gradually, the supply of finance to governments through the purchase of government bonds and bills may decline very rapidly. This might result in the state being unable to finance its current activity unless it resorted to monetary inflation to reduce the real value of its debt. (Such inflation would, from the point of view of business, cause the 'investment climate' to deteriorate further, thus prolonging the 'investment strike'.) Thus capital, and particularly money capital, has the power to indirectly discipline the state. In so far as many of the top financiers have access to the government leaders, this indirect power may be supplemented by direct lobbying, and gentlemanly arm-twisting. However, such arm-twisting is secondary to what can be termed the 'power of markets', notably the financial markets. This power constrains the participants in the market, including the government when it needs to raise finance for its activities. In this sense, given certain social and political conditions, markets can have a certain autonomy.

Whereas Lindblom's focus is largely on a range of pro-capitalist policies, seen from another point of view, business, and particularly big business, is not merely concerned with an appropriate short-term business climate (the concern of politicians seeking re-election), but also with long-term conditions for profit-making. This involves asserting its power over labour in a disciplinary way. Business is thus concerned with the wider macroeconomic conditions under which it operates. Thus, the more far-sighted, large-scale sectors of capital are prepared to sacrifice higher profits in the short run, in order to make profits under acceptable political conditions in the long run. They are better able to weather a recession, and indeed may be able to take over their weaker or bankrupt competitors towards the end of a slump in business activity. Such a phenomenon was noted as early as 1943 by Michal Kalecki who predicted that while governments could use macroeconomic policy to obtain full employment, they would not always do so, in order to sustain the appropriate long-term climate for business to flourish:

> It is true that profits would be higher under a regime of full employment than they are on the average under *laissez-faire*; and even a rise in wage rates resulting from stronger bargaining power of the workers is less likely to reduce profits than to increase prices, and thus affects adversely only the *rentier* interests. But 'discipline in the factories' and 'political stability' are more appreciated by the business leaders than profits. Their class instinct tells them that lasting full employment is unsound from their point of view and that unemployment is an integral part of the 'normal' capitalist system.[5]

For Kalecki the business cycle is ultimately a political phenomenon (with the state consciously pursuing deflationary policies), whereas for Marx, the cycle reflected certain contradictory economic aspects of capitalism. However, in effect what Kalecki's arguments imply is something which has been central to Marxist arguments about capitalism as a system: integral to the operation of capitalism are alternative periods of boom and slump, with the latter generating periodic unemployment. It is the actual or imminent existence of the 'reserve army of the unemployed' which puts labour on the defensive. With full employment the 'power of the market' tilts towards labour.

Some of the points made above fit in with the notion of a hegemonic framework of thought, one which serves the class interests of capital relative to those of labour. At the heart of this are the ideas that private property and accumulation are sacrosanct, and that without the private sector growth would be endangered. An example of the force of such ideas was the way in which monetarist ideas about the need to control inflation became widely accepted, and embodied in deflationary policies, in the Western countries during the late 1970s and early 1980s. Monetary targets rapidly became commonplace, mandating 'discipline' in goods and labour markets. Either wages had to be restrained, or, according to the logic of these policies, workers would 'price themselves out of jobs'. In Britain, Thatcherism was associated with the view that economic growth could only be achieved after the conquest of inflation, and the defeat of the powerful trade unions. Moreover, a central aspect of the project of Thatcherism was the promotion of the belief that economic conditions could not be properly controlled by governments (a centrepiece of the previous Keynesian consensus), and that somehow, economic outcomes were the product of 'natural' market forces. In this construct, the best that governments could hope to do was to aid the workings of the market, and consequently to promote economic efficiency in the private sector. In so far as this framework of thought came to be accepted by a large and growing number of people, as well as those in politically significant positions within the state, it implied a redefinition of the 'limits of the possible', as well as a shift in the 'terrain of contestability' in British politics towards the right. By this we mean the way the overall agenda for debate, and the arguments made in the debates, are shaped, within the political system. Acceptance and internalisation of such limits implied that 'there is no alternative' (to use Mrs Thatcher's favourite catch-phrase, 'TINA' for short), to Thatcherite policies. Taken with the existence of the power of markets, it can thus be argued that a Gramscian form of hegemony – of capital *vis-à-vis* labour – was being constructed.

3.2 The Power of Capital: International Applications

Given the rise of transnational corporations and of international capital mobility, an *international* analysis of the power of capital is essential. Realist analysis is backward here, although some neo-realists, stressing interdependence, have shown an awareness of the structural power of financial capital. Neo-classical economists have examined the bargaining power of transnational corporations, and the determinants of short-term capital flows, but have neglected the institutional and ideological aspects of power. These aspects are central to the Gramscian approach. Many Marxists have given growing attention to the power of transnational corporations.[6] However, they have not fully integrated the concepts of behavioural and structural power, in both its normative and material dimensions, into their analysis of modern capitalism.

We shall, as in the previous section, begin our analysis with the direct, behavioural aspects of the power of capital, and then deal with its structural dimensions.

3.2.1. Forms of Direct Power: transnational corporations, the internationalisation of authority, and international networks While Lindblom has distinguished between authority (associated with governments) and markets (associated with private enterprise), transnational corporations exert authority across national boundaries, in the way that they allocate resources. The headquarters of such firms often decide on the geographical location of production of a range of products and components. They make investment decisions on a global scale, shifting funds from one country to another, so affecting the jobs of millions of workers, and the levels of economic activity in a range of nations.

The market power of oligopolistic firms in certain industries operates at an international level. The classic case is that of the so-called 'Seven Sisters' in the international oil industry.[7] The seven oil 'majors' (five American-owned, one British, and one Anglo-Dutch) dominated the world oil industry from the 1920s until the end of the 1960s. They colluded over prices and in their bargaining with governments. For example, in the 1950s, India, when seeking to establish a refining industry, had to accept 100 per cent foreign ownership, since the Seven Sisters took a common stance to prevent Indian interests gaining a stake.

The case of oil also illustrates the way in which direct forms of economic and military power are interrelated. The inroads of Western, especially British, oil firms in the Middle East in the first four decades of the twentieth century were built upon British military power in the region. The profit-making interests of British Petroleum and Shell, and the security interests of the British Empire went hand in hand. BP lobbied the British government for military action when its Iranian assets were nationalised in 1953. However, while BP regained some of its Iranian stake, the price exacted by the USA for helping the British government to reinstall the Shah was a large stake for the American 'majors', that is their large oil companies operating in the region.

So far we have referred to transnational corporations lobbying their parent governments in order to obtain policies favourable to their operations overseas. Such lobbying also takes place with regard to host governments, as well as international organisations, such as the World Bank. Transnational corporations are heavily involved in the aid projects of the World Bank, and may try and use their influence with their parent government, in order to get contracts. In this respect, American companies have an especially privileged status, since the USA has the biggest voting stake in the Bank, and its President has always been American. Indeed, two past chairmen, Robert MacNamara and Alden Clausen, had been chief executives of giant transnational corporations (Ford Motor Company and Bank of America, respectively). The links between private enterprise and the World Bank are further strengthened through joint ventures, organised through the International Finance Corporation (a branch of the Bank). Transnational financial networks are particularly well developed, and the links between commercial banks, central banks, the IMF and World Banks are illustrated in a number of international forums. For example, the 'Paris Club' of creditors met regularly during the 1980s to review the debt problems of less-developed countries, partly to evaluate whether their indebtedness posed threats to the viability of the international financial system. Another forum is the Bank for International Settlements, which reviews the viability of the system, and publishes data on international financial flows.

The international patterns of elite interaction – between business, state officials, bureaucrats and members of international organisations – and the networks they generate, have not been thoroughly researched. As such, they are not well understood, at least in comparison with domestic networks. However, some organisations such as the Bilderberg meetings (which began in 1954), and the Trilateral Commission (formed in 1973) are explicitly concerned to foster such interaction and networks, as well as a shared outlook amongst the international establishments of the major capitalist countries. There is also a great deal of interaction within inter-governmental organisations such as the OECD, which organises conferences and research initiatives. What is crucial to note is that there is a common ideology, at least with respect to the role of international business and private enterprise, which cuts across all of these institutional forums. The people active in these networks are increasingly well served by a range of international periodicals, such as the *Financial Times*, the *Economist* and the *Wall Street Journal*, as well as by more specialised publications. The process of elite interaction and network-building helps to shape the agenda for those state policies which affect the operation of transnational capital. In so far as international organisations accept a framework of thought that serves the interests of capital, they are likely to exert influence and sometimes even pressure (for example, in IMF loan conditions) on national governments of a sort which is congruent with that exerted by business. Several writers have suggested that the elements mentioned above are coming together to produce a transnational capitalist class, with its own particular form of class consciousness.[8] This 'strategic' consciousness involves a long-term time-horizon, and consideration of the general conditions under which transnational capital operates, as well as more specific, immediate and 'crisis-management' issues. However, the time-horizons of fractions of transnational capital vary, with financial capital often displaying a more short-term outlook, and perhaps a lack of such a 'strategic consciousness'. An example of the latter was the way in which leading commercial banks, in their efforts to recycle surplus petrodollars, rushed into making loans to less-developed countries in the mid-1970s. The commercial banks did not adequately foresee the 'debt crisis' of the 1980s, and underestimated the special risks (to the banks) of the 'sovereign' debt of the developing nations.

3.2.2. Forms of Structural Power: international business climate, inter-state competition, and international mobility of capital In the 'domestic' section on the power of capital, we saw how central was the notion of 'investment climate', involving the concept of 'business confidence'. Today, capital is so internationally mobile, especially between the major capitalist economies, that the 'investment climate' of one country will be judged by business with reference to the climate which prevails elsewhere. Transnational corporations routinely appraise the legal freedoms (for example to remit profits), production costs, labour relations, political stability and financial concessions offered, of many different countries. They also examine the size and growth potential of a country's market. As a result, governments are increasingly constrained in their freedom of manoeuvre by the economic policies of other states, as well as by the investment decisions of internationally mobile capital.

The structure of the inter-state system of formally sovereign nations makes it all the easier for transnationals to play off one government against another in their search for concessions. Indeed, in some countries, different regions compete to win such foreign investment. This phenomenon is visible in countries as diverse in character as the USA, Britain and China. Indeed, in the Chinese case, there are several 'special economic zones' and also some coastal cities which have attempted to attract foreign capital and technology, issuing prospectuses and advertising in the Western press. The bargaining power of transnational corporations would be reduced if governments were able to coordinate their regulations and financial concessions. However, even supposedly like-minded and wealthy countries, bound together in a collective economic organisation like the EC, have not been able to discuss seriously, let alone achieve, this goal. Even if governments of some member states were so inclined, given the EEC voting rules, there would almost certainly be others (such as Britain) who would oppose such measures, and veto any such policy initiative. Thus this aspect of the structural power of transnational corporations, in contrast to national firms, owes much to the division of the world into many states. The threat of nationalisation is less crushing to a transnational company, since it is likely that only a small proportion of its assets would be expropriated by a single country. The purely national firm is more at the mercy of its own government. However, as we noted in the 'domestic' section above, even in this case there are structural pressures on the governments of capitalist countries to create favourable conditions for business.

We have already seen how business confidence in government may depend on its economic policies, including its macroeconomic policies. Ideas about 'sound finance' and 'fighting inflation' constrain governments. Such ideas may spread from one country to another. The pursuit of such policies is likely to attract more foreign investment. The response of firms to such policies and other determinants of the investment climate is often gradual, and spread over a number of years. As has been noted, financial capital can react to government policies, or expected policies, much more rapidly than productive capital. With the liberalisation of capital flows between the major capitalist economies (and some less-developed countries) the reaction of financial capital need not be one of postponement of investment (as in an 'investment strike'). Instead, huge sums of money can quickly flow out of a country to more attractive havens. The result of this can be a balance of payments crisis under fixed exchange rates, or a foreign exchange crisis (fall in the exchange rate) under floating exchange rates. A falling exchange rate brings with it increased risks of rising inflation, especially for a small, open economy. Hence the international mobility of financial capital can swiftly force governments which deviate from policies seen as suitable by the 'market', to change course. For example, governments may be driven to raise interest rates, tighten monetary policy, and thus create a rise in unemployment to offset a currency, or payments crisis. This is in fact precisely what occurred in Britain in 1976, although in this case, the Labour government was able to blame the IMF for imposing its austerity policies. The point was, however, that against a background of high inflation, Britain would have had to change its policies in this direction anyway or there would have been a further collapse in the international value of sterling. In a similar way, the Socialist French government changed course after 1981, because of the same types of international pressure.

From the above example, it is tempting to reinterpret the Thatcher slogan so that it becomes 'there is no alternative' in the long term to providing a business climate, attractive by international standards. In other words the conquest of inflation would be just one aspect of a wider doctrine. We have already noted how the major capitalist states adopted macroeconomic policies premissed on the 'war on inflation' from the late 1970s to the mid-1980s. One explanaton of the adoption of such policies is, of course, because of the power of markets. However, there is nothing inevitable or automatic about particular policy response to changes in market conditions, or to the business climate. What may have been crucial in the adoption of monetarist policies was perhaps the pervasive internalisation of a framework of thought amongst political leaders, as well as central and private bankers, which meant that no significant alternative (to monetarism) was actually contemplated, except in one or two major capitalist states, such as France. Where such policies are adopted, with almost no reflection on possible alternatives, the power of capital attains a hegemonic status.

The impact of increased capital mobility, and also of recessions, has worked to the advantage of large-scale transnational capital, relative to national capital. Transnational capital is not entirely dependent on the business climate of one country, in the way a purely national firm obviously is. When a recession in one country occurs, it will be easier for transnational corporations to survive, than it is for national firms. Indeed, the process of restructuring, whereby weak firms are either made bankrupt, or else taken over by the stronger survivors, is likely to work systematically to the advantage of transnational capital, particularly in the manufacturing sector. Thatcher's Britain in the 1980s was a clear example of this process at work.

While the structural power of transnational capital has risen relative to that of governments since World War II (except perhaps in primary products), it has also risen relative to that of organised labour. Transnational, but not national firms, can threaten unions with plant closures and relocation of investment to other countries. Countries with relatively weak, or pliant labour movements, will, other things being equal, tend to attract investment at the expense of countries with strong labour movements. For example, part of the American electronics industry shifted to Asian countries like Singapore and Taiwan in the 1960s. Such tendencies have also been at work within capitalist countries. An example of this is the USA, where, over the last two decades, there has been a shift of manufacturing industry towards the relatively non-unionised ('sunbelt') states of the South and West, away from the North-East and Mid-West (the 'rustbelt') where unionisation was traditionally strong. The wider point to be made here is that the 'new international division of labour', where manufacturing has increasingly been located in the so-called newly-industrialising countries (NICs), is partly a manifestation of the rising power of transnational capital, relative to national capital, and to labour, especially in the major capitalist states.

With regard to the structural concept of power, the key contrast at the international level is the relative mobility of capital, and the relative immobility of labour (although certain types of highly skilled labour, such as scientists, may be highly mobile). In the past, the power of capital implied in the new international division of labour might have been countervailed to a certain extent. In the 1950s and 1960s, organised labour was relatively stronger in the core states, and appeared to have the potential to organise internationally. By the 1980s, such a potential was substantially undermined. Workers of different states found themselves in a similar position to that of their national governments: that is, competing to attract foreign investment. At the same time, the low-wage labour of the developing countries was pitted against the high-wage labour in the developed countries. The Third World offered an enormous 'reserve army' of cheap labour. This indirectly served to 'discipline' labour in the developed countries. Indeed, the transfer of production away from the core occurred at a time when unemployment reached high levels in many developed countries.[9] In so far as governments compete for foreign investment by offering concessions (tax breaks, subsidies, etc.) which reduce the cost of capital, relative to that of labour, firms will be encouraged to use more labour-saving techniques. This results in a reduced demand for such labour, and tends to raise unemployment unless workers are absorbed into lower-paid, labour-intensive employment, such as services.

Finally, certain service activities, notably education and the media, play a key role in the shaping of ideas and values. In these areas, institutions are usually national, rather than transnational. Indeed, many centres of higher education, as well as radio and television companies are in the public sector. However, there are signs that the power of markets and their internationalisation, is on the increase. As a result, structural pressures, favourable to business, are also increasing.

4. THE POWER OF CAPITAL: LIMITS AND CONTRADICTIONS

The power of capital is partly limited by the scope (or extensiveness) of the market, that is by the existence of non-market structures, of which the state is the chief example. Others include the existence of pre-capitalist (subsistence) modes of production, the degree to which social life is commoditised (and labour is subordinated), the technological limits to the geographical size of market activity, and, finally, the existence of international political limits. These are mainly set by the character of non-market political economies such as communist states pursuing autarkic development strategies. In the rest of this section we focus on the relationship between the state and market structures within contemporary capitalism.

4.1 Domestic Limits: welfarism, mercantilism and the public sector

Capital needs the state, and the state needs capital in a capitalist system. However, the nature of their interdependence is a practical as well as structural question. From the perspective of economic liberalism, the market may not be the most efficient supplier of certain 'public goods' and services. Thus even extreme economic liberals argue for the necessity of the state in some aspects of economic life. The state has the means to regulate and coerce business, although its *will* to do so may be constrained for reasons noted earlier. The precise relationship between the state and capital varies between countries, and this relationship is crucial for the limits to the power of capital.

In many leading capitalist countries, for much of the post-war period, policies were pursued which would seem to be opposed to some of the interests of business, for example: nationalisation, price controls, restrictions on capital flows, unemployment benefits and some other types of welfare spending. The public sector has grown significantly in most countries, as a percentage of Gross National Product, and also as a proportion of the workforce (at least until the late 1970s). Such patterns have also applied to most less-developed countries. Indeed, sometimes industrial enterprises in the public sector of developing countries have outweighed those in the private sector, as in India. The social and political forces behind such policies, limiting the power of capital, have varied between countries but some common elements are discernible.

After World War II, there was a widespread reaction against the free market system as it had operated in the 1930s, and opposition embraced manufacturing business as well as labour. These productive, rather than financial or *rentier* interests were at the fore in the post-war reconstruction. Wartime experience, and the spread of Keynesian ideas made people, including some business leaders, more willing to accept government intervention in the economy. The military sector was boosted by the war effort, and particularly in the USA, the military gained a new legitimacy and permanence within the state structure. This was in contrast to countries like Japan, and to a lesser extent West Germany, where the military had been defeated and discredited. Their economies were reconstructed under US leadership so as significantly to limit the scope for military production. However, with the onset of the Cold War, the USA and its allies increasingly developed a militarised alliance to confront and contain the communist states.

In addition, after the insecure years of the 1930s, the idea of the welfare state became more widely accepted, both as a method of ensuring social cohesion, and for the maintenance of a high level of aggregate demand in the economy (also maintained by high military expenditures, especially in the USA). The 1930s was an era of economic blocs, and intense economic nationalism. These 'illiberal' tendencies were intensified during the war years. Thus capitalism, at this stage, was very 'national' in character, in contrast to what it was eventually to become in the post-war era. The post-war coalitions which came to power in the major capitalist states were mainly formed within this national capitalist mould.

Over time, in each of these capitalist states, the public sector grew, and at the same time the interests associated with the expansion of its interventionary power, and with the size of state expenditures also increased: there were ever more state employees, and an increasing number of voters who would back higher state expenditures. This tendency, allied to the interests promoting a bigger military sector, produced varying configurations of state–capital relations in different states. These configurations came to be known as the 'mixed economy'.

The ideology of the 'mixed economy' became the orthodoxy in the major capitalist states after 1945. A 'mixed economy' welfarist coalition became progressively 'embedded' in the political economies of Western capitalism. Business people often came to believe that major departures from full employment would lead to political as well as economic instability, such was the impact of the events of the 1930s on their consciousness. Thus, although the post-war policies discussed above can be taken as evidence of 'limits' to the power of capital, they can also be seen as proof of the power of ideas. They reflect the internalisation of a 'political Keynesian' model of the political economy of capitalism, even though its validity can be, and indeed, has been questioned (in the 1970s high unemployment returned, particularly in Western Europe).[10]

In less-developed countries the growth of the public sector was often associated with a nationalist ideology, sometimes born of struggles for independence. In countries like India, nationalist and socialist ideas were fused. Nationalist ideas favoured the growth of military spending and the establishment of arms production. State-sponsored military-industrial development often became a feature of some less-developed countries. This was sometimes based on the application of the Soviet model of central planning. It has been associated with a state capitalist class. However, this may be a transitional phase, reflecting the backwardness of some countries where at independence, a bourgeoisie was largely lacking. Public choice theory would see public sector workers (bureaucrats) as a vested interest.

Taken together, these statist forces, operating within capitalism, may be seen to impose certain limits on the power of markets. Certain elements in the 'private sector' worked to support this statism. In particular, declining industries (which have lost comparative advantage), and those nascent industries in less-developed countries (which have yet to gain comparative advantage) demanded protection in order to survive. Farmers in Japan and Western Europe (who lacked comparative advantage in certain crops) have been successful in gaining substantial state support and protection. Manufacturing industry in less-developed countries has often received substantial protection. These industries, although strictly speaking private, have become heavily dependent on the state for their prosperity and survival. As such they might be seen to comprise a 'quasi-public sector'. Defence contractors, for example in the USA, can also be seen as part of such a sector. Such state support is in the interests of certain sectors rather than others, and is usually in favour of 'national' capital, relative to 'foreign' capital. State support of this type has not always been restricted to the sectors and industries mentioned above: certain states have given considerable support to their more advanced sectors to help them to stay ahead (in terms of comparative advantage) and successfully to penetrate foreign markets.

In addition, some state support may be given with the objective of facilitating market adjustment to market forces, while keeping unemployment low. For example, the 'active labour market' policy of Sweden has been successful. Indeed, Sweden (and some other smaller developed capitalist countries like Austria) has combined a highly developed welfare state with a strong economic performance.

These different forms of mercantilism give priority to security (in a social and/or military sense) over a capitalist stress on efficiency (and the rigours of competition in the unfettered market-place). In consequence, the more that mercantilist-welfarist policies come to prevail, the greater will be the range of restrictions on the structural power of capital. As we have seen, this relies heavily on the power of competitive markets.

4.2 International Limits: inter-state rivalry, market imperfections and global macroeconomic instability

International and domestic aspects of the limits to the power of capital are closely knit. For example, the strength of nationalism, concern with security, and of the military/public sector interests are directly related to the intensity of inter-state conflicts. The 1930s saw economic nationalism, militarism and a tendency towards regional economic blocs. This heightened the tendency towards a global political economy of rival, national capitals. By contrast, the more 'orderly' periods of what realists call hegemonic leadership (Britain in the nineteenth century, the United States in the twenty-five years after World War II), gave more scope to liberal internationalist elements in domestic political coalitions. In these more liberal periods, there was a rise in the relative and structural power of internationally mobile capital. In contrast, such structural power declined between the two world wars. Internationally-oriented business has an interest in peace, rather than war (unless it is involved in arms exports, sales of *matériel*, or in financing wars). Indeed the defeat in war of a government of a capitalist country may provide one of the key preconditions for a successful socialist revolution.[11]

However, the significance of hegemonic leadership for the power of capital depends crucially on the nature of the political economy of the dominate state(s), and their domestic coalitions which control international economic policy. Both Britain and the USA were not only capitalist, but also in favour of liberal international economic policies. If the hegemonic state after World War II had been the USSR, then the power of capital would have been severely circumscribed, as it came to be in Eastern Europe. The enlargement of the communist sphere with the 1949 Chinese revolution extended the political constraints on the international mobility of capital, as well as making communist ideas more appealing, particularly in the Third World. A change in the ideas and policies pursued in the communist states, notably in the Soviet Union, towards a more liberal approach to private enterprise, markets, and international trade, therefore, would be a major enhancement of the power of capital. This would be because it would give more scope for foreign investment, and increase the number of states competing to attract foreign capital, as well as enlarging the world market.

While the structural aspect of the power of internationally mobile capital owes much to the division of the world into competing states, it may be weakened when inter-state rivalries are intense (especially among the major powers). The logic of military-industrial rivalry, which we discuss in the following chapter, may, under certain conditions, come to override the economic logic of the transnationalisation process. The ultimate example of this would be nuclear war, although conventional wars can now be extremely destructive. In this sense, the relationship between transnational capital and the state has a contradictory character.

What form of order would permit the forms of international competition favoured by transnational capital? Perhaps the power of internationally mobile capital would be maximised by a world confederation, with states competing to attract foreign investment (as they do within the EC and the USA). Cooperation in such a confederation would be easier, the smaller the number of states. Alternatively, for a large number of states, substantial cooperation is easier if power resources are concentrated in the hands of relatively few states. However, the structural power of internationally mobile capital would be enhanced by having a large number of relatively small states. There is no clear-cut ideal situation for transnational hegemony on a global scale, since any scenario involves contradictory elements. However, perhaps the best possible situation (for transnational capital) is the one which more or less exists in practice, that is where the bulk of transnational capital was headquartered in a small number of large capitalist states, states in which capitalist hegemony was firmly embedded. Moreover, in the majority of such states, the dominant coalition in the making of foreign economic policy would necessarily have to be internationalist. This would, following public choice theory, be most likely to generate cooperation within the core on setting the basic norms and rules for the system, as well as preventing any single state from deviating too far from the norms established (deviation might be punished by an 'investment strike' or 'investment flight'). In so far as there are any inhospitable socialist, or strongly nationalist states, pursuing autarkic economic strategies, transnational capital would perhaps prefer them to be neither large, nor geographically contiguous. Change in the USSR and China (in the sense of adopting a more welcoming attitude to foreign capital) is therefore of the first importance in this respect. Alternatively, the break-up of a large, relatively autarkic state (such as India) might be seen as a long-term political gain for transnational capital.

Another contradictory tendency within internationally mobile capital stems from the nature of markets, notably financial markets, in so far as they generate economic instability. Competition between banks can and has led to the creation of precarious debt structures and to myopic loans to some less-developed countries (as in the 1970s). Evidence shows that certain borrowing countries used such funds to bolster state capitalist enterprises relative to transnational manufacturing concerns, that is playing off one sector of international capital against another.[12] This suggests that the power of transnational capital was not sufficiently entrenched in such countries, so as to prevent the use of international finance for mercantilist purposes. This contradiction is increased when there is a glut of international finance, such that the balance between state capital and transnational capital is tilted more in favour of the former. This is discussed in more detail in chapter 10.

A wider contradiction inherent in the nature of international markets involves the danger of a prolonged recession following a major banking collapse or a setback to financial confidence as a result of fears of such a collapse. The debt crisis of the 1980s may, however, be a special case, although debt defaults (by Latin American countries) were a feature of the depression of the 1930s. More generally, the logic of the market ensures that investment will take place on the basis of expected profit yields, allowing for risk. This may mean that there may be insufficient investment in less-developed countries, so that they fail to become, from the point of view of international banks, more 'credit worthy' in the long term. There may be a shortfall in global economic growth because of this tendency.

An international hegemony based upon the concept of monetary discipline and 'sound finance' is beset by contradictions. If all countries compete to prove their 'monetary soundness' their deflationary policies will have negative multiplier effects. World recession is the natural outcome, if all deflate simultaneously. Such deflation could be seen as a mercantilist policy in pursuit of a trade surplus. The dangers of the hegemony of a strict financial orthodoxy were illustrated during the 1930s, particularly in the USA and the UK. In these countries a commitment to balanced budgets and monetary discipline made it difficult to reverse the slide into recession. Other countries more rapidly abandoned this othodoxy, to the point where some capitalist states actively pursued policies to constrain the power of markets. One extreme example of this was Nazi Germany. The wider macroeconomic issue is that what may appear to be 'rational' policy from the point of view of one country, may, if replicated elsewhere, add up to 'collective irrationality'. Economists call this the 'fallacy of composition'. The same type of fallacy was also involved in the attempts by countries to export their unemployment through competitive depreciation and the restriction of imports during the 1930s. This led to a fall in the level of world trade, exchange rate instability, and a growing climate of international uncertainty which sometimes writers claimed not only discouraged investment, but was one of the conditions which led to the outbreak of World War II. In contrast to the 1930s, in the 1980s, there were clear signs that politicians, bankers and economists were aware of the implications of this fallacy, and anxious to avoid them, in part through the international coordination of macroeconomic policies.

For example, in 1986–88 a common view was that unless West Germany and Japan took steps to expand their economies, a slowing of world economic growth was inevitable.

This implies that although a world confederation might be the ideal type of political authority for transnational capital, the more basic issue is the need for some type of international authority which can intervene to prevent market imperfections from having disastrous global economic consequences.

NOTES

1. Charles Lindblom, *Politics and Markets* (New York, Basic Books, 1977), pp. 170–88. See also David Marsh (ed.), *Capital and Politics in Western Europe* (London, Frank Cass, 1983); Frank Longstreth, 'The City, Industry and the State', in Colin Crouch (ed.), *State and Economy in Contemporary Capitalism* (London, Croom Helm, 1979).
2. Peter Bachrach and Morton S. Baratz, 'The Two Faces of Power', *American Political Science Review* (1962), Vol. 56, pp. 947–952; and their 'Decisions and Non-Decisions: an Analytical Framework', *American Political Science Review* (1963), Vol. 57, pp. 631–42.
3. Sidney Verba, 'The Silent Majority: Myth and Reality', *University of Chicago Magazine* (December 1970), Vol. 63, pp. 13–14, cited in Lindblom, op. cit., p. 202.
4. On the concept of structural power and its relation to the concept of action see Steven Lukes, 'Power and Structure', in S. Lukes, *Essays in Social Theory* (London, Macmillan, 1970); Anthony Giddens, *Central Problems in Social Theory: Action, Structure and Contradiction in Social Analysis* (London, Macmillan, 1979); David Knights and Hugh Wilmott, 'Power and Identity in Theory and Practice', *The Sociological Review* (1985), Vol. 33, pp. 22–47;

Katherine Betts, 'The Conditions of Action, Power and the Problem of Interests', *The Sociological Review* (1986), Vol. 34, pp. 39–64. On the concept of the structural power of capital, see Hugh Ward, 'Structural Power – A Contradiction in Terms?', *Essex Papers in Politics and Government* (1956), Department of Government, Essex University, Colchester.

5. Michal Kalecki, 'Political Aspects of Full Employment', *Political Quarterly*, (1943), Vol. 14, pp. 322–31. Reprinted in E. K. Hunt and J. G. Schwartz, *A Critique of Economic Theory* (Harmondsworth, Penguin Books, 1972). By *rentier* interests is meant those who are on fixed, or investment incomes, who may be vulnerable to inflation.

6. See, for example, Hugo Radice (ed.), *International Firms and Modern Imperialism* (Harmondsworth, Penguin Books, 1975).

7. Anthony Sampson, *The Seven Sisters: the Great Oil Companies and the World they Made* (London, Hodder and Stoughton, 1975).

8. See Robert W. Cox, 'Ideologies and the NIEO: Reflections on Some Recent Literature', *International Organisation* (1979), Vol. 33. pp. 257–302; Kees van der Pijl, *The Making of an Atlantic Ruling Class* (London, Verso, 1984); Stephen Gill, *American Hegemony and the Trilateral Commission* (Cambridge, Cambridge University Press, 1988).

9. Folker Froebel et al., *The New International Division of Labour: Structural Unemployment in Industrialised Countries and Industrialisation in Developing Countries* (Cambridge, Cambridge University Press, 1980).

10. Robert Skidelsky, 'The Decline of Keynesian Politics', in Colin Crouch (ed.), *State and Economy in Contemporary Capitalism*, op. cit.

11. Theda Skocpol, *States and Social Revolutions* (Cambridge, Cambridge University Press, 1979).

12. Jeff Frieden, 'Third World Indebted Industrialisation: International Finance and State Capitalism in Mexico, Brazil, Algeria and South Korea', *International Organisation* (1981), Vol. 35, pp. 407–31.

8   Military–Industrial Rivalry in The Global Political Economy

In this chapter we examine the logic of military-industrial rivalry and the way it affects state policies and arms production. In particular, we analyse the economic, political and social forces making for the rise of, and limits to, growing military expenditure and the spread of military-industrial complexes. The purpose of this is to begin to suggest answers to two related questions. The first is how far, and why, are arms production and military spending a systematic feature of the global political economy? The second is, what are the relationships between these systemic features and the propensity to war and peace in the post-war world?

1. 'CATCH-UP LOGIC' AND REALIST-MERCANTILISM

As has been noted, the oldest political economy approach, realist-mercantilism, has long paid particular attention to the relationship between economic and military strength (see chapter 3). In this section we focus on the implications of this perspective.

Some of the ideas of early Mercantilists (for example the concept of inter-state rivalry) have been taken up by modern Mercantilists such as Gautam Sen.[1] Sen has stressed how concern with national security has made industrialisation as much a military as an economic imperative. Strategic industries have been central to the industrial strategies and import-substitution programmes of many countries. Subsidies and trade barriers have been justified on the grounds of defence requirements. Mercantilist policies are needed to 'catch up' with other states: otherwise national independence may be compromised or even lost. Further, as Theda Skocpol has argued, national cohesion and political stability may break down as a state fails to 'catch up', or 'keep up' with its powerful neighbours and rivals. Social revolution is made either more likely, or at least more possible. For example, Japan and Germany were able to 'catch up' in the late nineteenth and early twentieth centuries, whereas Manchu China and Romanov Russia were not. Conservative reforms brought rapid industrialisation in the former two countries, whereas in the latter two, the pace of industrialisation was slower, and the state was unable to cope with external challenges. As a result social revolution occurred, sweeping away the old order.[2] Later, the Bolsheviks were able to mobilise and industrialise the USSR, and to build a large military apparatus whereas little industrialisation took place in China, leaving the country vulnerable to further invasion and occupation by Japan in the 1930s. Only with the coming to power of the communists in 1949 was an effective central state created, in contrast with nationalist China, enabling sufficient internal and external autonomy to promote industrialisation.

This 'catch-up' logic, which helps to promote a pattern of military-industrial development is consistent with the writings of Alexander Gerschenkron.[3] In his study of the contrast between Britain's 'early', and other states' 'late' industrialisation, in the nineteenth century, it is argued that later developers seem to require more direct state intervention because of the large capital needed to produce on an efficient scale. (Capital markets are often very underdeveloped in backward or less-developed countries.) Further, the state may be able to take a more long-term and strategic view, than may private enterprise. Thus the state will tend to mobilise funds and create or organise larger productive units which have greater economies of scale.[4] If states wish to avoid dependence on foreign capital (which may be seen as necessary for reasons of national security), they thus have no alternative but to introduce more state enterprises, across a range of 'strategic industries'.

The above logic of military-industrial rivalry explains and predicts a systematic tendency for arms and related industries to be more highly protected than most others. In less-developed countries, this usually means that the agricultural sector is discriminated against, so as to favour manufacturing industry. Only in already-industrialised countries can farmers hope to gain 'strategic' status for agriculture. Another implication of military-industrial rivalry is that in developing countries there will be pressures which lead to the expansion of the public sector, perhaps even relative to, or at the expense of, the private sector. Such a pattern of military-industrial development is usually associated with the growth of nationalist interests (for both capital and labour) and ideologies which together may set limits to the power of transnational capital (see the previous chapter on the role of the public sector as a potential limit to the power of capital). In effect, vested interests may 'wrap themselves in the flag'. If they are highly influential, they may come to form part of an historic bloc in which there is a hegemonic fit between the material capabilities of certain industries, nationalist and statist ideas, and elements of the state apparatus, as well as quasi-state institutions in the civil society (e.g. veterans' associations, reservists). The hegemonic concepts within this type of bloc are those of national security and territorial sovereignty. From this point of view, national self-reliance and self-sufficiency are of the essence.

A good example of what can be termed a military-industrial historic bloc was in inter-war Japan, where the military gradually came to dominate domestic politics, and there was a shift from the earlier leading role for light industries such as textiles (before 1914), to an emphasis on heavy industries, such as iron, steel and chemicals. The reasons for the triumph of militarism in Japan are to be found in a combination of internal and external factors. Japanese feudal traditions, through their stress on martial prowess, honour and loyalty to leaders were conducive to a militarist mentality and set of priorities. The Great Depression and the closing of foreign markets in the 1930s undermined the export-oriented growth (based on light industries) which prevailed up to World War I. A second example is India, since independence in 1947, where the growth of a large and dominant state sector has increasingly gone with attempts to build up arms production, especially since its humiliation in the war with China in 1962. India has turned to the Soviet Union for some of its military technology, as a means of gaining more self-sufficiency in military production in the longer term. Thus MIG fighter aircraft are produced in India. A third example is Israel, which has fostered a special military and industrial relationship with the USA, for similar reasons to those of India. Partly because of its small home market, Israel, to generate the necessary economies of scale, unlike India, has gone on to export a substantial proportion of its arms output.

Such military-industrial interests and ideas are to be found in most countries. However, their relative influence and political weight varies considerably. The hegemonic position they attained in inter-war Japan is an extreme case. In some countries military-industrial complexes have emerged, but they have been countervailed by other political forces (see later sections on this).

2. THE LEVEL AND DETERMINANTS OF MILITARY EXPENDITURES

World military expenditure is on a vast scale and grew substantially during the 1970s. Growth has continued in the industrialised countries in the 1980s but since 1982 there has been some decline in military expenditures in less-developed countries.

The Global Political Economy

Table 8.1: World military expenditure, 1975-84 (selected years)
(in $ billions at 1980 prices and exchange rates)

	1975	1981	1982	1983	1984	World share per cent
IMEs	257,534	290,278	307,827	324,230	348,697	53.7
NMEs	171,972	185,448	189,757	191,671	196,133	30.2
MOECs	33,352	45,143	48,598	44,874	44,988	6.9
RoW	43,452	54,238	61,862	60,018	57,419	8.8
World Total	507,480	576,860	609,900	622,800	649,070	100.0

Notes: Industrial Market Economies = IMEs; Non-Market Economies = NMEs; Major Oil-Exporting Countries = MOECs; Rest of the World = RoW.
Source: R. Luckman, 'Disarmament and Development – the International Context', IDS Bulletin (October 1985), Vol. 16, No. 4, p. 3.

The factors influencing these high levels of military expenditure, both globally and for individual countries are complex and difficult to unravel, particularly in a short chapter such as this. Some of the factors relate to the internal structure of national political economies, whereas others relate to the structure of the global political economy. Still others relate to economic factors such as changes in the level of technology. However, the internal and external factors are linked. Above all, security inter-dependence between countries means that decisions concerning the military expenditure of one country cannot be made independently of assessments of trends in other countries. In addition, decision-making is complicated by alliance networks. Let us now consider some of the explanations in the literature for the scale of military expenditures.

One explanation of the factors affecting military expenditures would use the public choice approach. Here the various factors would be considered in terms of political demand and supply. 'Demand' factors would include the perceived threats to the nation and a desire for security; a desire for national power and international status; the size of national income and wealth, especially as they affect the availability of resources for defence; the (opportunity) cost of defence equipment relative to the price of other goods and services; and the scope for free-riding on allies, thus transferring defence costs to other states. 'Supply' factors might include the price and profitability of arms production; the nature and influence of political institutions; and the alternative uses of funds for politicians and bureaucrats. The 'supply' factors concern the willingness and ability of governments to supply what is often seen as the 'public good' of defence.

In the case of Japan there has been a post-1945 consensus, promoted by the powerful Japanese bureaucracy, in favour of spending a very low percentage of gross national product on defence, at least when compared to most other major countries. Until the mid-1980s, this was less than 1 per cent, whereas in the United States and Britain it has usually exceeded 5 per cent of GNP. This relatively low (although in absolute terms quite high) level of military expenditures in post-war Japan, in contrast to the inter-war militarist period, can be explained with reference to some of the factors noted above. First, the Japanese leaders were concerned with post-war political rehabilitation, particularly as their war-time endeavours were widely condemned in other Asian countries. In addition, the United States had defeated and occupied Japan, and had written what came to be known as the 'Peace Constitution', which forbade the production of nuclear weapons, and restricted the functions of the Japanese military to a narrow definition of 'self defence'. The USA stationed its own military forces in Japan, and consistently provided what the Japanese call the 'nuclear umbrella' to protect Japan from China and the Soviet Union. Given the devastated condition of the Japanese economy in the aftermath of World War II, any attempt at high military expenditure would have resulted in even more malnutrition than occurred anyway. In this context, Japanese companies initially concentrated on the needs of economic reconstruction, and later began to see greater profitability and export opportunities in industries other than those concerned with arms production. In effect they have opted for peace, and victory in economic (notably trade) 'war'. A concept of economic security is at the heart of the new post-war outlook of Japanese leaders, premissed on being friendly with suppliers of raw materials, hosts to Japanese direct investment, and consumers of Japanese goods – in contrast to the imperialism of the Asian Co-prosperity Sphere of the 1930s. In consequence, the dominant business interests in post-war Japan have become those in consumer goods industries and in agriculture. This strategy has made Japan the world's second largest capitalist economy. Despite their recent wealth, and the ability to carry a heavier defence burden, there is a strong temptation to go on free-riding on American military power.

It should be noted that in the application of the public choice approach the demand and supply sides may not be independent of each other. In the above case there are very strong links between the Japanese bureaucratic leaders and the business elite, which arise because of common social background, education (at the University of Tokyo), and outlook. Some of those who are 'producers' on the supply side, are also active 'voters' and 'consumers' on the demand side. Where the public sector is large (its employees are also voters) this point may be of major consequence because politicians may be able to get sufficient popularity without either compromising their own preferences or coming into conflict with the bureaucracy. This is another way of explaining a mercantilist historic bloc.

The existence of such a bloc, and indeed of military-industrial complexes, is one of the various factors influencing military expenditure. We discuss this in a later section.

One shortcoming of the analysis above is that it avoids explicit attention to the interraction between states. Liberal theorists often resort to game theory to fill this gap, as in models of bilateral arms races, which are seen as involving zero-sum games, and perhaps the Prisoners' Dilemma (assuming little or no communication between states). More generally, higher expenditure in one country can lead to higher expenditure in other countries as others seek to catch up with the first country, or seek new allies to offset a decline in their relative military positions. Ratchet effects are likely in any arms race, with ever more arms needed to offset those of potential aggressors. Under certain types of international political conditions, any specific increase in demand for armaments in one country, perhaps due to pressure from vested interests, might trigger off a chain of similar demands in other countries. Military actions by one country might, of course, also produce such consequences, as others perceive their military interests as more threatened than before. Such pessimistic predictions are avoidable if models of arms expenditure are based on the Coordination Game, discussed in chapter 4. Concessions by any state in arms negotiations may be made contingent on concessions by the other side(s), with strict monitoring and verification. Parties might, in a practical sense, come to see arms reductions as mutually beneficial, in that apart from avoiding risks of an accidental war (for example through the launching of computer-controlled missiles), this would lead to a reduction in military expenditures, releasing resources for other purposes. In such a context, vested military-industrial interests would seek to hinder and block progress in arms reduction negotiations.

Game theory helps to illuminate some of the dynamics affecting the level of military expenditures. However, the 'game' at the international level involves many players, with different types of communication between them: in some cases communication (for example between allies) is relatively easy, in many others (between ideological enemies, and rivals), it is difficult or non-existent. This problem is compounded by the structure of the inter-state system, and in particular by the number of states within it.

The most militarily-intensive zones tend to be on, or close to frontiers. In a large empire or state, there is likely to be a vast, largely demilitarised area (although it may be heavily policed). If instead of such large empires there are many small states, often all parts of the country may be close to a frontier. In other words, there may be economies of scale in defending particular territories. During the heyday of the Roman Empire, approximately 300,000 troops patrolled a periphery which stretched from

Scotland to Egypt, and from Morocco to Romania. At the heart of the Empire, in the Mediterranean zone, apart from the powerful Praetorian Guard in Rome, there were virtually no troops. Pressure on one frontier was often relieved by transferring troops from another frontier which was going through a peaceful phase. Hence the break-up of a large empire is likely to raise the level of military expenditures.

Further, a rise in the number of states disproportionately increases the potential number of military (and diplomatic) interactions. This can be represented diagrammatically, as in Figure 8.1, below.

Figure 8.1 (i) shows the bilateral interaction of two states, in what is a single relationship. Adding a third state results in three relationships (Figure 8.1 (ii)). For each state added, the number of interactions increases arithmetically, in a progressive series. Thus the number of potential interactions in a world of many states is massive, although not all of these would be significant in military terms. None the less, a rise in the number of states is, other things being equal, likely to promote an increase in levels of militarisation. The interaction effects of arms races have more scope, the greater number of states.

Recent historical evidence supports this theoretical argument. Decolonisation, which greatly increased the number of states, has been followed by many wars in the Third World, and by regional arm races (as in the Persian Gulf and the Horn of Africa). These developments have been accompanied by higher growth rates for military expenditure in the Third World, as compared to the developed countries. This is one reason why the proportion of global military expenditures attributable to the superpowers has fallen dramatically since 1950 despite massively escalating costs of weaponry. The USA, for example, accounted for approximately 50 per cent of global military expenditures in 1950, a percentage which fell to about 23 per cent in 1980, a level thought by Western experts to be similar to that of the Soviet Union.[5]

3. THE COSTS AND BENEFITS OF MILITARY EXPENDITURES

The opportunity costs of military expenditures depend on many factors, such as the degree of spare capacity and labour, the import-intensity of military expenditures, the alternative uses of capital and labour which have to be switched to military expenditures, i.e. whether higher military expenditure is at the expense of consumption, investment, exports and/or research and development. These opportunity costs will vary according to the type of military expenditures, for example how capital- and skill-intensive it is. In the case of certain types of weapons development, there may also be significant social costs, such as the resources devoted to

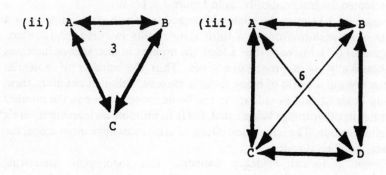

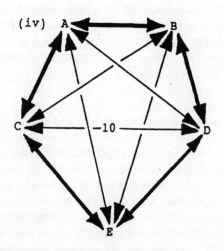

Figure 8.1: State proliferation and interaction patterns

protecting weapons installations, as well as the potentially massive cost resulting from accidents (such as from nuclear or chemical weapons). Another type of cost is more subtle and long-term, in that a large military expenditure might have political and social repercussions in terms of the distribution of political power resources, and dominant ways of seeing and interpreting the world: for example with regard to the loss of political freedoms in the face of pressing 'national security' problems. Such effects occur not just within particular societies, but also between them because of the dynamics of inter-state rivalry. This raises the issue of whether such effects are reversible, and if so under what conditions. Are there political 'ratchet effects' when military expenditure rises? The points made above refer primarily to increases in military expenditure under 'peace-time' conditions. However, the costs of military expenditure take on a new and more terrible dimension in war, with the loss of human life and also environmental damage.

Under conditions of spare capacity a rise in military expenditure may have little or no economic opportunity costs for a given state assuming that domestic firms are able to supply what is required. Such was the case in Germany in the 1930s. Indeed, for Hitler and the Nazi Party, there were political advantages since unemployment fell as military expenditures increased. Where little spare capacity exists there will be significant opportunity costs and the likelihood of inflationary pressures. These opportunity costs may be greater in the long run than the short run in so far as the stock of capital, skills and knowledge is reduced in the long term as a result of more short-term cutbacks in 'investment' programmes. The USSR, as a fully-employed economy, may face higher opportunity costs than its Western rivals in increasing military expenditures.[6]

There are national variations in the pattern and extent of arms production and the relationship between such production and that in other industries: some countries are much more self-sufficient than others. The import-intensity of military expenditure tends to be higher in the Third World, where a severe shortage of foreign exchange is common, relative to what is needed for economic development. Thus regional arms races and wars may adversely affect development: for example that between Iran and Iraq in the 1980s. A growing number of less-developed countries have developed their own arms industries and some even export, as well as import arms, such as Brazil. This development reflects not only a concern for security of arms supply and the conservation of foreign exchange: it can be part of a wider import-substitution industrialisation strategy, that is a part of 'catch-up mercantilism'. For such a strategy to be successful, there must a correct 'mix', and sufficient quantity of resources, such as trained personnel across a number of sectors. The shortage of skilled people in less-developed countries means that the opportunity cost of skill-intensive military expenditure (for example, pilots and engineers) is greater than that for unskilled, labour-intensive military expenditures (as with conscript infantry). Indeed, skill shortages can, while military spending rises rapidly, result in a crisis of absorptive capacity, as happened under the Shah of Iran in the 1970s, so adversely affecting both the pace of industrialisation and political stability.[7]

There are proponents of military expenditure who claim there are significant 'spin offs' – economic and political – from military expenditures. Such economic arguments focus on technology and the way in which high military expenditures (based upon a 'national' procurement policy) may contribute to the nurture of infant industries, and/or help maintain a nation's lead in high technology industries. Also, if the leading industries in a particular country are also the 'strategic industries', they may be boosted by strong military demand in addition to civilian demand, so obtaining scale economies and thus accelerating economic growth, for example in aerospace, high-speed computing and telecommunications systems.

The political arguments focus upon the degree to which high military expenditure helps to maintain the dominance of one state relative to others with correspondingly lower levels of military expenditures. For example, only countries with high technology industries geared to military production can give and use military aid as a means of political influence. Conversely, only by the development of such military-industrial power resources can such influence be resisted. Thus 'catch-up mercantilism' and 'keep ahead mercantilism' are two sides of the same coin. They both reflect a response to the structural condition of military-industrial rivalry. Military strength, in some historical circumstances, has been used to gain economic advantages, such as trading opportunities, investment rights, access to land, and better terms of trade. This has taken various forms, resulting in, for example, unequal treaties, puppet regimes and colonial conquest. Today, the scope for obtaining economic advantage from military actions may be less than it was, given the spread of weaponry and the wider acceptance of international norms of national sovereignty and self-determination. However, economic advantages may still be obtained by military aid in the form of training, advisors as well as subsidised weapons. An example is the granting of favourable fishing rights to the great powers by less-developed countries in exchange for military aid.

The problems of 'keep ahead mercantilism' are to do with both maintaining the range and quality of military-industrial innovation and preventing its diffusion to rival states whilst seeking access to the technology of other rivals (and also allies). The increased complexity of modern technologies, including the development of new industries and products (such as satellites, space shuttles, optical lasers, biotechnology) means that the investment requirements, both in terms of physical and human capital are greater than they once were. The costs of maintaining American military dominance are significantly greater than they were for Britain in the nineteenth century. In the *pax britannica* naval power was crucial, whereas today land, sea, air and space power are needed: this is indicative of the ever-expanding range of technologies and industries which are now central for military-industrial rivalry. Moreover, the rate of change within these contemporary industries is faster than for sea power in the nineteenth century.

4. THE POLITICAL ECONOMY OF ARMS

Technology of many types is diffusing faster than ever before. It is not always easy to separate civil and military technology, but even when this can be done technology is still likely to diffuse because of the structural force of international economic competition. To be competitive in many high-technology industries the realisation of scale economies is necessary, and if the home market is not large enough, exports are vital in order to generate the revenue to finance further research and development. Thus there is a contradiction between the structural dynamics of the inter-state system and those of international economic competition: for national security reasons states may wish to monopolise particular military-industrial technologies but the economics of technological innovation drive them to policies which facilitate diffusion. The spread dynamics noted here also interact with the quest by particular states (notably the superpowers) to maintain influence over other important states in part by supplying them with up-to-date weapons systems. The arms trade is a mechanism for the diffusion of armaments even where more fundamental technological capabilities are successfully withheld.

During the 1970s and 1980s there was a spectacular growth in the arms trade, much faster in the 1970s than the growth in world trade as a whole. Much of the arms supplied went to the oil-rich Middle Eastern states, fuelling a regional arms race between, on the one hand, Israel and the 'militant' Arab states, and on the other hand, between Gulf states such as Iran and Iraq. The major suppliers were the USA and the USSR, followed by France and the UK. Iraq was an example of a country which imported civilian nuclear technology, with a view to developing nuclear weapons – a venture which proved unsuccessful due to preemptive Israeli bombing. On the one hand, the West and Japan feared political upheaval in, and danger to, oil supplies from the Middle East; on the other, certain Western interests profited from arms sales to the region (as did the USSR).

The case of the Gulf conflicts of the 1980s illustrated simultaneously the ease with which Western arms could be sold, as well as the growing difficulty for the USA to use its own force to intervene in the region. Although the USA created a Rapid Deployment Force (Central Command) its usefulness in the Middle East was doubtful, given the proximity of the USSR, the large stock of weaponry in the region, the strength of nationalism, fundamentalism and anti-Americanism, and domestic constraints on the American use of force. The latter were, of course, tested by both American intervention in the Lebanon and also by the 1986 bombing of Tripoli. What seemed acceptable to the American public was intervention without American casualties. It should also be noted that the USA, USSR, France, Britain and Israel had a financial interest in the continuation of the Iran–Iraq War during the 1980s, in their role as weapons suppliers. The USA, the USSR, as well as other states, also had a military interest in a stalemate since then neither Iran nor Iraq could pose a serious threat to surrounding nations. These common interests were thus crucial to explaining the long duration of the War. Moreover, on the evidence of the 1970s and early 1980s, high arms sales to the Middle East have been associated with high oil prices. In this connection, it should be noted that the US took an ambiguous position on the oil price rises in 1973–74. American Secretary of State Kissinger was keen to see that the Shah had more money to buy US arms, so as to be the 'regional policeman' envisaged in the Nixon (Guam) Doctrine. This occurred at a time when the US government's military and space spending was in decline as a percentage of GNP, so that the American arms industry needed a big rise in foreign demand. Analysis of this example suggests that evaluation of the size and scope of the US military-industrial complex needs to consider arms sales and foreign policy as well as US domestic military spending. In 1986 the US found itself drawn into supplying arms to Iran in order to get the release of hostages. France faced similar dilemmas, yet neither country wanted an Iranian victory in the Iran-Iraq War. Ironically, the weapons of the Middle Eastern groups that have taken Westerners hostage have been supplied, in part by (private) international arms dealers.

The contemporary spread dynamics of military-industrial rivalry both contribute to, and in some ways undermine, a global military hierarchy, for example through nuclear proliferation and the massive arms trade. This is in contrast to the clear and rather easily defined military hierarchy of the nineteenth century. This argument thus sheds some doubt on the argument that there is now a relatively clear-cut 'New International Military Order'.[8] This may possibly be true for nuclear weapons, but even here the situation seems to be changing, and possibly becoming more unstable. However, the spread of arms production in the Third World is limited by the size of a country's GNP and resources, due to economies of scale and the burdens that high military spending can place on a country's economy.

Israel, perhaps the most successful small country in the production of arms, was forced to cancel its Lavi fighter programme in 1987 due to soaring research costs and the unwillingness of the United States to increase its subsidies. Neuman concludes that the 'inherent constraints of size and infrastructure will create a hierarchically structured world arms trade and production system as the military industries of states grow'.[9] The position of countries in the hierarchy will also depend on cultural and political factors that effect the mobilisation of resources and their scientific use.

5. THE NATURE AND SIGNIFICANCE OF MILITARY-INDUSTRIAL COMPLEXES

The notion of a 'complex' implies something more permanent than a temporary, tactical coming together of different interests for the purpose of pushing for increased military expenditures. It implies a shared framework of thought, overlapping and interpenetrating institutions, and a congruence between these social forces. It also implies a congruence between the 'the means of production' and the 'means of destruction'. If there is such a complex within a society, there is the possibility that military expenditures may grow in a way that is not just a function of inter-state rivalries and what some would see as basic security needs (which are often highly debatable). The very perception of these security needs is something that members of the complex have a vested interest in influencing and exaggerating. Arms producers have an interest in making more profits. Military bureaucrats have an interest in expanding their budget and prestige. 'Security intellectuals' have an interest in both promoting the indispensability of their expertise, as well as their ways of seeing and interpreting the problems of war and peace. Most fundamentally, the armed services have an interest in obtaining better and larger amounts of weapons, better pay and conditions, and as much status as possible within the society. At the heart of this complex is the concept of 'national security'.

In the American case it is embodied in the creation of such institutions as the USA's National Security Council, where the National Security Assistant (a position variously held in recent decades by Henry Kissinger, Zbigniew Brzezinski and Admiral Poindexter) has privileged access to the President as Commander-in-Chief and head of state on a daily basis. The task of the NSC is to coordinate the activities of a wide range of US institutions concerned with foreign policy: the Pentagon, the State Department, the Central Intelligence Agency, and the various intelligence and defence activities of other government departments. The NSC also takes account of international economic aspects of security. Such institutionalisation, which takes various forms in different countries, has been a significant ingredient in the emergence of military-industrial complexes.

Institutionalisation has been carried to remarkable lengths in the Soviet Union. Here its extensiveness involves the way that the economy is organised, primarily to provide the military with the best in terms of skills, technology, materials and finished products. It is almost as if the USSR were organised as a single military-industrial complex. National security is the number one priority for the Soviet state and its citizens. This has served to legitimate the Soviet military-industrial complex. Its power also rests on a strong consensus within the Communist Party that the military should play a important role within the Soviet state, although under Party control. However, in the mid-1980s the head of the KGB (secret police and intelligence) but not the Defence Minister had full membership of the Politbureau, in contrast to the Brezhnev era, which implied Soviet attempts to restructure its economic priorities.[10] In sum, in the 1980s a new Soviet consensus on the need for economic reforms developed, albeit less so on their precise nature. The influence of the military appeared to have weakened in this process, particularly since the coming to power of Secretary Gorbachev in 1985. In America, the interest of the military-industrial complex have been more partisan, and, as such, have faced often fierce public criticism in Congress.

In the USSR the very national and party-led nature of the military-industrial complex facilitates consideration of long-term national security interests. For both countries, arms control agreements and reduced spending on nuclear weapons can be seen as necessary for the economic growth of high-technology industries, which underpin military strength and spending in the long term. By contrast, in the US 'short-term rationality' may sometimes prevail given the business cycle, the strength of interest groups linked to the military-industrial complex and electoral pressures on politicians. However, long-term planning and continuity are striking in the US as well as the USSR. Thus although there are structural similarities between the two superpowers' military-industrial complexes, large differences in economic organisation, balance of political forces, political culture and military tradition distinguish one from the other.

6. THE SCALE OF AMERICAN AND SOVIET MILITARY-INDUSTRIAL COMPLEXES

The following figures suggest the scale of the military-industrial complexes of the USA and the USSR. One recent estimate of their military expenditures (which can only be indicative because of the difficulties of gaining precise information and establishing comparability of data) stated that together they accounted for around 50 per cent of total world military spending, and they held 96 per cent of the world's strategic nuclear forces.[11] American defence outlays in 1984 were $273.4 billion, and rose to approximately $300 billion in 1985, which meant a rise to approximately 7.55 per cent of GNP. The projected figure for fiscal year 1986 was $302.6 billion, and expenditures requested by the Reagan administration for 1986–88 would, if they had been fully appropriated by the Congress, have totalled over $1 trillion. Soviet expenditures are impossible to compare but supported total armed forces of 5.15 million people as opposed to the USA's 2.13 million. Western estimates of Soviet expenditures vary widely, ranging between 10 and 20 per cent of GDP. Western experts say Soviet expenditures almost rival those of the USA in absolute terms although the USA generally pays much higher prices and wages than the USSR, and gets less 'bang' per dollar than the Soviets have got per rouble. This seems to have increasingly been the case since the late 1960s as weapons have become more sophisticated and as Western prices have risen fairly rapidly.[12] These outlays compare with the entire 1983 GDP of the following countries, in $US billions: Greece ($37.69 billion); Mozambique (in 1981, est. $2.9 billion); Cuba ($15.44 billion, including heavy subsidies of Soviet aid); Australia ($155.7 billion); and oil-rich Saudi Arabia ($153 billion in 1982 and $120 billion in 1983).[13]

Another facet of this debate is the degree to which the influence of the military-industrial complex has an inertial effect on military expenditures within the economy, that is when a war ends is military expenditure slow to come down? Soviet military expenditure seems to be a fairly steady proportion of net material product (which equals gross domestic product, GDP, less services). In the USA military expenditure has shown some tendency to fall in the aftermath of wars, especially World War II, but also the Korean and Vietnam wars. Although the Pentagon continues to be the largest single purchaser of goods and services, its share has declined as the overall economy has grown:

While the military budget stayed the same, the ... [GNP] ... has almost tripled in real terms during the past three decades. As a result, the military's share of the GNP dropped from an average of 10% during the 1950s to an average of 6% during the 1970s. ... The military's share of government spending has also fallen, but by a smaller amount. Of the goods and services directly purchased by the federal government during the 1970s, the military consumed 70%. ... In the 1950s, the Pentagon's share averaged 85%. The military's portion stayed so high because much of the growth in civilian government spending has been in transfer payments, which are not direct government purchases.[14]

Most of these transfer payments concern pensions for veterans and war widows. These payments contribute substantially to the inertia of military expenditure. However, during the 1970s, in the post-Vietnam period, there was a significant fall in military expenditure, at the same time as expenditures for National Aeronautical and Space Agency (NASA) and other defence-related activities were also falling. Thus it would seem that the military-industrial complex in America cannot always hold its own in the face of other interests, whereas in the Soviet Union, at least until the mid-1980s, there has been less sign that the military have had to give ground in relative terms to more 'civilian' production. On the other hand, the forces of the American military-industrial complex, embodied, for example, in the activities of the influential Committee on the Present Danger, have staged a substantial comeback since 1977–78. Their arguments concern the degree to which consistently high levels of military expenditure in the USSR have eroded the security of the USA, and made the West more and more vulnerable to Soviet interventions in the Third World. This has helped to create a coalition of forces which have promoted an increase in the proportion of US GNP devoted to military expenditure, which exceeded 7 per cent in 1986. Although this is lower than the heights of the 1950s, it still represents a 25 per cent proportionate increase on the previous decade. Given that the US was in recession in the early 1980s the timing of this change fits in with the one aspect of neo-Marxist theories of military expenditures, that is the promotion of counter-cyclical government spending, via what is called 'military Keynesianism'.

However, the inertial power of the military-industrial complex in the United States, and of the military in the Soviet Union, reached a testing time in the latter half of the 1980s. Following the November 1985 Geneva summit between President Reagan and Secretary Gorbachev, the first meeting between American and Soviet leaders since 1979, progress in arms negotiations took place against a highly favourable background. The USSR was keen to slow down the growth in military spending for economic reasons. Some American politicians were concerned about the high budget deficit, itself partly caused by the substantial rise in military expenditures. President Reagan was concerned about his place in history, and diverting attention away from the Irangate scandal of 1986–7. With two well-established leaders in a hurry (for overlapping although different reasons), an agreement on medium-range weapons was reached in late 1987, with the promise of more to come. In addition, the US Congress was bent on cutting back on Reagan's pet programme, the SDI.

7. THE ECONOMIC AND POLITICAL IMPACT OF MILITARY-INDUSTRIAL COMPLEXES

An earlier American President, Dwight D. Eisenhower, who was the former General and Commander of US forces in Europe during World War II, warned, in his farewell address in 1960, against the dangers to liberal democracy which were created by the development of the military-industrial complex. (The latter term was in fact coined by Eisenhower.) More generally, these dangers can also be said to arise from the role of the state in military-industrial rivalry. Eisenhower warned that, unless subjected to consistent scrutiny and democratic accountability, the military-industrial complex, through a variety of means, could subvert the democratic process and threaten civil liberties. Others have suggested that what has emerged in the United States since 1945, is a 'state within a state', with secretive budgets and illegal activities rampant. These forces serve to undermine American constitutional guarantees and the separation of powers within the system.[15] In most countries, intelligence services and the armed forces are allowed a greater degree of secrecy than any other part of the state apparatus: all in the name of 'national security'. As a result, scope for public criticism of the security complex is severely limited. Those defending these forms of secrecy argue that there is a necessary trade-off between democratic accountability and national security, even though there is some evidence of abuse, corruption, inefficiency and incompetence in the security services. Given the veil of secrecy, what evidence there is of democratic abuses and inefficiency has to be viewed as the tip of an indeterminate iceberg.

With respect to the relation between military expenditures and economic performance, management scientist Seymour Melman has argued that the relative decline of the American economic and industrial system since 1945 was the consequence of 'the permanent war economy', in which the military fashioned a 'Pentagon capitalism' based upon permanent mobilisation for war.[16] The effects of this on the American economy have been predatory: they have eroded productivity, maximised waste and created a relatively parasitic group of producers who are not subjected to the pressures of market competition and who are able to inflate the prices of the goods they supply to the military because of inefficient procurement and 'logrolling'. The long-term effect of this has been to deplete the 'civilian' parts of the American economy of capital and technology, contributing to an erosion in the USA's technological lead. This has also, according to Melman, produced a military form of state capitalism. In addition, others, including the former Chairman of the Senate Foreign Relations Committee, Senator J. William Fulbright, have highlighted the use of propaganda by the Pentagon to sustain an ideological climate of anti-communism and an atmosphere of permanent crisis and insecurity. This is a technique for justifying military definitions of, and solutions to, the problems of world politics.[17]

The recent attempt by De Grasse to assess the impact of the military-industrial complex on American economic performance, adds weight to Melman's arguments. He does not rule out a favourable short-term impact, that is where there is considerable spare capacity, as in the late 1930s, and early 1980s. With respect to long-term effects, he argues that military expenditures have had little impact upon US unemployment levels, which have been significantly higher than in most Western capitalist countries until the 1980s. Military expenditures create fewer jobs than other government expenditures, and are concentrated in more highly skilled occupations, which have the lowest unemployment levels. Second, high levels of military expenditures have contributed to the relatively lower levels of investment and productivity growth than in the USA's main competitors, have skewed research and development priorities, and have tended to generate innovations with few commercial applications. Moreover, the nature of many military contracts is such as to 'feather bed' the suppliers, who charge often exorbitant prices for their products because they incur unnecessarily high costs, such as perks for managers. Many military producers have not been subjected to competition, especially from foreign producers.

The Reagan administration's military build-up (1980–86) was the largest in peacetime American history, only slightly smaller than that in the Vietnam War, and fuelled the already spiralling budget deficits which contributed to the international debt crisis of the 1980s. These may threaten the long-term stability of the American economy, despite the favourable short-term effects. De Grasse estimates that 48.6 per cent of Federal expenditures were spent on the US military in 1981. In 1986, the Pentagon was expected to use 59.2 per cent of the government's funds, whilst welfare and other social expenditures were being curbed.[18] Such economic burdens are much more severe for the USSR with its smaller GNP and more monopolistic and bureaucratic economy. The US can find it tempting to raise military spending so as to put pressure on the Soviet economy, even though this has adverse long-term effects on the American economy.

In terms of economic opportunity costs, Japan has been able to benefit from standing outside of such military-industrial rivalry and approach the US level of GNP per head.[19] If, and when, the Japanese will aspire to be a military superpower is one of the great unknowns of international relations. Despite the Peace Constitution there are still elements in Japanese culture which support such aspirations: for example in the writings of the neo-nationalist poet Yukio Mishima and the war memories and nationalist loyalties of men like the mid-1980s Prime Minister Nakasone. To date, most post-war Japanese leaders have been content to compete in economic rather than military terms. This might change if higher unemployment and barriers to export-led growth increase substantially since this would reduce the opportunity cost of higher military expenditure. (Signs of this possibility emerged with the rapid appreciation of the yen during 1986–87.) While this is speculative it is indicative of how wider developments in the global political economy might affect spending on arms.

The reformist tendencies of Gorbachev can be related to Mancur Olson's notion of encrustation, whereby vested interests, including those of bureaucracies, build up over time, unless checked by radical change and/or defeat in war.[20] The Stalinist state was successful in industrialisation, especially in arms-related industries. Its centralised planning was suitable to a certain stage of catch-up mercantilism, but perhaps less so to a higher stage. While this problem for the USSR reflects the more complex economy and technologies of the post-Stalin period, it can also be seen in terms of the bureaucratic consolidation of the Soviet state apparatuses: they, like Brezhnev, grew old together. Olson's stress on organisations and interests can, following Robert Cox's analysis of social forces, be extended to include ideas. In the case of the USSR, ideas about the virtues of centralised planning and the dangers of allowing markets and private enterprise much scope have been hegemonic (in a Gramscian sense) for decades. Under Gorbachev they are being cautiously challenged, more timidly than in China where there has been less time for encrustation since the communist victory in the revolution of 1949.

The pressures on states to reform their institutions come from economic as well as military competition. This is especially the case in the more integrated global political economy that has emerged since 1950. States compete not just for markets and foreign exchange, but for capital, skilled labour and access to new technology. For capitalist countries schemes like the Strategic Defence Initiative may result in 'brain drains' from other nations to the United States. High military spending may require high tax rates which may deter the inflow of capital and labour. In so far as high military expenditures (and government spending more generally) causes slow growth, it worsens what we have called, 'the business climate'.

The pressures on the USSR to moderate the growth of its military spending can be linked to a growing sense of economic failure compared to Japan and some of the newly industrialising countries. This is even more true for China. Further, improved global communications exert some pressure on communist governments to raise living standards, because of increased awareness of higher consumption in other countries.

Given the evidence on the economic burdens of defence, there is reason to think that there may be a conflict between developing a leading high-technology economy, as a basis for having a large arms industry and the maintenance of such an economy once a high defence burden is taken on. America's lead over other countries, both in technology and GNP per capita were built up in the first half of the twentieth century, at a time when (up to 1941) its industries were overwhelmingly geared to civilian rather than military production. After World War II, the years of American globalism were associated with the rise of the military-industrial complex, and from the early 1970s there was a near-stagnation in the growth of American productivity and real wages in most sectors.

8. CONCLUSIONS

While realist theory is very important in explaining military spending and the spread of arms production, economic, cultural and ideological factors need to be considered too. In particular, the effects of technological change, economies of scale and a more integrated world economy on military-industrial rivalry need to be considered. When countries are competing for mobile capital and labour, military spending can exert both positive and negative effects on growth rates. These need more research and analysis. At the ideological level there is a tension between the spread of nationalist ideas which go with a mercantilist stress on strategic industries and the spread of liberal economic ideas which cast doubt on the efficiency of monopolistic state enterprises and the effectiveness of an inward-looking import substitution strategy of development. Similarly there may be tensions between the spread of some aspects of militarism and consumerism. Above all, there is a tension between the attempts of states to gain a military technology gap and the economic pressures to sell both weapons and arms technology. This tension is especially marked for the smaller arms-exporting countries, including France and Britain, as illustrated by the proposed sale in 1978 of the Chieftain tank to the Shah of Iran before even the British army had it.

Still other tensions beset military expenditures. Even for the superpowers arms spending has caused economic problems through impairing long-term growth rates and so perhaps weakening their positions as hegemons within their respective blocs. More immediate and tragic are the pressures of military-industrial rivalry on poor less-developed countries which can ill-afford military expenditure. For some of their people it may be a matter of life and death – even if the arms are never used. All too often they are, not only in wars against rivals, but also in suppressing their own people – the latter use of weapons being in marked contrast to the situation in developed countries. It would be ironic if some disarmament proved easier to achieve between the superpowers than between countries in the Third World. However, such an outcome would also be logical in that the pressures of military-industrial rivalry are greatest on less-developed countries trying to establish their national identity, and to catch up economically.

NOTES

1. Gautam Sen, *The Military Origins of Industrialisation and International Trade Rivalry* (London, Pinter, 1984).
2. Theda Skocpol, *States and Social Revolutions* (Cambridge, Cambridge University Press, 1979).
3. Alexander Gerschenkron, *Economic Backwardness in Historical Perspective* (Cambridge, Mass., Harvard University Press, 1962).
4. See S. Deger and S. Sen, 'Military Expenditure Spin-Off and Economic Development', *Journal of Development Economics* (1983), Vol. 13, pp. 67–83. See also Robin Luckham, 'Militarism and International Economic Dependence', in M. Graham et al. (eds), *Disarmament and World Development* (London, Pergamon, 1986), 2nd edition, pp. 43–65; Mary Kaldor and Aisborn Eide, *The World Military Order: The Impact of Military Technology on the Third World* (London, Macmillan, 1979); M. Brozka, *Arms Production in the Third World* (London, Taylor and Francis, 1986); S. Deger, *Military Expenditures in Third World Countries: the economic effects* (London, Routledge and Kegan Paul, 1986).
5. Nobuhiko Ushiba et al., *Sharing International Responsibilities* (New York Trilateral Commission, 1981), p. 5; Fred Halliday, *The Making of the Second Cold War* (London, New Left Books, 1986), 2nd edition, p. 57. Halliday uses statistics from the Stockholm Peace Research Institute (SIPRI). These are generally regarded as the most reliable of the Western independent estimates.
6. Gautem Sen, 'The Economics of US Defence: The Military Industrial complex and Neo-Marxist Economic Theories Reconsidered', *Millenium* (1986), Vol. 15, pp. 179–95.
7. See Kamran Mofid, *Iran: Oil Revenues, Development Planning and Industrialisation – From Monarchy to Islamic Republic* (Wisbech, Cambridgeshire, Menas Press, 1987).
8. Jan Oberg, 'The New International Military Order: A Threat to Human Security', in Aisborn Eide and Marek Thee, *Problems of Contemporary Militarism* (London, Croom Helm, 1980), pp. 47–74.
9. Stephanie G. Neuman, 'International Stratification and Third World Military Industries', *International Organisation* (1984), Vol. 38, pp. 167–97.
10. C. Gluckham, 'New Directions for Soviet Foreign Policy', *Radio Liberty Research Bulletin*, Supplement, February 1986.
11. Marek Thee, 'Militarisation in the US and the Soviet Union', *Alternatives* (1984), Vol. 10, p. 95.
12. US figures are taken from Robert W. De Grasse Jr, *Military Expansion, Economic Decline* (New York, M. E. Sharpe/Council on Economic Priorities, New York, 1983), p. 20; and The International Institute for Strategic Studies (IISS), *The Military Balance 1984–5* (IISS, London, 1984), pp. 4, 15–16.
13. IISS, op. cit.

14. De Grasse, op. cit., p. 8.
15. Alan Wolfe, *The Limits of Legitimacy* (New York, Free Press, 1977).
16. Seymour Melman, *Pentagon Capitalism: The Political Economy of War* (New York, McGraw-Hill, 1970).
17. J. William Fulbright, *The Pentagon Propaganda Machine* (New York, Vintage Books, 1971); C. Wright Mills, *The Power Elite* (Oxford, Oxford University Press, 1956); Adam Yarmolinsky, *The Military Establishment: Its Impact on American Society* (New York, Harper and Row, 1971).
18. De Grasse, op. cit.
19. *The Economist*, 25 October 1986, p. 15.
20. Mancur Olson, *The Logic of Collective Action* (Cambridge., Mass, Harvard University Press, 1965).

PART III
THE POST-WAR SYSTEM

9 The Post-War Political Economy: Inter-state Rivalry, Transnationalisation and Globalisation

In this chapter we examine the emergence of a more institutionalised international economic order within capitalism than existed in the so-called liberal era of the *pax britannica*. After the Yalta settlement of 1945, the geographical scope of the capitalist system was further reduced, as it had been earlier after the Russian Revolutions of 1917. The USSR consolidated its power in Eastern Europe, and after 1947 the Cold War emerged, and a bipolar international system. The number of communist states was increased after the Chinese revolution which ended in 1949, and with the Cuban and Vietnamese revolutions. In consequence of these and other changes, the post-1945 global political economy has differed significantly from that of earlier periods.

The post-war period, at least up to 1973, saw the greatest boom in economic history. Since then there has been slower growth, marked by two recessions, which, some have argued, make this later period rather more like the condition of capitalism prior to 1939. However, in this more recent period, there are signs that a new stage in the development of the political economy has emerged, with conditions which differ considerably from those which prevailed in the 1930s. We call this the transnational stage in the development of capitalism. By this we mean a stage of capitalist international economic integration, in which internationally mobile capital, and transnational corporations in particular, have come to exert a systematic influence on government policies, consumer tastes and culture more generally. As yet, the communist states have not been fully integrated into the world economy, or substantially affected by the transnationalisation process.

Only since 1945 has the world lived under the threat of nuclear catastrophe, and the clash between the superpowers, expressed in the Cold War, has been of major concern to all nations. Also, since 1945, there has been a growth in the militarisation of the global political economy, in ways that are unprecedented. The growth and spread of military-industrial complexes is an important feature of this period. Yet another unique feature has been the character of the post-war military alliances, particularly that organised around the leadership of the United States. Since Yalta, there has been a massive process of decolonisation. This process has had repercussions for the spread of militarisation, and for the outbreak of over 160 wars, mainly in the Third World, in the post-1945 period.

To set the historical context for our discussion, we first shall briefly examine the global political economy prior to World War II, with particular attention to the 1930s. In particular, we examine the role of the United States during this period, since the United States was the key power in the shaping of the post-war capitalist order. Some of the post-war developments have been influenced by interpretations of and reactions to that decade of crisis.

1. SOME HISTORICAL ISSUES

Any significant historical account of the emergence of the contemporary global political economy must explain the decay of feudalism, the rise of industrial capitalism, the creation of a system of nation-states in Europe, and their subsequent international expansion, the development of world trading networks and the spread-dynamics of the capitalist mode of production. These issues have been the object of much debate amongst historians, and those who use the comparative historical method in the study of political economy.[1] It is beyond the scope of this volume to deal with this debate in the detail which it deserves, so we shall merely refer initially to some of the questions it encompasses.

The important issues in this debate concern the explanation of changes in the 'economic' structure, such as the collapse of feudalism (from the fourteenth to the sixteenth centuries or later); the rise of merchant capitalism; the transition to industrial capitalism, the movement from small-scale competitive capitalism to large-scale industrial capitalism, and the emergence of centrally planned 'state socialist' economies in the twentieth century. Also at issue are changes in the 'politico-military' structure or level, with the events of epochal significance such as the Thirty Years War (ending in 1648 with the signing of the Treaty of Westphalia), the Napoleonic Wars (1792–1815), the Great War – World War I (1914–18), the Russian Revolutions of 1917, and World War II (1939–45) as major periods of transition.

The emergence of a capitalist world economy is sometimes traced back to the sixteenth century (especially by world systems theorists such as Wallerstein), although other writers argue that this did not really occur until at least the end of the eighteenth century. None the less, it was not until the nineteenth century that industrial capitalism became firmly established, mainly in Western Europe, then the United States, and later in Meiji Japan. In the second half of the nineteenth century an integrated world economy began to emerge and take shape, with the industrialising manufacturing countries of the Atlantic region at the 'core' and primary producers (and exporters) on the 'periphery'. The emergence of this world economy was made possible by dramatic improvements in the technologies of transport and communications – themselves crucial aspects of the process of industrialisation.

The inter-state system of sovereign nation-states may also be traced back to the sixteenth century and to Western Europe. The termination of the dreams of Spanish kings of creating a Holy Roman (European) empire in the early seventeenth century was formalised in 1648 with the signing of the Treaty of Westphalia.

From around this time, political struggles took on an increasingly global character as the European powers sought to assert their international supremacy, or hegemony (in the realist sense) over other states.

2. THE INTER-WAR CRISIS AND AMERICAN HEGEMONY

One aspect of the historical debates noted above concerns the existence and importance of hegemonic powers. Realist theories, as has been noted in chapter 3, often associate periods of international stability (defined in terms of the absence of war amongst the major powers), with the presence of a hegemonic state.

Some writers have suggested that, in turn, the naval powers of Portugal, Holland and Britain were the hegemonic powers prior to the Napoleonic Wars.[2] However, no country during this period was able to assert its international dominance and leadership in a way compared with Britain in the decades after 1815, or with the United States in the immediate aftermath of World War II. The depression and growing international instability of the 1930s is often associated in the realist literature with the absence of a hegemonic state – or at least with the lack of will, or inability of, the United States to take over the mantle of international leadership from Britain, whose international power had been severely weakened by the Great War.

British strength in the nineteenth century rested heavily on its technological lead over other countries due to its primacy in industrialisation. Also, British financial institutions were more advanced than those of other countries, and this helped to mobilise economic resources for international, as well as domestic purposes. In addition,

British naval power was extensive. By the late nineteenth century, these advantages were declining in relative terms, first due to the rise of the industrial giants of the United States and to a lesser extent Germany, and secondly due to the industrialisation of France and Japan. The German challenge to British supremacy was mounted in the early years of the twentieth century, and was partly expressed through a significant build up of naval power. However, the City of London remained the leading financial centre up to 1914, and the City continued to play the pivotal role in the international monetary system of the period, based upon the Gold Standard.[3]

The United States had become the world's biggest economy by 1900, but until the twentieth century, its international activities were mainly focused in the Western hemisphere, notably in the Americas, and to a lesser extent the Pacific. The dominant political coalitions preferred an 'isolationist' stance with respect to 'entanglements' in continental Europe and, to a certain extent, elsewhere. Despite the 'isolationist' label, the United States had in fact engaged in a substantial feat of empire-building in the nineteenth and early twentieth centuries, successively enlarging its territory, either through war, annexation or purchase. A gigantic area from the Canadian border to the Gulf of Mexico was obtained in 1803 through the Louisiana purchase, in 1810–13 West Florida was wrested from Spain, and in 1819 East Florida was purchased from the Spanish; the independent republic of Texas was annexed in 1845, and through conquest it won a vast area, including California, Arizona and New Mexico from Mexico in 1848. The US seized the Philippines at the turn of the twentieth century from Spain, as well as securing various islands in the Pacific. Whilst it purchased Alaska from Russia, the US used military intervention in Central America and the Caribbean to extend its dominance in the Americas.

Indeed, the Monroe Doctrine of 1823, was in effect a declaration to the rest of the world [notably Europe] to keep out of the Americas:

> ... we should consider any attempt on their [i.e. the European powers] part to extend their system to any portion of this hemisphere as dangerous to our peace and safety.... Our policy in regard to Europe, which was adopted at an early stage of the wars which have so long agitated that quarter of the globe, nevertheless remains the same, which is, not to interfere in the internal concerns of any of its powers; to consider the government *de facto* as the legitimate government for us; to cultivate friendly relations with it, and to preserve those relations by a frank, firm, and manly policy, meeting, in all instances, the just claims of every power, submitting to injuries from none.[4]

The United States was none the less highly selective in the application of the Doctrine. For example, it did not oppose the British seizure of the

Falklands/Malvinas in 1833, and French and Franco-British intervention at the Rio de la Plata, respectively in 1838 and 1845. The greatest violation of the Doctrine was the overthrow of the republican government of Mexico by French troops in 1864, with the subsequent enthronement of Archduke Maximilian of Austria as the Emperor of Mexico. Through a series of corollaries, the Doctrine was gradually redefined to mean that the Americas were to be wholly in the American sphere of influence (for example by Secretary of State Olney in 1895, President Theodore Roosevelt, several times in 1901–5, and President Franklin D. Roosevelt in his 'Good Neighbour' policy of 1933).

However, the United States largely maintained its isolationist policy towards Europe until its entry into the Great War, and its attempts, in concert with other nations, to intervene in Russia in the aftermath of the Bolshevik Revolution of 1917. It then withdrew to its previous policy. Prevailing isolationist sentiment caused the US Senate to oppose ratification of the Treaty of Versailles of 1919,[5] although American banks and other firms continued to invest in Europe and elsewhere, and had, since the end of the nineteenth century, pressed for an 'open door' to the economies of other nations. The United States, in this sense, only gradually began to conform to the pattern of centuries of rivalry between the leading capitalist states, competing for captive markets, investment opportunities and colonies. Moreover, implicit in American objectives, were policies which, in the long term, were aimed at obtaining wider market access, and supplanting the European forms of colonial imperialism.[6]

The late entry of the United States into the mass carnage of the Great War made possible the Allied defeat of Imperial Germany, despite the collapse of Russia as an ally of Britain and France. As a result of its limited involvement in the conflict, the United States emerged stronger, relative to the European imperial powers, than it had been in 1914. (This was also true for Japan, the last of the great powers to industrialise.) New York came to rival London as the key financial centre, and the United States shifted its financial position from that of a net debtor, to a net creditor country. American banks lent money, of a primarily speculative type, to a number of European countries, especially Germany, to help with post-war reconstruction, and this contributed to a period of growth and financial stability in many parts of Europe during the 1920s. The chief symbol of such stability was the European return to the Gold Standard in the 1920s (with national currencies pegged to gold). This symbolised the resurgence of liberal internationalism during 1924–28. American involvement in Europe was heavily concentrated in the financial sphere.[7] The collapse of the Gold Standard during the early 1930s, following the Wall Street crash of 1929, was partly caused by a withdrawal of American short-term finance, and partly because Britain was unable convincingly to fill the gap this had created. Britain left the Gold Standard in 1931, after a crisis of confidence and flight from sterling following the announcement of a 1931 budget deficit of £100 million. Within a few days the value of sterling fell by about 25 per cent. The collapse of sterling as a major international currency contributed to a fall in world prices. Britain moved towards the abandonment of its traditional free-trade policy and the introduction of protectionism in manufactures and agricultural products. Even earlier, in 1930, the United States had raised its already high tariffs in the notorious Smoot-Hawley Bill.

While historians still argue about the causes of the Great Depression of the 1930s, there is substantial agreement that United States monetary policies were a significant factor in contributing to the severity and persistence of the recession. These policies permitted a dramatic fall in the US money supply. The inadequacies of the American banking system were exposed, and thousands of smaller regional and local banks collapsed. American economic policy was carried out with little regard for its international political and economic repercussions. The depression of the 1930s was also a crisis for liberal internationalism, and for the supremacy of international financial interests in the making of foreign economic policy in most of the major capitalist countries. The depression spread rapidly from the United States to the other capitalist countries (but not to the relatively self-sufficient Soviet Union), manifested in a series of financial collapses, and rising unemployment.

Germany was particularly hard-hit, especially since it had been highly dependent on American financial support. Unlike France and Britain, Germany was not able to take economic refuge in a colonial empire. The crisis in Germany gave Hitler and the Nazis an opportunity to bring down the Weimar system, with substantial popular support. Throughout Europe, and in the United States itself, there was a reaction against *laissez-faire* economic othodoxy, with the precise combination of state intervention varying from the Nazi, highly centralised model, to that of Franklin Roosevelt's Keynesian New Deal. The shift towards more direct interventionism tended to support productive interests, including organised labour, as opposed to those associated with the *laissez-faire* liberal internationalism. Karl Polanyi summed up this change in the title of his book, *The Great Transformation*, that is a historic change in the relationship between society and the market, and the state and capital in the major capitalist nations.[8]

In effect, American policy failures, in the context of the wider failure of *laissez-faire* orthodoxy, and the particular domestic conditions which prevailed in Weimar Germany, had contributed indirectly to the rise of Nazism, although President Hoover had offered a moratorium on the repayment of German reparations and inter-Allied war debts (which could never have been repaid anyway). The crisis in Germany between 1929 and 1932 grew to gigantic proportions. Germany's foreign and domestic sources of finance dried up almost completely (savings had been virtually wiped out by the hyperinflation of 1923), and it had no internal capital resources to draw on. It faced a war reparation debt of £100 million a year, roughly the same annual amount of foreign debt servicing, and a budget deficit of £60 million. Germany lost access to its most lucrative foreign markets in the general protectionism and slump of this period, and German exports fell from £630 million in 1929 to £280 million in 1932. Imports fell in the same period from £670 million to £230 million in 1932. Unemployment rose from two million to over six million.[9]

Even without Nazi leadership, Germany had been tempted to build an economic bloc in Central Europe (or *mittel-Europa*), in the form of the agreement with Austria to form a customs union in 1931. American (and indeed British) policy in fact promoted and exacerbated the 1930s tendency towards the formation of economic blocs, for example by its own measures of protection such as the Smoot–Hawley tariff increases of 1930 (reflecting the victory of the inward-looking, isolationist forces). Not only did American protectionism hit European exporters, it also meant that sustained export-led growth became impossible for Japan, particularly in the labour-intensive manufactured products where it held a comparative advantage. Instead, the path favoured by the Samurai military class was adopted: the construction of heavy industries and the production of weapons. Japan's imperial ventures in the Far East were partly inspired and justified by the need to sustain access to markets and raw materials. Japan invaded and occupied fertile Chinese Manchuria in 1931.

By 1932–33 the crisis reached its peak, with an estimated 15 million unemployed in the United States alone. The world financial system was on the verge of collapse, the dollar having depreciated by 30 per cent after the United States finally abandoned the Gold Standard in April 1933. The World Economic Conference of June 1933, involving 64 nations, designed to redress a worsening of the crisis, was a failure. States turned increasingly to economic nationalism and increased state interventionism to protect themselves from the effects of the international economic slump. This disintegration of the world economy occurred at the same time as political rivalry amongst the great powers was increasing, and as the international political climate worsened.

E. H. Carr has argued that the more that autarky was regarded as the goal of state policies, the larger economic units had to become. During the 1930s such units emerged and solidified into rival blocs:

The US strengthened their hold over the American continents. Great Britain created a 'sterling bloc' (the Ottawa Trade Agreements of 1932) and laid the foundations of a closed economic system. Germany reconstituted *Mittel-Europa* and pressed forward into the Balkans. Soviet Russia developed its territories into a vast unit of industrial and agricultural production. Japan attempted the creation of a new unit of 'Eastern Asia' under Japanese domination. Such was the trend towards the concentration of political and economic power in the hands of six or seven highly organised units, round which lesser satellite units revolved without any appreciable independent motion of their own.[10]

Many historians have argued that this configuration of the global political economy, into a series of increasingly antagonistic politico-economic blocs, created the structural conditions for the emergence of World War II. Other theorists, following the analysis of Charles Kindleberger, have argued that the crisis of the 1930s could have been averted if the United States had assumed leadership in the world economy, and helped to sustain its openness, to the general benefit of all nations.[11] Indeed, many economic liberals in the United States at the time, including Roosevelt's Secretary of State Cordell Hull, argued in similar ways. Why then was the United States limited in its capacity to pursue a far-sighted and coherent policy along these lines?

To answer this question we need to examine the balance of forces within the domestic political economy of the United States. Inward-looking, isolationist forces were in the ascendant, at least until the late 1930s, forces which served to constrain the more expansionist, cosmopolitan and far-sighted elements in the making of American foreign economic policy. Such forces would come together to form what Kees van der Pijl has called the 'New Deal synthesis' of internationally-oriented productive and financial interests which would press for a new economic globalism as the basis for the post-war international settlement.[12]

To explain the material basis of these forces, both Peter Gourevitch and Thomas Ferguson have developed a method of analysis which focuses upon different sectors and industries, and the factors which affect the formation of the political coalitions which influence economic policy-making.[13] These theorists assume that coalition of interests rationally pursues its own economic well-being when forming 'tactical alliances'. Industries that are not exposed to, or are able to cope with, international competition provide the basis of an 'internationalist' coalition which favours trade liberalisation and low levels of protection. Industries vulnerable to foreign competition provide the basis for a protectionist/nationalist coalition. Ferguson stresses differences between industries in the share of wages in value-added, because the more important wage costs are to a firm, the less willing it will be to become involved in a nation-wide coalition involving trade unions.

In the American case, the support for the Democratic Party from the 1930s until the early 1970s comprised a coalition between most organised labour and many industries with relatively low wage shares in value-added, and which were relatively invulnerable to foreign competition, and sought to extend production overseas. Ferguson argues that firms with the 'internationalist' characteristics rose in importance during the 1930s, and formed a 'multinational bloc' which pressed for a range of measures such as tariff reduction, social welfare programmes and to some extent, Keynesian policies. Business interests conceded more welfare spending in return for organised labour's support for some liberal measures. This was the 'New Deal synthesis'. Within the coalition the most internationalist elements were Eastern financial circles centred in New York City, which became more important in time as the dollar became a leading world currency after World War II:

The multinational bloc included many of the largest, most rapidly growing corporations in the economy. Recognised industry leaders with the most sophisticated managements, they embodied the norms of professionalism and scientific advance that in this period fired the imagination of large parts of American society. The largest of them also dominated major American foundations, which were coming to exercise major influence not only on the climate of opinion but on the specific content of American public policy.[14]

The rise of this 'multinational bloc' represented a powerful new force in the shaping of American foreign economic policy. Until the 1930s the United States had been mainly protectionist, particularly since the 1890s when the Republican protectionist coalition was in the ascendant. The highly restrictive Smoot-Hawley tariff and some of the measures of the first New Deal marked the high points of isolationist influence. However these successes owed much to short-term cyclical factors (severe depression after the Great Crash of 1929), while long-term structural changes in the American political economy were working against the established Republican coalition. However, any significant change was further constrained by the nature of the American constitutional system, which enabled conservatives to oppose, and successfully block, many of Roosevelt's initiatives. Indeed, several of the enabling statutes which were enacted to alleviate the crisis were judged unconstitutional by the Supreme Court.

Gradually, internationalists began to prevail, securing the Tripartite Agreement of 1936 which involved international monetary cooperation with France and Britain so as to limit exchange rate fluctuations. The internationalists were also influential in the orienting of American post-war plans for the world economy in a liberal direction. The New York Council on Foreign Relations was very much a reflection of this emerging coalition, and its personnel were heavily involved in the drafting of post-war plans. The internationalist liberal-Keynesian coalition underpinned Democratic dominance in the middle of the twentieth century. From the late 1960s this coalition began to unravel, contributing to the decline in the fortunes of the Democratic Party in the 1970s and 1980s.[15]

The predominance of the nationalist and protectionist interests in the United States until the early 1930s was related to the highly self-sufficient nature of the American economy. Unlike Japan and many European states, the USA was well endowed with raw materials. Unlike Britain it was a major food exporter. Further, the huge American domestic market meant that many of the mid-Western industrial producers, many headquartered in Chicago, and which were major elements in the isolationist coalition, had no need to seek foreign markets in order to reap significant economies of scale (for example in mass production). However, as large American manufacturing firms in new, high-technology industries (such as electrical goods and automobiles) faced a slowing-down in the growth of the domestic market for their products, they began to seek export markets, and to invest in production facilities abroad (for example General Motors, Ford and IBM in Germany).

In the 1930s, the United States did not just fail to take on the role of the hegemon in Kindleberger's sense of the term: it consistently failed to pursue policies which its leaders would later consider to be conducive to the long-term survival of capitalism. On the one hand, the banking collapse of the early 1930s was allowed to deteriorate with severe deflationary consequences for not only the United States, but also for the world economy. On the other hand, the supportive policies of the New Deal were piecemeal and inadequate. Moreover, as Theda Skocpol has noted, in the early 1930s, the United States simply did not have the administrative apparatus which was needed to implement a successful programme of public works, and at any event the divisions within the American business and political leadership meant that no coherent response was possible anyway.[16] At the heart of the inability to get to grips with the scale of the crisis was the hegemony of American anti-statist, *laissez-faire* ways of thinking which stressed the sanctity of balanced budgets, and strict limits to the intervention of the state in economic activity. It was only the wartime mobilisation catalysed by the Japanese attack on Pearl Harbor in 1941 which eliminated high unemployment in the United States. This, in effect, was the birth of an American variant of military Keynesianism, which, on this occasion, the Constitutional system of checks and balances was unable to abort.

3. PATTERNS OF POST-WAR GROWTH, DEVELOPMENT AND GLOBAL INEQUALITY

Let us now discuss the nature of the post-war order. The post-war boom contrasted sharply both with the inter-war years and the period between 1870 and 1913, as Table 9.1 demonstrates.

Table 9.1: Cyclical and growth characteristics of different periods (arithmetic average for sixteen countries)

Time-Period	Average Annual Growth Rate In:			Percentage maximum fall in GDP
	Output	Output per head of population	Non-residential capital stock	
1870–1913	2.5	1.5	2.8	– 6.7
1913–50	1.9	1.1	1.6	– 13.1
1950–70	4.9	3.8	5.6	+ 0.3

Source: M. Bleaney, *The Rise and Fall of Keynesian Economics* (Basingstoke, Macmillan, 1985) p. 96.

For the sixteen advanced countries considered by Bleaney, the rapid growth was more strongly associated with rising productivity than with the rise in population. The boom was remarkable for its absence of major recessions, as the extreme right-hand column of Table 9.1 illustrates. Furthermore, it was a boom which virtually all countries shared, both capitalist and communist, developed and less-developed. For the capitalist, as well as the communist countries, unemployment was very low in the 1950s, 1960s and early 1970s, as is partly shown in Table 9.2.

Table 9.2: Unemployment in selected countries 1950–73 (per cent)

	1950–60	1958–61	1962–73
Belgium	5.4		2.1*
France	1.3		2.2
West Germany	4.1		0.6
Italy	7.9		3.5
Norway	2.0		2.0
Sweden	1.7		2.1
United Kingdom	2.5		3.1
Canada	4.4	6.8	5.1
United States	4.5	6.1	4.6

Notes: With the exception of the figure for Belgium marked *, national figures have been adjusted where necessary to make them comparable with other countries.
Source: Bleaney, *op. cit.,* p. 94, from OECD figures.

It almost seemed as if some of the traditional problems of capitalism – unemployment and much unused capacity – had been solved. There was inflation, but at low levels, in the developed capitalist countries. Of these countries, Japan had the fastest growth, and the United Kingdom and the United States the slowest. Even the latter Anglo-Saxon countries had high growth by the standards of their past.

If there were any disappointment in this period, it was that most Third World countries had a slower growth of income per head than the average for the countries of the Organisation for Economic Cooperation and Development (OECD). The less-developed countries had absolute growth rates which were as high as the OECD group but their population was growing more rapidly. Indeed, most developing countries were experiencing a population explosion on a scale which was much greater than that of Europe in the nineteenth century, during its industrialisation. The other aspect of disappointment in Third World performance emerged in the late 1960s as it was noted that the gains from growth within less-developed countries were usually spread very unequally.

Table 9.3: Real per capita income 1960–84 (in $US at 1981 prices and exchange rates)

	1960	1965	1970	1975	1980	1984
Total OECD	5,304	6,458	7,718	8,540	9,685	10,220
OECD Europe	4,378	5,285	6,327	7,051	7,992	8,108
Japan	2,820	4,329	6,884	7,909	9,623	10,907
North America	7,891	9,248	10,222	11,060	12,386	13,150
Total of all Developing Countries	391	452	534	618	724	729
Africa	580	649	730	747	784	709
Asia	257	365	368	428	521	571
Latin America	1,400	1,572	1,838	2,190	2,488	2,276

Source: OECD Observer (1986), Vol. 143, p. 10.

The period since 1973 has seen major divergences in experience between different countries. In the 1970s Third World oil-exporting countries did well (in terms of growth rates) while many, especially African, oil-importing countries did badly. Some Asian economies grew very rapidly despite being oil-importers. Amongst this group were Singapore, Hong Kong, Taiwan and South Korea. On average in the 1970s, less-developed countries grew faster than the OECD countries. In practice it was the

Table 9.4: Average annual growth rates of real per capita income (per cent)

	1960–70	1970–80	1980–84
Total OECD	3.9	2.2	1.1
Japan	9.1	3.2	3.0
Total Developing Countries	3.1	3.1	0.0
Africa	2.2	0.8	–2.5
Asia	3.6	3.8	2.3
Latin America	2.6	2.9	–2.6

Source: See Table 9.3.

Asian newly-industrialising countries (NICs) and the oil-exporting countries which were closing up the gap between them and the developed countries, while many, especially African less-developed countries, fell behind. In the 1980s the Latin American countries, as well as the African countries, suffered outright decline. The contrast between these and the relatively successful Asian countries was pronounced. Amongst the Asian successes by this time was China. Examples of countries which have narrowed the 'development gap' to a significant extent include Singapore, whose income per head as a percentage of the OECD average per capita income rose from 24 per cent in 1960 to 65 per cent in 1984, Taiwan from 13 per cent to 30 per cent, South Korea from 10 per cent to 31 per cent, and Malaysia from 13 per cent to 20 per cent.[17]

The dramatic deterioration in the performance of some less-developed countries in the 1980s can be related to the so-called debt crisis. For example, Latin American countries such as Brazil, Argentina and Mexico have been driven to implement austerity programmes as their balance of payments situation deteriorated. In the case of sub-Saharan Africa, the deterioration was already marked in the 1970s and has received widespread media attention, owing to the disastrous scale of famine in the 1980s. The intensity of the African crisis has gone with a marked failure of food production to keep pace with population growth. Most black African countries were self-sufficient in food at independence, but they became increasingly dependent on food imports in the 1970s. The tropical African food crisis is partly bound up with growing threats to the ecological balance of the region by forces leading to deforestation and desertification. The food and growth situation in Asia has been much better than in Africa in this period, but even here there are similar signs of ecological breakdown. The progressive destruction of Amazonia is another ominous example of an impending ecological crisis. Certain patterns of growth in the post-war period may be unsustainable, not just in developing nations. Unsustainable global growth patterns have been stressed by a range of writers. The post-war pattern of growth was widely seen as extravagant in its use of some minerals, notably oil. Even though the first Club of Rome report, *The Limits to Growth*, may have displayed an exaggerated pessimism, the questions it raised about resource depletion and ecological degradation are the subject of growing environmentalist concern, in the North, as well as the South.[18]

4. INTER-STATE RIVALRY AND THE POST-WAR MILITARY ORDER

For all that there are unique features in the post-war period, there have, of course, been elements which have persisted. One of these is inter-state rivalry. However, the character of this rivalry, particularly between leading capitalist states, seems to have undergone a significant change. There has not been a war between these states since 1945, whereas there have been several wars and other forms of armed conflict between communist states (for example the border conflict between Vietnam and China which has lasted since the late 1970s, a conflict which is connected to Vietnam's invasion and occupation of communist Kampuchea, formerly Cambodia).

Institutionalised cooperation between the leading capitalist states often, but not always under American leadership, provides a contrast with both the inter-war years and the period of *pax britannica* in the nineteenth century. The bipolar structure, organised around the superpowers in opposed communist and capitalist military alliances, seems to have been a crucial condition for the virtual elimination in military conflict between the major capitalist states. Military conflict between the major capitalist and communist states has been largely restricted to Third World locations, mainly because each side has developed nuclear weapons which, if used against each other on a large scale, would lead to mutual annihilation.

In 1945 the United States found itself in a uniquely strong position, much surpassing that of Britain at the height of its power in the nineteenth century. With half the world's GNP, over three-quarters of the world's gold reserves and a technological lead in most manufacturing industries, the United States was well placed to induce cooperation in other countries. All of the former imperial powers were devastated by the war and needed American support for their post-war reconstruction efforts. That the Soviet Union did not accept the American embrace could be partly explained in terms of the USSR's wide range of natural resources which provided the capacity for relative self-sufficieny. Also, the USSR refused Marshall Aid because it claimed that the United States wanted not only economic, but also political reconstruction in Europe, along liberal-democratic lines, or at least in ways inimical to the development of communism.

1947 was the turning-point in terms of the evolution of the capitalist and communist alliance systems. After the Soviet refusal of Marshall Aid and the onset of the Cold War, the USSR strengthened its grip on Eastern Europe and the Western powers formed the North Atlantic Treaty Organisation (NATO) in 1949. This meant that the Atlantic part of the capitalist alliance became more militarised and institutionalised, under American command. The United States also moved to consolidate other military pacts to create a world-wide network of military alliances under its own leadership. These included the ANZUS pact (covering Australasia and the South Pacific), CENTO (covering the Middle East) and SEATO (covering South-East Asia). The United States also set up a world-wide system of military bases, an intelligence network, and had occupying forces still based in some countries, notably in West Germany and Japan. The USSR's military influence was largely confined to Eastern Europe and East Asia until it supported Cuba (with troops and munitions) and Egypt (with advisors) in the 1960s. The USSR's other major outreach came in the 1970s with the use of Cuban troops and Soviet advisors in Angola and Ethiopia. Thus the bipolar structure established initially within Europe took on an increasingly global character. The key symbol of this structure was the division of Germany into East and West, thus preventing the potential reemergence of German militarism, and a possible third military superpower. This containment of German military potential can be seen as in the interests of both superpowers as well as second-rank European powers such as Britain and France.

We call this American-centred military structure an organic alliance, implying something relatively permanent, and based upon shared and interpenetrating sets of interests and identities. This type of alliance can be contrasted with the wartime tactical alliance between the United States, the United Kingdom and the Soviet Union, which was easily broken after 1945, as well as the breakdown of the alliance between the USSR and China. This implies that the alliance between communist states, where it has persisted, has rested primarily on military might. Shared ideology is not sufficient to ensure an enduring military alliance. Some of the forces which have made for the emergence of this organic alliance are bound up with the process of transnationalisation which we discuss in the following section.

In contrast to the military stalemate between the superpowers, particularly in Europe, conflicts in the Third World have been frequent, often using arms supplied by the leading communist and capitalist countries. Less-developed countries have greatly increased in number since 1947 when India and Pakistan gained their independence from Britain. By the 1980s there were over 130 Third World states. The proliferation of boundaries has given added scope for regional wars and border disputes, especially since some of the colonial divisions of empire were arbitrary from a socio-cultural viewpoint. Territorial and tribal divisions often failed to coincide.

When empires had collapsed in earlier periods, it did not involve an orderly transfer of power, with economic (and sometimes military) aid being given by the former colonial power to the new state. While some new states came into being after a bitter and bloody war of independence (Algeria, Vietnam, Indonesia, Angola and Mozambique) most did not. Many of the smaller states have retained close links with the former power. Indeed, in many cases the number of resident Europeans in the former colonies has increased since independence, most notably in West Africa. Use of the imperial language – usually French or English – has often continued sometimes with the active encouragement of the former imperial state. The giving of large-scale and regular amounts of economic aid, officially for the purpose of economic development, is a novel aspect of the period since 1945. A total of 60 per cent of the gross aid programme in 1986–87 of the Overseas Development Association, ODA, was bilateral rather than multilateral in character, in line with the post-war pattern of aid-giving.[19] Such bilateral aid has helped to maintain links after decolonisation between the newly-independent states and their previous imperial powers. In addition, America and the Soviet Union have involved themselves in the giving of aid as part of their global competition. The unique character of the decolonisation process needs also to be put into the context of American leadership of an increasingly transnational capitalism. American pressure for decolonisation was considerable after World War II, especially on Britain and France. The United States wanted better access to markets, materials and foreign investment opportunities in Asia, Africa and the Pacific. The US developed post-war plans in the early 1940s for the achievement of a 'Grand Area', namely the maximum possible living space for the US economy to expand into. One reason that the USSR resisted the offer of Marshall Aid was because it would have entailed the opening up of Eastern Europe to American economic penetration, in order to maximise the Grand Area. The collapse of the old imperial order was another facet of this broader aim.

With the onset of the Cold War there was less United States pressure on the old imperial powers, and the US actively supported the French in Vietnam, before assuming the imperial mantle themselves. Some American pressure continued during the 1950s, particularly when the imperial habits of France and Britain began to reassert themselves in the Middle East, an area where the United States leadership was determined to secure American dominance. The USA opposed the armed intervention in Egypt by France and Britain in 1956. In the so-called Suez crisis, the US made its continued economic assistance conditional upon an Anglo-French withdrawal. The fact that the colonial territories were geographically distant from the imperial centre, made retreat from empire less threatening in terms of national security. At the same time, the American military presence in Europe and Japan meant that the concepts of national security held by the former imperialists necessarily had to change. The USA supported Israel in 1967 and in 1973 in its wars against the Arab states. This also underlined the eclipse of the old imperial powers within the region.

5. POST-WAR INTERNATIONAL ECONOMIC INSTITUTIONS

The institutionalisation of post-war military alliances was preceded by the construction of international economic institutions. These were designed to promote a liberal international economic order. In such an order, the United States, with its technological lead, could expect to gain substantially. However, various orthodox economic ideas influenced the design of these institutions. These ideas suggested that all countries could gain from more liberal trade, and also from increased flows of foreign investment. Such ideas stressed the virtues of the market mechanism and of private enterprise. The appeal of these ideas was enhanced by the experience of the 1930s which was widely seen as showing the folly of raising trade barriers and the disruptiveness of floating exchange rates. This made it easier for the USA to obtain agreement in principle at Bretton Woods on the need for institutions to promote freer trade and exchange rate stability.

The International Monetary Fund (IMF) and World Bank were established in 1945. The World Bank had two main branches, the International Bank for Reconstruction and Development (IBRD) and the International Development Association (IDA). However, the operational effectiveness of the IMF was limited during the years of post-war reconstruction by the financial supremacy of the United States which alone could give significant assistance to other countries. Marshall Aid was the main form in which assistance was given from 1948, following the enunciation of the Truman Doctrine in 1947 stressing the need to contain communism and bolster liberal democracy. This aid continued until the early 1950s. Resort to the IMF by developed countries began in 1947 and grew in the 1950s as their economies recovered.

The activity of the IMF was further increased by the rise in the number of less-developed countries. The IMF loans were from one to three years in duration and were meant to help governments avoid having to devalue their currencies. The fixed exchange rate system of this period was anchored on the dollar which for all countries (except the United States) was the pivot currency to which other currencies were fixed. The US dollar was pegged to gold at 35 dollars per ounce, with the US Federal Reserve (its central banking system) committed to buying and selling gold at this price. Stable exchange rates were thought to encourage trade, tourism and foreign investment through reducing uncertainty. However, during the 1960s certain exceptional episodes occurred in which speculation against the British pound and the French franc went with considerable uncertainty. Such episodes highlighted the lessening of restrictions on capital flows and their growing size. As early as 1958 full convertibility on current account transactions had been achieved by the West European countries, with Japan achieving this in the early 1960s.

Even this amount of convertibility permitted some speculation on exchange rates in that traders could hasten or delay their international payments. As IMF activities grew, more funds were required to meet demand, notably in other currencies than the dollar. The Group of Ten major capitalist countries was established in 1960 to provide these extra funds. In the same year the London Gold Pool was established in an attempt to keep the dollar price of gold down at the 35 dollar figure. This became necessary because of a shift from dollar shortage (1945–59) to dollar glut in the 1960s.

The early activities of the World Bank involved long-term loans to the major capitalist countries whose economies had suffered in World War II. During the 1950s it began to adopt its current rule, that is make loans to less-developed countries. To this end the World Bank borrowed on the international capital markets. Therefore its ability to charge below commercial interest rates was restricted by the amount of funds given by the leading capitalist countries to the International Development Association (IDA). Such low interest rate loans were limited to the least developed countries. Given that the main contributors to the IDA (and of capital to the IBRD) were developed countries, it was they who controlled the World Bank, just as it was these countries which dominated the IMF. Whilst the distribution of voting power in the United Nations was on the basis of one country one vote, the distribution of power within the world's two major international financial organisations was on the basis of the unequal distribution of economic resources. The richest countries carried the most weight, as they still did at the end of the 1980s.

The role of the IMF came into doubt in the 1970s with the breakdown of fixed exchange rates from 1973. Until the Nixon 'shocks' of August 1971, the fixed exchange rate system had been maintained quite successfully, with only occasional changes of parity. The IMF took on a new importance in the 1980s with the emergence of the so-called debt crisis. Here the IMF's stamp of approval was a condition for the granting of further loans from commercial banks to certain less-developed countries.

In the mid-1980s the World Bank began to be involved in this process. The growth in the activities of the IMF had been limited by the size and frequency of increases in quotas and the rules for access to loans. In the case of the World Bank, its activities were constrained, at least as regards the IDA, by the size of the capital contributions made by the leading capitalist countries. An indication of the scale of the activities of the World Bank is the total outstanding advances (loans) which were, on 30 June 1985, US $112.9 billion for the IBRD, and $36.7 billion for the IDA. Disbursements in 1985 were $8.6 billion for the IBRD and $2.49 billion for the IDA.[20] Net transactions with (that is flows of funds to) the Third World were $2.4 billion in 1985. It was estimated that such flows would be close to zero in the financial year ending June 1986 because of the scale of repayments by borrowing less-developed countries.[21]

Initially plans had been made for an International Trade Organisation (ITO), which would have included commodity agreements, but this was blocked in the US Congress. In its place, a more informal and limited institution, the General Agreement on Tariffs and Trade (GATT) was set up in 1948. It launched a series of rounds of negotiations designed to promote and liberalise trade from the 1950s onwards, notably the Kennedy Round of the mid-1960s and the Tokyo Round of the late 1970s. The guiding principles of GATT were to be multilateral trade bargaining with most-favoured nation, non-discriminatory, concessions granted to those countries which agreed to abide by its norms, rules and procedures. In such rounds the method was for countries to swop concessions so as to get reciprocal reductions in tariffs and other trade barriers. The resulting trade agreements involved the 'binding' of tariffs, that is, they were not to be increased under any circumstances, except in the case of dumping. Dumping occurs when exports are sold at prices lower than those which prevail in the exporting country. In this case punitive tariffs can be levied. Quota restrictions, however, might be used, on a short-term basis, in order to deal with balance of payments problems. This concession was made in order to make the adherence to fixed exchange rates more feasible. In the aftermath of war this involved the European countries and Japan placing many restrictions on imports because of their shortage of dollars. As their economies recovered from the war, these restrictions were eased during the 1950s.

The success of GATT and also the IMF and the World Bank in promoting liberalisation is evident in the faster growth of world trade than of world output since 1950. Real world GNP increased four-fold between 1950 and 1980, from about 2 trillion US dollars to about 8 trillion. Within this period, world exports as a percentage of global GNP (excluding inter-trade amongst China, Mongolia, North Korea and North Vietnam, from 1976 Vietnam) rose from 11.7 per cent in 1950 to 21.2 per cent in 1980.[22]

The following table also conveys the dramatic increase in trade intensity in the period since the early 1960s. Clearly the magnitude of the increase in the 1970s owed quite a lot to the rise in oil prices. This put pressure on non-oil-exporting countries to export a larger proportion of their GNP in order to obtain foreign exchange.

Table 9.5: Average propensity to trade for selected groups of countries (in percentages)

Country group	Average propensity to trade				Number of countries
	1963	1970	1975	1980	
Developed countries	17.9	21.5	28.9	35.0	23
All less-developed countries (LDCs)	26.8	28.0	39.2	45.8	99
Newly-industrialising countries	18.3	18.5	24.2	30.0	10
OPEC members	39.5	43.6	64.0	62.0	14
Other LDCs	36.4	37.2	42.9	46.4	75
All countries	19.3	22.5	30.8	34.0	122

Source: M. J. Gasiorowski, 'The Structure of Third World Economic Interdependence', *International Organization* (1985), Vol. 39, no. 2, pp. 331–42. Table 1.

6. TRANSNATIONALISATION

The rise of transnational corporations and the growth of short-term capital flows between countries are two of the most striking features of transnationalisation. However, there are other related aspects such as the spread of consumerism and ideas which stress the need for international market efficiency. The IMF itself is an organisation whose purposes are congruent with the forces promoting transnationalisation, since the IMF favours fewer restrictions on trade and capital flows. Both the IMF and the World Bank have encouraged less-developed countries to accept foreign direct investment. Indeed, one branch of the World Bank (the International Finance Corporation) makes loans in conjunction with mainly transnational private enterprise. Such encouragement was intensified in the first half of the 1980s due to pressures from the Reagan administration with its stress on 'market-place magic' as the answer to the economic problems of less-developed countries.

Foreign investment grew rapidly in the nineteenth century, but before World War II most of it took the form of portfolio investment, as with British funds invested in the American railroad system. After 1945 direct investment gradually became the dominant form with the rise and spread of transnational corporations.

Direct investment by transnational corporations needs to be distinguished from both long-term portfolio investment and short-term capital flows. Portfolio investment involves foreign ownership of assets in a country without foreign control of productive enterprises. This is because the object of such investment is to gain a high and steady source of income over a long period of time. Much portfolio investment is put into the national debt of borrowing countries, such as the acquisition by Japanese savings institutions of United States government bonds in the 1980s. Short-term capital flows involve funds which are highly mobile in response to changes in interest rates on short-term financial assets and expectations of exchange rate movement. By contrast, direct investment involves a stake in productive enterprise, and usually involves foreign control. One hundred per cent ownership of a subsidiary is not necessary for such control: sometimes less than 50 per cent may be sufficient. In the case of a joint venture, control may be shared between a local and a foreign enterprise. Direct investment also involves a package of managerial and technological inputs as well as capital flows. These are under the control of the parent (foreign) company.

In the post-war political economy there have been twin processes at work, each of which has had different implications for national autonomy and for patterns of development. Thus a distinction can be made between *internationalisation* and *transnationalisation* of capital and technology flows. Some international interactions and interdependence have developed without transnational control. For example, there has been an increase in technical collaboration agreements between firms of different countries, in technology licensing arrangements and in subcontracting. Western retail firms which sell clothing have had regular contracts with foreign textile producers, so that household names like Levi-Strauss market products produced in the Far East and elsewhere. Another example is that of American agribusiness firms with contracts to small peasants in Central America. In these contracts the peasant grows a crop such as strawberries and gets an agreed price along with certain inputs (fertiliser, pesticide, seeds) and credit. In this case, the subcontracting goes with technological and financial dependence, which may be cumulative as the peasants incur debts. At the same time, the peasants continue to own their land. Thus internationalisation has often gone with transnational control. On the other hand, licensing deals have, in some cases, led to the emergence of strong new competitors. After 1945 American and West European firms licensed technology to Japanese enterprises, little realising that within twenty years even their home markets would be faced with a Japanese challenge in fields such as electronics, optics and automobiles. Internationalisation and transnationalisation have developed at the same time, sometimes as substitutes, sometimes as complements, as in the agribusiness example (many American firms have subsidiaries in Central America). Improvements in transport and communications have faciliated both trends. An extreme recent example is the subcontracting of data processing by American companies to firms in Mexico and Europe via satellites.

Let us now examine the broad pattern of these processes. Decolonisation, and the movement towards a more liberal world economy fostered by the post-war international economic institutions facilitated a new and more diverse pattern of foreign investment, as well as new trade linkages. In this new pattern, the extreme dependence of the ex-colonies on the former imperial centres was reduced. Instead of foreign investment being limited to a few firms from one imperialist country, a more complex pattern of cross-investments emerged, invariably involving the emerging American transnational corporations entering the older spheres of influence and, in the 1970s and 1980s, an ever-increasing Japanese presence.

The American security presence in Europe helped to ensure an open door for American direct investment, especially in the consumer goods industries. However, a part of the capitalist post-war consensus in Western Europe was a commitment to a large, and in some cases expanded public sector. One aspect of this expansion was the welfare state, including health and education services. The proportion of government expenditure to gross national product (GNP) rose in all the major capitalist states in the post-war period, and in some cases, for example Sweden, it came to more than half of GNP. The growth of the public sector sometimes involved state monopolies, as in telecommunications. In addition to the public sector which was closed off from foreign control, were private industries considered so strategic that foreign takeovers of national firms was not allowed. Aerospace firms were one example, especially with respect to their role in arms production. In some countries, notably France and Japan (discussed below), opposition to foreign investment extended to a wide range of industries, at least in so far as foreign takeovers were concerned.

The first major surge of foreign investment in the post-war period was by American firms into Western Europe. This occurred in the years immediately preceding and following the formation of the European Economic Community (EEC) and the European Free Trade Area (EFTA) in the late 1950s. Indeed American support for the establishment of the EEC in 1957 was conditional on guaranteed investment access for its firms. Although American investment into the Third World also grew in this period, it was mainly in Latin America, and, in terms of scale, was much less than its new European investments. What Table 9.6 highlights is that the overwhelming majority of foreign direct investment since World War II was by firms from the developed countries investing in other developed countries. Whilst this continues to be the case, direct investment of this type is much more important (as a percentage of GNP) for the economies of the less-developed countries than is the case for the developed countries.

The relatively slow growth of foreign investment in the OPEC countries in the 1970s can be ascribed partly to their increased national ownership of their oil industries. Thus this showdown may have been in the nature of a one-off event, one temporarily extended by the impact of the Iran-Iraq War.

Table 9.6: Stock of direct foreign investment of developed countries in various host-country groups (in $ billions)

Country Group	1967	1970	1975
Developed countries	72.45	113.76	191.66
	(4.48)	(4.88)	(4.72)
All less-developed countries	32.55	44.24	67.34
(LDCs)	(11.03)	(10.40)	(7.28)
OPEC members	9.45	11.06	15.54
	(20.46)	(14.40)	(6.43)
Non-OPEC LDCs	23.10	33.18	51.80
	(9.28)	(9.25)	(7.58)
Tax havens	2.10	4.74	7.77
	(n.a.)	(n.a.)	(n.a.)
All countries	105.00	158.00	259.00
	(5.49)	(5.73)	(5.19)

Note: Figures in parentheses show direct foreign investment expressed as a percentage of the country group's total GDP.
Source: Gasiorowski, *op. cit.,* Table 3, p. 336.

The Third World experience is of course highly varied. Some newly-industrialising countries such as Singapore, Taiwan and South Korea had a rapid influx of foreign direct investment from the mid-1960s, whereas very little investment went to many small black African states.

The distribution of the ownership of the stock of direct investment between firms of the developed countries has changed significantly since the early 1960s. At this time the United States was still very predominant. Of foreign investment in the OECD area, US firms had 56.6 per cent in 1967 and 47.6 per cent in 1976, with the UK next in line with 16.6 per cent in 1967 and 11.2 per cent in 1976. In contrast, Japan's share rose from 1.4 to 6.7 per cent, and West Germany's from 2.8 to 6.9 per cent.[23] Much of the growth in foreign investment was two-way in character from the 1970s as first European, and later Japanese, firms moved into the United States. However, foreign investment in Japan remained relatively modest despite some growth from a very low level. For example, in the case of United

States foreign direct investment in 1982 (in current value in US dollars), 20.1 per cent ($44,509 million) was in Canada; 45.1 per cent ($99,877 million) was in Europe; 14.9 per cent ($33,039 million) was in Latin America and only 3.1 per cent ($6,872 million) was in Japan.[24] The low figure for Japan can be explained in terms of the lack of openness of the Japanese economy, rather than a lack of potential profitability of operating in Japan. The latter point is underlined by the success of Japanese corporations using Japan as an export base. Japan was, by 1988, the world's largest producer of cars, and in 1986 exported a car every five seconds.

Thus a striking exception to American insistence on the open door principle in the 1950s was Japan. Even before the end of American occupation in 1955 the Japanese government had placed severe restrictions on inward direct investment. This example reminds one of Sherlock Holmes' case of the dog which didn't bark in the night. Why did the United States not press the country which has now become its fiercest economic competitor for more access before the 1970s, that is when America was in a much stronger position to negotiate the terms? Whilst Holmes would undoubtedly know the answer, we, like Dr Watson, can only suggest some of the alternative explanations.

The first would be that the Americans were too busy watching the Russians and the Chinese, too obsessed (particularly during the height of McCarthyism) with the 'red menace' and the 'yellow peril' to understand the latent dynamism of the Japanese. The Americans were very concerned about the potential strength of the Japanese Communist Party, and this may have inclined the Americans to be more conciliatory towards the traditional elite, particularly those with *zaibatsu* connections. (*Zaibatsu* were military-industrial-financial combines or trusts controlled by the wealthy families which dominated the oligarchic inter-war power structure.) The second might simply be that they underestimated the Japanese because they had defeated them in war, they were not white, and the economy was very slow to recover after 1945. By the mid-1950s, many senior Americans still considered Japan to be an underdeveloped country, whereas France, Germany and Britain were seen as highly developed, with lucrative markets. This latter point perhaps meant that more attractive investment opportunities were available in Europe than Japan for the 1950s and early 1960s. Certainly post-war reconstruction proceeded more rapidly in Europe than in Japan. Japan did not surpass its pre-war production levels until 1959. The third reason would be that American cultural ties to, and knowledge of Europe were considerable, in contrast to their understanding of Japan. This perhaps explains why the occupation forces allowed some of the *zaibatsu* to re-emerge: they were needed to bolster reconstruction. Once they had reasserted themselves, in alliance with the powerful Japanese bureaucracy, these constellations of economic power pursued mercantilist policies which blocked the penetration of foreign capital. This reflected the fact that the Japanese elite was substantially united in its desire to exclude foreign economic influence. Their mercantilist outlook was embedded in the cultural experiences of centuries, and more recently in the economic successes of the Meiji Restoration. Indeed the opening-up of Japan remains a major challenge to the United States and its West European allies. Institutions like the Trilateral Commission, which involves elites from North America, Western Europe and Japan, have been developed partly with a view to overcoming this challenge.

While direct investment became the main form of long-term capital flow in the 1950s and 1960s between developed countries, in the 1970s there was a revival of portfolio investment (in the form of bond issues) along with a massive increase in short-term capital flows. This continued to grow in the 1980s as is illustrated in Table 9.7. The magnitude of these flows is evidence of the growing international links between national capital markets.

Table 9.7: International bond issues (in millions of US dollars)

Borrower	1983	1984	1985	1986*
Industrial countries	$60,309	$91,883	$140,531	$93,714
Developing countries	2,585	3,689	8,751	3,344
Latin America	71	216	953	839
Asia	2,302	3,118	6,956	2,310
Middle East and Africa	212	355	842	195
International organisations	13,410	11,723	18,027	8,514
Total	$76,304	$107,295	$167,309	$105,572

*First six months.
Source: Adapted from Morgan Guaranty Trust Co., reprinted in *Wall Street Journal*, 29 September 1986, p. 40D.

This growth in the international bond market followed on the much larger growth in short-term international assets, such as Eurodollars (deposits denominated in dollars in bank branches outside the United States). The estimated net size of the Eurodollar market (in US dollars at current prices) was $9 billion in 1964, £25 billion in 1968, £132 billion in 1973, $247 billion in 1976 and $475 billion in 1979 and around $1200 billion, by June 1980.[25] This may have reached $2000 billion by 1984.[26] The capacity of the Euromarkets to facilitate the rapid movement of capital is indicated by the daily volume of activity on foreign exchange markets. The average daily volume of trading in the American foreign exchange market by banks rose from $18 billion in March 1980 to $26 billion in April 1983, and to $50 billion in March 1986. At the latter date there was also $8.5 billion of trading by non-bank institutions.[27] On the basis of markets operating 365 days a year, and using the world exports figure cited earlier, we calculate that the daily volume of American exchange trading alone in 1980 was 3.64 times the size of the value of the average daily level of total nominal world trade. Of course, there are major financial centres other than American ones, especially London and Tokyo. Given that average daily trading has been increasing so rapidly the ratio of exchange dealing to world trade on a daily basis could well have been more than 25:1 by 1987.

As Table 9.7 reveals, the bulk of the funds raised by bond issues went to developed countries. In practice this meant principally the United States during the 1980s, because of its huge budget deficit. As a result, the United States emerged as the world's biggest debtor with net foreign liabilities of about $120 billion at the end of 1985.[28] Such indebtedness contrasts dramatically with the American position in 1945 when it was easily the world's biggest creditor nation. While the United States was absorbing vast amounts of capital, the Third World, since 1981, ended up transferring (net) capital to the richer countries. This net transfer rose from US $7 billion in 1981 to $56 billion in 1983, and to $74 billion in 1985.[29] These net capital flows do not include profit repatriation by transnational corporations or flight capital (for example, that removed from Nicaragua mainly to Miami by the dictator Somoza before the final victory of the Sandinista Revolution in 1979). From the 1950s until the 1970s there had been a net transfer of funds into the less-developed countries, in contrast with the 1980s.

Sources of external funds for the Third World have changed during the post-war period, as can be noted from Table 9.8.

Official development assistance or aid was the main source of funds up to the early 1970s. Bank lending was the main source from the mid-1970s until 1981, after which aid once again became the primary source of foreign funds for the less-developed countries. Direct foreign investment held third place, but grew substantially. What these figures also revealed was the growing importance of private sources of finance, relative to public sources (even including the World Bank, which got most of its funds in the private markets).

Thus the process of internationalisation has gone with a growth in the role of private institutions in development finance. The latter operated according to market criteria. One aspect of reliance on market criteria was acceptance of the influence of interest rates, the level of which was largely set by the developed countries. In the 1980s this meant that indebted less-developed countries whose debts were at floating rates (rates of

Table 9.8: Lending and development assistance, 1970–1983 (sums in billions of US current dollars)

	Net New Bank Lending	Net New Bond Lending	Net New Direct Investment	Official Development Assistance
1970	1	1	2	7
1971	1	1	2	7
1972	3	1	3	8
1973	5	1	4	9
1974	9	1	4	9
1975	15	1	5	12
1976	21	2	5	13
1977	15	3	5	15
1978	25	4	7	19
1979	40	3	9	22
1980	49	2	9	27
1981	50	4	13	25
1982	21	4	11	27
1983	13	3	8	27

Source: D. Folkerts-Landau, 'The Changing Role of International Bank Lending in Development Finance', *IMF Staff Papers*, Vol. 32, No. 2 (June 1985), p. 320.

interest which varied according to the London Inter-Bank market rate, LIBOR) had to pay much higher real interest rates than were paid in the 1970s. By the real rate of interest is meant the nominal yield minus the rate of inflation.

One feature of the last twenty years was the tendency for real interest rates in the OECD countries to move in the same direction. This can be taken as evidence of the growing international integration of capital markets. As Table 9.9 shows, real interest rates fell in the 1970s and rose in the 1980s. However, while in several major countries real rates in the 1980s were similar to those in the 1960s, this was not the case for the United States. American real interest rates were relatively low in the 1960s, and high in the 1980s. The contrast between these two decades is partly to be explained by the high demand for loans caused by the big budget deficit under the Reagan administration. The figures for 1984 revealed significant differences between the rates for each country. Thus whilst there was a good deal of integration in the international capital markets, this integration was less than perfect. Perfect integration would mean real rates would be equalised. In practice a country with a surplus of savings (such as Japan in the 1980s) has a lower real interest rate than a country with a savings deficit (such as the United States).

Even the partial integration of markets that existed was evidence of the growing financial interdependence between countries. This mirrored the

Table 9.9: Real long-term interest rates, 1965–84

	United States	Japan	Britain	West Germany
1965–9	1.8	2.1	3.1	4.7
1970–4	0.7	–3.4	1.0	3.2
1975–9	0.3	0.5	–2.2	3.0
1980–4	4.9	4.1	2.9	4.2
1983	8.1	5.6	6.2	4.6
1984	8.2	4.5	5.8	5.4

Note: A minus sign denotes that borrowers are lent money at a nominal interest rate which is less than the rate of inflation.
Source: S. Strange, *Casino Capitalism* (Oxford, Blackwell, 1986), p. 17, based on data from the Bank for International Settlements.

evidence cited earlier of increasing integration through trade and foreign direct investment. Economic interdependence also affected the labour markets, albeit to a lesser extent than for capital markets. An example of this was the movement of labour from low-wage Third World countries (for example Mexico), to high-wage, developed countries (for example the United States). The 'brain drain' into the richest countries, especially the USA since 1945, illustrated the famous statement from the *Book of Matthew*, 'to him that hath shall be added, and to him that hath not, even that which he hath shall be taken away.'

The mainly economic changes we have described in this section were also accompanied by the increasing efforts at international policy consultation and coordination, especially with respect to economic policy, amongst the major capitalist states, and certain less-developed countries. This took place at both informal and formal levels. Until the early 1970s these efforts were part and parcel of the Bretton Woods system, with most countries committed to fixed exchange rates. By this we mean that various countries (with the exception of the United States) had to design and implement their macroeconomic policies so as to defend a given set of exchange rate parities. The American dollar was the pivot currency of the system, around which other parities were aligned. The OECD collated information and fostered international economic debate through its publications. With the breakdown of some aspects of the Bretton Woods system in the early 1970s new channels were developed to supplement the continuing efforts of the IMF, the World Bank and the OECD. From 1975 there were annual economic summits between the leading five (now seven) capitalist countries. West European economic policy coordination has been promoted by the development of the EEC. A notable example of this was the operation of the European Monetary System (EMS) since 1979. The above examples relate to formal inter-governmental coordination. An example of a more informal process was the operation of the so-called

Paris Club. These were meetings of the leading creditor countries which coordinated responses to the demands of indebted countries.

7. TOWARDS A GLOBAL CULTURE?

Some of the the processes under discussion can also be linked to what has been variously called *cultural imperialism* and *cultural synchronisation*. The former term refers to the way that the values and norms of one country penetrate and change those of another, to the former's benefit. The latter term concerns the tendency for a set of values to emerge across a range of countries, such that popular outlooks and tastes become more homogenised. Cultural imperialism is thus more associated with what we call transnationalisation, and cultural synchronisation with the process of internationalisation. Some dependency theorists have argued, for example, that Walt Disney productions and artifacts, marketed in a wide range of countries, and consumed mainly by the young, tend to assist in the inculcation of American values, notably in Latin America. Thus the apparently harmless Mickey Mouse is a symbol of American individualism, and the aspiration to a better (that is North American) way of life. The world-wide market for Disney products allowed the parent company to develop economies of scale, such that it was able to outflank local competitors – the costs of animation and distribution were very high. This example can be extended to encompass a range of media and advertising concerns in the metropolitan countries, the largest of which were mainly American-owned. Though there was a growth of internationalisation in publishing, with the subcontracting of books, there was also a tendency towards concentration and transnationalisation.

Some writers even use the term 'globalisation of culture' in connection with some of the above processes. An example of this was the way internationally-marketed cultural products such as *Kojak* and *Star Trek* represented a particular sense of the world (or the galaxy), but more basically it concerned the pervasive spread of the values of consumerism, possessive individualism and status achievement. The more a tendency towards this type of global culture was reinforced, the greater was the scope for the increased power of transnational, relative to national, capital.

Improved transport and communication also promoted the spread of other types of cultural norms and values. An example of this was the revival and spread of fundamentalist Islam. Ayatollah Khomeini spread his revolutionary message from his base in Paris by means of cassettes, so contributing to the downfall of the Shah of Iran in 1978. Thus an irony of the revolution was that Khomeini used Western technology to undermine the very government which Western (notably American) interests sought to protect. A further irony was that Western radio broadcasts beamed into Iran spread information about growing unrest, and thus fuelled the flames of revolt. Since the Iranian revolution, radio broadcasts from Iran have spread the fundamentalist message to neighbouring Arab states and to Moslem parts of Soviet Central Asia, as well as to Afghanistan. Thus global communications facilitated resistance and challenges to the spread of materialist cultural and political values, of both East and West. The nature and extent of such challenges depends crucially on control of and access to communications networks.

The issue of access and national control was central to attempts in the 1970s and 1980s by some Third World and communist states to prevent the penetration of their cultures by the capitalist states and their media and communications transnational corporations (who argued for the free flow of information). Central to the strategy of the rulers of these states were attempts to create national monopolies over communications, partly in order to reduce the likelihood of challenges to their legitimacy provoked by 'bad news', and partly to prevent transnational corporations from gaining 'ideological access' to their countries. By limiting such access these countries' governments attempt to act as ideological gatekeepers in an attempt to control cultural and implicitly economic and political development for their countries. For example, socialist Tanzania under the leadership of Julius Nyerere practised such a policy of cultural closure, coupled with compulsory political education (in Swahili), which preached national self-reliance and independence.[30]

NOTES

1. See for example, Perry Anderson, *Lineages of the Absolutist State* (London, New Left Books, 1974); Immanuel Wallerstein, *The Modern World-System I: Capitalist Agriculture and the Origins of the European World-Economy in the Sixteenth Century* (New York, Academic Press, 1974) and *The Modern World-System II: Mercantilism and the Consolidation of the European World-Economy* (New York, Academic Press, 1980). The debate between their respective positions, for example on the origins of modern capitalism, is reviewed by Peter A. Gourevitch, 'The International System and Regime Formation: A critical review of Anderson and Wallerstein', *Comparative Politics* (1978), pp. 419–37.
2. George Modelski, *Long Cycles in World Politics* (Seattle, Wash., University of Washington Press, 1985). See also Richard Rosecrance, 'Long Cycle Theory and International Relations', *International Organisation* (1987), Vol. 41, pp. 283–301.
3. The Gold Standard involved the commitment by central banks to maintaining

the convertibility of their national currency into gold. Those on the standard were required to keep the exchange rate between gold and the national currency within narrow limits, that is having an official gold price. As a result, a country which was in balance of payments deficit would lose gold reserves to countries in surplus. Another central feature of the Gold Standard was the commitment by central banks to maintain a roughly fixed proportion between their official gold reserves and the money supply (of which gold coins were a significant part in the nineteenth century). See also chapter 10 on this.

4. 'The Monroe Doctrine', from President Monroe's Annual Message to Congress, 2 December 1823, reprinted in Robert A. Goldwin (ed.), *Readings in American Foreign Policy* (New York, Oxford University Press, 1971), 2nd edition, pp. 194–5.
5. E. H. Carr, *International Relations Between the Two World Wars, 1919–1939* (New York, Harper and Row, 1966), pp. 27–40.
6. On the economic interests related to this perspective, see Kees van der Pijl, *The Making of an Atlantic Ruling Class* (London, Verso, 1984), pp. 50–69.
7. Ibid., pp. 66–7.
8. Karl Polanyi, *The Great Transformation: the Political and Economic Origins of our Time* (Boston, Mass., Beacon, 1957).
9. Carr, *International Relations*, op. cit., p. 135.
10. E. H. Carr, *The Twenty Years' Crisis 1919–1939* (New York, Harper and Row, 1964), p. 230.
11. Charles Kindleberger, *The World in Depression* (Berkeley, Cal., University of California Press, 1973).
12. Van der Pijl op. cit., pp. 76–106; Lawrence Shoup and William Minter, *Imperial Brains Trust: the Council on Foreign Relations and United States Foreign Policy* (New York, Monthly Reivew Press, 1977); Gabriel Kolko, *The Politics of War: Allied Diplomacy and the World Crisis 1943–45* (London, Weidenfeld and Nicolson, 1969).
13. Peter A. Gourevitch, 'Breaking with Orthodoxy: the Politics of Economic Policy Responses to the Depression of the 1930s', *International Organisation* (1984), Vol. 38, pp. 196–217; and Thomas Ferguson, 'From Normalcy to New Deal: industrial structure, party competition, and American public policy in the Great Depression', *International Organisation* (1984), Vol. 38, pp. 41–94.
14. Ferguson, op. cit, p. 68.
15. See Stephen Gill, *American Hegemony and the Trilateral Commission* (Cambridge, Cambridge University Press, forthcoming), chapter 6.
16. T. Skocpol, 'Political Responses to Capitalist Crisis: Neo-Marxist Theories of the State and the Case of the New Deal', *Politics and Society* (1980), Vol. 10, pp. 155–201.
17. *OECD Observer* (1986), Vol. 143, p. 10.
18. Donella L. Meadows et al., *The Limits to Growth: a report for the Club of Rome's project on the predicament of mankind* (London, Pan Books, 1974).
19. *Financial Times*, 23 May 1986.
20. *Guardian*, 4 July 1986.
21. *Financial Times*, 23 June 1986.
22. N. Ushiba et al., *Sharing International Responsibilities* (New York, Trilateral Commission, 1983), p. 83.
23. Ushiba et al., op. cit., pp. 80–5.
24. M. Nishihara, *East Asian Security* (New York, Trilateral Commission, 1986), pp. 94–9.

25. D. Calleo and S. Strange, 'Money and World Politics', in S. Strange (ed.), *Paths to Political Economy* (London, Allen and Unwin, 1984), p. 96; W. P. Hogan and I. F. Pearce, *The Incredible Eurodollar* (London, Allen and Unwin 1982), p. 3.
26. S. Strange, *Casino Capitalism* (Oxford, Basil Blackwell, 1986), figure 2.2, p. 35.
27. *Wall Street Journal*, 29 September 1986, p. 40D, based on Federal Reserve Bank of New York figures.
28. *Guardian*, 9 January 1987.
29. Ibid.
30. We are grateful to Jill Kirby for pointing out this example.

10 Money, Finance and Macroeconomic Relations

INTRODUCTION

This chapter defines the nature and role of international money and looks at the major changes in international monetary and macroeconomic relations since the 1950s. In particular we examine the way in which such changes relate to the rise of transnational firms, especially those in banking and finance. In addition, we analyse the central place of the United States in the monetary structure.

First of all, however, we shall explain why we have placed this chapter before those on production and trade. Our argument is not that 'money' is necessarily above 'production' in the 'hierarchy of structures' in the global political economy.[1] The question of the nature and relationship of such structures is very complex.

The rise of transnational firms is best understood as part of a system which depends for its functioning upon a more integrated monetary order. Although some see the monetary situation in the 1980s as 'disorderly', we would argue that transnational capital is best placed to survive and flourish in this conjuncture. In this context we have four specific reasons for placing money before 'production'.

First, monetary disorders can have far-reaching effects, as was shown in the Great Depression of the 1930s. Trade wars were more a symptom, than the primary cause of the depression. Some of the effects of this slump have been outlined in chapter 9.

Second, a post-war lesson was drawn from this period, especially by senior figures within the United States. This was that open markets for both capital and goods required a new and more stable monetary order. Otherwise, capital market integration was likely to contribute to economic collapse. Since the early 1970s global financial integration has returned to a level akin to that which prevailed during the heyday of the Gold Standard. However, it has reached new heights in terms of the scale and speed of monetary transactions. This new integration has coincided with a period of slower growth, and with the recurrence of recessions not seen in scale since the 1930s. It has also been accompanied by an international debt crisis that has led to fears concerning the possible collapse of some leading banks. Hence the issue of monetary disorder is central to considerations on the prospects for the global political economy.

Third, the United States, which was most important in establishing the post-war monetary order, has continued to occupy the central place in the global monetary structure. The dollar continues to be the leading reserve asset, and as such, the impact of American actions (or lack of them) on international economic matters remains important to all other nations. The United States has been crucial to facilitating and enhancing the creation of international capital markets and also the spread of financial liberalisation. In particular, an example of American inaction (or what Bachrach and Baratz have called 'non-decision-making') was the failure to take effective steps to limit, prevent or regulate the growth of offshore markets for dollars. American banks sought to develop such markets in order to escape from the banking regulations which restricted their expansion within and beyond the United States. This non-decision, in combination with conscious decisions elsewhere (as in Britain) to allow banks to take dollar deposits, made possible the rapid growth of a huge market in Eurodollars.

Fourth, changes in money and finance serve to alter or maintain the prevailing distribution of power and wealth, not only between countries, but also within and between classes. In particular, transnational capital has benefited relative to other groups from the integration of capital markets. Within the category of transnational capital, there has been a rise in the relative power and influence of financial forms of capital. Part of this influence concerns the spread of monetarist, free-market ideas which, when expressed in policy, tend to favour internationally mobile capital at the expense of national capital and labour.

2. INTERNATIONAL MONEY

Money is both an important power resource and a means to promote efficiency though financing exchange. Efficiency is associated with specialisation and trade, both within and between countries. All manner of items have been used as money over the centuries, including iron bars, cowrie shells, gold coins, paper notes and bank deposits. Today the latter is the main form of money. To function as money, any medium of exchange must be widely acceptable. While economies function more efficiently because of the 'public good' of money, the creator of money (nowadays the state central bank and commercial banks) is especially privileged.

In Weber's classic definition, the state is characterised as having a relative monopoly of the legitimate use of force in a given territory. The state is also usually associated with a relative monopoly over the supply of money. Traditionally, this monopoly involved control over coinage. In the twentieth century, central banks came to control and to monopolise the issue of notes (private banks had issued notes widely during the nineteenth century). Through monetary expansion, governments were and still are able to finance government expenditures, including those for the police and the military.

For money to be an important power resource for the state certain conditions must be met. These include the widespread acceptability of the currency as a means of payment and as a store of value. Excessive monetary expansion can lead to a loss of acceptability or confidence in the currency, especially if severe inflation results. Indeed, it may contribute to a loss of political legitimacy, as occurred during the hyperinflation in Weimar Germany in the 1920s. In a capitalist country, high and unpredictable rates of inflation create uncertainty, which in turn may undermine business confidence and the wider 'business climate'. Investment may be adversely affected, resulting in a fall in economic activity, and the prospects for future growth.

The gains for a government from increasing the supply of money are sometimes referred to as 'seignorage'. The term is taken from the medieval lord or *seigneur*, who often minted and issued coins within his fiefdom. The acquisition of the right to create money, especially a monopoly, was (and still is) a source and a symbol of power (for example the head of the monarch on a coin). The possibility of international seignorage arises when the money of one country is used as a medium of exchange for international (or even internal) transactions by other countries. When non-American individuals and organisations hold and use the dollar, the United States gains a resource inflow. This is because to meet the foreign demand for dollars America must run a balance of payments deficit. These resources are provided at a cost: foreigners earn a rate of interest on their dollar deposits. However, if this rate is lower than the rate of return that the United States can obtain by investing these resources elsewhere, there is a seignorage gain.[2]

Whilst international exchange, in the form of trade, goes back over the millennia, widely acceptable international monies and seignorage gains from their creation are much more recent developments. During the merchant phase of capitalist development, from the sixteenth to the eighteenth centuries, international trade was financed through the use of national currencies based on gold and silver, supplemented by credit. During much of the nineteenth century there were fluctuating exchange rates between national currencies. By the late nineteenth century silver had declined in importance as the Gold Standard was adopted by the leading states. No country had a monopoly of the supply of the precious metal.

In the second half of the nineteenth century, the British pound sterling, which had a fixed rate of exchange against gold, gained a special acceptability. This was due to Britain's leading position in trade and investment and the highly developed financial markets of the City of London. These combined to ensure a large market in pounds. Money could be converted into pounds and invested in British government stock, so as to earn interest which was not obtainable if assets were held in gold. In so far as foreign funds were placed in British bonds and bills, then this tended to reduce the cost of servicing the British national debt. Alternatively, foreign funds could be invested, on a very short-term basis, in bank deposits. When central banks of other countries held some of their reserves in sterling assets (as opposed to gold) in London it meant that the pound had become a reserve currency. Crucial to this role as a reserve currency, or to the 'international money' status of the pound, was the maintenance of confidence in the convertibility of sterling into gold. If the gold reserves of the Bank of England were seen as inadequate there would be selling of sterling (a 'run on the pound'), as happened in 1931 when Britain was driven off the Gold Standard. However, many governments continued to hold sterling balances in London, accepting payment in this form during World War II. This helped Britain to finance its war effort, just as the United States was to be helped in financing the Vietnam War by foreign governments holding more dollars.

Since World War II the United States dollar became the main reserve currency for similar reasons to those which had earlier applied to sterling. The American dollar met all the requirements for being a reserve currency. First, the United States has been the leading trader, investor and aid giver since 1945, creating an international market for dollars. Second, the dollar has always been fully convertible, not just into other currencies, but also, until 1971, into gold. In contrast, the United States' superpower rival, the Soviet Union, has never allowed its currency to be convertible. Third, the dollar was credible, inspiring confidence partly because American inflation rates before the 1970s were usually below five per cent per year. Confidence was enhanced because the United States was the world's dominant economic and military power and as such its currency was regarded as secure and safe by investors. Further, liberal democratic capitalism was effectively unchallenged in the post-war United States, with little threat of a communist revolution dispossessing holders of dollars (in contrast to those who held roubles in 1917).

The dollar is held in the official reserves of nearly all countries. Other currencies sometimes held include the West German deutschmark, the

Japanese yen, the Swiss franc, the French franc and the British pound. With the rapid growth of the West German and Japanese economies since the 1950s, these two countries have expanded their trade to levels similar to that of the United States. As a result, their currencies have become more internationally useful, especially in the light of financial liberalisation. The other forms of reserve assets are Special Drawing Rights (SDRs) of the International Monetary Fund (IMF), and gold. SDRs are valued in terms of a weighted basket of major currencies. The interest rate on SDRs is less than that which can be obtained from reserves placed in national currencies. The lower return on the SDR is not accidental since it reflects the American interest in maintaining the status and standing of the dollar.

For purposes of intervention in foreign exchange markets by central banks, the dollar remains largely unchallenged. The exception to this is that some transactions within the European Monetary Systems (EMS), which began in 1979, use the currencies of members of the European Currency Unit (ECU) as its unit of account. The ECU consists of a weighted 'basket' of the member countries' currencies. In this basket (the collective value of the currencies of all EC members) the dominant currency is the deutschmark. A central bank (say of a developing country) can invest some of its official reserves in the Euromarkets, but have them denominated in ECUs. Another unit of account is the SDR. The attraction of using the ECU or the SDR as a unit of account is that risks of capital loss resulting from exchange rate movements are reduced. (See Table 10.2A.)

3. MONEY AND CREDIT

At both the domestic and international level, the nature and significance of money has been affected by the growth of credit. With the growth of commercial bank deposits from the nineteenth century (and even earlier in some countries) a form of credit emerged, that is as bank loans, matched by deposits. As this form of credit became widely acceptable, it took on the character of money. This meant that banks could create money as a multiple of their cash reserves.

The policy implication of this change was that banks were unlike other kinds of business, and required regulation by the state. This was because the state needed the power to restrict the money-creating ability of the banks, in the interests of financial stability. One means by which this is achieved is through reserve requirements, which stipulate the minimum ratio of reserves to deposits. A second method is through open market operations, where the government sells or purchases government bonds, in order to influence the availability of liquid assets to the banks.

The importance of such regulations was highlighted when many banks collapsed during the Great Depression. In the United States, a complex set of controls and rules was introduced. These consolidated the Federal Reserve System, and guaranteed the separation of banking from other types of business. Since then, other types of liquid asset have been developed, such as certificates of deposit and commercial paper. These developments have given rise to a debate amongst economists as to what actually is to count as money. If a narrow definition is adopted, then only short-term bank deposits are counted, along with cash. In this case there is no simple relationship between the stock of liquidity and the amount of money, given the vast array of 'non-monetary' assets. Alternatively, a very broad definition of money can be used, one which covers all types of liquid asset.

The consequences of this debate are not purely academic. In order to be able to control the creation of money, a banking authority needs to be able to define what it is trying to regulate. However, even if the authority succeeds in controlling a monetary aggregate, it is likely that 'financial innovation' will occur, in order to circumvent regulation. Certain organisations, which are not technically banks, may therefore come to deal in a variety of liquid assets in ways which involve the offer of banking-type services. The American financial services company Merrill Lynch is a case in point, given its active involvement in the market for commercial paper. The 'official' banks have complained of unfair competition and have lobbied for an easing of the banking regulations to which they are subject, with some success in the 1980s.

What is implied, in an economy which is credit-based and where financial innovation is free to take place, is that the best that a monetary authority can hope for is partial control over domestic monetary conditions. As a result, the definition and usefulness of domestic monetary targets is called into question. Also at issue is the government's authority and power to determine outcomes compared to the freedom of the banks to pursue their own ends.

Such targets were, however, a prominent feature of monetarism in the late 1970s. As we have seen, an adequate but not excessive supply of money and credit is needed to finance economic activity. In a world of constant financial innovation, it is far from clear how far the supply of money and credit should expand in order to finance a given level of economic activity. This casts doubt on the usefulness of Milton Friedman's suggested 'monetary constitution' for the United States. His 'constitution' would involve a fixed annual growth rate in the supply of money.[3]

Because of the problems of definition and control of the money supply there was a trend towards a reduced stress on the centrality of monetary targets in the policies of the developed capitalist countries in the 1980s.

Instead, there was a growing focus on using symptoms of monetary excess (or shortage) as signposts for changes in policy. Examples of such symptoms have included: a sharp rise (or fall) in the rate of inflation; a substantial rise (fall) in the rate of growth of nominal gross national product (GNP); and a marked depreciation (appreciation) of the exchange rate. In the context of the growing financial interdependence between the major capitalist economies, the exchange rate was seen as of special importance as a barometer for monetary policy.

At the global level, assets which are internationally acceptable, such as American dollars, have taken on an added dimension. This is because of the development of international credit markets involving new types of assets. The most notable of such markets is the Eurocurrency market, which involves many financial centres (notably London). There is also an Asia-dollar market (mainly based in Singapore, Hong Kong and Tokyo). In the literature, Eurocurrency markets are sometimes referred to loosely, to cover all offshore banking arrangements, not just those in Europe.

The vast growth of loans from the offshore markets has provided new opportunities for banks to expand credit. This is because banks are restricted if they take deposits in only the currency of the country where the branch is located. In the offshore markets, where deposits can be taken in any currency, reserve requirements have been minimal or non-existent. In consequence, banks seeking greater profits have had an incentive to concentrate their growth in the Euromarkets. In particular, in the 1970s, some of the major American banks obtained most of their profits from branches which were engaged in such markets. Some of the effects of these developments are discussed in section 7 of this chapter.

Finally, it should be noted that despite the ending of convertibility between the American dollar and gold in August 1971, the precious metal has continued to be held by many central banks and can be used to settle payments or as a security for borrowing. The Soviet Union resorted to increased gold sales in order to raise hard currency in the 1980s as its revenue from oil exports declined. South Africa, the other major gold producer, raised loans using gold as a security when its balance of payments ran into substantial deficit in the same period.

4. BALANCE OF PAYMENTS ADJUSTMENT

Neo-classical economists have suggested that three international monetary problems arise with respect to the promotion of economic efficiency and welfare in the world economy. These are the problems of 'adjustment', 'liquidity' and 'confidence'. So far we have referred mainly to liquidity and confidence.[4] In this section we focus on the problem of balance of

Table 10.1: Current account balances, 1978–86

	1978	1979	1980	1981	1982	1983	1984	1985	1986
Industrial countries	15.1	-23.2	-60.5	-19.0	-22.4	-19.8	-58.3	-50.7	-19.0
Canada	-4.3	-4.2	-0.1	-5.1	2.3	2.5	2.7	-0.9	-6.7
USA	-15.4	-1.0	1.9	6.9	-8.7	-46.3	-107.0	-116.4	-141.4
Japan	16.5	-8.8	-10.7	4.8	6.9	20.8	35.0	49.3	85.8
West Germany	9.0	-6.0	-15.7	-5.2	4.1	4.2	8.4	15.3	35.4
France	7.0	5.2	-4.2	-4.6	-12.1	-4.7	-0.8	-0.2	3.4
Italy	6.2	5.5	-10.0	-9.1	-6.2	1.6	-2.4	-3.6	4.1
Britain	1.9	-1.5	6.8	12.5	6.9	4.8	2.1	4.5	-0.2
Other industrial countries	-5.8	-12.5	-27.6	-19.2	-15.5	-2.7	3.7	1.3	0.5
Developing countries	-35.0	6.4	30.4	-48.5	-87.1	-64.0	-33.0	-23.9	-46.4
By region:									
Africa	-12.8	-3.4	-1.9	-22.4	-21.5	-12.2	-7.3	-0.2	-8.7
Asia	-5.2	-9.7	-14.4	-19.0	-17.4	-14.9	-4.2	-14.0	4.9
Europe	-9.7	-13.6	-15.6	-14.3	-8.7	-5.9	-3.2	-3.3	-1.7
Middle East	11.3	54.2	92.5	50.0	3.0	-20.1	-15.8	-2.2	-23.3
Western hemisphere	-19.0	-21.1	-30.2	-42.7	-42.5	-10.8	-2.6	-4.2	-17.5

Source: Financial Times, 17 September 1987.
Based on IMF Annual Report.

payments adjustment which can be seen in both economic and political terms.

The 'adjustment' issue concerns the requirements for overcoming unsustainable imbalances in international payments. Under a system of fixed exchange rates such imbalances appear as persistent deficits and surpluses in the overall balance of payments. This is usually defined to include the capital account as well as the current account (of which trade is a part). What is excluded are changes in official reserve assets (which may include loans from and repayments to the IMF). The flows on current and capital account have often been seen as autonomous, with changes in official reserve assets seen as a residual. Such assets decline when a country is in basic deficit, and vice versa. The rationale for the distinction between autonomous and official 'accommodating' transactions was weakened when governments began to borrow large sums in the Eurocurrency markets in the 1970s. These capital inflows were added to reserves.

Even without borrowing, a rise in reserves may be deliberately sought for mercantilist reasons. Liberal economists tend to see balance as a 'natural' equilibrium. This view is not universally shared, as David Calleo and Susan Strange have pointed out.[5]

Under floating exchange rates, if there is no intervention (that is 'pure' floating), then the basic balance will be zero. However, there may be a deficit on current account financed by net capital inflows. Sometimes these are viewed as 'unsustainable'. This was widely thought to be the case for the United States in the mid-1980s. As a result the dollar was seen as overvalued, with a fall in the exchange rate needed to reduce (correct) the current account of payments. This implied adjustment by other countries, in that their basic balances would have to worsen: one country's deficit is another country's surplus. Table 10.1 indicates the situation which existed at this time. Both Japan and West Germany were in surplus, the United States deficit was considerable, and other developed countries were either slightly in deficit, or slightly in surplus.

At the economic level, payments imbalances are often seen as a result of the misallocation of resources. A deficit country needs to shift resources into the production of traded goods – exports and import-competing industries. If there is no slack in the economy (that is no unused capital and/or labour) which can be absorbed profitably into the traded sector, then such a shift of resources must be at the expense of the non-traded sector – mainly services. The problem is which policies can help bring about this shift. Policies include those which reduce expenditures (such as deflationary fiscal and monetary policies) which release resources for exports and reduce imports. These policies can be alternated or combined with protectionist measures to switch expenditures such as higher trade barriers, export subsidies and attempts to engineer a fall in the exchange rate. These make the production of tradeable goods more profitable, both absolutely and relative to non-traded goods and services (see chapter 12).

At the political level, adjustment is a problem in that it requires policies which may be generally unpopular and may hit certain groups and interests more than others. Expenditure reducing and switching policies tend to raise unemployment. This is especially likely if capital and labour are not very mobile between different sectors of the economy. This is also the case if real wages are 'sticky', that is they tend not to fall in the context of deflationary conditions. In the case of a surplus country, higher unemployment from adjustment measures may be greatest in the export sector. In practice the burden of adjustment is often heaviest on the deficit country, since, in the absence of much economic slack, adjustment requires a reduction in living standards or at least in 'absorption' (which includes consumer, government and investment expenditure).

So far we have referred to the problem of adjustment between countries. However, it also relates to changes within countries, as one sector or region declines and another expands. For example, the country might lose its comparative advantage in one industry (in one region) and develop an advantage in another (perhaps located elsewhere). This might happen at the same time as the country's balance of payments was in fundamental equilibrium, with a sustainable balance. Adjustment problems are often linked to changes in trading patterns or the terms of trade, such as when oil prices fell after 1981, with a sharp drop in 1985–86. In this case the living standards of some oil-exporting countries were badly hit.

However, payments imbalances can also be caused by changes in the pattern of savings and investment, as well as by budget deficits. In macroeconomics, an equilibrium in the circular flow of income requires that the sum of investment (I), government expenditure (G) and exports (X), equals the sum of savings (S), government revenues (T) and imports (M):

$$I + G + X \ = \ S + T + M$$

By rearranging the terms so as to place the trade balance on the left-hand side:

$$X - M \ = \ S - I + T - G$$

Thus any excess in investment over saving, or in government spending over taxation must be accompanied by a trade deficit. Further, if there is a net capital inflow (in order to finance a budget deficit), then under a 'pure' float, the surplus on capital account must be matched by a deficit on the current account. An understanding of these points is vital to appreciating the macroeconomic origins of the vast American trade deficits of the 1980s.

Under certain conditions the adjustment problem becomes one of the maintenance of political stability in a given country, since the changes in macroeconomic policy which are implied may badly affect large sections of the population. For politicians, concerned about their popularity, there is often a temptation to postpone adjustment, or to shift its burdens onto other nations. Since one country's surplus is another's deficit, some nations must be prepared to see their surpluses deteriorate so that a deficit country is able to regain its basic balance. However, some surplus countries may 'free ride' on the efforts of others, sustaining or even increasing their surpluses. Not all countries can, in a mercantilist manner, be successful in sustaining a surplus – at least one must be in deficit. Thus the internal political stability of a country with a persistent imbalance may be vitally affected by the economic orientation of, and policies adopted by, other nations.

More generally, this problem relates to what Benjamin Cohen calls the problem of consistency (or inconsistency) between the balance of payments policies of different countries. Each country may set a target for its basic balance (or current account) in such a way that when all countries' targets are added together they do not equal zero. The same problem can also arise for liquidity targets if countries seek to increase their holdings of a reserve asset which is in relatively fixed supply (such as gold).

Apart from the problem of inconsistent current account targets, there is also an imperfect database to assess what is actually happening to balance of payment accounts. The IMF has estimated that in 1986, for example, instead of the sum of all national current accounts being (the theoretically necessary total of) zero, in practice they added up to $65 billion!

The contestable character of balance of payments (and adjustment) problems is also connected with disputes over whether an exchange rate is under- or overvalued. Much of the literature contains an implicit notion of a 'correct' or natural exchange rate. For economists, this usually involves a long-term balance for current and capital account taken together. 'External balance' is associated with 'underlying' long-term capital flows as opposed to short-term speculative flows. However, these long-term flows are dependent on economic policies pursued by the country and other countries since they affect the business climate. The direction and stability of such flows are partly bound up with how far the policies of a government are appealing to transnational firms.

Fred Bergsten and John Williamson have noted that the estimation of the degree of exchange rate misalignment is a difficult and, to some extent, a normative matter. They distinguish between different types of equilibrium. 'Fundamental equilibrium' refers to the 'real' exchange rate and reflects long-term forces, including a view of what constitutes the underlying capital flow. 'Current equilibrium' concerns short-term variations around the fundamental equilibrium due to cyclical factors, such as changes in interest rates. 'Market equilibrium' relates to the nominal exchange rate and is simply that rate which would clear the market in the absence of official intervention.[6] There is a tendency in IMF reports to see the 'correct' exchange rate as one which requires relatively liberal rules on trade and capital flows. Restrictions on these flows lead to an 'overvalued' exchange rate. IMF loans to developing nations have often been conditional on some easing of these restrictions. However, such restrictions have been used by political leaders in many countries to alter the distribution of income in favour of certain groups. For example, the urban population in Africa has benefited from cheap food imports while farmers supplying food have suffered, because of low prices for their own products. In this case, governments, rather than market forces, rule. More generally, on occasion, governments may find it in their interest to regulate and manipulate markets, just as they may see some domestic political advantage in expanding the money supply, for example to create a consumer boom before an election.

5. INTERNATIONAL MONETARY ORDERS

Benjamin Cohen suggests that international monetary orders can have only four alternative organising principles that can ensure a minimum degree of policy consistency among states: automaticity, supranationality, hegemony and negotiation. In practice, these principles may be combined.

The Bretton Woods system was largely 'hegemonic' in that the United States was spared balance of payments adjustment. The only element of discipline faced by the United States was the gold convertibility commitment. As this convertibility was eroded in the 1960s the Bretton Woods system (formally a gold exchange standard) increasingly became a 'dollar standard'. What mattered was that other countries' currencies were pegged to the dollar rather than the official pegging of the dollar to gold.

When countries were on the Gold Standard and gold convertibility was a regular occurrence, adjustment was largely 'automatic' in principle (though not always in practice). A deficit resulted in lower gold reserves and a smaller money supply. The Gold Standard of 1870–1914 was not fully automatic as governments retained some room for manoeuvre in so far as they could attract (or repel) capital inflows through variations in interest rates. In practice the Bank of England played a leading role in the management of the system. London was able to act as an ever-open market for the surpluses of other countries, as a lender of last resort at times of financial crisis and as a source of long-term counter-cyclical lending. Sterling balances were as good as gold at this time. In monetary relations Britain was the hegemonic power.

A common international currency issued by a world central bank would be an example of 'supranationality'. This ideal solution is politically virtually impossible to achieve in the current phase of development of the global political economy. Its establishment would require governments to surrender too much of their sovereignty to an international authority.

'Negotiation' approximates the condition which Cohen sees as characterising monetary relations since 1973, that is a struggle to attain 'consistency' through cooperation:

In a world of n sovereign states, only n − 1 external policies (be they adjustment policies or liquidity policies) can be independently determined. One country (the nth. country) is redundant. If all n countries try to set their policies independently, these policies will almost certainly be inconsistent − and as a result, the stability of the monetary order itself will be threatened. To preserve monetary stability, some means must be found to ensure consistency among national policies. Hence the consistency objective.[7]

The Bretton Woods system in effect solved the 'consistency problem' by allowing the America to be the privileged 'nth' country. Other countries could reduce or eliminate their deficits and surpluses by varying mixtures of macroeconomic policy changes and alterations of their exchange rate against the dollar (devaluation and revaluation). Adjustment through changes in the exchange rate was seen as a last resort when there was a 'fundamental disequilibrium'. If many countries wanted to be in surplus this was possible since the United States could run a deficit and indeed did so in most years of the 1950s and 1960s. A persistent deficit for the United States was possible because its currency was the main international reserve asset which the central banks and other countries were willing to hold in their official reserves. Many private firms and individuals outside of the United States also held dollars in the form of Eurodollar deposits at banks in Europe.

In some ways the United States was more privileged than Britain had been in the days of the Gold Standard. In the late nineteenth century all the major countries, not just Britain, were pegged to gold, so that all of them were subject to balance of payments 'discipline', that is they could not afford to run a persistent deficit. Under the Bretton Woods system the United States was pegged to gold and other countries' currencies were pegged to the dollar. It was a gold exchange standard that in practice became, in the 1960s and early 1970s, a dollar standard. The 'gold exchange' dimension depended on the willingness of the United States Federal Reserve to maintain convertibility between gold and dollars. For example, some West European countries were able to rebuild their gold reserves by converting dollars (gained by running a balance of payments surplus) into gold. However, once this convertibility was curtailed, as in the 1960s, and ultimately ended in August 1971, the Bretton Woods system became a pure dollar standard. Then the reserve currency status of the dollar permitted not just seignorage gains (which sterling had benefited from in the past) but substantial freedom from the 'discipline' of balance of payments adjustment.

With this greater degree of privilege went greater temptations. The United States could indirectly make other (surplus) countries finance its overseas military and diplomatic spending since the bigger the American deficit the more dollars held by these other countries. Unlike hegemonic Britain of 1870–1914, the United States in the 1960s and early 1970s was well able to adopt a policy of 'benign neglect' towards its balance of payments. For example, American interest rates remained below those of Western Europe in the 1960s, even though the United States had continuing and increasing balance of payments deficits. When Britain was the hegemon, deficits were soon alleviated through higher interest rates in order to attract capital to London.

6. INSTABILITY AND THE BREAKDOWN OF THE BRETTON WOODS SYSTEM

From the 'efficiency' angle, international monetary orders need to be analysed not just with regard to how they tackle the problems of adjustment, liquidity and confidence, but also as to how stable is a particular type of order.

While this second question has its technical aspects, it tends to highlight the political character of solutions. In the case of the Bretton Woods system up to 1971, the dollar was officially convertible into gold at $35 to an ounce of gold. Robert Triffin, as early as 1959, argued that this convertibility was not a stable solution so long as the rest of world used dollars as the main form of international liquidity. Rising demand for dollars as a reserve asset by central banks, firms and individuals could only be met if the United States ran a balance of payments deficit. United States dollar liabilities would come to exceed its gold reserves (as happened in 1960) by an ever-increasing amount so that a crisis of confidence in gold convertibility was inevitable, unless the price of gold was allowed to rise.[8]

However, the United States had political reasons for wishing to limit the role of gold and favour the dollar. America did not want to give a massive bonus to the main gold producing countries: the Soviet Union and South Africa. Acceptance of Triffin's analysis by American officials made the suspension of gold convertibility seem inevitable. From 1968 conversion of dollars into gold was minimal, as the major surplus countries, principally West Germany, chose not to 'rock the boat'. The overvalued dollar and United States deficits helped their export-led growth.

In its later years the Bretton Woods system came to be based on a fragile compromise between the United States, which gained from seignorage, and the EC and Japan, which were able to pursue growth in a mercantilist manner through trade surpluses. As early as 1968 the United States had vainly sought the cooperation of European countries in devaluing the dollar. American perceptions that the system was unstable merely served to raise the temptation to exploit the seignorage advantage to the full, before it could be curbed. The high government spending on social welfare (part of President Johnson's 'Great Society' programme) and the Vietnam War put inflationary strains on the American economy which could be eased at minimal cost, through running a bigger balance of payments deficit.

The spillover from expansionary United States monetary and fiscal policies to other countries contributed to the inflationary surge of the early 1970s. Not wishing to import inflation, West Germany let the deutschmark float upwards in May 1971. For Nixon, the 'shocks' of August 1971 were not just an attempt to obtain a devaluation of the dollar through the revaluation of other currencies: they were part of a domestic political game in which the prize was re-election as President in 1972. Nixon's measures appealed to industries hit by foreign competition and to nationalists wanting the United States to 'get tough' with 'awkward' foreign countries. The latter category included wealthy allies (especially Japan) who wanted export-led growth whilst free-riding on military and aid burdens borne by the United States.

President Nixon did not intend to end the system of fixed exchange rates. Gold convertibility might have been dead but a new set of exchange rates more favourable to American producers was alive as a possibility. However, the Smithsonian parities agreed in December 1971 did little to reduce the United States deficit and West Germany continued to be reluctant to 'import' American inflation. In consequence, the deutschmark was allowed to float upwards again in Spring 1973. The generalised floating of that year might have led to a new set of parities. However, the stability of the fixed exchange rate system was increasingly threatened by the growing volume of short-term capital flows. For example, huge inflows into West Germany in 1968–69 and 1971 boosted its dollar reserves and exerted an expansionary influence on the German money supply.

As restrictions on capital flows were eased and became less effective the central banks needed to intervene in foreign exchange markets on a much larger scale in order to peg (or hold) the exchange rate within narrow limits. For deficit countries this became less feasible as their foreign exchange reserves proved inadequate for the scale of intervention required. Thus there was a private 'confidence problem' in the stability of a particular pattern of exchange rates just as an official 'confidence problem' was threatening the convertibility of dollars into gold between central banks. In the face of the huge flows of short-term capital, governments had the option of constantly adjusting domestic monetary and fiscal policies to halt or reverse such flows. Under fixed exchange rates there were always major limits to monetary autonomy, but in an era of huge and volatile capital flows, these limits became greatly intensified.

Thus, a concern for the maintenance of some monetary autonomy contributed to the gradual acceptance of floating exchange rates during the 1970s. West Germany wished to be able to control its money supply with a view to keeping its inflation rate low. The British government, which floated sterling in June 1972, wished to pursue Keynesian expansionary policies in the run-up to the next election. In the case of the United States, the Bretton Woods system allowed it a monetary autonomy denied to other countries which it was reluctant to concede.

The move to floating or flexible exchange rates was made more appealing by the influence of optimistic analyses, which suggested that because of the stabilising effects of speculation, a 'market system' need not be disorderly. In this context, the views of Milton Friedman became more influential, especially in America.[9]

7. THE 'BRAVE NEW WORLD' OF CAPITAL MOBILITY AND OFFSHORE MARKETS

The increase in capital mobility which helped to undermine the viability of fixed exchange rates had far-reaching effects. Controversy over the nature of these effects has centred on the workings of the Euromarkets. One question concerns how far the rise of the Euromarkets has generated a dangerous 'credit pyramid'.[10] To examine this issue we shall first look at the way credit is generated at the domestic level.

Domestic banks use their initial inflow of deposits to issue loans in the form of other bank deposits and overdrafts. The scale of these loans can exceed the initial inflow of cash by some multiple (determined by the reserve requirements imposed by the government) as long as there is a consistent inflow of new deposits. These inflows replenish the bank's stock of reserve assets when borrowers liquidate their loans, as when they write cheques. This makes possible a 'banking multiplier' effect, where the ratio of final deposits created to the initial inflow is greater than 1:1.

At the heart of the controversy over the Euromarkets is the degree to which such replenishment effects occur. There is inadequate data available concerning the scale of inter-bank loans, which constitute a substantial fraction of the market. Moreover, there is considerable disagreement in the literature as to whether the multiplier is only slightly or substantially greater than 1. The dangers of the credit pyramid arise if the multiplier is much greater than 1. There is agreement, however, that the Euromarkets must add to the supply of money and credit in so far as they have lower reserve requirements than apply to national banking. In addition, the Euromarkets may also contribute to international inflationary pressures in that they may have facilitated a rise in the velocity of circulation, that is the rate of turnover of the money stock. Euromarkets have been associated with the rapid switching of funds between countries and currencies.

The effect of such rapid mobility of money and capital is to closely link the credit markets of the leading capitalist countries. One consequence is that the rates of interest in each of these countries and those of the Euromarkets have tended to move in a related manner (see Table 9.9). Because of the size of its money markets, and the special reserve status of the dollar, United States interest rates have the strongest national influence on Eurocurrency (especially Eurodollar) rates. This is partly because American companies can choose between raising dollar loans in the United States and borrowing on the Euromarkets, including the Eurobond market (for long-term loans).

National control of the domestic money stock, or more broadly, liquidity, is increasingly difficult because of the growing integration of money and capital markets. A tightening of monetary policy will often induce a large inflow of funds in response to a rise in interest rates. Further, such integration of markets may operate at both the relatively overt as well as covert levels. The most important covert aspects involve techniques such as transfer pricing by transnational corporations, which we discuss in chapter 11. As a result, even before exchange controls became as relaxed (or absent) as they were by the mid-1980s, transnational corporations were able to escape the pressures of a tight monetary policy in any single country. By contrast, smaller, national firms had no such escape. Another technique for evading controls is through the under- and over-invoicing of exports and imports. Less-developed countries suffered from 'capital flight' on a vast scale in the 1980s because of the use of this technique.[11] Indeed, one rationale for easing or abolishing controls on capital flows is that they are increasingly ineffective due to growing transnationalisation and trade interdependence. In so far as this point is valid, it implies that reference to trade, production and money 'structures' involves rather simplified (or parsimonious) abstractions: the structures are interdependent. Also, there is no going back to the 1950s.

The growth of integrated money and long-term capital markets also means that the use of figures on official international reserve assets held by central banks as an indicator of international liquidity is increasingly outmoded. Gross reserves figures do not allow for the increase in liabilities due to borrowing. Governments have borrowed large sums on the

Euromarkets to increase their holdings of foreign exchange. More generally, the ability to borrow reserve currencies when necessary is as important as the actual stock of reserves. This borrowing capacity serves to determine the 'potential reserves' of a country. Developed capitalist countries have usually been well placed in this respect, especially when they have been seen by the international banking fraternity as politically stable and sustaining a good business, or investment climate. A few of the newly-industrialising countries, such as South Korea, have also been able to borrow substantial amounts of foreign exchange. Access to international financial markets may be used by countries in an attempt to strengthen their position in the world economy and so in the inter-state system. As such, denial of such access is a major political setback.

Whilst many developing countries were able to borrow substantially in the mid-1970s, because of a relative glut of capital, this was no longer the case by the end of the decade. By the 1980s, the development programmes of many less-developed countries, including such relatively industrialised nations as Brazil and Argentina, were tightly constrained by limited foreign exchange reserves and export earnings. Economic backwardness, political instability and the debt crisis which have beset many developing nations adversely affected their access to international capital markets. One result was that they were driven to request IMF help and submit to the economic policies laid down in its conditions.

In sum, the ability to create money and credit is a source of power. This is also the case for the capacity to gain access to credit on favourable terms.

8. FLOATING EXCHANGE RATES AND THE DOLLAR

The 'non-system' of 'managed floating' that grew up after 1971 was eventually formalised as part of the Jamaica agreement of 1976, reached at a special meeting of the IMF's Interim Committee. This committee was the sucessor to the Committee of Twenty set up in July 1972 to examine reform of the international monetary system and related issues.

The Jamaica package did little more than normalise the existing situation. As regards balance of payments adjustment, countries were to avoid competitive depreciation, as they largely had done in the mid-1970s (in contrast to the early 1930s). In the 1960s, Japan and some European countries preferred to have an undervalued currency and a surplus position, as well as espousing other policies which were favourable to growth and keeping unemployment low. By 1976 priorities began to change as fear of inflation mounted, especially in the wake of the oil price shocks of 1973–74. In this new context, undervaluation was less appealing.

The reduced role for gold favoured by the United States found a place in the Jamaica Agreement. The obligation of IMF members to use gold in certain dealings with the Fund was ended. One-sixth of the Fund's gold was sold back to members at the former official price, directly in proportion to their quotas. Another one-sixth was sold on the open market. Most of the profits were then lent to poorer member countries through a new IMF Trust Fund. Special Drawing Rights (SDRs) with the IMF were made slightly more attractive through the use of a higher interest rate on SDRs. However this change was too modest to undermine the special position of the dollar. Thus from the 1970s the supply of international liquidity has been a mixture of gold, SDRs and reserve currencies (principally the dollar, though with a growing role for the deutschmark and the yen).

Whilst a large number of writers have argued that the Bretton Woods system collapsed in the 1970s, this claim can be overstated. The IMF continues to play an important role, the dollar remains the main reserve currency, the usual intervention currency, the most common unit of account and standard of deferred payment. Many developing nations, especially those in Latin America, peg their national currency to the dollar (though less of them than in the past). The ending of gold-dollar convertibility and the move to floating rates between the United States, Japan and Western European countries reflected the policy preferences of these countries, particularly those of the United States. It was the United States which initiated the Bretton Woods system, and it was the United States which ended gold convertibility. American actions provoked the first period of widespread floating in 1971, American veto power blocked the establishment of a substitution account to eliminate the 'overhang' of surplus dollars in the 1970s. This was because such an account would have threatened the dollar's status as a reserve currency.

Floating exchange rates did not result in the kind of order which had been anticipated. Speculators took a short-term view. Since there was no clear or agreed model of the world economy for the developed capitalist countries, there was only an imperfect basis for 'rational expectations'. While asset markets for bonds, bills and commodities were flexible and responsive, this was less the case for goods and labour markets, which adjusted much less rapidly. As a result, the new 'non-system' was very prone to 'over-shooting' of exchange rates: several currencies experienced significant fluctuations in value within relatively short periods. Initially it was tempting to attribute the gyrations in exchange rates to unusual shocks (such as sharp rises in oil prices), but this seemed less plausible as the volatility continued through the 1980s. Attempts to constrain the effects of such volatility led to a number of institutional innovations and agreements among the major capitalist countries, notably the European Monetary System (EMS), and the Plaza and Louvre accords of, respectively, 1985 and 1987, among the biggest (the Group of Five; later Seven) of these countries. These agreements reflected attempts to coordinate the macroeconomic and exchange rate policies of these countries in order to bring about an orderly depreciation of the dollar. The dollar had come to be seen as overvalued in the mid-1980s.

Fixed exchange rates would have been easier to sustain if the leading capitalist countries had been more willing to restrict capital flows and use import licences in the way many countries did in the 1950s and to a lesser extent, in the 1960s. Even the United States had controls on capital outflows in the late 1960s, for balance of payments reasons. They were abolished by President Nixon. Such controls complicated and restricted the activities of transnational corporations and financial institutions interested in overseas portfolio investment. Since then capital controls have been eased in Japan and Europe and rules on banks and other financial institutions have been liberalised. Both Japan and Germany have had misgivings about the use of their currencies for reserve purposes. Japan's liberalisation has come later than that of Britain, where the financial interests of the City of London have long been strongly entrenched. Industrial exporters exerted more political influence in Japan and Germany than in Britain during the 1960s and 1970s. Even in the early 1980s there was a strong contrast between the very high interest rate policies of Britain which lifted the pound sterling on the foreign exchange markets (and were good for banking profits) and low Japanese interest rates with an undervalued yen.

In the American case there was a dramatic contrast between the willingness, even the desire, to see the dollar depreciate on the foreign exchange markets in the early and mid-1970s and the tight monetary policies at the end of the decade. These policies led to a severe recession which hit American industrial interests. However, the stronger dollar of the early 1980s, along with high interest rates, was good for American bank profits and discouraged Arab, European and Japanese investors from switching out of dollars to further diversify their assets. In the mid-1970s the shift to floating exchange rates had already led to some diversification away from the dollar, reducing its share in reserve currency holdings.

David Calleo has argued that these policy changes (initially prompted by a desire to avoid a collapse in the value of the dollar) amounted to a near-revolution in American economic policy.[12] Mark Amen has suggested that they reflected the triumph of the American 'banking complex' and of the monetarist ideas within the United States.[13] This 'complex' of ideas, institutions and material capacities included some Friedmanite economists, commercial and investment banks, the Federal Reserve, the Treasury Department and many members of Congress. Its policy triumph was at the expense of those sectors of American industry and agriculture that were most vulnerable to foreign competition. The cautious easing of monetary policy in 1982 and 1985 can be related to the fears of American banks over the emerging debt crisis which, if debtors defaulted on their interest payments, would threaten their solvency.

While the credit crunch imposed by the Federal Reserve under the chairmanship of Paul Volcker in Autumn 1979 signalled the political strength of United States financial interests, it also marked the new limits of the dollar standard. Now the United States had to have high interest rates to get foreigners to hold dollars, whereas in the 1960s American interest rates were below the European average, including that on the Eurodollar market. Monetary discipline, akin to the IMF's balance of payments 'medicine' for borrowers, had come to prevail in the United States. If foreign funds were not forthcoming the dollar would have to decline and the United States would have to 'adjust' its current account. However, given the attractions of the large American financial markets, foreign funds continued to flow to the United States. As soon as the dollar strengthened, President Reagan pressed Volcker to loosen monetary policy. (In practice Volcker was more cautious, insisting on the necessity of restoring foreign confidence in American policy.) At the same time, Reagan proceeded with an expansionary fiscal policy (involving massive increases in military expenditures). This led to enormous budget deficits. By 1987, after two years of a substantial (but desired) fall in the value of the dollar, American interest rates were raised once again in order to protect the dollar and to curb a rise in inflation. The fall in the dollar from autumn 1985 had American support as evidenced by the 'Baker initiative' of the then US Treasury Secretary which led to the Plaza Agreement of September 1985 between the Group of Five.

The developments we have just outlined suggest that the price of the privilege of having a reserve currency may change over time. This was very evident in the British case in the inter-war period, and again in the 1950s and 1960s when high interest rates were adopted to defend the sterling exchange rate against the dollar. This resulted in less investment in domestic manufacturing industry and reduced economic growth. However, the United States is in a much stronger position than was Britain because there is so far little chance of any serious rival to the dollar as a reserve currency. In this context, it was no accident that the so-called 'Volcker shift' occurred soon after the formation of the European Monetary System (EMS) with the European Currency Unit (ECU) as its unit of account.

It has been suggested by Riccardo Parboni that the ECU might become a rival to the dollar if it became a medium of exchange as well as a unit of account.[14] Our view, however, is that this is unlikely in the near future because the European members would not be prepared to lose more of their monetary autonomy, and because it would be opposed by West Germany, given the German fears of absorbing inflationary tendencies transmitted from other countries. Further, Britain, with its highly developed financial markets, would be crucial to extending the role of the ECU. Britain was still outside the EMS in 1987, preferring to let sterling float.

Table 10.2: International role of the United States dollar

A. Percentage of Official Reserves

	End-1974	End-1974
United States dollar	75.0	57.0
Japanese yen	0	4.8
West German deutschmark	5.8	11.0
British sterling	5.4	2.6
Swiss franc	1.4	1.9
French franc	1.0	1.0
ECU	0	11.0
Other	11.4	10.6

B. International Bond Issues, 1984

	Values in billions of United States dollars	Percentage of total
United States dollar	100.0	60.6
Japanese yen	12.6	7.6
West German deutschmark	11.2	6.8
British sterling	6.35	3.8
Swiss franc	14.5	8.3
French franc	1.6	1.0
ECU	7.3	4.4
Total	165.0	92.7

C. International Bank Lending, 1985

Currency denomination	Value in billions of dollars, September 1985	Percentage
United States dollar	210.9	70.0
Japanese yen	3.0	1.0
West German deutschmark	48.7	16.0
British sterling	2.8	0.9
Swiss franc	14.8	4.9
French franc	1.3	0.6
ECU	6.0	2.0
Total	301.2	97.4

D. *Exchange Rate Base, 1974 and 1981*

	Percentage of developing countries pegging their currencies to different countries	
	1974	1981
Dollar peggers	62	32
Sterling peggers	9	1
French franc peggers	13	12
Special drawing rights peggers	0	12
Own basket peggers	0	16
Other currencies	1	3
Other approaches	14	22

Source: Financial Times, 8 April 1987.
Based on IMF Annual Reports.

The continuing relative decline of the dollar during the 1980s was uneven, and varied according to the type of use. This is revealed in Table 10.2, A–D.

Increased American willingness jointly to manage the foreign exchange markets was reflected both in the Plaza Agreement of September 1985 and in the Louvre Agreement of February 1987. However it was still doubtful that the United States was prepared to pay the full price to achieve exchange rate stability. A stabilisation of the dollar would involve not just changes in monetary policy, but also a major reduction in the American budget deficit. This deficit had been sucking in foreign capital for several years, thereby guaranteeing a deficit on current account.

The United States has, during the past three decades, become accustomed to pursuing its fiscal and monetary policies without much reference to external interests and international repercussions. The Volcker shift was a sign that attitudes were changing with regard to monetary policy. However, the persistent budget deficit of the 1980s suggested that little had changed with respect to fiscal policy. It took the global stock market crash of October 1987 to force President Reagan and senior members of Congress to revive their discussions concerning how to reduce the budget deficit. The price of inaction was a further plunge in the value of the dollar on the foreign exchanges. The United States hoped this fall would improve its trade balance and sustain economic growth in the election year of 1988. However, too severe a decline would weaken the status of the dollar as the major international currency. By January 1988, the United States had resumed intervention in support of the dollar on the foreign exchange markets, along with the other members of the Group of Seven (G7). Thus the 1980s can be seen as a decade of growing, but inadequate collective management of floating exchange rates.

9. THIRD WORLD DEBTS: BANKS AND STATES

Whilst the debt crisis surfaced dramatically, when Mexico was unable to maintain its debt payments in summer 1982, it had its roots in the mid-1970s. It was then that banks came to lend on a massive scale to less-developed countries, in the context of the vast growth of the Euromarkets and the recycling of petrodollars. In the second half of the 1970s about half of the foreign loans of transnational banks went to the Third World. In practice most of these loans went to just a few countries: Brazil, Mexico, Argentina, South Korea, Chile, Venezuela, the Philippines and Nigeria.

At one level the crisis can be traced to the failings of banks and borrowers: their greed, incompetence, inexperience, shortsightedness, imperfect information and misfortune. Not since the 1920s had there been a large flow of portfolio (bond) investment to the Third World. At an institutional level the crisis can be traced to the lack of regulation and monitoring of the Euromarkets and to what has been termed 'moral hazard'.[15] The latter arises when those engaged in a risky activity have reason to think that others, such as governments, have an interest in bailing them out. Could the US afford to see Brazil and Mexico trapped in a vicious circle of economic decline and political instability? Could the leading capitalist countries afford to let several major banks collapse, given the knock-on effects on other banks and financial confidence, generally?

The centrality of the United States was highlighted by the global impact of its deflationary monetary policy in the early 1980s. The volume and the value of Third World exports fell. Interest rates on Third World debts rose with American rates, since loans had been made on the basis of floating rates linked to the Euromarkets. As the United States budget deficit increased, real interest rates rose further, crowding out the less-developed countries from the markets. From 1973 to 1980 the interest rate on Third World debt averaged 10.2 per cent, while the export growth rate for non-oil developing nations averaged 21 per cent per annum. In 1981–2, the interest rate averaged 15.8 per cent while export growth averaged only 1 per cent.[16]

While various parties may have an interest in bailing out countries and firms, they may fail to combine forces due to ignorance, haggling over burden-sharing and free-riding. The handling of the debt crisis in the 1980s (in contrast to the 1930s) demonstrated the existence of substantial collective capacities in modern capitalism. These forces were of an international character and were represented in the close and growing links between commercial and central banks, governments and international organisations.

The United States government moved quickly to help Mexico by means of loans and oil purchases and also some easing of monetary policy. A bankers' cartel for handling Third World debts was organised by the IMF and central banks with the active support of the big banks in 'whipping-in' the smaller banks. The commercial banks made further loans to debt-ridden countries on the basis of programmes approved by the IMF.[17] New IMF loans were made conditional on the commercial banks playing their part as 'lenders of the last resort'. In order to cope with what was initially seen as a crisis of liquidity (rather than of solvency) various committees of bankers and the members of the 'Paris Club' (of sovereign creditors) negotiated the rescheduling of debts.

This approach to crisis management was revealed as inadequate by 1985. The scale and duration of the debt burden was by then so great that it became clear that the problem would continue, well into the 1990s. The terms of trade of developing countries were still weak and the oil price began to fall sharply. Continued stagnation or decline in countries whose debt payments exceeded their capital inflows was a recipe for default and potentially, political instability. The net transfer of capital from the Third World to the developed capitalist countries rose from $7 billion in 1981 to $56 billion in 1983 and to $74 billion in 1985.[18]

Thus for the first time in post-war history less-developed countries became net capital exporters. In addition, there was a substantial flight of capital from the Third World. In this context, the stress of dependency theorists on capital drain and underdevelopment took on added meaning. Indeed, in many parts of Africa, which were suffering from agricultural crisis and ecological disaster, the drain of capital was acute. For most

Table 10.3: Debt to export ratios of selected countries, 1982–85

	Debt to export ratios*			Outstanding debt ($bn in 1984)	
				Total debt	Bank debt
	1982	1984	1985		
Argentina	406	473	483	47.8	32.0
Brazil	339	322	368	102.0	73.7
Chile	333	402	442	20.4	15.6
Ecuador	240	260	254	7.6	4.7
Mexico	299	293	322	95.5	77.1
Peru	250	330	370	13.4	4.7
Venezuela	169	177	201	34.9	27.6
Nigeria	85	165	180	19.2	5.7
Philippines	270	312	342	26.2	13.4
Yugoslavia	167	166	160	18.5	7.9

Note: *Average of gross external debt at beginning and end of year as per cent of exports of goods and services.
Source: Financial Times, 23 and 28 September, 1985.

African countries the debt crisis was chiefly one of official, not bank debts, in contrast to Latin America. African external debts grew from $6 billion dollars in 1970 to over $82 billion in 1985. While these 1985 figures were much smaller in absolute terms than those for Latin America, debt level as a percentage of GDP was 62 per cent for Africa compared to 58 per cent for Latin America.[19]

Again it was the United States which took the lead in the next phase of managing the debt crisis, with the so-called 'Baker Plan' of Autumn 1985.[20] The IMF was to continue its role as an assessor of policies, but in conjunction with the World Bank whose long-term structural adjustment loans were to be increased to help ensure some economic growth. The World Bank was essential since commercial banks were still reluctant to lend more to most debtor countries. However, this required an increase in the Bank's capital which the United States Congress was reluctant to appropriate. The Congress insisted that loans made by multilateral agencies such as the World Bank were to be conditional on economic reforms favouring private enterprise and the market mechanism. Eventually, more generous packages, including some rescheduling, were negotiated with Mexico and Argentina. However, the slump in oil prices led to a second Mexican package with contingency loans as a new element. These loans (from the IMF and commercial banks) were to be made if economic growth and export earnings were less than projected.

By 1987 the inadequacy of the Baker Plan became clear. New commercial bank lending to developing nations was negligible while the export earnings of these countries grew slowly as world economic growth faltered. In consequence, rescheduling on more favourable terms to debtor countries was accepted by the commercial banks. By this time the banks had realised that a large percentage of the debts would be lost and they were forced to make substantial provisions for bad debts. Sometimes these were written off against tax (as in Japan and Britain). In March 1987, Citicorp, a leading American bank, made public its bad debt provisions and other banks followed suit.

The securitisation of bank debt (that is, its conversion into long-term bonds) began to be discussed. Debt-equity swaps became more common. Debt-equity swaps were a means by which bank debt was either turned into long-term assets or sold off at a discount. Such swaps occasionally involved the creditor bank buying up a local financial institution and cancelling a part of the debt in the process. More often they involved the sale of the debt at a discount to a transnational firm that was planning to buy up a local firm. The transnational firms then used the local currency proceeds from the debt. Proceeds were also used to finance new factories.

If the banks had shown they could act unwisely, as in the rush into syndicated loans to sovereign states in the 1970s, they had demonstrated, in the 1980s, their collective power and influence, and an ability to learn from past mistakes. However, the costs of learning for them were far less than for the many millions of mainly poor people in the Third World whose living standards fell significantly. They paid the biggest costs of adjustment.[21]

In December 1987 there was another Baker Initiative on Third World debts. The United States arranged a scheme whereby Mexico could hope to swap new debt for old – at a discount. For Mexico, this would facilitate both a writing down of the value of its debts and a reduction in the burden of debt servicing. In addition, a new IMF fund to help the poorest developing nations was set up: the Enhanced Structural Adjustment Facility. Thus, belatedly, governments showed signs of appreciating the wider nature of the debt crisis. There was a shift from the earlier view that the crisis was one of liquidity, to the view that it involved the long-term solvency and even political stability of a range of countries.

10. POLITICAL CONSEQUENCES AND CONCLUSIONS

As was noted at the outset of this chapter, money is a source of power and influence. Moreover, changes in the nature of the international monetary order, and in the workings of the system have differentiated political, economic and ethical consequences. Changes in monetary relations have significant repercussions for the distribution of income and wealth, the level of economic activity, and the political stability of different nations. Moreover, these changes have class, as well as international dimensions. In our conclusion we shall discuss a limited number of such consequences, and in particular seek to highlight the growing power and influence of internationally mobile financial capital to set the conditions for macroeconomic policy.

In the mid-1970s there was an unusual glut of capital while petrodollars were being recycled mainly through the Euromarkets. The glut also reflected the huge increase in dollars in foreign hands in this period because of United States balance of payments deficits. To an unprecedented extent, not only conservative, but also nationalist and social democratic governments were able to raise funds and postpone adjustment. Nationalist developing countries were able to borrow funds and in some cases, such as Brazil, Mexico and Argentina, use this finance to fund state capitalist development, expanding the public sector.[22] In the 1970s Brazil, Colombia, Venezuela, Algeria, Nigeria, South Korea and Indonesia had little or no recourse to the IMF.[23] It was not until the 1980s that the tables were turned. In this context it is important to note that when the IMF made conditional loans the most common effect was to reduce the share of labour in national income.[24] By contrast the effect on current account has tended to be relatively insignificant.

The burden of balance of payments adjustment to a variety of shocks may be spread very unevenly within a country. The painful adjustments in many developing nations in the 1980s have been for the mass of the population, rather than for the elite. The wealthy elites have been able to get capital out of their countries, to escape from the face of deprivation by travelling abroad, and to have superior access to foreign goods even in periods when exchange controls have been severe and exchange rates have been overvalued. In the case of Mexico a huge capital flight occurred in the early 1980s, prior to the devaluation of the currency. Some of the outflow returned afterwards, with resulting capital gains for the rich. From the point of view of dependency theory it is the mid-1970s, not the 1980s which looks to be atypical.

In the mid-1970s in some European countries, notably Italy and Britain, profits were squeezed while inflation accelerated. However, this led to capital outflows, falling exchange rates and, in Britain, difficulties in selling government bonds.[25] IMF loans were requested and policies more favourable to business were adopted. Thus even in countries with strong labour movements, the nature of internationally mobile capital caused a shift in macroeconomic policy.

We believe the evidence on post-war monetary relations points to a cumulative increase in the power and influence of internationally mobile capital, especially financial capital notably during the last two decades. While international bankers nowadays seem unusually good at international cooperation (witness the management of the debt crisis) they have also made mistakes. However, even without any cooperation and the advantage of close contacts with government officials, such mobile capital has substantial structural power. Investment 'strikes' and capital flight do not need to be organised: they can develop through spontaneous individual action, as long as they are not blocked by controls. By contrast, labour is less mobile, is faced by many, not always effective, immigration controls, and trade unions find it difficult to organise on an international basis.

Small-scale national capital is also at a disadvantage in an age of high capital mobility. Transnational firms are better able to cope with the high uncertainties of the era of floating exchange rates. The latter are a problem for some, but not all: just as with balance of payments adjustment.

Transnational banks have been particularly mobile: witness the influx of first American and later Japanese banks into Western Europe.[26] In their turn, European banks have been taking over some American banks. As the growing number of bank branches in tax havens illustrates, banking (and finance) is one of the most footloose industries: much more so than oil.

Competition by governments to attract transnational banks is an excellent example of a response to such structural power. For these banks, deregulation and increased uncertainties (as from volatile exchange rates) are an opportunity and a challenge. Even if the banks concerned have to write off half the value of their Third World debts this will have been more than matched by the massive profits from historically high real interest rates, compounded through debt rescheduling. In 1970 the seven largest United States banks obtained just 22 per cent of their profits from foreign (mainly Third World) operations. In 1982 their foreign profits were at a record 60 per cent.[27]

It should also be noted that the debt crisis has been a major blow to the state capitalism of several countries. In consequence, some privatisation has occurred and governments have had to woo foreign firms, with debt-equity swaps being one way of doing this.

Another aspect of the changes which have accompanied the growing mobility of transnational capital is at the level of ideas about the management of the economy: the weakening of Keynesian and interventionist ideas. Monetarist and market-place ideas gained a new cutting edge. However, there is a contradiction between traditional monetarism (with its stress on monetary targets and tight regulation of financial institutions) and a *laissez-faire* approach to markets. What President Reagan has called 'market-place magic' is related to financial innovation, capital mobility and the erosion of monetary rules and targets. In this approach, the ultimate disciplinarian is mobile capital, forcing governments to raise interest rates when the exchange rate spirals downwards. However, such discipline has volatile and sometimes highly unpredictable effects.

Even the United States now faces some balance of payments discipline because of capital market integration and the existence of rival reserve currencies and units of account. With high interest rates and floating rates, the gains from seignorage have been eroded. However, the United States is still, in Susan Strange's phrase an 'extraordinary' monetary power, and is uniquely well-placed to attract foreign capital. Whereas capital was being drained from many developing countries in the 1980s, it was pouring into the American economy. In 1985–87 dollar debts owed to Japanese investors were written down (devalued) by about one-third because of the rise in the value of the yen against the dollar. A similar fate befell many other foreign investors, although not by the same proportion.

The various problems in international monetary relations discussed in this chapter have been exacerbated by the growing scale and extent of capital mobility. None the less the 1980s witnessed the widespread easing of exchange controls and the extension of financial deregulation. Different financial centres have competed for business and bank branches with the assistance of their home governments. John Plender likens such financial competition to a zero-sum game between nations:

It is also a moot point whether competitive deregulation and effective supervision are at all compatible. Any attempt to clamp down on imprudent financial practice risks driving business and jobs away to other more lightly regulated centres.[28]

Susan Strange has echoed these concerns in the era of what she calls 'casino capitalism'. She sees the current system as a threat to ethical values, economic growth and political stability.[29] Strange advocates that the United States Federal Reserve should become a global lender of the last resort, but one which should increase the surveillance of and control over, global banking and finance. The Federal Reserve's new role would be made conditional on banks and financial firms meeting a stricter set of rules and divulging much more information. Other central banks could then follow the United States lead, and be incorporated into a new system.[30] Christopher Bliss has said of that this proposal hinges upon the continued dominance of the dollar:

The United States is to use the leverage implicit in the dollar's dominance in international exchange to regulate international banking. How long the dollar's dominance would survive such an attempt would be interesting to discover.[31]

Bliss implies that alternative centres of financial power and the growth in alternative reserve currencies are perhaps enough to put major American financial interests at risk. In other words, the vested interest of the United States 'banking complex' might object and attempt to veto the proposal. If Bliss is correct, it is difficult to see how the current monetary order will be substantially reformed, unless the world were to witness a major banking collapse, or more of the chaos in global stock markets which triggered the biggest crash in Wall Street and world-wide stock values since 1929, in October 1987.

NOTES

1. Susan Strange, *Casino Capitalism* (Oxford, Basil Blackwell, 1986).
2. H. G. Grubel, *The International Monetary System* (London, Penguin Books, 1977), 3rd edition, pp. 140–5.
3. Milton and Rose Friedman, *The Tyranny of the Status Quo* (Harmondsworth, Penguin Books, 1983), pp. 40–70.
4. Benjamin Cohen, *Organising the World's Money: The Political Economy of International Monetary Relations* (London, Macmillan, 1978).
5. David Calleo and Susan Strange, 'Money and World Politics', in Susan

Strange (ed.), *Paths to International Political Economy* (London, Allen and Unwin, 1984), p. 96.

6. C. Fred Bergsten and John Williamson, 'Exchange Rates and Trade Policy', in William Cline (ed.), *Trade Policy for the 1980s*, (Washington DC, Institute for International Economics/MIT Press, 1983), p. 104.
7. Cohen, op. cit., p. 74.
8. R Triffin, *Gold and the Dollar Crisis: the Future of Convertibility* (New Haven, Conn., Yale University Press, 1960).
9. M. Friedman, 'The Case for Flexible Exchange Rates', in Friedman, *Essays in Positive Economics* (Chicago, University of Chicago Press, 1953). On the influence of such views on United States officials, see J. S. Odell, *United States International Monetary Policy: Markets, Power and Ideas as Sources of Change* (Princeton NJ, Princeton University Press, 1982).
10. On this question see P. .Schnitzel, 'Testing for the Direction of Causation between the Domestic Monetary Base and the Euro Dollar System', *Weltwirtschaftliches Archiv* (1983), Vol. 119, pp. 616–28.
11. Richard Lapper, 'Policing the Fast Trade Lanes', *South*, October 1987, pp. 16–17.
12. David Calleo, *The Imperious Economy* (Cambridge, Mass., Harvard University Press, 1982).
13. M. M. Amen, 'Recurring Influences on Economic Policy-Making: Kennedy and Reagan Compared', in P. M. Johnson and W. R. Thompson (eds), *Rhythms in Politics and Economics* (New York, Praeger, 1985), pp. 181–200.
14. On this see Riccardo Parboni, *The Dollar and its Rivals: Recession, Inflation and International Finance* (London, New Left Books, 1980).
15. Peter Nunnenkamp, *The International Debt Crisis* (Brighton, Wheatsheaf Books, 1986).
16. William R. Cline, *International Debt* (Cambridge, Mass., MIT Press, 1985), pp. 6–7.
17. M. P. Claudon (ed.), *Multinational Institutions in the Global Debt Crisis* (Cambridge, Mass., Ballinger, 1986); H. S. Bienen and M. Gersovitz, 'Economic stabilisation, conditionality and political stability', *International Organisation* (1985), Vol. 39, pp. 729–54.
18. Frederick Clairmonte, 'Impossible debt on the road to global ruin', *The Guardian*, 9 January 1987.
19. T. Parfitt and S. Riley, 'The International Politics of African Debt', *Political Studies* (1987), Vol. 35, p. 2.
20. P. Conway, 'The Baker Plan and International Indebtedness', *The World Economy* (1987), Vol. 10, pp. 193–204.
21. For a Marxist perspective on the debt crisis, see P. K. Korner, G. Maars, T. Siebold and R. Tetzlaff, *The IMF and the Debt Crisis* (London, Zed Books, 1986).
22. Jeffry Frieden, 'Third World Indebted Industrialisation: International Finance and State Capitalism in Mexico, Brazil, Algeria and South Korea', *International Organisation* (1981), Vol. 35, pp. 407–31.
23. R. E. Wood , *From Marshall Aid to Debt Crisis* (Berkeley, Cal., University of California Press, 1986), p. 261.
24. M. Pastor Jr, 'The Effects of IMF Programs in the Third World: Debate and Evidence from Latin America', *World Development*, Vol. 15, pp. 244–62.
25. On the British case see J. Coakley and L. Harris, *The City of Capital* (Oxford, Blackwell, 1983).

26. On the Japanese case see M. Fujita and K. Ishigaki, 'The Internationalisation of Japanese Commercial Banking', in M. Taylor and N. Thrift (eds), *Multinationals and the Restructuring of the World Economy* (London, Croom Helm, 1986), pp. 193–227.
27. Clairmonte, op. cit.
28. John Plender, 'Deregulation gains add up to zero', *Financial Times*, 29 August 1985.
29. Strange, *Casino Capitalism*, p. 2.
30. Ibid., pp. 176–81.
31. Christopher Bliss, review of *Casino Capitalism*, in *The Economic Journal* (1987), Vol. 97, pp. 779–80.

11 Transnational Corporations and Global Production

1. INTRODUCTION

Because of their often immense size, decisions about the location of investment, production and technology by transnational firms influence not only the distribution of power resources between states and classes, but also the levels of aggregate welfare in various nations and throughout the world. The growth in the size and extent of transnational operations is the essence of the 'transnational stage' in the development of capitalism. Such firms are illustrative of some aspects of the power of internationally mobile capital. In consequence the analysis of transnational firms is not confined to this chapter, since their operations relate very directly to one of the two main themes of this book.

A widely accepted definition of a transnational corporation (sometimes called 'multinational' companies) is that of the United Nations Department of Economic and Social Affairs. This definition covers:

all enterprises which control assets – factories, mines, sales offices and the like – in two or more countries. This definition has the advantage that no important aspect of the phenomenon (e.g. finance or services) or of the problem (e.g. questions associated with nationally oriented enterprises or small firms) is arbitrarily excluded.[1]

Our discussion in this chapter is limited to those firms which are most active in global production and the transfer of technology (rather than banking and finance which we have discussed in the previous chapter). This is because we are concerned to analyse the production and knowledge structure of the global political economy, and the role of the transnational corporation in this context. What is common to the relationships between transnational companies and local states, producers and workers is the crucial importance of knowledge as a factor of production.

In placing the chapter on transnationals before that on trade we are giving priority to production and knowledge structures in our analysis of the dominant aspects of the contemporary global political economy. Transnational corporations, through their decisions on investments, sourcing and technical collaboration, are well placed to influence the volume and direction of trade and distribution of the gains from it.[2] This is partly because a substantial proportion of trade in manufactures and raw materials now takes the form of 'intra-firm' trade between the subsidiaries of transnational corporations.[3] It is also because they dominate the marketing of many commodities, such as wheat, coffee, cocoa, pineapples, tobacco, copper, iron ore and bauxite.[4] Further, through their investments and training programmes transnational firms serve to change the international distribution of factor endowments, notably of capital, skilled labour and knowledge. As a result they modify, as well as respond to, sources of comparative advantage. Finally, trade policies have increasingly become part of the wider industrial strategies of states. Such policies are often aimed at increased output and productivity, and gaining a favoured position in the global structure of production. In this respect national policies on investment grants, government spending on infrastructure, as well as trade barriers (or exemptions from them) are different ways of encouraging foreign firms to locate their production in a given country.

2. THE NATURE AND DEVELOPMENT OF TRANSNATIONAL CORPORATIONS

Transnational firms are of three main types: those in extraction, manufacturing and services. Before World War II, most foreign direct investment was in extraction and plantations, such as in oil, primary products and tropical fruits. This reflected both the demand of industrialising countries for raw materials and the political dominance of the European powers in Asia and Africa and of the United States in most of the Western Hemisphere. The colonial precursors of the modern corporation, such as the British East India Company, had not only considerable resources in finance and technology, they also had what were in effect standing armies which could be used to reinforce their economic power.

Modern transnational corporations do not possess such direct military capacities (although many of them produce military technologies), and therefore often rely on political influence, market power, control over finance and technology, and the structural power of the market to reinforce their control. None the less, the vast expansion of transnational activity since 1945 has taken place in the context of the post-war international economic order, itself partly founded upon America's global military power. Moreover, since World War II, foreign direct investment has grown much more in manufacturing than in primary products, particularly where developing countries are concerned. Post-war trends are partly reflected in Table 11.1.

John Dunning has estimated that the stock of foreign direct investment rose from US$14.3 billion in 1914 to $386.2 billion in 1978. Of this, the most rapid growth, a six-fold increase, took place between 1960 and 1978.[5] In effect, by the mid-1970s the world was returning to a similar situation to that which prevailed in 1914, in terms of the weight of foreign investment in the world economy, after a precipitate fall between the two World Wars. However, the post-war growth took place in the context of the longest and most protracted boom in modern economic history.

George Modelski has summarised some of the post-war changes in terms of a shift from an economy which was essentially a World War II-type military-industrial complex (involving motors, steel and aviation) to an economy where most of the major firms were in the energy field, as well as in electronics and computers. None the less, these firms still embodied what Modelski described as 'the sinews of contemporary military power'.[6] Since he wrote, transnational banks have become increasingly prominent, especially Japanese banks. By June 1986, there were seven banking and financial concerns in the world's 20 largest public companies.[7] According to Modelski, by a conservative estimate, the world's 50 largest industrial corporations accounted for between 10 and 15 per cent of the industrial output of the non-communist world in 1975, and they probably controlled as much as one-third of all international investment.[8] By 1987, transnational corporations employed 30 million of

Table 11.1: Major industry groups among the biggest 50 industrials

Industry group	Number of firms among top 50 firms		Per cent share of top 50 sales		Per cent change in
	1955	1975	1955	1975	1955–75
Oil	11	17	27	46	+19
Electrical	3	7	6	12	+ 6
Chemical	3	7	5	9	+ 4
Steel	6	5	10	6	− 4
Aerospace	5	—	4	—	− 4
Auto and tyre	9	10	30	21	− 9
Consumer	9	4	15	6	− 9

Source: George Modelski, *Transnational Corporations and World Order* (San Fancisco, W. W. Freeman, 1979), p. 51.

the 90 million manufacturing workers in the countries of the Organisation for Economic Cooperation and Development (OECD).[9]

The evolution of the biggest 50 firms reflects the changes in the post-war industrial structure. Since 1975 companies in information technology and telecommunications have risen to challenge the energy complex and the auto manufacturers within the rankings. Moreover, since the 1950s American dominance in the sphere of transnationalisation has been undermined by the rise of West European and Japanese companies, although the latter have moved much more slowly into international production, preferring to focus their efforts on exporting Japanese manufactures. Until the mid-1970s the most internationally-oriented type of Japanese transnational was the trading company.

Transnationals are of three organisational types: vertically integrated, horizontally integrated and conglomerate. Vertically integrated transnational corporations are common in minerals where they are often involved in the extractive and smelting stages. In petroleum they are often involved in the distributive stage, owning many petrol stations. In manufacturing there has been a growth of transnational corporations which make components in certain countries and assemble them in others, for example Japanese and American electronics firms have assembly plants in 'cheap labour' countries like Taiwan.

Horizontal integration occurs when a firm has the same sort of plant in many countries. An example of this is Union Carbide which has many chemical subsidiaries, the most infamous of which was at Bhopal in India, where the terrible accident occurred in 1984. An example of a conglomerate firm is the British-based Lonrho which has interests in newspapers, mining, oil, ranching, brewing and plantations, amongst others. Lonrho is especially active in black Africa.[10]

Transnational companies vary enormously in terms of their orientation towards global production and sales. A firm may be called a transnational even if it has only one or two foreign subsidiaries accounting for only a small proportion of its output. By contrast, some firms carry out most of their production and trade outside of the parent country, such as the Swiss transnational, Nestlé. Some transnational firms only have subsidiaries in one region, whereas others are more truly 'global' with branches all over the world, in twenty countries or more. Further, the outlook and planning of the firm may be more or less 'global' in character. For example, Ford and General Motors have developed automobile models (the 'world car') which can be marketed in more or less any country which has reasonable roads, as well as constructed in a variety of production locations. The United Nations study referred to above has attempted to categorise such variations as follows:

On the basis of their orientation, corporations are also distinguished into 'ethnocentric' (home-country-oriented), 'polycentric' (host-country-oriented) or 'geocentric' (world-oriented). When internationalism is taken to the limit the corporation may be considered to be 'anational' and hence be referred to as 'denationalised', 'supranational' or a 'cosmocorp'.[11]

As regards ownership and control, however, the dominant pattern is national, with relatively few instances of sharing of such control with non-nationals, at least until the 1970s and 1980s – hence our use of the term 'transnational', as opposed to 'multinational' in this book. (The latter term may carry the implication that control and ownership is shared fairly equally between a number of different countries, which is still relatively rare.) One implication of such ownership and control patterns is that governments of 'host' countries are sometimes fearful that the foreign firm will limit their economic sovereignty and even serve the foreign policy of the parent country's government.

In practice the transnational corporation, like other firms, is most concerned about making profits, corporate growth and increasing its market share. In pursuit of these goals its interests may diverge from those of both the host and the parent countries. However, managers may sometimes be so loyal to the government policy of their parent country that they are willing to sacrifice some of their potential profits for national goals. For example, Japanese car firms consistently bought tyres from Japanese producers in the 1950s and 1960s, even though their products were substantially inferior to those made by firms in America and Europe. However, by the 1970s, the quality gap between Japanese manufacturers and those overseas was closed.

As has been indicated, transnational companies are also responsible for the bulk of the world's foreign direct investment. Of such investments, the bulk is located within the developed capitalist countries (over 75 per cent of the total stock by 1975), with the remaining proportion in developing countries. In addition:

The share of foreign capital received by the developing countries has steadily fallen from a peak of around 30% in 1967; this mainly reflects the expropriation of assets of foreign based multinational enterprises, especially in the oil and other extractive industries, and the increasing attractiveness of developed countries as maufacturing outlets.[12]

As John Stopford and others note, not only is foreign direct investment heavily concentrated in the developed nations, but also within the OECD grouping four countries take the bulk of such investment:

Of the developed countries, Canada, the United States, Great Britain and West Germany are the leading host countries to the affiliates of foreign multinational enterprises; in the late 1970s they accounted for nearly two-thirds of foreign direct investment in developed countries and nearly one-half of all foreign direct investment. In the 1970s, the growth of inward direct investment was fastest in the United States and West Germany, and slowest in Canada.[13]

In 1978, the United States was the leading country of origin, accounting for 45.5 per cent of all foreign direct investment, although its share had fallen since the 1960s. The next largest country of origin was the United Kingdom, but its position was being strongly challenged by West German and Japanese transnationals, whose combined investment totals had risen from 3.9 per cent in 1967 to 15.9 per cent in 1978.[14]

Since the 1950s there has been a remarkable rise in the number of subsidiaries, especially in manufacturing. The biggest 500 transnational firms now hold at least 80 per cent of all foreign affilitates (subsidiaries).[15] In the early 1970s, production by the affiliates of American transnationals was almost four times greater than the value of United States exports. By 1970, 62 per cent of United States exports were by such firms and 34 per cent of United States imports.[16] This was because the international production of transnationals was growing more rapidly than both international trade and world output.

In 1977, the United States had 2826 transnationals; Britain had 1706 and West Germany had 1450. The American share of total transnational firms from developed countries was 26.3 per cent. The United States share of total affiliates of transnationals was 32.6 per cent compared to 26.5 per cent for Britain.[17] Since 1977, Japanese transnationals have grown rapidly as have some from Third World countries, such as Tachung from Taiwan. In consequence, it would appear that American domination of the transnational phenomenon has been declining. None the less, American transnationals tend to be the more efficient and profitable firms within the American economy. These firms performed impressively in the 1960s and 1970s, much more so than did the United States economy as a whole:

The competitiveness of US firms, as measured by their share in world exports in manufactured goods, decreased much less than did that of the US as a geographic entity. The share of US multinationals in US exports (up to 1977), including exports by all their foreign affiliates, actually increased. The reasons for the difference are that US multinationals increased their exports from the US faster than did firms with no overseas operations and increased exports from their foreign affiliates still more.... The implication is that the decline in US shares in world manufactures exports in the late 1960s and 1970s was not, as sometimes alleged, to be found in deficiencies in American management or declines in American technological leadership.[18]

Such findings may not have held good in the 1980s when the share of the Pacific Rim countries, notably South Korea and Taiwan, has increased and Japanese companies have made further inroads into the American market. In addition, simply concentrating on export shares is an inadequate basis for judging comparative firm performance. Direct investment by non-American firms has enabled them to increase their American market shares, as in the case of Japanese car companies which have set up plants in America. From 1985 there was a huge increase in Japanese direct investment in the United States at the same time as the dollar declined and trade barriers rose. Many European firms, notably British ones, had joined in the rush to invest much earlier, as had Canadian investors. Whereas much of the Japanese investment involved new factories, the Europeans more often took the the takeover route into the United States. Recent developments are partly reflected in Table 11.2.

Table 11.2: Publicly recorded takeovers in the United States

Purchasers	Number of deals						
	1980	1981	1982	1983	1984	1984	1986
United Kingdom	50	80	54	41	48	78	89
Canada	57	62	36	28	36	25	64
West Germany	14	14	6	2	4	12	19
Japan	9	9	4	6	6	9	16
Sweden	8	7	4	3	8	7	11
Netherlands	6	8	5	7	5	17	9
France	20	14	12	7	7	4	6

Source: Financial Times, 8 August 1987.

Table 11.3: Average foreign content of the world's 350 largest industrial corporations (in millions of US dollars and per cent)

Item and year	Total ($)	Foreign	Foreign share (per cent)
Sales 1971	1,769	527	30
1980	7,084	2,822	40
Net assets			
1971	956	300	31
1980	2,417	803	33
Net earnings			
1971	83	41	49
1980	266	140	53
Employment			
1971	63,318	23,958	39
1980	68,669	31,914	46

Source: Michael Taylor and Nigel Thrift (eds), *Multinationals and the Restructuring of the World Economy* (London, Croom Helm, 1986), p. 2. Based on United Nations, Centre on Transnational Corporations, statistics.

Partly because of the substantial appreciation of the Japanese yen since 1985, by the middle of 1986 Japan had 33 of the world's 100 largest companies, compared to 50 for the United States.[19]

A more general trend has been for the largest industrial firms to become progressively more transnational and global in character as Table 11.3 shows. This is also true for British transnationals, as is illustrated by Table 11.4.

Table 11.4: Average foreign content of 50 of the largest British-based industrial corporations (in millions of pounds sterling and per cent)

Item and Year	Total (£ million)		Foreign Share (per cent)
Total sales 1981/82	1,440	Overseas production as per cent of sales	44
Overseas production 1981/82	639	Exports as per cent of sales	15
Exports 1981/82*	209		
Total employment	43,119		—
Foreign employment**	17,851		41

Notes: *Only 42 corporations provided export figures.
** only 45 corporations provided foreign employment figures.

Source: Taylor and Thrift, op. cit., p. 2. Based on Labour Research statistics.

Transnational firms also vary as to how far they are involved in production activities which do not conform to the usual type of direct foreign investment, that is involving a majority ownership of subsidiaries (in terms of effective control of operations this may mean upwards of 30 per cent, but may sometimes reach 100 per cent ownership). Unlike portfolio investment, control over production and sales is the essence of direct investments. It involves a package (or 'bundle') of knowledge, skills and funds.

Transnationals sometimes engage in joint ventures, where control is in principle shared (although the transnational firm, because of its expertise, may dominate day-to-day management). In a third type of foreign activity, the management contract, ownership is not in the hands of the transnational but it holds most of the the key management positions. Yet another possibility is the turn-key project, where the transnational is paid for supplying and establishing an entire plant and for training the local workforce. Here the transnational company does not have any equity stake in the plant. In the latter case, a limited relationship may continue after the plant is handed over to the local owners, in the form of management consultancy and technical collaboration. Sometimes, transnational companies may simply buy inputs and products from overseas suppliers. For example, local producers may supply the transnational on the basis of sub-contracting. Frequently, local producers have become dependent on such foreign customers. Indeed, in some cases transnational companies have been much more than customers, sometimes supplying loans, inputs and technical advice to local producers.

As has been noted, one aspect of transnational activity has involved the growth of intra-firm trade. The scale and significance of this trade is hard to interpret, since most of the available data is aggregative, but its scope is considerable. Excluding petroleum from the figures, Murray has concluded:

It would seem that, contrary to widely-held views, vertically integrated transnational enterprises may not be taking over increasing shares of developing country trade. At least as far as US-based enterprises are concerned, the much discussed increasing internationalisation and vertical integration of production is confined to Western Europe and Canada.[20]

This form of vertical integration is also supplemented by trends towards conglomeration and more recently towards growing collaboration and joint ventures between transnationals from different countries. For example, General Motors has a joint venture in California with Toyota. Ford has a stake in Mitsubishi Motors. Collaborative research agreements have been signed between General Motors and Isuzu for the development of a new truck and between Ford and Kawasaki for the design of new assembly production systems. Similar collaboration arrangements exist in telecommunications equipment and aircraft.[21] While arrangements of this sort may reduce (share) risks and realise economies of scale in research, they also promote tendencies towards concentration and oligopoly.

3. THEORIES OF THE TRANSNATIONAL CORPORATION

Theories about the growth and behaviour of transnational corporations have proliferated since the 1960s. Initially, theorists focused on the foreign direct investment of American firms, especially manufacturing ones, in Western Europe. These firms were often in oligopolistic industries which, in the United States, were approaching market saturation. The financial, technological and managerial advantages of these American firms enabled them to establish themselves in Western Europe and elsewhere. The

Marxist writer, Stephen Hymer, pioneered the transnational oligopoly approach. Hymer used it to stress the hierarchical and exploitative character of transnationals, with power concentrated in the metropolitan headquarters.[22] Early theories of the 'product cycle' sought to explain why, and at what point in a firm's development, it would begin to invest and produce abroad.[23]

Early theories focused mainly on economic and geographic factors, in their explanations of why American companies chose to invest in Western Europe. Product-cycle theory highlighted the 'maturing' of a product as its production technology became standardised and known abroad. Foreign direct investment was therefore seen, for the original leading firms, as a defensive strategy which attempted to secure or maintain market share by producing in countries where production costs were, at a given stage of the product cycle, lower than those prevailing in the technological leaders. In addition, foreign direct investment was motivated by the need to overcome the effects of tariff and trade barriers, by producing within, rather than outside them.

Another way of representing this was to suggest that 'location-specific' factors relating to cost, combined with 'ownership-specific' advantages to make it more profitable for American firms to produce in Europe than to go on exporting from the United States. Amongst the location-specific factors were labour costs and the taxation policies of governments. Just as low effective company tax rates and special grants may have attracted transnationals to Europe, generous American tax allowances on foreign investment income also encouraged American firms to invest abroad. For example, in the American case provisions were made to avoid 'double-taxation' of overseas profits, and extra allowances were granted for foreign investments in oil.

A firm with a technological advantage has another option to exporting and direct investment: it can engage in licensing and technical collaboration agreements. However, this type of strategy runs the risk of building up strong foreign competitors in the future (as American firms have discovered with regard to the Japanese). From a monopolistic viewpoint, direct investment may be a preferable way to maximise 'rents' to technological knowledge and related human capital (highly-skilled labour) within the firm. Attempts to explain the basis for such strategies, with reference to how a company is organised, has led to the development of theories which pay more attention to the internal aspects of transnational firms, whilst still paying attention to the types of factors which concerned product-cycle theory.

Organisation theory, when applied to transnational companies, pays particular attention to vertically integrated firms and the way in which the coordination of successive stages of production can bring economies of scale and reduce risks. This is in contrast to a situation where there are separate firms at each stage of production who negotiate at 'arm's length'. For example, where secret commercial information is concerned, coordination between two stages may be at its greatest if they are controlled by the same firm. Thus where highly-specific equipment, geared to one customer is involved, the investment will appear less risky if the customer is part of the same firm. Loyalty is 'built in'. John Dunning has tried to combine a theory of the advantages of 'internalisation' with the earlier stress on ownership specific advantages and location-specific factors in an eclectic theory often referred to as the OLI (organisation, location, internalisation) paradigm.[24]

In the light of these theories it is appropriate to stress the role of technological changes in facilitating the rise of the transnational corporation. The emergence of mass-production and research-intensive industries in the twentieth century contributed to the growth of entry barriers and oligopoly. It was in such industries as chemicals, automobiles, computers and electronics that manufacturing transnationals were most dominant after World War II. For much of the twentieth century the pattern of industrial growth had shifted towards such industries.

More recently, transnationalisation has developed in a range of service industries, notably finance and banking, data processing, telecommunications and in the media. Satellite communication and data processing have made technically possible the global integration of financial markets, as well as access to global data bases and the spread of information processing. More generally, the cost-effectiveness of internalisation and vertical integration of all transnational companies has been greatly enhanced by improved transport, and communications and data processing capacity.

Transnationalisation has also made some headway in retailing, a sector which, tourism apart, is not engaged in international trade since proximity to the customer is usually essential. In the case of a successful British firm, J. Sainsbury, with extensive holdings in supermarkets and other retailing outlets, the company adopted the strategy of purchasing foreign companies which had developed new technology which could improve productivity.

In this case the product-cycle explanation for overseas expansion, that those firms which are knowledge-leaders expand abroad to maximise their profit return on their research and development, was reversed. However, this case may be seen as significant if it were placed in a wider theory of transnationalisation. Apart from risk-avoidance and market control, in a situation characterised by significant competitive pressures, firms must both seek out and develop knowledge in order to survive and grow. As Modelski and others have noted, the largest companies have often been the most conservative, preferring to avoid risks, using their financial power to buy up younger, smaller and more innovative enterprises which develop new ideas and applications. This search for new technologies is now world-wide. In order to finance this pursuit of knowledge firms need vast funds, since companies compete to buy up technology (as well as other potentially profitable resources). To finance such purchases this may require sales in many countries, particularly the major markets of North America, Western Europe and Japan. These two factors combine to increase the incentive to transnationalise operations.[25] Foreign investment, if it is politically possible, may be the most effective way to obtain the sales, the funds for research and, sometimes (through takeover), the technology.

Over time, given the right kinds of global political conditions, transnational firms will gain relative to purely national ones. This is by virtue of the fact that transnational firms benefit from economies of scale, internalisation, access to more varied and cheaper sources of capital, as well as lower effective tax rates. Lower tax rates are due to the ability of transnational companies to use 'transfer-pricing' techniques. These techniques involve the under-pricing and/or over-pricing of materials, components, goods, equipment and loans which take place between branches of the same firm in different countries. Therefore transfer prices may differ considerably from what are called 'arm's length' prices, that is prices which reflect market conditions. In consequence of the transnationals' ability to engage in such intra-firm trading, in a country where corporate taxes are high, company profits can be made to appear lower than they actually are. This can be done, for example, by under-pricing components transferred to subsidiaries in other, low-tax countries. In effect, the profits can be made to appear where it is most convenient for the firm. Since some governments lose tax revenue this is a major bone of contention between them and the transnationals which are practising tax avoidance.

The theories which are outlined above all focus on mainly economic explanations for the growth and power of transnational companies. However, a fuller appreciation of political conditions is essential for fully explaining the rise of and limits to, the power and growth of transnationals. Some of these conditions were outlined in chapter 7 in our discussion of the power of capital. For example, in the past, some communist governments have not allowed foreign direct investment, while many capitalist countries have prevented significant foreign ownership in large parts of their economies, especially in strategic industries. The major barriers are created by states pursuing highly mercantilist strategies, or even autarkic forms of economic development. In addition to political conditions, location decisions are affected by cultural factors such as the historical experience gained in the colonial period and language. For example, a large proportion of early Japanese direct investment was in Korea, Taiwan and South-East Asia.

In practice most foreign direct investment since 1945 has been between developed capitalist countries in which liberal economic ideas have been entrenched (the major exception was Japan). These countries have also been close allies of the United States, which has pressed for an open door policy. America's allies are not only dependent on America for their security, their producers often also depend on access to the vast American market. As such, their government policies are unlikely to substantially discriminate against foreign firms, especially American ones. In other words, a crucial condition for the power of transnational capital has been the way that the international economic order has been associated with the American-led alliance systems, especially NATO.

4. CONFLICTING PERSPECTIVES ON TRANSNATIONAL CORPORATIONS

There is more controversy over the interpretation of the political, economic and cultural effects of transnationals than there has been over explanations of their rise. There are basically two arguments: the first suggests that the effects of transnationalisation have been generally beneficial. The second sees such effects as undermining autonomy and national development, increasing economic inequality in the host nations, and as such denying economic sovereignty to a range of countries.[26]

Liberal political economists and some Marxists have stressed the ways in which the presence of transnational companies and foreign investment raises efficiency and increases economic growth. The rapid growth of the West European countries in the 1950s and 1960s, is attributed partly to the influx of American firms. Similarly, the success of newly industrialising countries in the Third World is partly explained in terms of foreign investment and policies which have attracted transnationals. However, a correlation between direct investment and growth is not proof of causation, nor does it establish the weight to be attached to the role of transnationals. Where the conditions for market growth are seen as favourable, and where transnational companies feel satisfied with the political character and stability of the host nation, direct investment is most likely to occur. Success breeds success, with agglomeration economies being realised at attractive 'growth poles'.[27]

Liberal political economists do not argue that foreign direct investment necessarily promotes efficiency and welfare. They argue that if such investment is simply attracted by trade barriers and subsidies to capital, then it may promote inefficient import substitution that does not generate economies of scale, or do much to increase employment. The poor growth record of most Latin American countries is often cited here. Brazil is sometimes seen as a partial exception, because of its size (economies of scale being easier to realise) and greater export orientation for much of the period after 1964.

Most Marxists and dependency theorists have stressed the unequal and distorted nature of the growth associated with the transnationals. What has been called the 'branch factory' economy is dependent on outside suppliers, and is controlled from the headquarters of transnationals (Canada is a good example of this). In the Third World, a nation's economy may lack integration because of large imports of capital goods and spare parts. However, a large country like Brazil has achieved a substantial measure of self-sufficiency in capital goods, partly due to foreign investment in the machinemaking sector. Where Brazil has conformed to radical expectations is in its capital-intensive bias. This has been linked to success in developing large-scale and high-technology industries. Above all, radical writers point to the unequal distribution of income and wealth in Latin American countries where there is a large stock of foreign direct investment. However, severe inequality has a long history in Latin America, preceding the influx of foreign direct investment. National policies, including low effective taxation of the wealthy, have done little to lessen inequalities in most Latin American countries. These policies might have been adopted even in the absence of foreign investment.[28]

Ultimately, different interpretations of the role and impact of transnationals have to focus on the relationship between these firms and the states they deal with. How far are the policies, strategies and goals of the state *influenced by transnationals? How far can states* influence the behavior of transnational corporations so as to meet 'national goals'? In answering the first question it is necessary to consider a variety of channels of influence which are available to transnational companies, and how these might be used. These include: (i) direct political influence within a country; (ii) indirect political influence, through the behaviour of an external power or organisation; and (iii) structural power stemming from certain features of the global political economy seen as a world system. (See chapter 7 on these.)

According to Richard Barnet and Ronald Muller all states may be seen as increasingly subject to the power and influence of transnational corporations. None can escape their 'global reach'.[29] All countries may need to attract some foreign direct investment and find the best way to deal with foreign firms. In coming to terms with transnationals, all states face constraints, but as with the animals in Orwell's farm, some are more constrained than others. A more differentiated view of things is that the power of a transnational company, or of transnational capital as a class *fraction* varies relative to the type of state under consideration. In world systems' terminology, it would depend on whether the state in question is in the core, periphery or semi-periphery.

However, put this way the power of transnationals appears as an external force, whereas within states, especially 'core' ones, the influence of transnational capital may be considerable. Indeed, some Marxist writers, like Harry Magdoff, seem to assume that the American state is dominated by the interests of American transnationals.[30] Thus while the external aspects of the direct power of transnationals may be less significant in relative terms in the larger 'core' states, within such countries their structural power may be at its greatest, especially at the ideological level.

As we have seen in chapter 7, partly by virtue of the widespread legitimacy of ideas supportive of the capitalist system in countries such as the United States, Japan, West Germany, France and Britain, and the impact of business confidence and the business climate on the level of economic activity and the behaviour of the state, the power of capital may have achieved a near-hegemonic status. Providing that the basic liberal rules of economic activity are maintained, the internationalisation of the business climate means that the structural power of internationally mobile capital may be very great indeed. This argument is the other side to the coin of the dominant realist interpretation of the power of transnational companies. Realists stress the autonomy of the state and the dominant influence of ideas about the 'national interest' which prioritise security. In this view, transnationals are able to flourish in so far as it suits the most powerful states. The argument outlined here and in chapter 7 is that there cannot be a straightforward separation of the forces of state and civil society in these countries. Therefore, the state's policies should be analysed not simply from a 'national' point of view. The policies pursued by states, and the constraints within which these are developed (both internal and external) are also related to class interests, and the interests of fractions of classes. This point is taken further in the next section.

5. TRANSNATIONALS, THE UNITED STATES GOVERNMENT AND AMERICAN FOREIGN ECONOMIC POLICY

Given its power and influence in the global political economy, the United States case is of special importance. Political sociologists investigating the presence of business interests within the American political system have long concluded that business is well represented in both major parties, especially the Republicans, in what the Librarian of Congress and distinguished historian Daniel Boorstin once called the 'great democracy of cash'. In America, at least since the late nineteenth century, there has been a consistent circulation of political and business leaders to and from the upper echelons of the American executive branch and corporate sector, a fact well documented in recent years by Thomas Dye's extensive and detailed studies of elites in the United States.[31] In addition, in many sectors of the economy, the United States government has devolved regulatory power to large corporate interests, in effect extending the economic authority of private business into political authority.

In Presidence Carter's cabinet, for example, there were at least three members who had been on the board of IBM, the world's biggest industrial corporation. Many of the general interests of blue-chip corporate capital in the United States are represented on the private Conference Board. This influential organisation provides not only advice and policy recommendations to the United States government, but also many of its members (who are the chief executives of the biggest American companies) take high government office. A good example of this type of figure was Reagan's second Secretary of State George Schultz, who had been Dean of the University of Chicago School of Business and a Vice-President of the world's largest private company, the California-based Bechtel Corporation (Reagan's first Secretary of Defence, Caspar Weinberger, was also a Vice-President at Bechtel at the same time as Schultz).

Dye also adds that the most powerful man in the United States in the 1980s was not President Reagan, but a private individual, David Rockefeller. The vast Rockefeller holdings stretch into virtually every key sector in the American economy, and through philanthropic foundations, American society. In addition, Rockefeller is the North American Chairman of the prestigious Trilateral Commission (which brings together many of the political and business leaders of North America, Japan and Western Europe) and of the influential New York Council on Foreign Relations (CFR). CFR members, often with links to Rockefeller activities (such as John Foster Dulles and Henry Kissinger) have traditionally filled the position of Secretary of State, as well as a large number of other key positions (usually Secretary of Treasury) in American administrations since the CFR's foundation in the 1920s.

The place of large-scale corporate interests (most large American companies are transnationals) in the American system is captured in Figure 11.1. In Gramscian terms, this might be viewed as the framework of a hegemonic, historic bloc in the United States. The figure further indicates the centrality of civil society in the American political process, and the crucial importance of the corporate sector in generating much of the resources which shape the contours of policy in the United States. Policy planning groups are organisations like the Conference Board and the CFR. Because of these and other links between the American state and

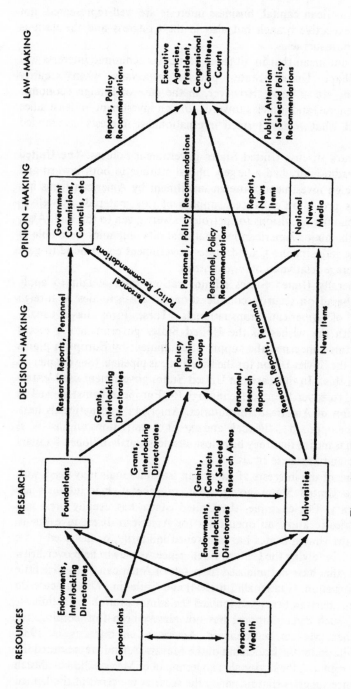

Figure 11.1: Corporate influence in the US policy-making process

Source: Thomas Dye, *Who's Running America?* (Englewood Cliffs, NJ, Prentice-Hall, 1979), p. 212.

large-scale American capital, business interests are well represented, not only in the executive branch but also in the Congress and the various government bureaucracies.

This does not mean that in all cases particular economic interests will inevitably shape United States policies, especially when security considerations are at issue. However, in the case of foreign economic policies in general, and policies towards foreign investment, at least since World War II, what we have termed 'internationalist' interests have tended to prevail.

We shall now discuss United States government policies. The United States has traditionally had a largely liberal attitude to both inward and outward foreign investment. Foreign investment by American firms has been seen as providing enhanced supplies of raw materials as well as profits. Special tax provisions for petroleum were given to this end. Also, in so far as the major American international oil companies were able to dominate the industry the United States government could hope to gain strategic leverage relative to other countries.

More generally United States administrations have sought to apply restrictions based on security considerations to the activities of foreign subsidiaries of American transnationals. These firms have usually complied with the wishes of the United States government. A recent example of this concerned the supply of equipment by European plants and firms to the Soviet Union for the Siberian gas pipeline. (See chapter 15 for detail on this.) In this case the United States government used 'extra-territoriality' to cover licensed technology (to European firms) as well as the production of American subsidiaries. American transnationals have generally been opposed to the scale and extent of restrictions on East-West trade. This has meant that they have lost business worth billions of dollars to European and Japanese rivals.

While some of the interests of American transnationals may clash with those of the United States government, in general their interests are complementary. For example, the United States has usually pressured other countries to allow an open door for American direct investment. Sometimes the United States has intervened militarily, or has used more covert means, involving the Central Intelligence Agency to help overthrow governments that have nationalised the assets of American firms with little or no compensation. Guatemala (in 1954) and Chile (in 1973) are cases in point where American firms had lobbied the administration for action.

However, such direct support has not always been forthcoming, for example when Mexico nationalised American oil interests in 1938. Whereas Chile under the leadership of the Marxist Allende represented the 'communist menace', the nationalist government of Mexico did not. Much of the evidence suggests that normally the security concerns of the United

States government dovetail with the economic interests of American transnationals. When there has been a clash between the two, the state has usually, but not always, prevailed. An example of the latter was when in 1973–74 American oil majors helped enforce the Arab embargo on supplies to the United States (see chapter 13 for discussion of this).

Another way of looking at this is the argument that American transnationals may work against long-term United States interests even when there is no conflict with the administration. Robert Gilpin has argued that the outflow of direct investment from the US in the 1960s and 1970s has weakened the material basis of American dominance.[32] Lack of investment in the United States has slowed its growth rate while technology transfer abroad by transnationals has reduced the productivity gap between the United States and other countries. In addition, he noted that foreign investment has strengthened the position and earnings of capital relative to labour. Foreign investment outflows have helped to increased economic inequality in the United States (see Chapter 16 for detailed discussions of this). We suggest that this last point of his needs to be seen as one instance of a more global phenomenon: greater mobility of capital in all its forms works to the relative disadvantage of labour that is immobile. Real wages have shown little or no growth for the vast majority of Americans since the 1960s (see Tables 16.2 and 16.3), a period which saw a massive wave of foreign direct investment by American transnationals.

In view of the threats to jobs and real incomes which have been generated by these outflows of capital, American unions have increasingly lobbied for restrictions on outward foreign investment. However, reflecting the weakness of organised labour in the United States, these attempts have failed, such as the one embodied in the Burke-Hartke Bill of the early 1970s. Since the early 1970s, American unions have further declined in political weight. This failure may be contrasted with the success of American transnationals in obtaining legislation to create tariff loopholes for their overseas production when it is imported into America.[33]

While in the 1980s liberal economic ideas have been challenged on nationalist grounds in America, with a large number of protectionist Bills in Congress, the restrictions sought have been on trade rather than on the activities of multinationals (across-the-board protectionist measures faced a presidential veto). Also, in so far as higher trade barriers encouraged an influx of foreign firms into the United States, this may serve to reduce domestic concern over foreign investment by American workers. One attempt was made by the United States to place restrictions on the activity of transnationals, by prohibiting bribery of foreign customers, following the Lockheed bribery scandal of 1975–76. These restrictions were actually intended to support transnational activities in the long run, since it was feared that the legitimacy of transnational business was being undermined by the scale of corrupt practices. However, legislation was repealed in the late 1970s after a government study revealed that American companies had lost considerable business in the Third World to European and Japanese competition, where similar legislation had not been enacted.

American attitudes to inward direct investment have been and remain very liberal, except for certain 'strategic industries' such as aviation, shipbuilding, nuclear output and communications. In 1987 two proposed takeovers of American firms with some defence business were vetoed for security reasons by the Pentagon, but many more defence contractors have been taken over by non-American companies, albeit sometimes with Pentagon-approved proxies on the board to filter out sensitive technical data and prevent it reaching the foreign owners.

Similar practices to those of the United States are to be found in other capitalist nations. Britain has long been very liberal except for certain restrictions for balance of payments purposes which were gradually eased in the 1960s and 1970s before being abolished in 1979. Indeed, even traditionally nationalist countries like France and Japan, have moved in the American direction. Ironically, perhaps the most striking difference between the United States and Japan on the one hand and Europe on the other, is the vast and growing array of national financial inducements that the West European states employ in competing with each other to attract transnationals. However, in using trade barriers as an inducement to pull in foreign (especially Japanese) investment there are many similarities between Europe and the United States. Furthermore, at the state and city levels within the United States, there is substantial political competition to attract firms.

With regard to outward direct investment in less developed countries there are many parallels between France, Britain and the United States. All use bilateral aid and trade credits to promote and protect foreign investment (as well as trade). French military interventions and bases in Africa have been in or close to areas where French firms have interests.

With the interpenetration of foreign investment between the leading capitalist countries, there is good reason to expect a strong and continuing consensus in each of these countries on the importance of keeping an open door to foreign investment. Nevertheless, France and Japan have tended to be more nationalistic and restrictive in their approach to foreign transnational companies, in contrast to the more liberal stance of Britain, West Germany and the United States. However, there are strong signs that this situation has changed recently. Where both competition and conflict has arisen, is over the range of investment incentives and conditions, especially when it affects trade patterns. An example of this is when special tax concessions are made conditional on a substantial part of the output of a subsidiary being exported. The use and abuse of such 'performance requirements' is one issue the United States intended to raise during the Uruguay Round of trade negotiations in the late 1980s.[34]

6. TRANSNATIONAL COMPANIES AND THIRD WORLD STATES

Many writers have noted a contrast in policies on foreign direct investment between the developed and developing countries. In particular, developing countries seem to have been more suspicious of, and restrictive towards transnational firms, especially those engaged in producing primary products, such as minerals. Many developing countries have nationalised mines and plantations owned by transnationals. By contrast, developing nations often have sought to attract foreign direct investment in manufacturing in various ways. Tax concessions, government-subsidised services, trade barriers and localised exemption from these barriers (as in export processing zones) have been adopted by many countries, notably in the 1970s and 1980s. Despite these general patterns of response, there are national differences in policy towards transnational firms that need to be explained. For example, India has pursued more restrictive policies towards transnationals than have Kenya or Singapore, although some easing of Indian policy has occurred in the 1980s.

The North–South contrast can be explained in terms of a variety of factors which Robert Kudrle, using a public choice approach, has classified under four headings: impact transparency, ideological consonance, the distribution of costs and benefits, and the institutional context.[35] The ideological consonance between transnational firms and governments tends to be greater in the North than the South. In the South attitudes are less favourable towards the market mechanism, competition and sometimes private enterprise. This is because many developing countries have viewed international trade as a market system which has worked better for the North than the South. Dependency theory has contributed to such views. Thus restrictions on private enterprise, especially transnational firms, are often seen as necessary either to obtain a greater share of the benefits from trade and foreign investment and/or to enable the development of infant industries to take place.

In India, apart from general restrictions on big business, policies have discriminated against foreign firms while a large public industrial sector has been developed, partly to avoid 'excessive' dependence on transnational firms in such industries as chemicals, pharmaceuticals and oil refining and extraction. Even a pro-capitalist state such as Brazil built up a large public sector, including industrial enterprises, in the 1960s and

1970s. This reflects the continuing importance of nationalism, not least among Third World bureaucrats.

Impact transparency concerns the extent of public awareness of the opportunity costs of restricting or excluding transnational firms and therefore of relying on public sector or domestic companies to produce many important manufacturers. Local firms may be less efficient than transnationals so that the consumer has to pay a higher price and/or accept inferior quality goods. In practice public knowledge of these opportunity costs of restricting and excluding transnationals is low, according to Kudrle. He suggests that this lack of impact transparency may be especially great for mining and plantations. Thus, when such activities have been nationalised, there has been little awareness of costs in other parts of the world. Policies that are hostile to transnational firms are seen as more obviously contributing to national security and economic independence than they are seen as reducing economic prosperity. Reductions in the latter may be widely spread over the mass of consumers whereas policy decisions may reflect the interests of urban elites which often stand to benefit from protection against imports and transnational firms.

This need not result in the exclusion of transnationals: instead there may be an insistence on joint ventures enabling local urban elites to participate in the profits. The influence of elites reflects the very unequal distribution of political power, wealth and knowledge in most developing countries.

Nationalisation of foreign enterprises has been most common in the primary producing sector. This is due to the colonial experience in which foreign domination was associated with this sector, upon which the economy came to depend. The primary products produced for profit contributed significantly to GNP and were the main source of foreign exchange. This situation persists for many developing nations, such as in the case of copper for Zambia. In the Zambian case, the nationalised industry has remained partially dependent on transnational companies, this dependence taking the form of 'management contracts' with the previous transnational owners of the industry. Ironically, this arrangement has ensured that Zambia, rather than the companies, has borne the brunt of low copper prices in the late 1970s and first half of the 1980s.

In the 1980s there were signs that developing countries were becoming less hostile to transnational firms than was the case in the 1960s and early 1970s. By this time many developing countries had secured a large measure of control of 'their' mines and plantations. With the oil price shocks of the 1970s the oil-importing developing nations often found themselves with balance of payments problems. They needed to earn more foreign exchange and one way of doing this was to attract investment by transnationals in manufacturing for export. This was a major reason for the proliferation of export-processing zones. These balance of payments problems worsened in the early 1980s because recession in the developed countries meant a reduction in demand for the exports of the developing countries. As a result many developing nations have borrowed from the International Monetary Fund (IMF) and sought loans from the World Bank. Both these institutions use their influence to encourage developing countries to place increasing reliance on private enterprise, including transnational firms and the market mechanism.

7. BARGAINING WITH TRANSNATIONALS

The exact nature of the relationship between Third World governments and elites on the one hand and transnationals on the other hand, has been the subject of much debate. Dependency writers have tended to minimise the autonomy of Third World governments while liberal writers like Raymond Vernon have stressed their growing ability to bargain with transnationals, an ability highlighted by the successes of the Organisation of Petroleum Exporting Countries (OPEC) in the 1970s which led to the nationalisation of oil fields in Venezuela and the Middle East, as well as a higher oil price.

A more complex picture emerges in the work of Peter Evans on Brazil.[36] Evans found a mixture of competing and complementary relationships between foreign and local capital and various elements in the state apparatus. Certain industries where local capital was less in need of foreign technology were reserved for Brazilian firms while in other industries joint ventures were encouraged, unless the technology was very advanced. Since he wrote, Brazilian computer firms have made significant progress with state support.[37] Thus whether the technological dependence of developing countries is inevitable is still an open question. The United States government put pressure on Brazil to reduce its discrimination against foreign firms, especially IBM, and threatened retaliatory measures against Brazilian exports. As a result, in 1986 Brazil made some concessions, notably guaranteeing full copyright protection for imported foreign software.[38] However, Brazil blocked some imports in the mid-1980s, notably those of the American firm Microsoft. This led to the United States government to threaten retaliation if Brazil did not back down.

Steven Langdon, when reviewing the situation in Africa, stressed the importance of intimate social networks which involve foreign and local capital, officials and politicians, as well as widespread joint shareholding in countries such as Kenya, Ivory Coast and Nigeria. These linked together the domestic power structures with transnational capital.[39] However, there are so many differences between Third World countries that generalisations are unwise. In this respect much can be learned from case-studies, some of which are considered below.

The evidence from national case studies on foreign direct investment by transnational firms is consistent with the view that many factors affect the balance of bargaining power between governments and transnationals. A government will be in a weak bargaining position when the transnationals have something (such as technological know-how) the government wants very much. The government's position is further weakened if a transnational (or a group of transnational firms colluding) has many alternative countries to choose between when making its investments. On the other hand, if transnationals (and/or other foreign suppliers of technology) are competing to invest, the bargaining position of the country may be strengthened.

We shall now discuss in more detail the Indian case we mentioned briefly in chapter 7. In the 1950s India wished to develop an oil-refining industry and had to initially concede the companies a 100 per cent ownership stake. At this time the leading oil companies worked together closely so that India was unable to play off one company against another. By the 1970s there was much more competition between oil firms so that some developing countries anxious to establish an oil industry were able to do so through joint ventures. In the Indian case the oil companies were forced by the 1960s to accept less than 100 per cent ownership after India had acquired refining technology from the Soviet Union. Soviet technology was also helpful to India's bargaining position with transnational firms in the pharmaceutical industry. In both cases the Soviet Union was concerned not just to promote Indian economic development but also (and perhaps mainly) its political links with India, and to strengthen its geopolitical position. The Indian example also illustrates the way in which the balance of bargaining power becomes more favourable to the host country as technology is transferred, local labour is trained and the transnationals build up an investment stake which is a 'hostage', such that nationalisation becomes a realistic possibility.

India's experience of obtaining more favourable terms over time has been repeated in many developing countries, especially in mineral extraction, the best example being that of the OPEC countries. For example, in 1979, Nigeria expropriated the stake of the United Kingdom's oil majors, Shell and British Petroleum. This move drove the British government to back more effectively the transition to black majority rule in Rhodesia (soon to become independent Zimbabwe). Such cases are examples of what has come to be called the 'obsolescing bargain', a process which has often been associated with an increased ability to negotiate with, and monitor, transnational firms. This ability has grown with experience and an increasing number of highly-educated nationals.[40]

Cases of the 'obsolescing bargain' cast doubt on the long-term validity of the more determinist versions of dependency theory which has often stressed the dependence of developing countries on transnational firms and the capacity of the latter to exploit Third World countries. Whilst this dismal picture was largely correct for the colonial era when European rule favoured transnationals (especially those from the colonial power), it became much less accurate after 1945. Post-independence governments sought, with varying degrees of success, to secure more favourable terms in their dealings with transnational companies, especially in minerals and agricultural products – the main export industries established in the colonial era. In addition, a number of countries developed industries which could compete with those of the 'core', as technology and investment diffused production capacities, hence the term, 'newly-industrialising countries'.

Another factor affecting bargaining power is the market size and natural resources of the host country; that is to what extent a country has something of value to transnational corporations. Some developing countries have large and growing home markets which they can deny to foreign firms by imposing trade barriers and restricting foreign investments. As has been noted, transnational manufacturing firms may require access to, and sales in, all of the world's major markets in order to obtain sufficient profits to maintain research and development spending at a level comparable to that of their rivals (each other). This is especially true of corporations in high-technology industries.

Returning to the Brazilian case, this country managed to develop a telecommunications equipment industry which was not entirely dependent on transnational firms, mainly by using its control of access to the substantial and fast-growing Brazilian market through the state-owned telecommunications monopoly, Telebras.[41] Initially the transnationals were 'driven' to invest in Brazil because Telebras adopted a policy of buying equipment from firms which carried out some production of equipment in Brazil. Over time pressure was brought to bear on the foreign companies to accept a large Brazilian equity stake. Further, Telebras preferred transnationals which carried out some research in Brazil, and, partly by virtue of this, developed its own research capacity.

A large country which can deny market access to foreign firms is better placed than a small country when it comes to licensing technology on favourable terms. In this respect Brazil was following the Japanese example, as were India, China and South Korea. The South Korean government played an active role in deciding which industries to develop, which foreign firms to deal with, and what terms in technology deals were acceptable. Further, it closely monitored the operation of such deals, and sometimes forced through a revision of the terms.[42]

Foreign investment in small countries is often geared to exports either of primary products (such as bauxite and sugar from Jamaica) or manufactures (for example, radios from Singapore and Taiwan). In the case of manufactured goods transnational firms can choose between many countries. They will favour countries which have relatively low production costs given an adequate infrastructure and a favourable 'investment climate'.

In developing countries production costs are often low because of cheap labour. However, low wages may be offset by low labour productivity and high capital costs (for example in some cases transnationals might have to build their own electricity generators due to unreliable local supplies). In the 1960s and 1970s manufacturing transnationals shifted production from developed countries to developing nations for the more labour-intensive stages of production, such as the assembly of electronic goods. One country that was very successful in attracting transnational firms in this period was Singapore which had excellent transport and communication facilities, was politically stable (with a very autocratic 'democracy') and very welcoming to foreign capital.

However, in the mid-1980s Singapore's rapid economic growth came to a halt partly because transnational firms found that wages were by then significantly lower in other Asian countries such as Malaysia and Indonesia. Large wage increases in Singapore in the early 1980s reduced its comparative advantage in some labour-intensive manufactures. In consequence, the Singapore government combined policies of wage restraint with tax concessions to foreign firms to attract more foreign investment. By 1987 Singapore was again growing rapidly as Japanese investments flooded in. This example shows how little room for manoeuvre small countries can have where factors affecting production costs are concerned.

Apart from bilateral bargaining, what cooperative methods might less-developed countries use to increase the benefits they receive from transnational firms? One policy measure which developing countries might attempt to use in order to maximise their tax income from transnational companies is unitary taxation, although to be able to do this would require considerable powers of collective action. Unitary taxation is when the tax levied on the subsidiary of the transnational firm is based on exacting a proportion of the global earnings of the company. In effect this means that one government (or state within the American union) may succeed in taxing profits originating from outside the country. American states, such as California, recently used this system (much to the annoyance of non-American companies with investments in the United States). Less-developed countries would need to bring in unitary taxation together. Failure to do this would result in transnational firms switching investment to those countries not adopting a collective, 'Third World' line. (On why such unity is unlikely, see chapter 14.)

A second collective means at the disposal of developing countries is information-sharing and monitoring. The latter is one area where the United States Federal government has led the way, so as to prevent the abuse of 'transfer-pricing' techniques in intra-firm trade. Many other countries now have, like the United States, special tax offices concerned with transfer pricing. Indeed the United Nations Centre on Transnational Corporations has been helping developing and developed countries to monitor transnational firms more effectively.

8. LABOUR AND TRANSNATIONALS

Bargaining between organised labour and transnational firms can take several forms. First, a national trade union may bargain with a transnational over wages and working conditions for subsidiaries in its country. Secondly, the union may combine with unions from other countries in negotiating with the company: this is what Robert Cox calls a 'transnational strategy'.[43] Thirdly, unions may attempt to bring their national government and public opinion into the bargaining arena.

Of these three bargaining approaches the 'transnational strategy' is the most difficult but the most desirable from the general point of view of the unions. Transnational companies can threaten to relocate production or new investment (and therefore jobs) to other countries. Unless trade unions work together on a transnational basis this type of threat cannot be countervailed effectively. Transnational labour cooperation is difficult because of different wage levels, conditions, and political outlook between the unions of different countries. In particular, workers in a 'low-wage' country may hope to gain in jobs and pay at the expense of 'high-wage' workers in another country.

Some attempts have been made at international cooperation through the formation of international federations of trade unions, such as the International Federation of Chemical and General Workers (which coordinated a confrontation with the French transnational Saint Gobain) and the automotive industry where the International Metalworkers Federation organised a series of world company councils. While such efforts have not got very far, especially as regards combined strike action and gaining the involvement of workers in developing countries, they have proved useful for sharing and comparing information on particular firms. Recently, shop-floor representatives of 140,000 Ford workers in 16 countries agreed to world-wide mutual support in the event of any plant being in dispute with its local management. When there is a dispute in one country, Ford workers in other countries will not allow the company to increase or substitute production elsewhere or to import substitute vehicles or parts. Further, a central information bank has been established to provide the unions with international reports on Ford activities.[44]

The first and third bargaining approaches amount to a national strategy which has been easier to pursue, especially in countries with strong trade unions linked to a socialist or social democratic party. At the domestic level unions can hope to get some support from 'national' firms, if such firms are under competitive pressure from transnational firms. In addition, unions and local firms may combine to lobby the government to keep out a foreign company which is considering investment in that country. At a more general level, unions may seek to mobilise public opinion and gain political allies in support of tighter controls on transnational firms, such as greater disclosure requirements which may help the unions in bargaining. In the United States, unions have sought tax changes which will discourage foreign investment by American firms, although they have had little success.

Trade unions have used their influence at the international level, both directly and through their national governments, to try to establish international codes of conduct for transnationals. The European Community (EC) and OECD guidelines on transnational firms have not gone as far as the representatives of much organised labour would have wished, particularly as regards disclosure. For example, the EC (Vredeling) Directive which was intended to ensure information and consultation rights to workers in transnational companies was watered down: information has to be supplied annually as opposed to every six months; scope for retaining secret information was introduced; a clause giving workers access to central management was dropped; and mandatory consultation before decision-taking was changed to consultation before actual implementation.

One case where guidelines on foreign investment seem to have had some effect is that of foreign direct investment in South Africa, at least where American and EC firms are concerned. In the 1970s and 1980s, especially in the United States, public opinion was widely aroused, and pressure was placed on Congress and Presidency to take action against the South African government. This provided some elements of labour with allies to form a coalition for change in South Africa.

In general, when broadly-based political coalitions in favour of controlling transnational activities exist, the ability of labour to achieve its ends is at its greatest. However, in so far as such a bloc of forces is able to achieve some success in developed countries, there is an increasing likelihood that transnational firms will shift production to developing countries, notably those which adopt repressive policies with regard to organised and other labour. Such relocation of production has been occurring in the 1970s and 1980s, and is bound up with the 'new international division of labour'. This has led to growing political demands in the developed capitalist countries for trade barriers against 'cheap labour' manufacturing imports from developing countries.

Thus, in trying to cope with the structural power of transnationals, labour (like governments), is likely to end up backing measures designed to attract these firms. One reason for this is to be found in the consistent backing given by social democratic political parties and associated unions to the importance of national sovereignty and self-determination. This has the effect of dividing workers of different states, and, in effect, causing them to compete against each other. These divisions are partly reflected, for example, in the fact that organised labour in many developed countries has usually favoured the imposition and retention of strict immigration controls. By analogy, the backing given by developing countries to the United Nations principle of national self-determination has the similar structural effect of dividing their collective potential and the possibility of a shared identity upon which to build their collective action.

In contrast, transnational capital, divided by capitalism's condition of perpetual competition, is none the less informally linked on an international basis through forums such as the Trilateral Commission, the Club of Rome, and the Saltzburg Seminars (many of which are for the heads of transnational companies). Indeed, many Social Democrats and Labour Party leaders have been engaged in these forums, although in smaller numbers than their Liberal and Conservative counterparts. In addition, the interests of transnational capital are both generalised and reflected in the policies of international organisations such as the IMF and World Bank, as well as in the OECD.

9. CONCLUSIONS

The transnational corporation epitomises the era of transnationalism, and the mobility, technological prowess and financial power of such companies is central to understanding the dynamics and development of the contemporary global political economy.

Whilst there are various types of transnational corporation, the development of truly global 'cosmocorps' has a long way to go. In particular the location of a substantial proportion of their production abroad is a very recent development for Japanese firms. The trend towards increased Japanese foreign direct investment is likely to continue throughout the 1990s, further consolidating the cross-cutting pattern of direct investment that has emerged since 1970. This has been reinforced by a wave of mergers, international takeovers and transnational alliances which has occurred during the 1980s.

The American 'domination' of the ownership of transnational corporations will continue to decline. On the other hand, as a location for direct investment there are signs that the United States is becoming increasingly important, so confirming the centrality of the United States within the global political economy. In this respect, the political relationship between state and large-scale transnational capital within the United States (and also Japan and West Germany) is crucial for assessing the future potential for the power of transnational capital.

Neither the nation-state nor transnationals have superseded the other. Transnationals are dependent on the state for political goods and services, an attractive business climate, the provision of infrastructure and for various forms of direct and indirect economic support. In a world of sovereign states, there is considerable competition among the various countries to attract foreign direct investment, and the technology, management expertise and foreign links this may bring with it. On the other hand, some nation-states, many of which are in the Third World, have grown more sophisticated in their monitoring of and bargaining with transnational companies. This is partly because, on occasion, they have been able to 'unbundle' the direct investment package. In consequence, the power of transnationals has been reduced.

The situation in developed countries is such that there is often a close identity of interest between transnational capital and the state. Therefore, the 'internal' and 'external' dimensions of the autonomy of the state need to be taken account of in reviewing the relationship between the state and transnational capital. The bargaining situation varies enormously. Some developing countries, like South Korea and Brazil, had successes, whereas the situation in Mozambique is best described as neo-colonial. Here some plantations owned by transnational companies are almost akin to a 'state within a state' with their own mercenary soldiers to guard them. The structural power of capital is so great and the poverty of some left-wing Third World states so extreme, that there countries are impelled to introduce welcoming foreign investment laws. In 1987 Nicaragua and Vietnam followed in the footsteps of China. Vietnam's foreign investment code offered, in some cases, up to 100 per cent foreign ownership, tax holidays and full rights to repatriate capital.[45] This included, of course, the corporations of its former adversary, the United States.

In the post-war period, labour has been less resilient and sophisticated in its dealings with transnationals than national governments have been. Whereas governments draw strength from the cultural identity of the nation, for unions and for the socialist political movements which are generally espoused by organised labour, nationalism is an obstacle to the kind of transnational alliance they need to achieve to countervail the power of internationally mobile forms of capital. The prospects for such an alliance in the 1990s do not appear to be very encouraging for socialists and trade unionists.

NOTES

1. United Nations Department of Economic and Social Affairs, *Multinational Corporations in World Development* (New York, United Nations, 1973), p. 5.
2. Stuart Holland, *The Global Economy: from Meso to Macroeconomics* (London, Weidenfeld and Nicolson, 1987), especially chapter 4.
3. On intra-firm trade, see Mark Casson, *Multinationals and World Trade* (London, Allen and Unwin, 1986).
4. Holland, op. cit., p. 143.
5. John Dunning, 'The History of Multinationals During the Course of a Century', Paper, Institute for Research and Information on Multinationals Conference, Paris, November 1982, cited in C. J. Dixon et al. (eds), *Multinational Corporations and the Third World* (London, Croom Helm, 1986), p. 7.
6. George Modelski, 'International Content and Performance Among the World's Largest Corporations', in Modelski (ed.), *Transnational Corporations and World Order* (San Francisco, W. H. Freeman, 1979), p. 51.
7. 'Global Finance and Investing', Special Report, *Wall Street Journal*, 29 September 1986.
8. Modelski, op. cit., p. 45.
9. *The Economist*, 24 January 1987.
10. S. Cronjé et al., *Lonrho: Portrait of a Multinational* (Harmondsworth, Penguin 1976).
11. United Nations, op. cit., p. 5.
12. John Stopford, John Dunning and Klaus Haberich (eds), *The World Directory of Multinational Enterprises* (London, Macmillan, 1980), p. xv.
13. Ibid.
14. Ibid., pp. xiv–xv.
15. John Stopford and John Dunning, *Multinationals, Company Performance and Global Trends* (London, Macmillan, 1983), p. 3.
16. Robert Gilpin, 'The Multinational Corporation and American Foreign Policy', in Richard Rosecrance (ed.), *America as an Ordinary Country* (Ithaca NY, Cornell University Press, 1976), p. 176.
17. R. E. Lipsey and I. B. Kravis, 'The Competitive Position of United States Manufacturing Firms', *Banca Nazionale del Lavoro* (1985), No. 153, p. 144.
18. Stopford et al., *The World Directory of Multinational Enterprises*, Table 1, p. 3.
19. 'Global Finance and Investing', op. cit. Figures given are by market value on 30 June, converted into US dollars at the exchange rate for that date. IBM was the largest company with a market value greater than the next two biggest companies combined (Exxon and General Electric). Fourth biggest was Tokyo Electric.
20. R. Murray (ed.), *Multinationals Beyond the Market* (Brighton, Harvester Press, 1981).

21. See James Caporaso (ed.), *A Changing International Division of Labour* (Boulder, Colorado, Lynne Reiner, 1987), chapter 2; J. M. Kline, 'Multinational Corporations in Euro-American Trade: Crucial Linking Mechanisms in an Evolving Trade Structure', in Theodore Moran (ed.), *Multinational Corporations* (Lexington, Mass., Lexington Books, 1985), pp. 199–218.

22. Stephen Hymer, *The International Operations of National Firms: A Study of Direct Foreign Investment* (Cambridge, Mass., MIT Press, 1976); Stephen Hymer, *The Multinational Corporation: A Radical Approach* (London, Cambridge University Press, 1979), edited by R. Cohen et al.

23. Raymond Vernon, 'International Trade Investment and International Trade in the Product Cycle', *Quarterly Journal of Economics* (1966), Vol. 80, pp. 190–207.

24. John Dunning, *International Production and the Multinational Enterprise* (London, Macmillan, 1983). See also, R. E. Caves, *Multinational Enterprise and Economic Analysis* (Cambridge, Cambridge University Press, 1982).

25. K. Ohmae, *Triad Power: the coming shape of global competition* (New York, Free Press, 1985).

26. As suggested in the title of Raymond Vernon's book, *Sovereignty at Bay: the Multinational Spread of US Enterprises* (London, Longman, 1971). For a public choice approach which attempts to combine economic and political factors, see F. S. Schneider and B. S. Frey, 'The Economic and Political Determinants of Foreign Direct Investment', *World Development* (1985), Vol. 13, pp. 161–75. For a Marxist approach, see Hugo Radice (ed.), *International Firms and Modern Imperialism* (Harmondsworth, Penguin Books, 1975).

27. R. Murray, 'Underdevelopment, international firms and the international division of labour', in J. Tinbergen (ed.), *Towards a New World Economy* (Rotterdam, Holland, Rotterdam University Press, 1972), pp. 159–248.

28. On Latin America, see R. Newfarmer (ed.), *Profits, Progress and Poverty: case studies of international industries in Latin America* (Notre Dame, Indiana, Notre Dame University Press, 1985).

29. Richard J. Barnet and Ronald E. Muller, *The Global Reach: The Power of the Multinational Corporations* (New York, Simon and Schuster, 1974).

30. Harry Magdoff, *The Age of Imperialism* (New York, Monthly Review Press, 1969).

31. Thomas Dye, *Who's Running America?* (Englewood Cliffs NJ, Prentice-Hall, 1979).

32. Robert Gilpin, *US Power and the Multinational Corporation: the Political Economy of Foreign Direct Investment* (New York, Basic Books, 1975).

33. On American policies and the influence of American transnational firms, see R. T. Kudrle and D. B. Bobrow, 'US Policy Toward Foreign Direct Investment', *World Politics* (1982), Vol. 35, pp. 363–79; C. F. Bergsten, T. Horst and T. H. Moran, *American Multinationals and American Interests* (Washington DC, Brookings Institution, 1978); C. P. Kindleberger and D. B. Audretsch, *The Multinational Corporation in the 1980s* (Cambridge, Mass., MIT Press, 1983).

34. S. E. Guisinger, 'Do Performance Requirements and Investment Incentives Work?', *The World Economy* (1986), Vol. 9, pp. 79–96.

35. Robert Kudrle, 'The Several Faces of the Multinational Corporation: Political Reaction and Policy Response', in W. Ladd Hollist and F. Lamond Tullis,

(eds), *The International Political Economy Yearbook* (Boulder, Colorado, Westview Press, 1985), pp. 175–97.

36. Peter Evans, *Dependent Development: the Alliance of Multinational, State and Local Capital in Brazil* (Princeton NJ, Princeton University Press, 1979).

37. E. A. Adler, '"Ideological Guerillas" and the Quest for Technological Autonomy: Brazil's domestic computer industry', *International Organisation* (1986), Vol. 40. pp. 673–705.

38. 'Brazil cools conflict with US', *Financial Times*, 28 October 1986.

39. Steven Langdon, 'Multinational Corporations and the State in Africa', in J.J.Villamil (ed.), *Transnational Capitalism and National Development* (Brighton, Harvester Press, 1979), pp. 223–240.

40. Vernon, *Sovereignty at Bay*, op. cit. Despite the title of this book, Vernon has stressed the obsolescing bargain and the complexity of the relationship between transnationals and states. See also his more recent work, *Storm over the Multinationals: the real issues* (London, Macmillan, 1977).

41. M. Hobday, 'The Impact of Microelectronics on Developing Countries: The Case of Brazilian Telecommunications', *Development and Change* (1985), Vol. 16, pp. 313–40.

42. R. Leudde-Neurath, 'State Intervention and Foreign Direct Investment in South Korea', *Institute of Development Studies Bulletin* (1984), Vol. 15, pp. 18–25; J. Enos, 'Government Intervention in the Transfer of Technology: the Case of South Korea', *Institute of Development Studies Bulletin* (1984), Vol. 15, pp. 26–37. For a good review of case study material on Brazil, India and South Korea see Katherine Marton, *Multinationals, Technology and Industrialisation* (Lexington, Mass., Lexington Books, 1987).

43. Robert W. Cox, 'Labour and the Multinationals', *Foreign Affairs* (1976), Vol. 54, pp. 344–65.

44. I. Hamilton-Fazey, 'Ford workers agree to worldwide mutual support', *Financial Times*, 18 March 1985.

45. T. Fawthrop, 'Vietnam's Opening Door', *South*, October 1987, pp. 9–13.

12 Trade and Protectionism

1. INTRODUCTION

Trade is just one channel of global interdependence and one aspect of social integration within and between countries. It has often been seen as the major force linking countries. With the rise of capital mobility and transnational capitalism, we think that a reappraisal of the place of trade in the global political economy is needed.

The first half of this chapter examines the importance, and changing place of trade in the global political economy, and its relationship to economic growth. In the second half of the chapter it is argued that although demands for protection are common and have been growing in the 1980s, there are many social forces which serve to keep world trade growing at a faster rate than world output. Economic interdependence through trade will continue to be a major feature of the global political economy, even though it is secondary, in structural terms, to money, finance and transnational production. In this context it is argued that Western liberal political economists have tended to place an exaggerated stress on protectionism when expressing fears about the possible collapse of the liberal international economic order.

We shall first, however, discuss trade in terms of its economic importance for developed and developing nations, and second, as a means of economic integration, and as a possible source of conflict or peace in international relations.

2. THE IMPORTANCE OF INTERNATIONAL TRADE

The export and import of goods and services directly affects most people on the globe. Even if they do not work in the export sector – and most do

224

not – it is likely that they possess imported items or items which contain imported materials. While millions work in service activities many of which are largely non-traded in character, such work often makes use of imported items, such as spices and exotic foodstuffs in restaurants. Indeed, the modern fast-food service industry uses natural and synthetic ingredients from most parts of the world.

The scale of trade varies for different countries, but for most economies it is a significant proportion of gross domestic product (GDP). For example, in 1985 total imports as a percentage of GDP at current prices was 9 per cent for the United States, 10.8 per cent for Japan, 24.8 per cent for West Germany, 21.1 per cent for France, 24.8 per cent for the United Kingdom, 24.2 per cent for Italy and 22.1 per cent for Canada.[1] Trade is of much greater importance for the vast majority of developing countries. Their average propensity to trade in 1980 was 45.8 per cent, whereas for developed capitalist nations it was 35 per cent. (See Table 9.5.) If these figures seem less than spectacular it should be remembered that they only cover goods, not services, such as tourism, transport, insurance and banking. Many of these services are required for the export of goods and also for the activities of transnational firms.

International trade is, of course, a major way in which world economic integration takes place. From the sixteenth century until the nineteenth century it was the main means of integration, (although some flows of capital and labour also occurred). Hence it was tempting, in the interests of theoretical parsimony, to develop theories of trade (like that of David Ricardo) which assumed no factor mobility between countries. In practice, in the mid-nineteenth century, trade, capital and labour flows were linked. The settlement of the American West was facilitated by railways which were often financed by British capital. Soon the prairies were exporting food to Britain. Foreign investment in mines and plantations in Asia, Africa and Latin America contributed to the emergence of an international division of labour with 'core' countries exporting manufactures to 'peripheral' regions in return for primary products and manufactures.

After World War II trade continued to outweigh capital flows in quantitative terms for many years. In the 1970s, however, short-term capital flows came to dwarf trade values. Further, a large proportion of trade, especially in manufactures, took the form of intra-firm trade: that is between subsidiaries of the same firm in different countries. Trade in manufactures between developed capitalist countries has soared and far exceeds their imports of primary products from the Third World.

The importance of trade for developing countries is often related to Robert Keohane and Joseph Nye's concept of 'vulnerability' interdependence.[2] Many less-developed countries are highly vulnerable because of their extreme dependence on imports of certain essential goods and services. These include machinery, arms, know-how and, often, food. Their vulnerability arises because of their limited domestic capacities, such that changes in policy are insufficient to change their basic condition. This means that their trade and wider economic relations are generally characterised by structural dependence (see chapter 6, section 3). (This issue is discussed at length in chapter 14 on North–South relations.) Such vulnerability is a basis for the unequal power which is manifested in international exchange relations, and in international relations more generally.

While exchange promotes social interaction both nationally and internationally (buyers need sellers, and vice versa), these relations are characterised by varying degrees of inequality. In our discussion of 'market power', for example, we pointed out how a group of oligopolists may collude to gain 'power over' more vulnerable consumers. Thus, whilst exchange through the market is a means of social integration, it is also a means of social stratification.[3] At the international level, a system of international exchange is bound up with an international hierarchy of nations and classes.

In Hegel's discussion of master and slave, and their social relations, both parties are changed through their roles in a situation of inequality. Hegel's insight can be applied to the global political economy. For example, the unequal exchanges of the colonial period (such as the slave trade) have left a legacy of racism in many Western countries. In addition, the attitudes and institutions which shaped (and are still shaping) the identity of people in developing countries have been significantly changed by the adoption of foreign lifestyles and aspirations, religions, and forms of government. Thus interdependence, partly fostered by trade, is a complex cultural and social phenomenon, as well as one which involves economic relations and structures of power.

Does more trade promote a lessening of international conflict? Whereas economic liberals do not necessarily expect trade to promote peace, liberal idealists have often argued that the growth of trade can reduce the likelihood of war. On the one hand, the opportunity costs of war are increased by greater interdependence. On the other hand, trade may lead to interactions between countries which promote better mutual understanding between nations. E. H. Carr, and more recently, Barry Buzan, have criticised such liberal idealism, pointing to the example of World War I which followed a century of rapidly growing trade.[4] In other words, the question posed at the start of this paragraph is still an open one. For example, the realism of E. H. Carr has been developed by world systems writers who see competition between states and also between firms in world trade as a structural necessity of the capitalist 'world system'. This contrasts with the earlier non-capitalist 'world empires' (which were, in practice, regional empires). Notable examples of the latter were Imperial China and perhaps Mogul India, whose leaders saw trade as a marginal activity. Marxists too, have seen trade not only as a means of global integration and stratification, but also as a source of inevitable inter-capitalist conflict. For classical Marxists, the growth of trade was driven by the expansionary needs of the capitalist system. This was the case for both the merchant stage and the later monopoly or imperialist stage in the development of capitalism. However, for this later stage, the export of capital was seen as more important than trade. (See chapter 5, section 3.) By contrast, trade between socialist states was expected to promote peaceful economic integration.

This debate is, however, a complex one and cannot be resolved in the context of a single chapter. Our own view is that it is unwise to generalise on the basis of one historical era. Furthermore, it is important to ask 'what is being traded – guns or butter?' We have seen in chapter 8 how trade has played a crucial role in the process of militarisation, especially since World War II. The relationship between trade and the propensity to war might well vary according to the range and nature of international economic linkages of a given era. In particular, what might hold for a period characterised by 'national' (or imperial) political economies might not hold for an era characterised by significant transnational linkages. In consequence, liberal fears that a decline in trade openness might lead to conflict, disorder and perhaps war, may be based on an historical analogy which is inappropriate. For such closure to occur it would necessarily entail a wider restructuring of capitalism back towards the 'national' pattern. We think this is, however, unlikely, for reasons discussed in previous chapters, and outlined for example, in Chapter 17.

3. LEVELS OF ANALYSIS AND KEY QUESTIONS

We find it useful to distinguish between the macro-, meso- (or intermediate) and micro-levels in the analysis of international trade. The macro-level concerns the degree of openness and closure (expansion and contraction) in the world trading system. The micro-level relates to patterns of openness and closure in particular industries. There are also contrasts at an intermediate or meso-level, combining macro- and micro-aspects, for example between different groups of countries. At each of these levels, distributional questions are involved. These concern the costs and benefits of trade for different people, firms, groups, classes and countries.

A principal task of the political economy of trade is to explain variations in the degree of openness, and the relationship of this to global economic growth. In particular, the contrast between the extreme closure of the 1930s and 1940s and the open ages of the mid-nineteenth century and the period since 1950, requires explanation. (In addition, this task includes an account of how and why the emergence of a capitalist world economy involved increasing openness to European commercial penetration.)

One major problem within this task is how to measure openness and closure. Such measurement depends upon how the terms themselves are defined and applied. Openness is normally associated with the absence of trade barriers (such as tariffs, quotas, voluntary export restraints), or protectionism, narrowly defined. However, protection takes many forms. Some types of protection may encourage, rather than restrict trade, such as export subsidies, trade credits, tied aid to developing nations, and investment incentives for exporters, as in special economic zones which allow privileges to foreign firms.

A broad definition of protectionism would cover the impact of all methods used to make some branch of economic activity more profitable, that is to raise its value-added. In consequence, investment incentives which encourage import-substitution and even manipulation of exchange rates can be protective: for example, a low exchange rate increases export competitiveness while making imports less competitive. Other less overt methods of protection include health and safety rules, and bureaucratic discretionary powers. Each of these instruments may have a different impact on trade, but some (such as the predisposition of bureaucrats to process applications for credentials for importers) may be impossible to measure.

A further and growing problem in measuring protection has been the increase in 'counter-trade'. The latter involves barter deals between countries with implicit prices that can diverge significantly from normal arm's-length (market) prices in trade. Some developing nations, desperate to save foreign exchange, have dumped their primary products in the markets of developed countries by means of counter-trade. This type of deal does not show up clearly in trade statistics, and its size is a subject of some debate. Some writers suggest that it may have grown by the mid-1980s, to about 20 per cent of all trade. In effect, counter-trade can be another form of protection, which may sometimes be equivalent to an export subsidy. Examples of this are inter-governmental deals, involving oil for manufactures, as between Nigeria and Brazil.[5]

There is clear evidence of substitution between different instruments of protection: as tariffs have fallen since 1945, so non-tariff barriers have risen.[6] Table 12.1 shows how subsidies tended to rise for the biggest six capitalist economies between 1956 and 1980. Italy, for example, increased its subsidies in precisely those areas where European Community regulations mandated the abolition of tariffs.[7]

Table 12.1   Subsidies as shown in national accounts statistics as a percentage of gross domestic product, 1956–80

Country	1956	1964	1972	1976	1980
United States	0.20	0.44	0.59	0.34	0.43
Japan	0.26	0.65	1.12	1.32	1.32
France	2.71	2.03	1.99	2.68	2.51
Germany	0.20	0.99	1.48	1.49	1.59
Britain	1.76	1.56	1.82	2.78	2.32
Italy	1.30	1.23	2.29	2.60	3.01

Source: Adapted from G. C. Hufbauer, 'Subsidy Issues After the Tokyo Round', in William R. Cline (ed.), *Trade Policy in the 1980s* (Washington DC, Institute for International Economics, 1983), p. 328.

The most common method of measuring the protection afforded to an industry is to calculate the 'effective rate' of protection.[8] This is the proportional change in value-added as a result of all forms of protection. The calculation allows for both direct and indirect policy measures by the home state. By indirect measures is meant those which alter the cost of inputs into the industry. However, such calculations may fail to show how 'effective' protection is, due to the ways that trade barriers may be circumvented. Voluntary export restraints are usually made for specific goods from a particular country. That country might succeed in re-routing its exports through other countries. It might also alter the mix of its products which it exports, so as to avoid the specific restriction. Evidence has been found to suggest that newly-industrialising countries succeeded in doing this in the 1970s.[9]

Despite such problems of definition and measurement, there is a consensus that protection designed to restrict trade in manufactures fell, at least for trade between the developed capitalist nations during the 1950s and 1960s. Since the 1970s, such protectionism is thought to have risen for trade between these countries, for both agriculture and manufactured products. This is particularly the case for production subsidies and voluntary export restraints (such as Japanese car manufacturers restricting their exports to Western Europe and the United States, under threat of loss of market access). By contrast, protection in the newly-independent developing nations has substantially exceeded that of the colonial period. This has often taken the form of quota restrictions and exchange controls, whereby imports are rationed according to state priorities.

After discussing recent trends in trade, we shall return in more detail in subsequent sections of this chapter, to our key questions at the macro-, meso- and micro-levels.

4. POST-WAR TRADE DEVELOPMENTS

We shall now discuss changes in trade since 1913, notably since 1945. World trade since World War II has grown rapidly, both in absolute terms and as a percentage of world gross national product (GNP). During the period 1950–80, world GNP rose from $845.4 billion to $11,269.1 billion in current prices, and from $1,981.5 billion to $7,977.8 billion (in 1975 dollars at constant prices, 1950–80).[10] Between 1950 and 1970, annual growth in total world output was 4.9 per cent. Between 1913 and 1950, growth in world output was only 1.9 per cent. (See Table 9.1.) In the 1913–50 period, trade growth fluctuated considerably. It was fastest in the 1920s, and declined in absolute terms in the 1930s. Using 1913 as the base year (=100) the index for trade in manufactures rose to 129 in 1929 but fell to 107 in 1937. For all primary products the volume index rose to 138 in 1929 and fell to 131 in 1937.[11] Because of the fall in the price level, especially for primary products, the fall in the value of trade exceeded the decline in volume. By 1935, world trade had fallen to one-third of the level of 1929, measured in gold dollars, and by 45 per cent when measured in paper pounds.[12]

Table 12.2 illustrates the predominance of the major developed capitalist countries in post-war trade, which rose as a percentage of world GNP from 11.7 per cent in 1950 to 21.2 per cent in 1980. The contrast between the figures for Western Europe, with and without intra-European trade, highlights the rapid growth of such trade. This tendency for European countries to do more of their trade with each other was largely due to attempts at economic integration, notably through the establishment and extension of the European Community (EC).

In Table 12.3 the relatively minor role of the Soviet bloc (Eastern Trading Area) in the world trade is clear, as is the somewhat larger, but still minor role of developing nations (except the oil-exporting countries). Despite increased exports by developing nations to the Eastern bloc, they still remained mainly dependent on Western markets: their exports to the developed capitalist countries were more than twelve times greater than those of the Eastern bloc in 1970. This in turn was almost four times as much as the trade the developing nations did with each other in 1970, whereas in 1953, trade among developing countries was a little over a third of the size of their exports to developed capitalist countries, indicating an increased reliance on Western and Japanese markets.

Exports between the developed capitalist countries were growing especially rapidly in the decade before 1973. Between 1973 and 1978 their exports to developing nations began to grow more rapidly than trade amongst the major capitalist nations. Since many developing nations were hit hard by the oil price rises, a disproportionate share of the increased

Table 12.2 Exports 1950–80

[A] *Exports FOB billions of current dollars*

	1950	1960	1970	1980
World total	60.8	128.3	313.9	1,855.7
Major developed capitalist countries*	34.0	81.0	214.0	1,224.3
United States	10.1	20.4	42.6	220.7
Japan	0.8	4.1	19.3	130.5
Western Europe**	20.1	51.0	136.0	806.1
Western Europe***	n.a.	25.6	44.1	256.1
West Germany	2.0	11.4	34.2	192.9
Britain	6.3	10.6	19.3	115.2

[B] *Exports as a percentage of GNP and of World Exports*

	Exports as a percentage of GNP				*Exports as a percentage of World Exports*	
	1950	1960	1970	1980	1950	1980
World	11.7	11.3	12.6	21.2	100.0	100.0
Major developed capitalist countries	7.3	8.8	10.5	17.2	55.9	66.0
United States	3.5	4.0	4.3	8.4	16.7	11.9
Japan	5.6	9.4	9.5	12.5	1.3	7.0
Western Europe (including intra-European trade)	13.8	15.5	17.8	25.1	33.1	43.4
Western Europe (excluding intra-European trade)	n.a.	7.8	5.8	8.0	n.a.	13.8
West Germany	8.5	15.8	18.4	23.5	3.3	10.4
Britain	17.0	14.7	15.6	22.2	10.4	6.2

*Major developed capitalist countries are the USA, Canada, the EEC member countries and Japan.
**Western Europe: including intra-European trade.
***Western Europe: excluding intra-European trade.
'World' excludes inter-trade amongst the following: China, Mongolia, N. Korea, and North Vietnam (from 1976, Vietnam).
Source: Nobuhiko Ushiba et al., *Sharing International Responsibilities* (New York, Trilateral Commission, 1983), pp. 81, 83.
Based on Eurostat and United Nations statistics.

Table 12.3 World trade, 1963–78 (in billions of US dollars, figures round, FOB)

Origin	Year	Developed capitalist	Destination Developing nations	Eastern bloc
Developed capita-				
list countries	1963	69.2	21.9	3.5
	1973	288.9	68.7	18.2
	1978	578.8	199.6	42.0
Devoping coun-				
tries	1963	22.1	6.7	1.7
	1973	79.5	22.5	5.3
	1978	215.1	68.7	12.9
Eastern bloc	1963	3.5	2.5	12.4
	1973	15.4	6.5	32.4
	1978	33.4	18.4	69.4

Source: Adapted from James Foreman-Peck, *A History of the World Economy* (Brighton, Harvester Press, 1983), p. 294.

exports by developed countries to developing nations went to oil-exporting countries.

In the 1960s, clear signs could be discerned of a change in the autarkic stance of the Eastern bloc countries, as they came to import more Western technology, reflected in the persistent trade deficits of the Eastern bloc countries with the developed capitalist countries, whilst, however, they maintained consistent surpluses with developing nations. (See chapter 15.)

Growth in trade slowed during the recession of 1979–82: indeed there was no growth in trade in real terms in 1981, but growth picked up again in 1984. The severity of the setback to trade growth can be seen in Table 12.4. The figures somewhat exaggerate the slowdown because of the appreciation of the US dollar.

Table 12.4: Total trade 1979–84 (in billions of US dollars)

	World	Imports of developed countries	Of which from developing nations (per cent)	Imports of developing areas
1979	1635	1117	26.6	353
1980	1989	1342	29.2	455
1981	1963	1269	29.0	498
1982	1844	1183	26.5	466
1983	1807	1175	24.8	431
1984	1915	1271	24.5	433

Source: 'Change and Continuity in OECD Trade in Manufactures with Developing Countries', *OECD Observer* (1986), Vol. 139, p. 4.

Amidst the generally dismal position for less-developed countries there was growing success in exporting manufactures to developed countries. Indeed by 1984 the countries of the Organisation for Economic Cooperation and Development (OECD) imported more by value of manufactures from developing countries that they did of non-oil primary products. In 1986 developing countries even earned more foreign exchange from selling manufactures than from exporting either fuels or other primary products.[13] By 1984, the OECD countries were buying nearly 10 per cent of their imports of machinery and equipment from developing countries, not the kind of outcome dependency theory would lead us to expect! However, developing countries were most prominent as suppliers of textiles, clothing, footwear and other light industrial products. Most of these are consumer goods, with the notable exception of electronics components.

As has been noted, a notable feature of trade patterns in the 1960s and 1970s was the tendency for the countries of the EC to do more of their trade with each other. In the case of food a greater degree of self-sufficiency was achieved and agricultural surpluses were sometimes dumped on world markets. Food exporters, such as Canada, Australia, New Zealand and the United States lost out as a result. So did some less-developed countries exporting wheat (such as Argentina), beef (Argentina, Brazil, Botswana) and sugar (the Philippines, Mauritius and most Caribbean countries). With the entry of Spain, Portugal and Greece into the EEC, the Mahgreb countries of Morocco, Tunisia and Algeria also were disadvantaged.

5. TRADE AND GROWTH

The association of rapid economic growth with fast-growing trade, sometimes with the rate of trade surpassing that of the rate of economic growth, has given rise to a variety of interpretations. Liberal economists have interpreted the association as one where causation runs from freer trade to faster trade growth to faster economic growth. However, trade might grow faster than output because rapid growth makes the reduction of trade barriers politically easier to achieve. Reduction in such barriers may, in turn, facilitate growth through encouraged trade. Reduced transport costs enable trade to outgrow output. How then might trade promote growth? That is, how might it alter the rate of increase, not just the absolute level of output, productivity and living standards?

Traditional mercantilists argued that higher exports could increase output by reducing under-employment. Since the employment gain from exports would be cancelled out if imports rose by the same amount, a balance of trade surplus was crucial for economic growth (and hence for national power). Liberal economists doubted this claim, arguing that such a surplus was not sustainable for monetary reasons. A surplus country would gain gold, a deficit country would lose gold. As a result the price level of the deficit country would fall, relative to that in the surplus country. This would increase its competitiveness and its trade performance, thereby eliminating the initial advantage to the country which had obtained a balance of payments surplus.

Both the early mercantilists and their liberal critics assumed a relatively fixed supply of global money, based on the precious metals. With the growth of paper currencies, bank deposit money and ultimately, international reserve currencies, the zero-sum assumption of the early political economists no longer holds. Thus, if one country is able and willing to run a deficit sufficient to allow other countries their desired surplus, increasing the global money supply in the process, then the mercantilist growth effect could apply at a global level. This is the role often assigned to United States balance of payments deficits during the period from the early 1950s to the early 1970s: precisely the period of the post-war boom.

The early liberal argument for freer trade made by Adam Smith and David Ricardo was that a reallocation of resources could lead to a one-off improvement in efficiency and productivity. The reallocation of resources would arise if the labour of countries became more highly specialised in activities for which they had an absolute productivity advantage (Smith) or a comparative advantage (Ricardo). For example, the European textile industry has contracted since the 1960s, while that of the Far Eastern countries has expanded, partly through exporting to the West.

An extension of the arguments of Smith and Ricardo is the idea that trade makes possible the attainment of economies of scale, and hence a one-off increase in productivity. Freer trade could thus delay the approach towards the 'stationary state' or no-growth condition. One way in which this static analysis might be adapted to suggest a basis for faster growth is that higher incomes make possible higher savings and investment. Higher investment, in response to changes in trade patterns (improving allocative efficiency) may serve to extend the production possibility frontier. This may then result in a period of faster growth, until a new production possibility frontier is reached.[14]

Much analysis of trade has been on the basis of the exchange of consumer goods. However, a substantial proportion of trade takes the form of capital goods. Imports of capital goods may be a condition for maximising the economic growth potential of a country. This is particularly the case for many developing countries which have little in the way of capital goods industries. A similar point applies to trade in technology (such as licensing). Increased knowledge also extends the frontier of production possibilities.

Freer trade may heighten competition with positive dynamic effects. Again, this can take the form of a one-off improvement as 'X-inefficiency' is reduced (and as 'productive' efficiency is increased). An X-efficient firm is one that produces a given level of output (and quality) using the least-cost combination of factors of production. For example, an X-inefficient organisation may have significant overmanning, pay its executives unnecessarily large perks, and not use the cheapest available sources of raw materials and supplies. Improvements in productive efficiency often are one-off gains.

By contrast, increased competition might lead to a continuing improvement in productivity, through what might be termed 'innovative' or, in Joseph Schumpeter's term, 'dynamic' efficiency. This arises because of increased effort in generating and developing innovations (of both an organisational and productive nature) in order that a firm can assure its long-term survival and expansion. Some economists have found that productivity-raising innovation has made a major contribution to economic growth in the post-war period. Thus the argument concerning innovative efficiency may be (empirically) the most important in favour of open trade.[15] The innovative efficiency effect of trade, from this analysis, might be at its smallest in a capitalist economy with a very large market, and with many domestic producers engaged in fierce competition. However, foreign direct investment by transnational firms can also serve to transfer technology and may enhance competition.

6. GAINS FROM TRADE

According to Ricardo, when countries specialise in the production of those goods in which they have a comparative advantage, and trade ensues, there is an absolute gain in welfare for both economies. On this basis he advocated free trade, suggesting that Britain export manufactures and import foodstuffs. However, this would have involved reduced demand for British agricultural output, threatening the incomes (rents) of the landowning class. In principle, the gains for the urban capitalists would be more than sufficient for them to be able to compensate the landowners. In practice, such a suggestion attacked the basis of the class power of the landed aristocracy. Whether compensation was paid was a political question.

As Marx noted, Ricardo's model implied a potential class struggle between the old landowning aristocracy and the rising industrial bourgeoisie. Marx himself suggested that in the long-term the landowning class would come to be just one more fraction of the wider capitalist class. The more fundamental class conflict was between capital and labour. Ironically, the neo-classical Heckscher–Ohlin theory of trade highlights this basic class conflict.

The Heckscher–Ohlin theory of trade predicts that, on the basis of opportunity costs, a relatively capital-rich nation (country A) will export capital-intensive goods.[16] A nation with relatively plentiful supplies of labour will export labour-intensive goods (country B). In the simplest version of this theory, the capitalist class of nation A stands to gain if trade expands. Freer trade raises the demand for the goods of A which embody considerable capital; it lowers demand for goods which require a lot of labour, since these will be imported at lower cost from country B. As a result the profit rate rises in A, and the wage rate may decline. Conversely, in country B, which has an abundance of labour, the capitalist class stands to lose from freer trade, whereas labour may gain. Hence capitalists in B will favour policies of protection, whereas those in A will favour free trade. Likewise, labour in A will favour protection,whereas labour in B will favour open trade.

Later, in the 1960s the simple two-factor Heckscher–Ohlin model was modified to allow for skill-intensive labour, embodying 'human capital'. A country relatively rich in skilled labour will export skill-intensive goods; for example, products involving a lot of research and development. Hence in a country rich in skilled labour there will be a division of interest between the skilled workers who will favour free trade, and unskilled workers who will favour protection.

In his analysis, Ricardo assumed, like many modern liberal theories of trade, a perfect mobility of factors between sectors, so that full employment was not endangered. However, factors are only imperfectly mobile between sectors, and adjustment costs are unevenly distributed among workers and capitalists. Such costs will be greater, the more that capital and labour are 'industry-specific', that is tied to a given type of production. This necessarily means a struggle will occur as producers attempt to defend their threatened positions. Thus, even in a capital-rich country, capitalists as well as workers in a given sector may combine to demand protection against imports.

Neither Heckscher–Ohlin nor Ricardian theory allowed for factor mobility between countries. If capital is mobile in the form of foreign direct investment, then the export sector of one nation may be owned by capitalists from another. These foreign owners may repatriate most of their profits. Such was the experience of the primary product sectors of many developing nations during, and sometimes after, the colonial period. Some of the gains from trade which went primarily to the export sector left the country. This loss was especially great in mineral extraction since the share of capital in value-added was high, partly because of the low level of wages. In some of these countries the export sector accounted for a large proportion of national income.

In some of the colonies monopsonistic (single buyer) powers were granted by the imperial country to a chartered company (such as the Royal Niger Company for palm oil in Nigeria). In consequence the prices paid to peasant producers were depressed below the competitive market rate. Once again the profits were often remitted to the imperial power. While such grants of privilege came to an end with independence, some of this monopsony power has survived in primary product industries, in which the marketing is dominated by a few transnational corporations. A result of such power is to make the net barter terms of trade less favourable for the developing country, than would be the case under a competitive market system. The net barter terms of trade is given by the ratio of the price of exports to the price of imports. Where many commodities are involved, this means the ratio of two price indices. The significance of adverse terms of trade with monopsony power may be appreciated as the reader contemplates the price of a cup of coffee. In the mid-1980s, of this price just over 5 per cent went to plantation workers, 33 per cent to others in the producer country and 62 per cent to those, mainly in the consumer countries, engaged in wholesaling, packaging, transport, retailing and advertising.[17]

Writers from various perspectives have given reasons as to how and why developing nations may receive poor, or even deteriorating, terms of trade. For example, the 'immiserising growth' analysis of Jagdish Bhagwati was based on the view that the demand for Third World primary products was highly price- as well as income-inelastic. Thus, as output expands (and the supply curve shifts to the right) the price falls substantially. As a result, despite extra output, export earnings may decline.[18] In this circumstance the gains from output growth are more than offset by worsened terms of trade. Of course, in this case, the fall in living standards in some less-developed countries is matched by an increase in economic welfare of developed countries.

Raoul Prebisch and others have given various reasons for expecting the terms of trade to deteriorate in the long-term for developing nations.[19] One of these was that income- and output-elasticities of demand for primary products were inelastic, that is below 1. For example, as incomes rise in the richer nations, little of the extra income is spent on tropical foodstuffs and beverages such as coffee. The demand for manufactures (such as consumer durables like cars and stereos) is, by contrast, income-elastic, that is it rises more than in proportion to income. Thus Third World countries which continued to specialise heavily on primary products would find the pattern of demand growth was biassed against them, in ways which worsened their terms of trade.

Prebisch also suggested a line of thought which was later taken up by W. Arthur Lewis, a liberal development economist, and Arghiri Emmanuel, the Marxist writer.[20] Prebisch contrasted the persistent low wages of workers in less-developed countries with the steadily rising real wages of workers in the industrialised metropolitan nations. Productivity gains in the latter were shared between workers and capitalists. In developing nations such gains were likely to reduce the price of exported primary products to the advantage of consumers in developed countries. Using the labour theory of value, Emmanuel argued that the labour embodied in Third World exports was greater than that which was embodied in their imports of manufactures. Therefore North–South trade was characterised by an 'unequal exchange' of labour values. Lewis came to a similar conclusion, based upon the idea that there was an unlimited supply of rural labour to the 'modern sector' (including mines and commercial agriculture) in developing nations. In the absence of effective trade unions this would tend to hold down the wages of unskilled workers. When this has occurred it has often involved coercion of workers and suppression of unions by governments anxious to maintain their political control and a favourable business climate for foreign investment.

While the above picture of what John Spraos has called 'inequalising trade' fits much of the evidence from the colonial era, theoretical and empirical criticisms can be made of its relevance today.[21] If real wages rise in the metropole (as they have), then there may be a growing incentive for manufacturing firms in these locations to transfer production to locations where labour is cheaper, such as in developing nations. Much depends on the political stability and the adequacy of infrastructure in such countries. In practice, there has been a post-war growth of direct investment by transnational firms in manufacturing plants in the Third World. While some of this investment has been geared to the home markets of developing countries (import-substitution), more recently much of it has been geared to exporting back into the developed countries. As was noted in chapter 11, this capital mobility has weakened the position of labour in the metropolitan countries.

As industrialisation has spread to certain developing countries, transnational firms have been well placed to capture a larger proportion of the gains from trade in manufactures. One reason for this, also discussed in chapter 11, is that intra-firm trade has conferred special advantages on transnational companies. Such trade constitutes a major proportion of world trade in manufactures and some primary products.

In addition, the new international division of labour which relates to these changing patterns of trade, also operates at the intra-firm level. As transnationals shift their production from one location to another, one section of the firm's labour force may gain at the expense of another.

Indeed, it may be that the power relationship between owners and managers (capital) on the one hand, and workers on the other, tilts appreciably in favour of capital as production is transnationalised. Hence the class conflict implied in the simple Heckscher–Ohlin theory is likely to manifest itself more clearly in the age of transnational capital. This is in contrast to earlier periods when most manufacturing was national capitalist in nature. Thus even if capital has an industry-specific character, the mobility of capital means that transnational capitalists have less interest than national capitalists in forging alliances with organised labour. National capital and associated labour have a strong incentive to combine and press their government for protection under these conditions.

One influential liberal explanation of changing sectoral patterns of trade is Raymond Vernon's 'product cycle' theory, which we introduced in chapter 11.[22] This, like our preceding discussion, combines trade with foreign direct investment. The choice between exporting and foreign direct investment is related to the changing 'maturity' of a product. At the earliest, and most innovatory stage of the product cycle, production will be home-based, with foreign markets supplied by exports.It is at this stage that the monopolistic rents to the technological know-how embodied in the product are at their greatest. Further, at this stage the demand for well-paid, highly-skilled labour is at its peak. Here the gains from trade to the firm and to the home economy are highest. As such new products 'mature', the know-how diffuses so that production and 'comparative advantage' ultimately shift to developing nations. It is at this late stage in the cycle that the market for the product is at its most competitive, and at which the rent element is close to zero. For mature products, transnational firms will often face significant competition from local firms, since the technology is by then widely diffused. There is controversy over how far transnational companies have speeded up the transfer of technology in their attempts to maximise profits, thus shortening the product cycle.

Paul Krugman has developed a North–South model of innovation, technology transfer and the world distribution of income, built from the product cycle theory.[23] The higher incomes of the North reflect monopolistic rents and a return to human capital. The income gap between North and South depends on how rapidly products mature and technologies diffuse. This model implies an international division of labour with research-intensive industries in the North and more mature and labour-intensive industries in the South. In practice, this would involve a hierarchy of industries and related gains from trade. Certain left-wing writers have made similar use of ideas drawn from the theory of the product cycle in order to explain what they call the 'new international division of labour'.[24] There is empirical evidence that the rate of diffusion of technology has accelerated, which on Krugman's analysis would imply a narrowing of the North–South gap. However, his model does not distinguish between the interests of national and transnational capital. In practice, a large part of the gains from a hierarchical global division of labour might be captured by transnational firms. The latter might remit much of their profits back to the metropolitan countries.

One implication of Krugman's analysis is that it will pay a government to subsidise the development and production of high-technology goods which yield monopolistic rents. This may be rational even if it lowers the export price of such goods, so long as price exceeds the marginal cost of exports.[25] Hence his analysis helps to account for some (non-military) high-technology protectionism, which contrasts with protection of lower-technology declining industries in developed countries. Governments facing demands for protection by declining industries have a choice between opposing or promoting adjustment. The 'adjustment costs' associated with decline involve unemployment of labour and capital and, perhaps, the demoralisation of certain towns or regions which have been dependent on one or two industries. In sum, governments with limited financial resources have faced the dilemma of choosing between high-technology protection, and support of a defensive nature for their declining industries.

7. THE MACRO-LEVEL: GLOBAL OPENNESS OR CLOSURE

We identify three main approaches to the analysis of the macro-level, each of which has some merit in helping to explain changes in global openness. The most common and influential approach stresses the influence of the relative concentration of power, especially in a hegemonic state. A second approach focuses on the impact of slower economic growth, marked by recessions. The third approach highlights the changing character of capitalism as a global system, with particular attention being paid to increasing interdependence and social and political integration. In our analysis, explanations of openness or closure require an understanding of the nature, dynamics and contradictions of the transnational stage of capitalism.

Writers from many perspectives have stressed the importance of hegemony, usually in the sense of dominance. They have seen a decline in American hegemony as leading to a weakening, or even breakdown of the post-war liberal economic order. Realists and world systems theorists have debated whether hegemony is a necessary and/or a sufficient condition for an open trade system. A second, related question, is whether the existence of such a system is likely to contribute to the long-term erosion of hegemony, and an outbreak of global economic conflict. There is a large measure of agreement that a liberal order promotes the diffusion of technology. Since this reduces the hegemon's material dominance, liberal orders are said to 'self-destruct'. These questions have also been central to much Marxist writing, for example that of Fred Block.[26] In this context, there are signs of an 'unholy consensus' of Liberals, Marxists, realists and world systems theorists, which has been described by David Sylvan as the 'newest Mercantilism'.[27] Hence the most common forecast is that openness will continue to decline, and the regionalisation of trade become much more pronounced.[28]

The early versions of the Theory of Hegemonic Stability, discussed in chapter 4, implied that American dominance was a necessary condition for the establishment and maintenance of an open order, and thus for relatively free trade. The theory stressed the willingness of the United States to invest resources in the construction of a pro-trade regime (the GATT), thus providing a 'public good'. This version of the Theory of Hegemonic Stability sees hegemony in 'benevolent' rather than 'coercive' terms. However, the years immediately after World War II saw little effective reduction of trade barriers even though American primacy was at its height. The United States was prepared to allow Europe and Japan time to reconstruct their economies, while political pressures in European countries were such as to make trade liberalisation difficult. United States policies on trade were influenced by security concerns, that is to make Western Europe and Japan safe from communism.

The failure of the United States to act like a hegemonic power in the 1930s has been a subject of much debate. In this context, a specific problem for hegemonic stability theory is the need to explain the substantial tariff increase in the United States in the early 1930s. It is one thing to explain a lag in the development of pro-trade American policies: it is another thing to explain increased protectionism for the emerging hegemon's economy.

Some of the reasons for the slow development of an internationalist coalition in the United States were discussed in chapter 9. They included the size of the American market, the substantial scope for capital accumulation on the basis of this gigantic market in the 1920s and American self-sufficiency. From another viewpoint, a key factor was the relative security from invasion which facilitated the persistence of the 'isolationist' outlook. However, the increased protectionism of the Smoot–Hawley Act has also to be understood as made possible by monetary disorder within the United States, Congressional log-rolling and what might be termed an ignorant insularity. This is why American leaders were taken aback at the scale of damaging retaliation, even though foreign diplomats had given considerable warning. Thus an explanation which relies heavily on the distribution of material power resources is likely to be excessively parsimonious and misleading.

The Theory of Hegemonic Stability, when applied to trade, often assumes that a hegemon's first-best policy is free trade. This is because of its technological lead, which enables the hegemon to reap a substantial proportion of the gains from trade.[29] The largely unilateral adoption of free trade by Britain in the nineteenth century is often cited in this context. However, liberal economic theory suggests that the size of the hegemon in the world economy is likely to be large enough for it to exert some monopsony and/or monopolistic power by means of an 'optimal tariff'. Further, the hegemon can influence the distribution of the gains from trade liberalisation by using its leverage, for example whether it allows foreign access to its large home market. The hegemon may not always allow freer trade to be a 'public good'. Indeed, trade liberalisation on a global scale may require the hegemon to avoid making large unilateral tariff cuts, since then its leverage can be used to get other countries to reduce their trade barriers. The hegemon, by using its economic centrality, as well as its military strength, can act as an 'enforcer', curbing the free-riding tendencies of other states.[30]

In addition, despite the predictions of Hegemonic Stability Theory, hegemonic decline may not always be associated with policies of increased protection. A comprehensive theory would integrate 'domestic' and 'international' levels of analysis. To explain the British case after 1870 requires an examination of the strength and persistence of 'internationalist' forces in British 'domestic' politics. These forces can be likened to a Gramscian historic bloc, since they involved both workers and internationally-oriented capitalists. At the heart of this bloc were the material interests associated with the City of London, and the hegemony of liberal ideas. The eventual shift towards substantial protectionism in Britain came long after Britain's relative economic decline had begun (often dated to the 1870s). It took the onset of economic depression and a World War, involving ferocious rivalry between the leading capitalist states before the move towards protectionism occurred. In this vein, other writers, such as Susan Strange and Roger Tooze, have noted the higher demands for protection made in industries with surplus capacity and more generally, in times of recession and slow growth.[31]

Various factors have been suggested by public choice theorists which affect the demand for protection. Producers will demand more protection the greater are the expected gains ('rents') relative to the costs of getting organised and lobbying. The gains may appear greater in recessions assuming firms are averse to risk since in such periods the survival of firms is often at stake and the likelihood of new entrants into the industry is minimal as Timothy McKeown has argued.[32] Hence industries with surplus capacity will tend to have a higher demand for protection than those with little slack. Slower growth makes the elimination of such surplus capacity much more difficult. This is especially so if slower growth occurs at the same time as there is a process of global restructuring and changes in comparative advantage, as during the 1970s. By the end of the 1970s the impact of transnationalisation and the rise of the newly-industrialising countries was becoming much more marked.

G.M. Gallarotti finds the empirical evidence is consistent with the influence of the business cycle on changes in tariff levels in the cases of West Germany, the United States and Britain.[33] P. Cowhey and E. Long find that the existence of surplus capacity in automobiles is the most significant factor in explaining changes in protection when compared to the influence of hegemonic decline.[34] However, they suggest a possible synthesis of the surplus capacity and hegemonic decline theories:

A decline in hegemony may constitute a necessary, but not sufficient, condition for the collapse of a regime. Conversely, as long as a hegemonic power exists surplus capacity may also be only a necessary, but not sufficient, condition for regime change.[35]

Those stressing the role of the hegemon need not accept this compromise since they could argue that slower growth is itself due to the decline of American hegemony. Following the mercantilist argument of section 5 of this chapter, the breakdown of the Bretton Woods system could be seen as disrupting a beneficial mixture of trade surpluses and increased dollar liabilities. Also, as we have seen in chapter 10, the threat of diversification away from dollars in 1979 was one factor in the adoption of a severely deflationary policy in the United States, which helped to provoke a global recession. These developments are sometimes seen as symptoms of American decline. However, such arguments, in their turn, ignore increased international financial integration and the growth of transnational firms, both of which contributed to the move away from fixed exchange rates.

The growth in demands for protection need to be seen in the context of growing economic interdependence and exchange rate volatility. More economic openness has raised the burden of adjustment costs, especially for workers and national capitalists in developed capitalist nations. The demand for protection has been increased partly because of exchange rate volatility which has, in periods of overvaluation, intensified foreign competition. Unmanaged floating has had a 'ratchet' effect on levels of protection. This is because those threatened by foreign competition in countries with overvalued currencies have demanded, and obtained protection. Such protection tended to continue even after the exchange rate declined.

In this respect the policies of the pro-trade Reagan administration have been perverse. Adjustment assistance to uncompetitive industries in the

United States was severely cut shortly before the dollar reached high levels in 1982–85. This was painful for American industry. The high dollar partly reflected capital inflows to finance the American budget deficit.

E. V. Clifton has studied the influence of exchange rates on import penetration, and found that they were a significant influence for the United States, but somewhat less so for Britain, for the 1963–80 period. Clifton also found that exchange rate volatility seemed to have a 'ratchet' effect on protection.[36] Thus policies to limit exchange rate fluctuations and the 'overvaluation' of some currencies may help dampen demands for protection. These findings are important in that import penetration seems to be the key variable triggering protection, except if the country is heavily engaged in exporting. This is consistent with the study by William Cline who estimated 'protection functions' for the United States, Britain, Canada, West Germany and France.[37]

It might be asked why, when calls for and measures of protection appear to have risen to a crescendo during the 1980s, it is still possible for trade to grow slightly faster than world output: indeed why it is possible for trade to grow at all? On the one hand, demands for protection partly reflect structural changes bound up with the growth of transnational capitalism. On the other hand, such demands can be seen as part of a process of structural change in the global political economy which may reinforce the strength of social forces favourable to the maintenance of open trade. This is a dialectical process, the precise outcome of which is difficult to predict.

With the spread of transnational production there is a new rationale for raising trade barriers: to induce foreign direct investment. Workers and national capitalists have often combined to lobby for protection in the past.[38] However, now such lobbying can take on a different character. Many workers may increasingly come to perceive that their long-term job security is enhanced by the influx of foreign transnationals. Hence, whereas in the past demands for protection could be seen as a manifestation of the defensive behaviour of national capitalism, today the situation is more complex. Some organised labour makes its demands for protection because they think that higher trade barriers will cause transnationals to invest more in the workers' country. In effect, such workers and their unions (and their governments) are operating with a new concept of economic necessity, one that is no longer nailed to the nationalist mast. Other workers, in exporting and importing industries, continue to have an interest in open trade. Workers, as consumers, will also to an extent share this interest. As such, the interests of a wider range of workers may be incorporated into an emerging historic bloc of social forces favouring further transnationalisation of the world economy.

In a sense, the workers, by attempting to raise the level of protection, may be able to undermine the threat of transnational firms relocating elsewhere, particularly if they are from a country which has a large domestic market. This will, in this particular nation, serve to limit the structural power of transnational productive capital. Hence, transnational corporations, seeking to avoid this, will have a long-term interest in the maintenance of open trade, particularly in the nations which have the biggest markets. Low trade barriers enhance the credibility of threats by transnational companies to relocate their production in another country.

Vertically integrated transnationals have a special interest in low tariffs on assembled and intermediate goods such as base chemicals, not least since this enables them to gain more from the technique of transfer-pricing. The scope for transfer-pricing is reduced if quotas are imposed, since tariffs can be circumvented. From the point of view of labour, however, quotas are preferred, since by limiting the physical quantity of imported items, the level of production in their plants may be more easily sustained. Thus there is a struggle, not just over the level, but also over the form of protection.

The interest of transnational firms in open trade is, however, subject to certain qualifications. For example, when transnational firms have invested in some developing nations, to supply these markets, their decision has often been influenced by high trade barriers. Removal of these barriers would threaten the profitability of these investments. Even in cases where transnationals prefer open trade, the intensity of their demand for such openness will tend to be less than that for a national capitalist firm in an export sector. Unlike such national capitalist firms, transnationals are able to jump tariff barriers. In addition, when import competition grows, a transnational may shift production from a country (even the parent country) and survive in a way which would be impossible for a smaller national firm.

On balance, the greater the share of transnational corporations, as compared to national ones, in world output, the lower will be the demand for protection. Given the transnationals' long-term interest in keeping location options open, they are likely to ally themselves with national firms (and associated labour) engaged in exporting and importing. In so far as this complex of political forces is successful, it will be partly because the autarkic and protectionist fractions of national capital will be unable to survive in their competitive struggle with transnational capital.

8. THE MESO-LEVEL: ARMS PRODUCTION AND NORTH-SOUTH CONTRASTS

Our discussion of the meso-level differs from that of Stuart Holland, since we focus on some differences in the level and sectoral mix of protection which have a global and systemic character. Holland uses the term with special reference to the role of transnational corporations in trade, which we have already elaborated in this chapter and in chapter 11.[39]

In both North and South, capitalist and communist countries, high protection is usually afforded to defence-related industries, especially armaments. This often takes the form of subsidies and national preference in state purchases, sometimes backed by elaborate systems of industrial surveillance. Even foreign direct investment, in the form of majority-owned subsidiaries, is exceptional in the arms sector. Licensing, joint ventures and subcontracting are much more common.[40] As noted in chapter 8, many Third World nations have sought to develop their own arms production. Thus the influence of security considerations, stressed by realists and world systems writers, is amply confirmed.

Another global pattern is that the level of protection in manufacturing (and some services) is much higher in developing nations than in developed capitalist countries. One of the first policy changes made by most of the newly independent countries was to raise tariff barriers. Further, unlike developed capitalist countries they have frequently resorted to quotas, often for balance of payments reasons. A striking feature in many Third World states is the extent to which there is discrimination against agriculture, in favour of industry. This contrasts with the high level of protection given to farmers in most developed countries, such as in the Common Agricultural Policy of the EC.[41]

In the developed countries, agricultural interests have traditionally wielded substantial political influence. For most of the post-war period this has been disproportionate to the share of agriculture in both output and employment. In the developed countries, there is more large-scale farming, agricultural lobbies are well organised and vocal, and their interests are frequently represented in conservative parties. Indeed, the support of such interests is crucial for conservatives in Japan, West Germany, France, Italy and is still important in Britain. Farming lobbies have been associated with supplier and food processing industries, notably the large chemical companies. In many countries these lobbies have established a special relationship with 'their' ministry of agriculture which works on their behalf within the wider political process. In those developing countries where industrialisation and urbanisation have reached fairly high levels, such as in Taiwan and South Korea, there is also positive effective protection for agriculture.

This contrast in patterns of protection also reflects a concern by developing nations to diversify their economies and make them less vulnerable to changes in the world economy, especially changes in the markets of developed capitalist countries. For many years import-substitution industrialisation was seen as a way of doing this. Developing nations considered that they had more 'infant industries' to protect and develop, so justifying high tariffs. One realist interpretation of these contrasts and concerns is that, for reasons of national power, security and prestige, Third World governments have sought to change the dependent structure of their economies. In a similar vein, a world systems approach sees developing nations as driven to adopt such policies by structural forces of inter-state rivalry and capital accumulation. These forces are particularly strong in the periphery and semi-periphery. It is as if protected agriculture is a luxury which only the richer and more industrialised nations can afford.

The protection afforded to manufacturing in the Third World can be related to the global pattern of protection for arms industries noted earlier. Successful arms production requires the development of related strategic industries. However, in order to establish an adequate industrial base, developing nations often have to welcome foreign direct investment, even though they tend to prevent such investment in arms production itself, which is usually in the public sector. In consequence, Third World attempts at increasing national power and reducing the effects of structural dependence are beset by contradictions. Studies have shown how this contradiction manifests itself in practice. Often, attempts to reduce one kind of dependence, have led to another. For example, the persistent priority given to manufacturing has discouraged the growth of agricultural output, resulting in growing food imports in many African countries.[42]

More empirical research needs to be done on establishing what constitutes the demand for protection in developing countries. Using a public choice approach, one hypothesis which might be tested is the degree to which urban interests (especially those of the rich and the bureaucracy) predominate in the shaping of trade policy, relative to those of the rural majority. The latter are more widely dispersed, harder to organise and less well informed than the urban elites. Urban elites may hope to benefit substantially from industrialisation since it raises urban land values, and opens up business opportunities, including involvement in joint ventures with foreign transnationals. A hypothesis couched in Marxist terms would qualify the town versus countryside distinction to incorporate the balance of class forces, both within the ruling class and within the workers and peasantry. In particular, some fractions of 'rural capital' (landowners, the biggest farmers) might be expected to be more favoured in terms of protection than would the peasantry (or at least less discriminated against than the peasants). There is evidence in some Third World countries that cheap loans and technical advice have tended to favour the largest and most capital-intensive farmers.[43]

Another, more specific and practical hypothesis drawn from development studies is that tariff protection will vary with the development of the tax and financial system. In many developing nations the systems are underdeveloped so that they use tariffs in order to gain a large part of their revenue. For example 66 per cent of central government revenue for Gambia came from taxes on international transactions.[44]

9. THE MICRO-LEVEL: THE INDUSTRY COMPOSITION OF PROTECTION

There are pronounced industry variations in protection, within and between countries. Concentrating solely on the general factors which affect global openness and closure tends to obscure the significance of these micro-level variations. To examine these a less parsimonious approach is needed, to take account of the conditions which are specific to different industries.

Micro-level questions include the following. Is the industry geographically concentrated within a nation, so possibly enhancing the industry's political weight? How far is the industry transnationalised? How much scope exists for intra-industry trade? Is the industry young or mature? Is the industry research-intensive, capital-intensive or labour-intensive?

Certain sectors have been much more highly protected than others. For example, agriculture has been kept largely outside of the GATT, originally at the request of the United States in the 1950s. In addition, many services that are often provided by the public sector have been monopolies favouring home suppliers, such as in telecommunications. Within manufacturing certain industries have been highly protected. For example, textiles and clothing have had a special regime of their own, the Multifibre Arrangement, since 1962. Since then non-tariff barriers have grown in the steel, automobile and electronics sectors. A public choice approach would explain these sectoral contrasts in terms of variations in the demands for protection.

Some industries, such as textiles and steel, are often geographically concentrated, so that their workers can make a major impact on election results. Geographical concentration tends to raise the social costs of adjustment. Some of these industries in the West have suffered from mounting import competition as comparative advantage has been lost to Japan and/or the newly-industrialising countries. In addition, surplus capacity has been a widespread problem in some industries, as in steel, ship-building and shipping. The presence of surplus capacity will raise the demand for protection. Further, these traditional heavy industries are usually national rather than transnational in character. The technology involved in such manufacture is widely available.

Empirical work using the public choice approach has been growing in recent years. Studies on America have found that a significant positive correlation exists between both nominal tariff rates and effective rates of protection, and the relative labour intensity of manufacturing industries. Low wages and labour intensity may be used as an indicator of the severity of import competition which in turn will be related to the size of the 'rents' that can be obtained by protection. T. A. Pugel and I. Walter conclude:

A company facing more severe import competition, both in a static sense (as measured by the initial tariff rate) and dynamically (as measured by the increase in import penetration) is more likely to oppose or view unfavourably trade-liberalising legislation. A company more likely to benefit from easier access to foreign markets (as measured by R & D-intensity) is more likely to favour liberalising legislation. The evidence on the role of internal risk-pooling capabilities (as measured by the extent of product diversification) indicates a tendency for more diversified firms to favour trade-liberalising legislation.[45]

The European Community provides a classic case of trade growth involving substantial intra-industry trade.[46] Such trade involves countries importing and exporting the same good in large quantities. In consequence, what some firms lose through increased import competition is often offset by what they gain from higher exports. The adjustment costs associated with intra-industry trade are much lower than they are for inter-industry trade. The latter relates to the case considered as normal in most trade theory, when discussing comparative advantage. The normal view of comparative advantage involves a country exporting certain goods and importing different goods. Indeed, when it comes to consumer goods, the Japanese have been accused of adopting a 'laser beam' approach: that is establishing a strong comparative advantage in specific products, highly targeted on foreign markets, especially those of the EC and the United States. By contrast, EC countries, happy to trade with each other, increasingly attempted to construct an anti-laser shield of export restraints and quotas to repel Japanese penetration of their markets. The Japanese riposte was to increase its manufacturing and financial investment in the EC, notably in Britain, and thus gain automatic access to Community markets.

10. FROM TOKYO TO URUGUAY

We shall now discuss the way trade negotiations have been conducted during the 1970s and 1980s, and the background to the Uruguay Round.

The Tokyo Round of trade negotiations in the GATT was more or less completed in April 1979. Unlike previous trade rounds it paid substantial attention to the growth and persistence of non-tariff barriers such as voluntary export restraints. Another contrast with previous rounds was the reduced willingness of the United States to make large concessions and stand strictly by international norms.[47]

The agreements reached included tariff reductions, several codes covering non-tariff trade barriers and sectoral agreements for dairy products and aircraft. These agreements made some contribution to the maintenance of an open trade order. None the less there were certain departures from the GATT norm of unconditional most favoured nation status. These were embodied in the government procurement, subsidy, and proposed safeguard codes, as well as the revision of some GATT Articles. These departures reflected a tacit acceptance of the interests of developing countries and of some interest groups from the developed nations (such as farmers). For example, the subsidies code banned the use of export subsidies on manufactured products from developed capitalist countries. However, it did not prohibit subsidies for raw materials (defined to include foodstuffs of which the EC has a surplus). Furthermore, there was no outright injunction against the use of subsidies by Third World countries.

The issue of safeguards against unfair competition and 'serious injury' remains controversial. Many developing nations have been dissatisfied with the demands of the developed countries, especially those made by the EC. The existing Article XIX of GATT allows the use of safeguards. However, it does so in such a restrictive way that it has hardly ever been used. Of Article XIX, Stephen Krasner comments:

It also obligates the country to consult with other members of GATT that might be affected, and allows affected parties to retaliate by withdrawing 'substantially equivalent concessions or other obligations' ... [Countries] have, instead, acted under other provisions of GATT, sanctioned arrangements between private groups and negotiated voluntary export restraints (VERs) with exporting countries.[48]

The European Community has insisted on the right to act unilaterally and selectively (that is against any exporting country) on the safeguards issue. Thus the Tokyo Agreement failed to establish provisions which could check the growth of voluntary export restraints. Indeed, a brief review of developments in international trade negotiations and agreements suggests a trend towards bilateralism rather than an adherence to the multilateral principles of the GATT.

In the mid-1980s mounting protectionist demands in the United States meant renewed Congressional involvement in trade policy, an involvement which harked back to the Smoot–Hawley tariff of 1930. Demands were couched in terms of bilateral reciprocity and 'fair trade'. Such demands, as other nations were swift to point out, were completely contrary to both liberal economics and the 'multilateral' spirit of the GATT. As part of its bilateral trade offensive, the United States negotiated a free trade treaty with Israel in 1986 and with Canada in 1987.

Some bilateral trade deals have been negotiated between the EC and other groups of nations, such as that with some Mediterranean and Third World countries. The Yarbroughs have argued that such arrangements may help sustain the growth of world trade since they are easier to monitor and enforce, despite the fact that they contravene the principle of non-discrimination.[49]

Similar types of tactics have been deployed by United States, allowing it to bargain over the conditions of access to its huge market. This method has been used to extract trade concessions from newly industrialising countries. In the mid-1980s South Korea agreed to United States demands for some trade liberalisation, while Singapore committed itself to enforcing intellectual property rights so as to maintain access to the low duties of the Generalised System of Preference scheme (designed for less developed countries in the early 1970s). In 1986 the United States unilaterally withdrew some duty-free concessions under this scheme from Taiwan, Hong Kong, South Korea, Brazil and Mexico.

In 1987 the United States raised tariff duties on a variety of Japanese consumer goods in response to claimed violations of the United States–Japan agreement on silicon chips for semiconductors. This was intended to improve market access for American firms in Japan, as well as restricting Japanese exports to the United States.

In consequence of these developments, the Uruguay Round began, in 1987, under a protectionist cloud. In the Uruguay Round, agriculture and services were to receive more attention than previously. The United States was the most active advocate of this new agenda. The developing countries were more cautious, notably the more industrialised ones, such as India and Brazil. Before entering into new negotiations, they sought assurances that the developed countries would agree to some 'roll-back' of restrictions on their manufacturing imports. Third World nations pointed out that such restrictions were inconsistent with the rules and the spirit of the GATT. In addition, they sought a commitment from the developed countries to establish a new comprehensive agreement on 'safeguard' measures. The United States was opposed to this since it was keen to use 'safeguards' and thus access to its markets as a means of leverage. The United States was using trade concessions in the field of manufactures, in order to gain the liberalisation of services and agriculture. Third World countries were anxious to minimise concessions on services.

The American interest in the new agenda has stemmed from a perception that while the United States may have lost some of its comparative advantage in a growing range of manufactures, the opposite seems to be the case for some services. American transnationals retain a competitive advantage in some fast-growing service sectors, such as banking, insurance and computer software. Other countries tend to see certain services as closely bound up with sovereignty and the 'national interest'. For example, telecommunications is seen as bound up with national security while control over national savings is seen as vital to attaining economic development and minimising external vulnerability. Moreover, many suspect that the real argument is about foreign investment, including banking. This suspicion is confirmed by the stated American desire to see the GATT rules extended to cover capital mobility.

The other important but difficult area in the Uruguay Round will be agriculture where conflicts between the EC and the United States have been intense. Growing export subsidies by these countries are not only a burden on the tax payer but also operate to the substantial disadvantage of some developing country exports (such as sugar).

11. CONCLUSIONS

Those who fear growing protectionism often invoke the 1930s. Some writers see another trade round as necessary to maintain commitment to the liberal GATT regime. This has been labelled the 'bicycle theory' since to stop pedalling (trade liberalisation) is to risk a crash (retaliation and trade wars).[50] However, trade growth has continued in most years in the 1980s despite rising trade barriers. This is not to suggest that this process is straightforward, nor that it is not without contradictory tendencies. Further, the trade system is bound up with, and, in a variety of respects, subordinate to the security, production and money structures of the global political economy. Monetary disorder could, and indeed to some extent has raised demands for protection. While such disorder can be linked to the changing position of the United States in the global political economy, there is no simple relationship between trade closure and hegemonic decline, or indeed the propensity to war.

In the light of our 'complex integrationist' argument, we suggest that there was, by the mid-1980s, a set of social forces sustaining the level of trade openness. In another context, Susan Strange has outlined a 'web-of-contracts' model, which supplements our analysis by adding quasi-legal factors to the social forces we identify.[51] Trade links have also been intensified for technological reasons as transport costs have fallen and communications have improved. Some countries, notably the United States have become less self-sufficient in fuel and raw materials than they once were. Such trends are likely to continue.

In addition to the material forces which have been the major focus of this chapter, there are signs that the role of liberal pro-trade ideas and institutes has been growing more important for much of the 1970s and 1980s. Liberal economic ideas have been promoted by many organisations, for example liberal institutes such as Chatham House in Britain, and the Council on Foreign Relations in America, as well as more right-wing institutes such as the American Heritage Foundation, the Adam Smith Institute in Britain and the international Mont Pelerin Society, founded after World War II by F. A. von Hayek. The obverse to this has been the decline of Keynesian political economy, and the doubts and divisions in social democratic politics in the face of a liberal and conservative ideological offensive. Increasing numbers of leaders within mainstream political parties in the developed countries have been persuaded by liberal economic views. At the international level, the IMF, World Bank and the GATT have also encouraged trade liberalisation, as a part of a wider pro-market reform programme.

NOTES

1. *Financial Times*, 3 March 1987.
2. Robert O. Keohane and Joseph S. Nye, *Power and Interdependence* (Boston, Mass., Little, Brown, 1977).
3. Peter Blau, *Exchange and Power in Social Life* (Chichester, John Wiley, 1964).
4. E. H. Carr, *The Twenty Years' Crisis, 1919–1939* (New York, Harper and Row, 1964); Barry Buzan, 'Economic Structure and International Security: The Limits of the Liberal Case', *International Organisation* (1984), Vol. 38, pp. 597–624.
5. G. Banks, 'The Economics and Politics of Countertrade', *The World Economy* (1983), Vol. 17, pp. 159–82.
6. On non-tariff barriers, see R. E. Baldwin, *Non-Tariff Distortions of International Trade* (Washington DC, Brookings Institution, 1970); William Cline (ed.), *Trade Policy in the 1980s* (Washington DC, Institute for International Economics, 1983).
7. E. Grilli and M. LaNoce, 'The Political Economy of Protection in Italy: some Empirical Evidence', *Banca Nazionale del Lavoro* (1983), Vol. 145, pp. 143–61.
8. Bela Belassa, *The Structure of Protection in Developing Countries* (Baltimore, Johns Hopkins University Press, 1973).
9. David B. Yoffie, *Power and Protectionism* (New York, Columbia University Press, 1983).
10. Nobuhiko Ushiba et al., *Sharing International Responsibilites* (Trilateral Commission, New York, 1983), Table 2, p. 81 (world GNP), Table 4, p. 83 (exports), based on UN and Eurostat statistics.
11. P. Yates, *Forty Years of Foreign Trade* (London, 1959), cited in James Foreman-Peck, *A History of the World Economy* (Brighton, Harvester Press, 1983), p. 199.
12. Ibid., p. 213.
13. 'Costs and Benefits of Protection', *OECD Observer* (1985), Vol. 134, p. 20.
14. Hywel G. Jones, *An Introduction to Modern Theories of Economic Growth* (London, Nelson, 1975).

15. Edward Denison, *Why Growth Rates Differ* (Washington DC, Brookings Institution, 1967); Angus Maddison, 'Long Run Dynamics of Productivity Growth', *Banca Nazionale del Lavoro* (1979), Vol. 128, pp. 3–44.
16. On trade theories, see P. R. D. Wilson, *International Economics: Theory, Evidence and Practice* (Brighton, Harvester Press, 1986); R. A. Johns, *International Trade Theories and the Evolving International Economy* (London, Pinter, 1985).
17. Jon Bennett and Susan George, *The Hunger Machine* (Oxford Polity Press/ Basil Blackwell, 1987), p. 128.
18. See Wilson, op. cit.; Johns, op. cit.
19. Raoul Prebisch, 'The Role of Commercial Policies in Underdeveloped Countries', *American Economic Review: Papers and Proceedings* (1967), Vol. 49, pp. 251–73.
20. W. Arthur Lewis, *The Evolution of the International Economic Order* (Princeton NJ, Princeton University Press, 1978); Aghiri Emmanuel, *Unequal Exchange: A Study of the Imperialism of Trade* (New York, Monthly Review Press, 1972); A. Brewer, *Marxist Theories of Imperialism* (London, Routledge, 1980), pp. 208–32.
21. John Spraos, *Inequalising Trade* (Oxford, Clarendon Press, 1983).
22. Raymond Vernon, 'International Trade Investment and International Trade in the Product Cycle', *Quarterly Journal of Economics* (1966), Vol. 80, pp. 190–207.
23. Paul Krugman, 'A Model of Innovation, Technology Transfer, and the World Distribution of Income', *Journal of Political Economy* (1979), Vol. 87, pp. 253–66.
24. Folker Froebel et al., *The New International Division of Labour* (Cambridge, Cambridge University Press, 1980).
25. Paul Krugman, 'New Theories of Trade Among Industrial Countries', *American Economic Review: Papers and Proceedings* (1983), Vol. 73, pp. 343–7; B. J. Spencer and J. A. Brander, 'International R & D Rivalry and Industrial Strategy', *Review of Economic Studies* (1983), Vol. 50, pp. 707–22.
26. Fred Block, *The Origins of International Economic Disorder* (Berkeley, Cal., University of California Press, 1977).
27. David Sylvan, 'The Newest Mercantilism', *International Organisation* (1981), Vol. 35, pp. 375–9.
28. John Palmer, *Europe Without America? The Crisis in Atlantic Relations* (Oxford, Oxford University Press, 1987); Robert Gilpin, *The Political Economy of International Relations* (Princeton NJ, Princeton University Press, 1987).
29. David A. Lake, 'Beneath the Commerce of Nations: A Theory of International Economic Structures', *International Studies Quarterly* (1984), Vol. 28, pp. 143–70; Robert Gilpin, *US Power and the Multinational Corporation* (New York, Basic Books, 1975); Stephen D. Krasner, 'State Power and the Structure of International Trade', *World Politics* (1976), Vol. 28, pp. 317–47.
30. B. V. Yarbrough and R. M. Yarbrough, 'Free Trade, Hegemony, and the Theory of Agency', *KYKLOS* (1985), Vol. 38, pp. 350–1.
31. Susan Strange, 'The Management of Surplus Capacity: or how does theory stand up to protectionism 1970s style?', *International Organisation* (1979), Vol. 33, pp. 303–44; Susan Strange and Roger Tooze (eds), *The International Management of Surplus Capacity* (London, Allen and Unwin, 1982).

32. Timothy J. McKeown, 'Firms and Tariff Regime Change: Explaining the Demand for Protection', *World Politics* (1984), Vol. 36, pp. 215–33.
33. G. M. Gallarotti, 'Toward a Business-Cycle Model of Tariffs', *International Organisation* (1985), Vol. 39, pp. 155–87.
34. P. F. Cowhey and E. Long, 'Testing Theories of the Regime Change: Hegemonic Decline or Surplus Capacity?', *International Organisation* (1983), Vol. 37, pp. 157–88.
35. Ibid., p. 186.
36. E. V. Clifton, 'Real Exchange Rates, Import Penetration, and Protectionism in Industrial Countries', *IMF Staff Papers* (1985), Vol. 32, pp. 513–36.
37. William R. Cline, *Exports of Manufactures from Developing Countries: Performance and Prospects for Market Access* (Washington DC, Brookings Institution, 1984).
38. Stephen P. Magee, 'Three Simple Tests of the Stolper–Samuelson Theorem', in Peter Oppenheimer (ed.), *Issues in International Economics* (Oxford, Oriel Press, 1980), pp. 138–53.
39. Stuart Holland, *The Global Economy: from Meso to Macroeconomics* (London, Weidenfeld and Nicolson, 1987).
40. C. J. Dixon et al., *Multinational Corporations in the Third World* (London, Croom Helm, 1986). See especially, S. W. Williams, 'Arming the Third World: the Role of the Multinational Corporation', pp. 66–90.
41. R. C. Hine, *The Political Economy of European Trade* (Brighton, Harvester Press, 1985).
42. Bennett, op.cit., p. 174.
43. Keith Griffin, *The Political Economy of Agrarian Change: an essay on the green revolution* (London, Macmillan, 1974).
44. Bruno S. Frey, *International Political Economics* (Oxford, Basil Blackwell, 1984), p. 23.
45. T. A. Pugel and I. Walter, 'US Corporate Interests and the Political Economy of Trade Policy', *Review of Economics and Statistics* (1985), Vol. 67, pp. 465–73.
46. See Hine, op.cit.
47. Stephen D. Krasner, 'The Tokyo Round', *International Studies Quarterly* (1979), Vol. 23, pp. 491–531.
48. Ibid., p. 521.
49. B. V. and R. M. Yarbrough, 'Cooperation in the liberalisation of international trade: after hegemony, what?', *International Organisation* (1987), Vol. 41, pp. 1–26.
50. Susan Strange, 'Protectionism and World Politics', *International Organisation* (1985), Vol. 39, pp. 233–59.
51. Ibid., pp. 241–2.

13 Energy and the Case of International Oil

1. INTRODUCTION

In this chapter we examine the case of oil, in the context of the political economy of global energy. We outline the factors which have affected the demand for, and supply of, energy, and changes in prevailing global arrangements since the turn of the century, in particular since the early 1970s. We also discuss oil in the context of Middle Eastern, global and superpower politics. We pay specific attention to United States policies and their effects on the United States position in the global political economy. The case also provides evidence in support of (or against) some of the major propositions contained in the perspectives. These are discussed in the penultimate section of this chapter. The final section concerns future prospects.

2. THE IMPORTANCE OF OIL

Oil's importance lies in the fact that it has been, and still is, the major form of energy consumed in the post-war world. Oil, because of cheapness, availability, flexibility and relative ease of transportation, became the primary energy source for most industrial nations. For economic and military reasons, all states have been concerned to assure stable supplies of energy as an essential aspect of their security. Because so much rests upon energy supply, it would be plausible to claim that energy industries, and oil in particular, are strategic industries, *par excellence.*

As such, an interesting aspect of the history of international oil for much of the twentieth century, and notably for the post-1945 period was the willingness of a large number of countries to allow (or not to challenge) the control over supply by the giant transnational oil companies, the so-called 'Seven Sisters', namely Exxon, British Petroleum (BP), Royal-Dutch

Shell, Gulf, Mobil, Standard Oil of California (SoCal) and Texaco (see Table 13.1). This is an instance of what we have called the 'internationalisation of authority' implying considerable potential power for the Sisters relative not only to the producer, but also the consumer states. Moreover, the oligopolistic market power of these companies held back, at least for much of the first half of the twentieth century, new entrants into the international oil industry. Under the auspices of the Seven Sisters, which are diversified energy corporations, based mainly, but not exclusively in oil, the oil business became the world's biggest international industry. The assets and sales figures of these companies came to dwarf the gross national product (GNP) of many small states. Because of their mobility, technological prowess, vast cash reserves, and an uncanny ability to cooperate with each other and to play the game of international politics and diplomacy, by the late 1950s, the power of the Sisters seemed largely unchallengeable. An exception, to a limited extent, was in the United States, where the rising power of 'independent' oil companies such as Getty and Occidental was important. As a result, by 1969 the Seven Sisters controlled 76.1 per cent of the international oil market.

Table 13.1 Seven Sisters' control over international oil, 1950–69 (production shares of world oil market, in percentages)

	1950	1957	1969
Largest four companies (Exxon, BP, Shell, Gulf)	82.6	69.5	55.8
Largest seven companies (big four plus SoCal, Texaco, Mobil)	98.3	89.0	76.1
All others	1.8	11.1	23.9

Source: M. A. Adelman, *The World Petroleum Market* (Baltimore, Johns Hopkins University Press, 1971), pp. 80–1.

The so-called 'energy crises' of the 1973–74 (following the Arab-Israeli October war) and 1979–80 (after the Iranian revolution) dramatised the dependence on foreign sources of oil, for many of the developed and as well as many less-developed countries. The vulnerability to disruptions in the supply of such oil, especially from the volatile areas of the Middle East, forced these countries to engage in conservation programmes, attempts to use energy more efficiently, and to diversify their consumption and sources of energy, in favour of non-oil sources. This is reflected in Table 13.2. From the 1960s on, the entry into the market of larger numbers of oil companies undermined the oligopolistic market structure. A more competitive structure emerged, which began to resemble the markets for other primary commodities. There emerged a worldwide glut of oil in the 1980s, and real prices fell substantially, as they had to a lesser extent in 1976–78. The emergence of a more complex, and more competitive oil industry also brought with it a decline in the power of the Organisation of Petroleum Exporting States (OPEC) to control prices in international markets for oil. This control had been considerable during much of the 1970s.[1]

Table 13.2 Composition of world energy consumption, 1979–84

	oil	natural gas	coal	hydro	nuclear	total
1979	45.0	18.4	28.5	5.9	2.2	100
1981	42.4	19.3	29.2	6.2	2.9	100
1983	40.3	19.2	30.3	6.8	3.4	100
1984*	39.3	19.7	30.3	6.8	3.9	100

* Estimated.
Source: Union des Chambres Syndicales de L'Industrie du Pétrole, *L'Industrie Française du Pétrole, 1984* (Paris, UCSIP, 1985) p. 28, cited in Zakhir Mikdashi, *Transnational Oil: issues, policies and perspectives* (London, Pinter, 1986), p. 24.

As has been noted, for much of the post-war period, the real price of oil fell in the industrialised countries. As a result, consumption rose dramatically between 1960–73, at a compound rate of 7.5 per cent per year, as oil increasingly helped to fuel the long post-war boom in the West and in Japan. The demand for oil is, in the short term, relatively inelastic, so that when real prices rose by 23 per cent between 1973 and 1982, consumption only fell marginally by 0.7 per cent, as is shown in Table 13.3. This allowed the producer countries, who by this time had obtained more control over their own production, to obtain significant economic rents and substantial increases in income. At the same time, total energy consumption per unit of GNP fell by a factor of some 25 per cent in the biggest seven capitalist nations between 1973 and 1984, partly because of recession and slower growth, industrial restructuring and increased energy efficiency.[2]

Table 13.3 Non–communist energy and oil consumption, and oil prices, 1960–82 (compound average annual percentage change)

	1960–73	1973–82
Energy consumption	5.3	0.6
Oil consumption	7.5	-0.7
Real price of crude oil	-0.1	23.0

Source: Chase Manhattan Bank, *The Petroleum Situation* (New York, August 1983), p. 1, cited in Mikdashi, op.cit., p. 23.

These developments indicate that the importance of oil as the world's primary source of energy is declining, but that it is still the central energy source. In addition, the distribution of reserves means that it will continue to be of crucial importance within the global political economy, since most other sources cannot be as easily transported, and have less flexibility in use. In addition, nuclear power has yet to prove a safe and satisfactory alternative (and its spread is linked to the proliferation of nuclear weapons), and coal-fired power stations have significant pollution costs, for example producing acid rain. (Oil-fired power stations also have significant pollution costs.) Safer and cleaner forms of energy, for example solar power and wave power, have not yet been fully exploited, although the Soviet Union is reported to have embarked on an ambitious solar power venture which would involve the use of giant mirrors in space, erected by using the Energia rocket. (See chapter 15 for discussion of this.)

Because of the experiences of the 1970s, and in view of continuing qualitative importance of oil, there is uncertainty as to how far a return to the growth rates of the 1950s is possible. Many in the West fear that rapid growth could result in a third oil price hike. Such fears are, however, somewhat overstated since new patterns of industrial production are based upon more efficient and the lower level use of energy, and supplies are more diversified than was the case in the 1970s.

3. CHANGES IN INTERNATIONAL OIL

As has been noted, for most of the post-war period, oil was the world's biggest industry, yielding great profits to the transnational oil companies. The maintenance of an oil order based on Western control of international oil between 1918 and 1970, with dominance passing from the United

Table 13.4 Political organisation of the international oil system, 1918–74

Year	Dominant Power	Type of actor acceptance	System character
1918–28	Britain	Principles and rules introduced	Order creation
1928–39	Britain	Accepted principles and rules	Order
1939–54	USA	Accepted principles and rules adjusted	Order creation
1954–70	USA	Accepted principles and rules	Order
1970–74	—	Decaying acceptance of principles and rules	Order/ disorder

Source: Hans Jacob Bull-Berg, *American International Oil Policy: Causal Factors and Effects* (London, Pinter, 1987), p. 151.

Kingdom to the United States is reflected in Tables 13.4, 13.5 and 13.6. These tables summarise the basic features in the political organisation of international oil. This order originated in the late nineteenth and early twentieth centuries, when a small number of companies came to dominate the global oil industry, backed by the strategic power of Britain and the United States. Because of very low marginal costs of production, Middle Eastern oil 'took off' in the inter-war period, and helped to fuel the post-war boom. Middle Eastern oil, as a share of internationally-traded oil, rose substantially, and British control was gradually supplanted by the United States.

Table 13.5 Control by major powers in key producing areas outside the United States, 1929–39 (percentage)

Year	Power	Producing Areas		
		Western Hemisphere	Middle East	Far East
1929	United States	58	—	5
	Britain and Holland	39	100	90
	Others	3	—	5
1939	United States	48	16	19
	Britain and Holland	36	78	78
	Others	16	6	6

Source: Bull-Berg, op.cit., p. 142.

Table 13.6 Control by major powers in key producing areas outside the United States and the Soviet Union, 1938–53 (percentage)

	1938	1945	1953
United States	33	41	53
Britain and Holland	53	41	33
Others	14	18	14

Source: Bull-Berg, op.cit., p. 144.

The key actors in this order were governments and transnational oil companies, especially the Seven Sisters, or 'majors' and their consortia. The majors operated an oligopoly pricing convention of (administered) 'posted prices', relative to those for oil arriving in the ports of the Gulf of Mexico for the American market. The majors ensured market stability and high profits and consumers developed the expectation of uninterrupted supply. The operations of the transnational oil companies were backed by the military capacity (with threat of or actual intervention) of the 'sponsoring' British and American (and also French) governments. The oil-producing states had few power resources to offset such Western domination. This enabled order to persist despite wide-ranging political changes, including two world wars, from the late nineteenth century, although leadership passed from Britain to the United States. Thus strategic power was actually a condition for the organisation of the oil system, although its operations were conducted principally by the majors.

Built into this order were certain contradictions, which helped to bring about its demise. The high profits of the industry gradually began to attract new producers, called 'the independents', who came to supply a growing market share and compete with the majors. The 'bargain' of the transnational oil companies (with the producer countries) began to 'obsolesce' as skills and knowledge grew in the producer countries, and as the (hostage) investments of the transnational oil companies increased, an obsolescence enhanced by the rising tax revenues of the producer governments. This helped to develop their internal power resources. The producer countries began to move towards the nationalisation of their oil assets.

Of particular interest within this order was the behaviour of the United States government. The distribution of power in the American oil industry, and the strength of domestic vested interests, well represented in Congress, circumscribed United States foreign policy, even in wartime. This made coherent long-term oil policy impossible, in contrast to the United Kingdom, where the state had demonstrated its autonomy with respect to oil policies. This meant that transnational oil companies in effect controlled the international order with little direct United States government control over its domestic production. Robert Keohane has called this a 'drain America first' policy, developed under pressure from domestic independent producers who favoured import quotas (introduced in the 1950s).[3] As Keohane suggests, this policy appeared irrational from the perspective of American strategic interests, since foreign oil could be obtained very cheaply at this time, and American military power could safeguard such supplies. In the 1960s, United States import quotas kept American oil prices above world prices. This policy contributed to the fall in the real price of oil paid by the main importing countries, since the United States imported less than it would otherwise have done.[4] The United States was unique amongst major countries in having no national oil corporation. The effects of this policy on American spare capacity are reflected in Table 13.7.

The long-term implications of this were felt by the West when OPEC imposed its boycott during the 1973 October War. At this point, Aramco (a consortium of American majors operating in Saudi Arabia) functioned as an agent for its hosts, rather than its parent government. The American government ignored Aramco's warnings concerning the costs of supporting Israel, and in consequence the Arab countries later imposed an

Table 13.7 United States spare capacity 1956–73*

	1956	1960	1967	1970	1973
US spare capacity	2080	2706	2122	1331	0
US spare capacity as a percentage of Middle Eastern and African oil	—	55	8.3	7.7	0

Note: *In relation to oil exports of the Middle East and Africa, in millions of barrels per day and as a percentage.
Source: Bull-Berg, op.cit., p. 150.

embargo. During the embargo the true ambiguity of the oil transnationals' role became more apparent, as they obeyed Arab instructions and imposed tight controls over the supply and distribution of oil. The United States and Holland (which was also pro-Israeli) were made prime targets of the boycott.[5] The post-war American-dominated oil order began to break down, and effectively ended in 1974.

The period 1974–82 was characterised by what can be described as a new, OPEC-dominated order in international oil, although the period manifested relatively few of the attributes of stability associated with the previous order. OPEC was formed in 1960, as an organisation of producer countries. The West became increasingly dependent on Middle East oil in the 1960s and the early 1970s. In the boom of 1972–73, the demand for oil began to outpace the supply. After the 1967 Arab–Israeli War, Arab political and economic cohesion increased and was expressed in the formation of the Organisation of Arab Petroleum Exporting Countries (OAPEC). The 1973 October War led to Arab use of the oil weapon against the West, and against the United States in particular, in order to gain support for their case against Israel. Realising the advantage of high oil prices, other members of OPEC cooperated with their Arab counterparts. Between early 1971 and late 1973 the price of Persian Gulf oil rose from US $1.80 to $11.65 per barrel of crude. Between 1974 and 1978 the price of such oil fell slightly in real terms and rose again in mid-1978. But when supplies from Iran (which at the time produced about 17 per cent of total OPEC exports) were halted, prices rocketed to almost $30 per barrel. Nominal prices peaked at almost $40 in 1982, with a precipitate fall in 1986, briefly to about $8, rising again to a fairly stable level of around $18 per barrel in 1987.

These developments occurred at the same time as oil transnationals pursued a policy designed to increase their rates of return, and to boost profits. In 1981, Data Resources, Inc. reported that oil company profits rose an average of 2.6 per cent during 1956–72, and soared in the period 1973–80 to 20.8 per cent. In current dollars, profits rose from $6.8 billion in 1972 to \$15.9 billion in 1974. American oil company profits declined for three years (when the real price of oil fell), then rose to \$16 billion in 1978, and then doubled to \$32.8 billion in 1980. Thereafter such profits fell to \$29.2 billion to 1981 and \$29.8 billion in 1982.[6]

Most of the increased cost of oil was borne by consumers worldwide. The most badly hit consumers have been low-income groups, for whom energy costs are a larger proportion of disposable income. This is particularly the case for low-income groups in developing nations.[7] One factor which assisted the rise in OPEC power was the strong boom in the world economy in 1972–73, partly fuelled by a surfeit of dollars. This created an inflationary environment in which many commodity prices rose.

Part of the explanation for the rise in prices in 1971–74, and especially in the period immediately after the October War, was the inability of the major Organisation for Economic Cooperation and Development (OECD) consumers to organise a collective response to the Arab members of OPEC. All they were able to do was to join with the United States in forming the International Energy Agency (IEA), which agreed emergency provisions. (France did not join.)

What lay behind the inability of the OECD countries to combine and become a monopsony buyer was the differing degree of vulnerability which each had with respect to the price and supply of Middle Eastern oil. Some countries had very little energy resources, for example Japan, Italy and Denmark. At the time (and even today) these countries were very dependent upon OPEC. In order to secure supplies, they were prepared to pay high prices. A second group of countries was able to supply much of its energy requirement from domestic solid fuels but were dependent on the world market for their supplies of oil, such as France, West Germany and the Benelux countries. Thirdly, some countries had relatively unlimited energy resources of all kinds, and were not inevitably dependent upon the world market, for example the United States and to some extent, Canada.[8] The producers of these countries have an interest in higher oil prices. The fourth category comprised countries, like Britain and Norway, which, because of North Sea oil, became exporters, and had an interest in higher oil prices.

The interest of consumers however, were in lower oil prices, and it may well have been the case that during the post-war boom, they were important in orienting OECD policies towards cheap oil, despite the growing vulnerability to disruptions in supply from the Middle East. On the other hand, because of their diversified economies, OECD countries had the possibility of coping flexibly with rising prices, and funding alternative sources of primary energy, in contrast to the developing countries.

In consequence of the developments noted above, OPEC revenues rose rapidly, for example between 1971 and 1980, Algeria's revenues from oil increased from US $321 million to $10,787 million, Nigeria's from $846 million to $20,000 million, Saudi Arabia's from $1,886 million to $102,212 million. Total OPEC revenues rose from $11,023 million to $264,025 million. The bulk of the increase came between early 1974 and 1980. OPEC members' rapidly growing finances and other assets were often held in Western banks. This was especially true of Saudi Arabia. In addition, OPEC members generally increased their quotas, and thus their influence within the IMF. OPEC members also were able to increase their stocks of knowledge and skills, and begin to develop new industries, such as petrochemicals in Saudi Arabia.

OPEC consolidated its position in various ways: (i) by stabilising prices; (ii) by playing off the Western countries against each other; (iii) channelling funds to selected developing countries and supporting the Third World's demands for a New International Economic Order; (iv) channelling funds through Western and Japanese banks to ease the balance of payments problems of oil-importing countries, strengthening their links (interdependence) with the West; (v) by contributing funds to the IMF oil facility; and (vi) by purchasing Western technology, goods and above all, weapon systems, so as to build up their power resources and reduce their vulnerability. These military procurements helped create a regional arms race (see Table 13.8).

OPEC coped with the oil surplus of 1975–78 by agreed production cuts. The Iranian revolution of 1978 was followed by large increases in oil prices in 1979–80. An oil glut returned after 1981, as Iranian supplies were resumed, although at lower levels than before. Demand for OPEC oil was reduced on a long-term basis. This resulted in a drop in both the real and nominal price of oil after 1981. None the less, in the 1970s, OPEC and other non-OPEC oil exporters had increased their share of the oil revenues, in the form of royalties, taxes and untaxed profits (through nationalisation). The balance of power between the oil transnationals and the oil exporters shifted substantially.

In this second post-war order, the major actors were governments, transnational companies, OPEC and increasingly consumers, who were important in that they cut back on their consumption of oil. Within OPEC, Saudi Arabia and Kuwait, the swing producers, were the most important actors since they were able to restrain production to maintain the price of oil. OPEC strategy was worked out in regular meetings, which set target prices and levels of production.

The contradictions for the OPEC states in the new order can be seen as in some ways similar to those which undermined the power of the majors: new entrants threatened OPEC's partial cartel. High profits from oil led to more non-OPEC oil production, for example North Sea and Alaskan oil.

Other consumer countries began to use their energy more efficiently, developed alternative sources of oil and other forms of energy, and thereby attempted to minimise their vulnerability to disruptions in the supply of Middle Eastern oil. This has led to a much more competitive market structure in international oil. There was a shift from a system based upon market power (first by the transnational oil companies, then by the OPEC producers in alliance with the majors), to a system more characterised by the 'power of the market', with prices reflecting supply and demand factors in a rather more transparent way.

A second contradiction was that oil wealth encouraged and 'fuelled' regional ambitions, and a growing militarisation of the Middle East. Iran sought to establish a regional dominance, initially under the Shah, and later under Ayatollah Khomeini. Although Islamic fundamentalism and anti-Americanism were important mobilising forces in the Iranian Revolution, it contributed to a fall in the political cohesion of OPEC, as other states felt threatened, notably Saudi Arabia, and, of course, Iraq. The political cohesion of OPEC, which had never been great, was substantially weakened by the outbreak of the Iran–Iraq War in 1980. The United States increased its military capacities in the Middle East, for example by creating the Central Command, or Rapid Deployment Force after the regional 'policing power' of Iran, central to United States strategy in the Middle East, was 'lost'. Gradually, the Soviet Union sought to increase its influence in the region in the 1980s, sharing a common interest with the United States, Arab 'moderates' such as Saudi Arabia, and its allies Iraq, and in 1987, Syria, in preventing Iranian expansion. The Soviet Union also shared an interest with OPEC in preventing lower oil prices.

4. EAST AND WEST, NORTH AND SOUTH

The world has become accustomed to looking at OPEC and the OECD countries as respectively the major producers and consumers of oil. In fact the two superpowers are the world's biggest producers and consumers of not only oil, but of all forms of primary energy (the United States is, of course, an OECD member). Thus, any systematic account of the political economy of energy must explain the effects of their policies, not only on themselves, but also on their allies, rivals, and for world energy supply and demand.

Indeed, control over the international oil industry by American companies is often cited as a major factor in sustaining post-war American dominance in the non-communist world. Likewise, Soviet dominance in energy supply to communist states has been crucial for its political control of Eastern Europe. Some writers have therefore argued that as the post-war order in international oil broke down, one of the central pillars of American hegemony was weakened. In this period, however, it can also be argued that the rise in oil prices emphasised the vulnerability of other industrialised oil-importing nations to a disruption in supplies, particularly of Middle Eastern oil. Since the United States had, and still has, significant domestic supplies, and is the central 'national' actor in the Western oil markets, it is much less vulnerable than its major competitors. Despite the loss of American dominance over Middle Eastern oil, the resource advantage of the United States over Western Europe and especially Japan, has continued and was emphasised by high oil prices.

The Soviet Union is the world's biggest producer of oil and gas, and is second only to the United States in terms of the production of coal. In the 1970s and 1980s, oil accounted for about 60 per cent of Soviet hard currency earnings. In 1984, the two superpowers consumed 45 per cent of world oil, half of coal and nuclear energy, and 70 per cent of gas. The United States alone consumed about one-third of non-communist energy supplies in the 1980s. China was third largest, but accounted for only 7.5 per cent of world energy consumption, with Japan, the fourth largest consumer, at 5 per cent.[9] Although the Soviet Union supplies Eastern Europe, it has a production surplus which enables it to export oil and gas to Western Europe. Energy supplies from the Soviet Union to these countries are still less than 5 per cent of their total energy consumption.

As well as the East–West aspect of energy the political economy of energy also has a North–South dimension, and it is perhaps worth noting that the post-war oil order, at least until 1973, reflected a basic North–South divide, and the dependence of the OPEC states on the transnational oil corporations and the OECD consumer countries. Since then a more differentiated picture has emerged, with North and South more interdependent.

The nature of the oil-producing countries in OPEC is, however, extremely varied. Some have small populations and plentiful supplies (such as Saudi Arabia), whereas others have large populations and need to sell as much as they can (for example, Nigeria). There are also considerable differences in political regime and culture (compare the feudal monarchies of the Arabian Gulf with the non-Arab Islamic republic of Iran), as well as in levels of development. Kuwait, Qatar and the United Arab Emirates had per capita incomes roughly twice as great as those in Britain in the mid-1980s, whilst Indonesia's per capita incomes were only about 5 per cent of those in the United Kingdom. Most of the OPEC members are developing countries, massively dependent on a single export, whereas most of the major consumer nations are developed countries with highly diversified economies and much higher standards of living. Apart from the superpowers, some oil-producing countries have developed economies

(Britain, Canada and Norway), whereas other developing countries which produce large quantities of oil for export are not OPEC members (for example, Mexico).

Of the OPEC states, Saudi Arabia is the most important, since its resource endowments enable it to act as the 'swing producer', in effect indirectly controlling the price at which OPEC oil can be sold on the international markets. Not only are its oil wells massively more prolific than those elsewhere, it also has enormous reserves, when compared with the superpowers (measured in terms of the ratio of production to recoverable reserves). United States and Soviet reserves vary between ten and fifteen times current output:

This compares with an average of forty to fifty times for major OPEC countries in the Middle East ... due to two combined factors: the discovery of giant prolific fields, and/or production considerably below capacity to prevent prices from falling. In terms of absolute productivity, it is worth noting that the Gulf region comes first, with an average of 3,163 barrels per day per well in 1983 (Saudi Arabia ranking highest with 6,490). By comparison, the United States had fourteen barrels per day per well in that year.[10]

This situation is offset by what has been called a 'special relationship' between the United States and Saudi Arabia – a relationship which is, however, clouded by American support for Israel. Because of its massive reserves, Saudi Arabia has an interest in discouraging the use of alternative sources of energy and using its vast revenues to obtain Western assets. However, the Saudis are highly dependent on the United States not only for military protection, but also for the operation of much of their industry and basic services (for example, the United States Army Corps of Engineers had a substantial presence in the 1980s). As Mikdashi notes, this relationship was reflected in the sale of five American Airborne Warnings and Control Systems (AWACS) in 1981, for which the Saudis paid US $8.5 billion in cash. In effect this sale provided not only a massive profit, but also a flying intelligence base, for the United States. The operating conditions attached to the sale were so stringent that the former American Ambassador to Saudi Arabia was quoted as saying, 'the real question is whether the United States will give all the information that the AWACS gather to Saudi Arabia, not whether the United States will have access to it'.[11]

The AWACS sale can be related to the growing interdependence between American military producers and some Middle Eastern states. Indeed, all the major weapons-exporting states (notably the Soviet Union, also Britain, France, West Germany and Italy) have signficantly increased their dealings with the countries of the region. This is partly reflected in Table 13.8, compiled before the AWACS deal, and the start of the Iran–Iraq War.

Table 13.8 The ten largest third world weapons importers 1977–80 (in millions of constant, 1975, US dollars)

Importing country	Total value	Percentage of Third World total	Largest exporter per importer
Iran	3446	8.7	United States
Saudi Arabia	3133	8.0	United States
Jordan	2558	6.5	United States
Syria	2311	5.9	Soviet Union
Iraq	2172	5.5	Soviet Union
Libya	2107	5.4	Soviet Union
South Korea	1987	5.0	United States
India	1931	4.9	Soviet Union
Israel	1778	4.5	United States
Vietnam	1220	3.1	Soviet Union

Source: Adapted from Andrew J. Pierre, *The Global Politics of Arms Sales* (Princeton, NJ, Princeton University Press, 1982), p. 133. Based on Stockholm International Peace Research Institute (SIPRI) figures.

5. AMERICAN POLICIES

The evidence from the post-war period shows that the United States is dominant relative to other major capitalist powers in the energy sphere. Despite its consistent support for Israel (meaning its loyalties are divided in the Middle East) the United States is much less vulnerable than either Western Europe (except Britain and Norway) or Japan, to a disruption in Middle Eastern supplies. Indeed, energy policy, particularly since the early 1970s, has been a continuing source of tension between the United States and its allies.

The United States enjoys much greater flexibility than most of its allies, trading partners and economic competitors in the trade-off between economic policy and energy policy. Oystein Noreng notes that before 1973 energy prices were higher in the United States than in Western Europe or Japan, which was a competitive disadvantage for American industry, as well as an incentive for domestic oil production. The difference in prices could have been eliminated if the United States had dismantled import controls and permitted domestic oil prices to move to world market levels, or if world market prices rose to American levels. He argues that between 1971 and 1973 the United States encouraged OPEC to raise its prices, and after the oil crises the United States supported the 'price radicals' of OPEC, primarily Iran.[12] Moreover, much of the surplus of 'petrodollars' was channelled into the United States, and much of the financial recycling was carried out by American banks. This strengthened American transnational finance capital, relative to its competitors, although many American banks made ill-considered loans of such funds to Latin American governments. However, despite Noreng's claims, there is little direct evidence that American political leaders had adopted a policy of raising oil prices (at least until President Carter's attempts to decontrol domestic oil prices). Publicly at least, the United States took a rather confrontationist stance towards OPEC in 1974 (much to the annoyance of several of its key allies). The United States leadership appeared to resent the way that OPEC had undermined American dominance over Middle Eastern oil. In addition, even if it is true that the position of the United States was strengthened relative to Western Europe and Japan, this need not have been a planned outcome (although it might well have been a predicted one). Indeed, where the United States did have conscious aims in its policies, the consequences may not have always been those which its leaders intended. The fall of the Shah and the rise of Islamic fundamentalism are examples of this latter point.

Moreover, as the political and military conflicts in the Middle East intensified, much of the income earned from oil in the 1970s was used to purchase weapons systems. The major Western supplier of arms to the Middle East was the United States, followed by Britain and France (who were much less important). In the 1973–80 period, the chief oil producers who were also the recipients of American arms transfers were Iran, Saudi Arabia, Canada, Great Britain, Kuwait, Venezuela and Indonesia. These transfers were US $2 billion in 1967, $5 billion in 1973, $11 billion in 1974 and $16 billion in 1975. The total then declined to $14 billion in 1978, but then rose to $22 billion in 1982.[13] The Soviet Union's supply of arms to its Middle Eastern allies, however, was of similar magnitude to the United States'. Thus, the recycling process involved a boost to the American military–industrial complex, and to its arms producers in particular, at a time when the United States government's military expenditures had fallen in the aftermath of the Vietnam War. Petrodollars also boosted the Soviet military–industrial complex, as well as increasing the Soviet Union's supply of foreign exchange.

Noreng argues that in the mid-1970s the United States sought simultaneously to improve its competitive position, relative to other OECD countries, and to integrate them into an American-dominated consumer organisation, the International Energy Agency. Noreng adds, however, that the United States had different and sometimes very contradictory 'national' interests with regard to oil, and thus pursued seemingly inconsistent and changing policies. The United States allowed oil imports to rise in the 1970s, but maintained domestic price controls, so that the average level of energy prices was lower for the United States than either Western Europe or Japan: this gave a competitive advantage, at least in the short term, to American industry. Moreover, by increasing imports, and supporting worldwide price rises, the United States was able to slow down the rate of depletion of its domestic oil and gas reserves, ensuring greater future supplies, as well as increased profits for American-based oil transnationals. American prices were brought into line with world prices after decontrol, leading to an equalisation in the early 1980s, so removing the competitive advantage which American producers had held in the 1970s.

American policies cannot be described as unequivocally successful, for a number of reasons. First, the success of OPEC, which the United States arguably encouraged, inspired demands for a New International Economic Order, which was committed to promoting the further transfer of wealth from the rich, industrialised 'North' to the poorer (non-oil-producing) 'South'. Also, the recycling of petrodollars created a glut of capital, enabling developing nations to obtain loans from the OECD countries at real rates of interest which approached zero. In the short term at least, this undermined the influence of international institutions such as the International Monetary Fund, in that countries had less need to turn to them as lender of last resort and accept stringent conditions to the granting of loans. Thus many developing nations were able to pursue economic policies which were not always favoured by the United States, the major contributor to the Fund.

Secondly, and probably more important for United States strategy, it can be argued that American leaders made a major error in not anticipating the socioeconomic effects of rapid increases in income in certain Middle Eastern countries. In Iran, for example, which the United States encouraged to increase its prices after 1973, the 'modernising' policies of the Shah, allied to the brutal repression of internal dissent, were major driving forces in the Islamic revolution. The leaders and followers of the Iranian fundamentalists were violently opposed to the 'American Satan', and held United States diplomatic personnel hostage for some 444 days after they had taken power. President Carter, under pressure from Henry Kissinger and David Rockefeller (both of whom had been personal friends of the Shah, and the latter of whom had substantial oil interests in the Middle East), allowed the Shah to enter the United States, and further antagonised the Iranians. The hostage crisis was a major turning-point in the Carter presidency and was an important factor in his failure to gain re-election in 1980.

More fundamentally, American policy in the region was massively damaged. The Iranian revolution sent shock-waves across the Middle East. The United States sought to compensate for its strategic loss of Iran by bolstering the military capacity of Saudi Arabia, and consolidating its position in Egypt. The political instabilities of the region led increasingly to a spiralling arms race, which made Israel more demanding of weapons. Thus the Middle East countries became the major importers of weapons from the major powers, fuelling a political and military situation which was already explosive. American policy in the region became more and more dependent upon the goodwill of Saudi Arabia. In this country, however, the fears of an Islamic revolution mounted.

In the longer term, American policies were bound to lead to the opening-up of non-OPEC reserves, as well as alternative sources of energy, which would become more economically viable with higher prices. Again, of the major capitalist nations, the United States, with its lead in oil technology and massive financial resources, had the companies which would be best placed to take advantage. There was evidence, however, that by 1987 France had a lead in the construction of cost-effective nuclear power stations and Sweden led the field in deep-drilling for gas (see the final section of this chapter). The United States, partly because of the setbacks to its nuclear energy industry in the wake of the Three Mile Island accident, had, by the late 1980s, begun successfully to build power stations which used alternative forms of energy. Such power stations were more acceptable to the influential American environmentalist movements.

On the other hand, the increased price of oil, and the high profits to be gained within the industry, have meant that other nations and corporations have also developed their capacities. Thus its initial acceptance of OPEC price rises in the early 1970s must be balanced against longer-term aspects of American policies, which tended to reduce OPEC's power.

6. PERSPECTIVES AND INTERPRETATIONS

We shall now return to the question of how far the energy case provides evidence for or against some of the major propositions contained in the perspectives. We might ask, for example, how far does the case of energy 'fit' the dependency view of a relatively fixed, dependent relationship between core and periphery? In our account of the effects of the first and second post-war oil crises, it is clear that a substantial transfer of income from the OECD to the oil-exporting countries of OPEC took place, and that OPEC, using its power to control the supply of oil, to a certain extent reversed the domination of the West over their economies. Indeed, particularly Europe and Japan, were extremely vulnerable to the actions of OPEC, that is, to a large extent, in the energy sphere, they were dependent upon the oil-rich nations of the Middle East, as well as on United States policy and its major oil companies.

A second problem for dependency theory is that the Soviet Union was the world's biggest oil producer, but its role in world markets was much less important, for the OECD countries at least, than was the OPEC group. Dependency theory often treats the Soviet Union as a member of the core, but it can be argued that it, along with the United States, had a national interest in higher oil prices, which would enable it to gain more leverage over the economies of its allies, to whom the Soviet Union was the major supplier of oil. Thus there were clearly rival interests among the core economies, as well as in this case clear economic transfers taking place from core countries to a specific group of developing nations.

By contrast, some elements of the realist/mercantilist perspective seem appropriate to analysis of energy. Those countries most self-sufficient in primary energy resources were least exposed to the actions of OPEC. Both superpowers were largely self-sufficient in this respect, and thus less vulnerable to disruptions in supply of overseas oil: although the United States began to import much more oil it still had vast reserves. Moreover, as Noreng's analysis of US policies tends to indicate, American policies in the 1970s appeared to be directed at gaining competitive advantage for American capital, *vis-à-vis* its economic rivals. The realist analysis of the United States position, as a hegemonic power, pursuing its national interests at the expense of others, is also partially supported by United States strategy in the Middle East, embodied in both the Nixon Doctrine (which promoted the militarisation of Iran and Israel as 'regional policemen') and in the Carter Doctrine, which expressed military support for 'moderate' Arab states, as well as Israel, to hold back the threat of Islamic fundamentalism.

With respect to the other question which seems important for the mercantilist perspective (that is, why did so many countries allow themselves to become dependent on Middle Eastern oil after World War II?) it would appear plausible to argue that such countries believed that American dominance in the region, as well as relatively cheap supplies of oil, would continue. At a certain point, their consumption patterns were such that the opportunity cost of alternatives became very high. By the early 1970s these countries had benefited greatly from cheap oil imports, and their belief that the American-led order was self-sustaining perhaps meant that their policies deviated considerably from long-term mercantilist principles. On the other hand, we have noted that the last two decades have seen producer countries asserting increasing control over their oil resources, often at the expense of foreign capital. Particularly in the last twenty years, many Western and most developing nations have established national oil corporations either to develop and/or purchase oil supplies, and as such have changed their policies to increase state control and minimise vulnerability. This fits the mercantilist perspective on the state, in that, it is argued, states will seek to minimise their external vulnerabilities, and where possible develop self-sufficiency in primary energy.

Another interesting aspect of the changes in the oil order since World War II is that the market structure has shifted away from oligopoly, towards more competition. The public choice and liberal economic approaches seem to be particularly strong (because of their stress on the role of domestic interests, particularly in the United States, constraining state autonomy, and because of their emphasis on competition eventually undermining monopoly) in explaining the way in which a competitive structure emerged in international oil, as well as for explaining why the United States government was unable directly to shape its energy policies, particularly in the post-war period, when the United States drained its own reserves very rapidly. This example undermines the usefulness and validity of the realist assumption of the autonomous state as a rational actor, at least for the United States.

Viewed from an orthodox Marxist perspective, the movement away from oligopoly appears to reverse the predicted tendency towards the concentration of capital, although international banks have become more important in managing the flow of petrodollars, and as such this aspect perhaps would fit with the proposition that transnational finance capital has become more powerful. None the less there has been a wave of mergers in the 1980s, which tended to concentrate the industry, although to nothing like the same extent as in the 1960s (see the next section). Moreover, the move towards a more competitive market structure implies that there has been a long-term change in the character of power in and of, the oil markets. Initially this could be characterised as 'market power' (of the Seven Sisters, then of OPEC), whereas by 1987 the 'power of the market' would appear to have prevailed, with no single grouping of actors dominant, and with consumers less exploited by suppliers than was the case for much of the 1970s and 1980s. The explanation for this outcome is bound to be complex and defies any straightforward ascription of developments to class interests. Can the rise of the Arab producer states be analysed in terms of proleterian struggles?

If, as some Marxist arguments seem to imply, the United States government had been 'hand in glove' with big oil 'monopoly capitalists' (despite the fact that they were, strictly speaking, oligopolists), it seems likely that different American policies would have emerged, that is policies which would have prevented a challenge to their market dominance, or the threat of nationalisation. On the other hand, a coalition of domestic class forces, in the rising South and West, helped to cause the American government to adopt policies which were irrational in the long-term when viewed from the mercantilist perspective of America's national, strategic interests. In the domestic class struggle over oil, smaller-scale national capital (in the form of the independents) appeared victorious over transnational 'monopoly-capital' in the 1950s. However, the American independents later became increasingly transnational themselves. This made it easier for Third World governments to play off the majors against the 'maverick' independents (notably Libya with respect to Occidental Oil in 1960–70).

7. PROSPECTS

Although the 1970s brought with it a number of doomsday scenarios, such as that in the Club of Rome, *Limits to Growth* study, it would appear that, for at least the next 100 years, no serious long-term oil and energy shortage will emerge, although short-term supplies may occasionally fall below the level of demand. This is not to deny the existence of an energy crisis for millions of people in the Third World who cannot afford kerosene and depend on firewood as their basic fuel. Further, their crisis has global consequences because deforestation provokes changes in climate. In addition, the example of lack of firewood highlights the differences between demand (backed by money) and 'need'.

One ground for technological optimism concerning future supplies of energy was the recent discovery of a massive subterranean gas field beneath the Siljan Ring by Sweden. This discovery was based on the theory that oil and gas are not, as is normally believed, fossil fuels. Instead, it is believed by Professor Thomas Gold, a Cambridge University astrophysicist, that oil and gas are natural products which originated when the earth was formed. If this theory proves to be correct, it may be that oil and gas are present in quantities so enormous that they could meet consumption needs for millions of years.[14]

With respect to estimates of energy reserves based upon traditional theories, John Portella has pointed out:

As with other proven and ultimately recoverable reserve estimates, academic sources advise that most ultimately recoverable US reserve estimates have been systematically understated by the oil industry. They point out that estimates of ultimately recoverable US oil reserves have shown steady increases, not increasing scarcity in the period from 1948 to 1983 [thus] there is a strong possibility that proven reserve estimates have been systematically understated in order to mislead the government and avoid taxes.[15]

This is also the case for world reserves. Portella notes that the 1968 United States Geological Survey of world reserves estimated that there were:

'10 trillion barrels of crude oil ... of which 6.2 trillion barrels may be found.' At the 1978 consumption level, 6.2 trillion barrels would last the world some 270 years. The 1978 survey estimated recoverable world reserves at 6.0 trillion barrels, of which nearly one-third was in developing countries. In 1979 the *Petroleum Economist* estimated ultimate reserves, including heavy oil and tar sands at 7.4 trillion barrels.[16]

With respect to short- and medium-term considerations, as will be noted from Table 13.9, Western countries are much less dependent on OPEC supplies than was the case in 1979, and there was, by 1987, substantial unused production capacity outside the Gulf in countries like Mexico, Venezuela, Indonesia and Nigeria (approximately 2–3 million barrels per day). There was also an even larger unused capacity in Saudi Arabia (of approximately 7 million barrels per day), large quantities stored outside the OECD in floating containers, and the equivalent of more than one month's supply at sea. Government and company stocks were also far larger than in 1979.[17]

Excess supply forced prices down during the 1980s, to a low point of US $8 per barrel, in 1986. An OPEC agreement was forged in December 1986, and members' production was reduced in 1987 to below 15.8 million barrels a day, forcing oil companies to run down huge stocks built up during the glut of 1986. This resulted in prices stabilising at around $18 per barrel. The price collapse of 1986 was the result of Saudi attempts to undermine the search for other sources of energy, by, in effect, pricing them out of the market. However, the price of $18 per barrel represented a compromise, since other OPEC states lost considerable revenue. This price was set at a level which, the Saudis hoped, would enable OPEC to regain control of the oil market in the 1990s, since high-cost production would be uneconomic at less than this price.[18]

Table 13.9 Non-communist world oil supply and demand, 1979–87 (millions of barrels per day)

	1979	*1986*	*1987**
Consumption			
OECD	41.6	34.8	35.2
Non-OECD	10.8	11.8	12.0
Total**	52.4	46.6	47.2
Supply			
Non-OPEC	22.1	28.2	28.4
OPEC	31.6	19.3	—
Total	53.7	47.5	—

Notes:
* Estimate assumes annual economic growth of 2.25 per cent in 1987.
** Includes marine bunkers, refinery fuel and non-conventional oil.
Source: International Energy Agency, cited in *Financial Times*, 5 August 1987.

Whether OPEC's resolve will hold in the longer term is an open question. During the 1980s many countries refused to keep production down to their allotted quota levels, using a variety of means, such as bilateral countertrade (barter) deals, to increase their sales. Ironically, OPEC was, at times, aided in its efforts to limit production since 1980 by the Iran–Iraq War. Despite the fact that, from an economic perspective, many parties would appear to have an interest in the continuation of this conflict, it may ultimately come to an end. When it does end, it may well mean that OPEC's efforts to maintain price levels are undermined. Both the Iraqi and Iranian governments are likely to maximise their output to pay for reconstruction after the war.

There are other reasons, quite apart from OPEC actions, why there may be limits to the further emergence of a competitive market structure for oil and to a dramatic drop in its price below $18–20 per barrel during the late 1980s and early 1990s. A number of pieces of evidence suggest that the potential for a strong transnational coalition of forces emerged in 1986–87, to sustain the price at these levels. Having said this, the diverse character of such a coalition meant that international cooperation between its constituent interests was difficult.

Lower prices were inconsistent with the profitability of certain energy investments, such as the North Sea and Alaskan oil, and with the profitability of the high-cost fields in the United States, such as in Texas and Oklahoma. With this in mind it is interesting to note that whilst the Reagan administration, obsessed with American dependence on imported oil, had massively built up the Strategic Petroleum Reserve when prices were low in the early to mid-1980s, the United States Congress was also scrapping a major energy conservation measure and raising the highway speed limit from 55 to 65 miles per hour. Both these measures, plus American diplomatic pressure on Saudi Arabia to stabilise prices around $18 per barrel, can be seen as means of indirectly supporting the American oil industry. The Reagan administration estimated that a $10 per barrel price (which prevailed in March 1986) would reduce American economic growth by over $30 billion per year and result in the loss of 400,000 jobs outside the oil sector in the United States economy.[19] For slightly different reasons, the Soviet Union also supported OPEC moves to sustain oil prices, after a collapse in its hard-currency earnings in 1986.

Lower oil prices also threatened a number of large oil companies in the West and since 1979 there was a spate of mergers and rationalisations leading to a shift back to a more concentrated industry. Six large oil companies fell in multi-billion dollar take-over deals between 1980 and 1987, the largest being Chevron's purchase of Getty Oil for $13.2 billion in 1984.[20] These companies can be expected to lobby for policies which will prevent the price of oil from falling too far.

International bankers, as well as Western political leaders, were also worried that sustained low prices would threaten the political stability of certain oil-producing developing countries, such as Nigeria and perhaps Mexico, as well as inhibiting their ability to service their debts to foreign banks. Low oil prices were seen as inconsistent with containment of some aspects of the debt crisis, since they might indirectly provoke a major default and the collapse of one or more of the highly-exposed Western banks. Thus despite their general commitment to economic liberalism, these interests recognised that their economic security might be incompatible with the relatively competitive market structure which emerged in the 1980s, in the same way as many governments acknowledged that the free market might not provide energy security in the long term.

Finally, it should be noted that the content and timing of the growth in the literature on the political economy of oil mainly reflects the fears and interests of the rich nations of the earth. In this context, we suggest that political economy research on energy should pay more attention to other sources than oil. It should also be informed by a concept of human need, as well as the concepts of effective demand, power and wealth.

NOTES

1. Original OPEC members were Iran, Iraq, Kuwait, Saudi Arabia and Venezuela. Since 1960, when OPEC was formed, eight nations have joined: Qatar, Libya, Indonesia, Algeria, Nigeria, the United Arab Emirates, Ecuador and Gabon.
2. Zakhir Mikdashi, *Transnational Oil: issues, policies and perspectives* (London, Pinter, 1986), p. 24.
3. For a brief review of the first oil order, see L. P. Frank, 'The First Oil Regime', *World Politics* (1985), Vol. 37, pp. 586–98. He reviews I. H. Anderson, *Aramco, the United States and Saudi Arabia: a Study of the Dynamics of Foreign Policy 1933–50* (Princeton NJ, Princeton University Press, 1981); P. J. Baram, *The Department of State in the Middle East 1919–1945* (Philadelphia, University of Pennsylvania Press, 1978); W. Stivers, *Supremacy and Oil: Iraq, Turkey and the Anglo-American World Order 1918–30* (Ithaca NY, Cornell University Press, 1982); and M. B. Stoff, *Oil, War and American Security: the Search for a National Policy on Foreign Oil, 1941–47* (New Haven CT, Yale University Press, 1980). Also relevant for this order are M. A. Adelman, *The World Petroleum Market* (Baltimore, Johns Hopkins University Press, 1971); John Blair, *The Control of Oil* (Pantheon, New York, 1976); Leon Lindberg, *The Energy Syndrome* (Lexington, Mass., Lexington Books, 1977). For a review of literature mainly focusing on developments since the late 1960s, see Ernest J. Wilson III, 'World Politics and International Energy Markets', *International Organisation* (1987), Vol. 41, pp. 125–49. Wilson reviews Hans Jacob Bull-Berg and Magne Holter, *Discussing*

the Politics of Oil 1954–74 within the Framework of the Regime Concept (Polhodga, Norway, Fidthof Nansen Institute, 1983); Peter Cowhey, *The Problems of Plenty: Energy Policy and International Politics*, (Berkeley, Cal., University of California Press, 1985); Martin Greenberger, *Caught Unawares* (Cambridge, Mass., Ballinger, 1983); Wilfred Kohl (ed.), *After the Second Oil Crisis* (Lexington, Mass., Lexington Books, 1982); William Quandt, *Saudi Arabia in the 1980s* (Washington DC, Brookings, 1981); Steven Schneider, *The Oil Price Revolution* (Baltimore, Johns Hopkins University Press, 1983); Mary Ann Tetreault, *Revolution in the World Petroleum Market* (Westport CT, Quorum, 1985); Miguel Wionzek (ed.), *World Hydrocarbon Markets* (Oxford, Pergamon, 1983); Daniel Yergin and Martin Hillenbrandt (eds), *Global Insecurity* (Boston, Mass., Houghton Mifflin, 1982). See also M. E. Ahrari, 'OPEC and the Hyperpluralism of the Oil Market in the 1980s', *International Affairs* (Spring 1985), Vol. 6, pp. 263–77; Paul Kemesis and Ernest J. Wilson III, *The Decade of Energy Policy: Policy Analysis in Oil Importing Countries* (New York, Praeger, 1984); Franklin Tugwell, 'Energy and Political Economy', *Comparative Politics* (1980). Vol. 13, pp. 1–4; Dermot Gatley, 'A Ten-Year Retrospective: OPEC and the World Oil Market', *Journal of Economic Literature* (1984), Vol. 22, pp. 1100–14. For a sophisticated application of the public choice approach to oil, see James E. Alt, 'Crude Politics: Oil and the Political Economy of Unemployment in Britain and Norway, 1970–85', *British Journal of Political Science* (1987), Vol. 17, pp. 149–99.

4. Robert O. Keohane, 'Hegemonic Leadership and United States Foreign Economic Policy in the "Long Decade" of the 1950s', in William P. Avery and David Rapkin, *America in a Changing World Political Economy* (London, Longman, 1982), pp. 49–76.

5. Louis Turner, *The Oil Companies in the International System* (London, Royal Institute of International Affairs, 1980).

6. John L. Portella, 'Oil politics and economics', Paper, 26th Annual Convention of International Studies Association, Washington DC, 8 March 1985.

7. L. P. Frank, *The Third World Economic Handbook* (London, Euromonitor Publications, 1982), pp. 25–6, 19. Data cited is from OPEC and the World Bank.

8. Portella, op. cit.

9. T. Scanlan, 'Impact of the Superpowers' Energy Balances on World Oil', *Energy Policy* (1985), Vol. 13, pp. 5–12. See also Hans Jacob Bull-Berg, *American International Oil Policy: Causal Factors and Effect* (London, Pinter, 1987).

10. Mikdashi, op. cit., p. 26.

11. James E. Akins, 'The Influence of Politics on Oil Pricing and Production Policies', in the symposium, 'Oil and Money in the Eighties', London, 28–29 September 1981. Cited in Mikdashi, op. cit., p. 52.

12. Oystein Noreng, *Oil Politics in the 1980s* (New York, McGraw-Hill, 1978), pp. 50–1.

13. United States Arms Control and Disarmament Agency, *World Military Expenditures and Arms Transfers, 1971–80* (Washington DC, US Government Printing Office, 1983), pp. 117–19; 'Arms Trade', *Washington Post* (30 January 1983), p. 2, cited in Portella, op. cit, pp. 32–3.

14. Robert Temple, 'Sweden taps a gas bonanza', *The Observer*, 10 May 1987.

15. Portella, op. cit., pp. 13–14, 18.

16. Ibid., pp. 9–11. See also, Peter R. Odell, 'The Prospect for Oil Prices and the Energy Market', *Lloyds Bank Review* (July 1987), pp. 1–14.
17. *Financial Times*, 5 August 1987.
18. *The Guardian*, 26 June 1987. See also Theodore Moran, 'Modeling OPEC Behaviour: Economic and Political Alternatives', in J. M. Griffin and D. J. Teece (eds), *OPEC Behaviour and World Oil Prices* (London, Allen and Unwin, 1982), pp. 94–130.
19. William Hall, 'US faces up to oil market contradictions', *Financial Times*, 20 March 1987.
20. *The Observer*, 3 May 1987.

14 North–South Relations

1. INTRODUCTION

This chapter examines the nature of, and structural forces underlying, North–South tensions, with special reference to the Third World demands for a New International Economic Order. The failure of less-developed countries to obtain satisfaction of these demands is explained. The problems of cooperation between less-developed countries are analysed with specific reference to commodity agreements, cartels and regional associations. The political economy of aid is also briefly discussed.

The terms 'North' and 'South' are crude and contestable labels. By the North is usually meant the industrialised countries of the West, Japan and the Soviet bloc. By the South is usually meant the countries of Asia (except Japan) Africa and Latin America. Australia and New Zealand may be southern in location but are counted as part of the affluent West. The 'less developed' countries, or, more optimistically, the 'developing' countries of the South are extremely varied not only in gross national product (GNP) per head, but also in their broader economic, political and cultural aspects.

Indeed, countries as industrialised as Brazil, Singapore, South Korea and Taiwan might well be considered developed in some respects. The economic gulf between the dire poverty of Ethiopia and oil-rich Saudi Arabia might be considered greater than that between Mexico and the United States. On average, however, the economic gap between 'North' and 'South' is vast. In 1980, for example, the World Bank estimated that the gross domestic product (GDP) per capita of the developed capitalist countries to be US $10,444, whereas it was only $650 per capita in the developing countries.[1] Moreover, when measured in terms of criteria which are not directly economic (such as infant mortality, life expectancy, nutrition, health care, literacy and life-chances), the gulf in basic living conditions between most 'Northern' and most 'Southern' countries is gigantic.

2. PERSPECTIVES ON NORTH–SOUTH RELATIONS

The political economy of the relations between the developed capitalist countries of North America, Europe, Japan and Australasia, and the less-developed countries of Africa, Asia, and Latin America have been the subject of increasing analysis and controversy since the 1950s. It has been suggested by dependency and Marxist writers that the world capitalist system makes inevitable the exploitation of less-developed countries by developed capitalist states. The developed capitalist states have been accused of pursuing policies (often through their control of international institutions such as the International Monetary Fund, IMF), which widen the economic gap between North and South. The very notion of the 'Third World' is for radical dependency and Marxist writers a concept that is historically rooted in centuries of colonialism, imperialism and exploitation. It is not simply to be equated with low incomes and low output per head and industrial backwardness. At issue is how far the present international economic order (or at least its North–South dimension) either can, or should, be changed. Reforms of an interventionist and redistributive type were favoured by the first *Brandt Report* (1980). The report suggested commodity agreements to raise and/or stabilise primary product prices and an international tax on armanents, the revenues from which would go to promoting Third World economic development.[2] This 'social democratic' approach can be contrasted with a liberal one which favours changes to increase the reliance on the market mechanism and private enterprise. Thus with respect to the question of reforming the North–South system, while the present international economic order is predominantly capitalist, from the liberal viewpoint it is not capitalist enough. Some Marxist approaches have no use for social democratic reforms except as a tactical manoeuvre that hastens the birth pangs of a socialist international economic order. A realist approach would predict neither reform nor revolution unless there is a change in the power resources between nations, and especially between North and South. Such 'realism' contrasts with the global ecological awareness of parts of the *Brandt Report* when it suggests that there are common, long-term interests that transcend those of nations, races, continents and classes.

3. THIRD WORLD ECONOMIC INTERDEPENDENCE

The evidence on trade and investment flows is consistent with the view that less-developed countries (especially small ones) suffer from the effects of 'asymmetrical interdependence'. On average, they are much more 'sensitive' in their economic interdependence than are developed capitalist states. For example, less-developed countries tend to have a higher propensity to trade as indicated by the ratio of the sum of imports and exports to gross domestic product (GDP). (See Table 9–5 above.)

In addition it should be noted that less-developed countries often tend to rely on the export of a small number of goods so that they are highly sensitive to changes in the demand of their main markets in the developed capitalist countries. For example, 97 per cent of Iraq's total export value in 1977–79 was from oil, while for Saudi Arabia it was 94 per cent, for Iran 90 per cent, for Nigeria 88 per cent, and for Indonesia, 58 per cent. Uganda obtained 93 per cent, of its export earnings from coffee, while for Ethiopia the figure was 72 per cent, for Colombia it was 62 per cent and for Guatemala it was 42 per cent. Sudan got 57 per cent of its import earnings from cotton, while Zambia got 89 per cent of its export value from copper.[3] Since the commitment of resources to their export sector often involves very limited flexibility, less-developed countries find it hard to adjust to large changes in demand; that is they are vulnerable as well as sensitive to such changes. This export inflexibility (inelastic supply of exports) is one reason for the much sharper price fluctuations for primary products as compared to manufactures. Further, it should be noted that a substantial proportion of developing country imports consists of food, machinery and spare parts which are essential rather than luxury goods. The machinery is vital to economic development. Hence a fall in foreign exchange earnings, as in the early 1980s, had severe repercussions on living standards and economic growth.

Interdependence in international capital flows affects most countries. However, many less-developed countries have become rather dependent on external sources of finance, for example aid in the case of most African countries and commercial loans in the case of most Latin American countries. The 'drying up' of new bank loans to Brazil, Mexico, Chile and Argentina precipitated the debt crisis in 1982. As for foreign direct investment in less-developed countries, it was roughly twice as high relative to domestic economic size as it was in developed capitalist states (see Table 9.6 above.)

While many developed capitalist states are heavily dependent on international trade, most of this trade is between themselves rather than between them and less-developed countries. By contrast, as we saw in chapter 12, the Third World does most of its trade with the West and Japan.[4]

Most world trade takes place between developed countries. They have the biggest markets. Developing countries need access to these markets far more than developed countries need access to Third World markets. Thus, international economic relations would seem to be more of a threat to the sovereignty of less-developed countries. Changes in demand, interest rates, and in rules and procedures affecting trade and capital flows will often have a major impact on the economies of less-developed countries, to which they will find it difficult to adjust. The modest share of less developed countries in world trade reflects not just low prices of primary products but the fact that most value added is at the processing stage. This stage is most often done in developed countries, as was noted in the case of coffee in chapter 12.

4. THIRD WORLD CONSCIOUSNESS AND THE INTER-NATIONAL ECONOMIC ORDER

Third World consciousness developed with the rise of nationalist movements in Latin America, and later in Asia and Africa. This contributed to the achievement of political independence for scores of new states between 1947 and 1980. Racial and cultural contrasts with the West were partly a basis for Third World nationalisms. This was not so true for Latin America, particularly its largely white elites, oligarchies, or ruling classes. However, the elites of Africa, Asia and Latin America have shared an interest in reducing their economic dependence on the West, an interest linked to the diversification and industrialisation of their economies. This 'interest' has been associated with the somewhat mercantilist belief in the link between national power, wealth and manufacturing industry. Latin American intellectuals, such as Raoul Prebisch, have taken a leading role in questioning the rationality and fairness of the international division of labour in which the 'peripheral' economies of Asia, Africa and Latin America specialised in exporting primary products while importing manufactures. Such views became influential in many less-developed countries, not just those in Latin America. Thus certain shared values (economic independence and national strength) combined with similar beliefs and some objective economic similarities to give birth to a Third World consciousness that included Latin America. At the elite level, this development was facilitated by improved transport and communications and the establishment of institutions such as the United Nations and related bodies.

When the liberal international economic order and associated institutions were being established in the 1944–48 period, less-developed countries were little involved since most of them had yet to attain their independence. By the 1960s, Third World countries were numerically dominant within the United Nations General Assembly, having a clear majority of the votes. This contrasted with the distribution of voting power in certain key 'liberal' institutions, for example the IMF and the World Bank.

As for the General Agreement on Tariffs and Trade (GATT), the conditions of membership were less appealing to less-developed countries. This was partly because the key principles of the GATT regime are those of non-discrimination in trade policy and reciprocity in trade negotiations. With their relatively small home markets, most less-developed countries have had little leverage in negotiations based on reciprocal tariff concessions. Indeed, less-developed countries have been anxious to provide trade protection for their infant industries. Thus trade liberalisation was seen as a luxury that wealthier capitalist states could afford, but less-developed countries, bent on 'development', could not. Latin American countries have used a combination of trade barriers and multiple exchange rates to promote import-substitution industrialisation. Other less-developed countries have tended to follow their example. Such policies and practices are not favoured by the GATT, the IMF and the World Bank. Disaffection with these institutions, especially GATT, led to the establishment of the United Nations Conference on Trade and Development (UNCTAD) in 1964 with Prebisch as its first Secretary-General.

Given the economic asymmetries that afflict less-developed countries and the lack of leverage they have because of their small markets and technological backwardness, Stephen Krasner has argued that less-developed countries have a rational preference for international regimes which favour an 'authoritative', as opposed to a 'market', allocation of resources. In multilateral institutions, less-developed countries may be able to bring their numerical superiority to bear in a way that is not possible in international markets, where wealth, rather than numbers, counts. Thus conflict between North and South over the international economic order in general, and the trade and money regimes in particular, can be seen as a long-term structural phenomenon.[5] Many liberal economists reject this line, arguing in favour of export-led growth and citing the success of South Korea, Singapore, Hong Kong and Taiwan.

5. THIRD WORLD DEMANDS

One example of the 'authoritative' allocation of resources desired by less-developed countries is the allocation of Special Drawing Rights from the IMF on a basis favourable to themselves, as in the 'link' scheme in which new Special Drawing Rights would be created and assigned only to less-developed countries. Such a measure would enable developing countries to share in the gains from seignorage that result from the creation of international (and national) reserve assets. In the absence of a Special Drawing Rights link scheme, such gains will continue to be shared between a few developed capitalist states whose currencies are desirable because of these countries' large role in world trade and investment. Another example concerns the proposed United Nations Law of the Sea Treaty under which a Sea-Bed Authority will allocate mining rights and set up joint ventures with transnational coporations. This Treaty was meant to ensure that less-developed countries had a dominant voice in sea-bed mining and would gain a significant proportion of the revenues from such mining, instead of all the revenues going to the transnational corporations which together had a monopoly of the required technology. Both the United States and Britain refused to ratify the treaty. In world shipping, the Liner Conferences are seen by less-developed countries as biased in favour of developed countries. Here, they seek a larger allocation of shipping routes for themselves: similarly with certain air-routes.

The most prominent demands of less-developed countries in the 1960s and 1970s concerned trade. The UNCTAD favoured commodity agreements between producing and consuming countries. Less-developed countries hoped that such agreements would serve to raise and/or stabilise the prices of primary products for which they were the main exporters. In the 1970s the Third World called for an Integrated Programme for Commodities with a Common Fund which would make loans to commodity councils set up by particular commodity agreements. Most of the finance for the Common Fund would be provided by the developed countries, that is the scheme would involve an element of income redistribution from North to South. Such a scheme, it was hoped, would lead to the negotiation of many more commodity agreements since only a few existed in the 1960s (for example tin, coffee and sugar). Less-developed countries also sought improved access to the markets of developed countries, especially for their exports of manufactures. The General System of Preferences of the EEC, Japan and the United States, granted in the early 1970s, met one of their demands. However, due to quota restrictions on Third World exports it has been of only modest value. It should be noted that this preferential system went against the GATT principle of non-discrimination. Concern with improved market access fits in with liberal economic views about trade. By contrast the commodity agreement proposals were anti-market in orientation, especially in that less-developed countries hoped to keep prices above the 'free market' level, so as to improve their terms of trade.

At the institutional level, less-developed countries have sought an increased 'voice' and vote in the IMF and the World Bank. As for trade matters, they hoped to make UNCTAD, rather than GATT, the main forum for negotiation. Some of the trade concerns of less-developed countries can be traced back to the late 1940s when negotiations for an International Trade Organisation took place but foundered on opposition in the United States Congress. In general, developing country demands on trade matters have been aimed at securing a greater share of the gains from trade while being able to press on with the protection of their 'infant industries'.

6. THE NEW INTERNATIONAL ECONOMIC ORDER AND THE NORTH–SOUTH DIALOGUE

While Third World consciousness and views on international economic relations and policy proposals were developing in the 1950s and 1960s, it was in the mid-1970s that Third World demands became more insistent. These demands were aggregated in the United Nations resolution of May 1974 calling for a New International Economic Order. The timing of this resolution was much influenced by the dramatic success of OPEC in securing higher oil prices which resulted in a massive transfer of income from the developed capitalist nations to the oil-exporting countries. The West was seen as being on the defensive, not least because it was more anxious about its supply of raw materials and fuel than it had been in the 1960s.

The OPEC cartel was seen as a great example of how market forces could be controlled and harnessed by less-developed countries so as to increase their export revenues. In retrospect, less-developed countries may have underestimated the importance of a high level of demand for oil in causing the oil price rises, just as they may have over-generalised from one rather special commodity. However, in 1974–75 less-developed countries were very optimistic about the possibility of imitating OPEC either through producer associations (such as that for bauxite) or through commodity agreements. This optimism contributed to Third World unity, despite the severe repercussions of the oil price rises on many oil-importing less-developed countries. This unity was strongest at the United Nations where the less-developed countries had established arrangements for consultation and mutual support, based partly on the Middle Eastern countries backing African resolutions on South Africa in return for African support on resolutions over Israel/Palestine.

The developing countries which imported oil supported, or at least did not criticise OPEC, because (i) they hoped to obtain special trade deals with OPEC, (ii) they hoped to receive economic aid from some OPEC countries, (iii) they hoped to imitate OPEC, and (iv) they wanted OPEC's support over their New International Economic Order demands: the 'oil weapon' would strengthen their hand in negotiations with the West. Third World unity was helped by the willingness of the OPEC countries to give aid to certain, largely Moslem, less-developed countries. The OPEC countries were conscious of the need to avoid an alliance between developed capitalist states and developing country oil importers against themselves.

7. THE FAILURE OF THE NEW INTERNATIONAL ECONOMIC ORDER DEMANDS

Various conferences involving North and South took place in the 1970s and culminated in the Cancun conference of 1981. However, for all the talk there was very little action, or concessions by the developed capitalist states. It is true that these developed countries ultimately accepted the idea of an Integrated Programme for Commodities, including the Common Fund proposal, in 1980. However, many developed capitalist countries failed to sign and ratify the treaty. Only in 1987, when the Soviet Union belatedly signed, was the way opened for the establishment of the fund in 1988.[6] In consequence of these reactions, up to 1987 the fund had not become operational. After the initial shock of the oil price rises of 1973–74, the developed capitalist nations gradually recovered their self-confidence They realised that oil was a special case since it is, in value terms, much the most important primary commodity. Above all, they realised that they still controlled key institutions like the IMF and in terms of wealth and technology were in a strong and privileged position.

During this period the Western countries were suffering from higher inflation and unemployment. As a result, and because of the impact of the oil price rises on living standards, Western governments were less able and willing to make concessions to less-developed countries. This was reflected in a decline in the flow of aid to less-developed countries in real terms (that is, after allowing for inflation) during the 1970s. Thus the developed capitalist states decided to adopt a strategy of 'much talking and few concessions'.

The European Community, in its renegotiation of the Lomé Convention in 1975, made some concessions because of its concern over supply of commodities. These concerned the Stabex and Minex schemes which involve the commitment of EEC funds to the stabilisation of the export earnings from certain primary products of the African, Caribbean and Pacific (ACP) countries associated with the Community. In the IMF, the developed capitalist nations backed measures which helped less-developed countries. Examples of this were the Oil Facility, gold sales so as to subsidise interest payments on loans to poor less-developed countries, increased access to IMF loans, and an increase in the size of IMF quotas favourable to less-developed countries. However, these concessions were limited and temporary in some cases (for example, the Oil Facility) and reflected the increased availability of commercial bank loans and

Eurobonds to less-developed countries which had the effect of reducing their need to go to the IMF: indeed in 1977–78 the IMF became concerned to gain new customers. The glut of credit on the Euromarkets came to an end in the early 1980s at the same time as the world economy went into recession and United States and worldwide interest rates were driven upwards by American monetary and fiscal policy.

These changes transformed the situation of most less-developed countries which now faced a prolonged shortage of foreign exchange and found it hard to obtain a net capital inflow from Western and Japanese banks. OPEC's power declined along with the fall in oil prices after 1981. Thus the bargaining position of the South which had always been quite weak, deteriorated significantly in the early 1980s. Despite all the rhetoric, resolutions and conferences in the 1970s, the South made little more progress (in gaining concessions) than they had in the 1960s when they had benefited from such measures as the Compensatory Finance Facility of the IMF.

The failure to bring about the New International Economic Order can be explained by reference to certain realist arguments, that is regime formation requires substantial investments and/or commitments by countries with the greatest amount of power resources. The less-developed countries were unable to persuade the developed capitalist states that most of the New International Economic Order demands were in their interest. Further, they were not very successful in persuading the Soviet Union to back their New International Economic Order demands, beyond obtaining some diplomatic support. The Soviet Union has traditionally been reluctant to open up its market to less-developed countries because of its rather rigid planned economy and a tradition of substantial autarky: for example, it replaced imports of natural rubber with home production of synthetic rubber during the post-war period. This implied that most less-developed countries, even 'socialist' ones, will usually have to rely heavily on trade with the West. It was not so much what the Soviet Union did do (it stayed on the side-lines claiming that it had no part in the exploitation of the Third World) as what it did not do, that is it did not offer greater financial support to developing countries. The Soviet Union could not afford to subsidise more developing countries in the way it subsidised the Cuban economy (notably through a high price for sugar from Cuba). The burdens of military spending on a sluggish economy were such as to limit severely Soviet economic competition with the West in the Third World. The Soviet Union has concentrated its competitive efforts on military rather than economic aid. With respect to commodities, the Soviet bloc in 1976 came out in favour of the Integrated Programme for Commodities. By the end of 1979 the Soviet Union was participating in the agreements for tin, sugar, wheat, coffee and cocoa.

The bargaining tactics and strategy of the South have been questioned by some writers. For example, it has been suggested that the New International Economic Order demands were too many, and in some cases too ambitious, even impractical. In particular, it has been argued by Jagdish Bhagwati[7] that the emphasis on the Integrated Programme for Commodities was unwise, given the many difficulties of establishing and maintaining commodity agreements (these are discussed in a later section). However, the ambitious and wide-ranging nature of the demands, and the insistence on negotiating them together (as a package) was, perhaps, unavoidable given the large number and varied interests of the less-developed countries. The negotiating package had to be such as to have something in it for all of them.

The focus on the Integrated Programme for Commodities was natural in so far as most less-developed countries exported primary products. However, the Integrated Programme for Commodities needed to be organised in a way that affected many commodities. Hence the stress on a Common Fund which might lend to a wide variety of commodity groups, especially in that part of the fund was intended to be for 'diversification' purposes; that is loans to less-developed countries to develop either new primary product exports or the processing of existing exports. Many such proposals were formulated more with an eye to maintaining a precarious Third World unity than to persuading the developed capitalist states that there was something in it for them. As Robert Rothstein has said of the less-developed countries' negotiating organisation, the 'Group of 77' (in practice over a hundred developing countries), it

made the fundamental error of emphasising too exclusively Third World development as the key norm. This failed to satisfy enough of the interests of the holders of power, it ignored the fact that the conceptual basis for such a principle was doubtful, and it did not consider that a genuinely stable international regime of regimes must incorporate concerns other than, but not less than, development.[8]

The phrase 'international regime of regimes' presumably refers here to a common principle of redistribution and equity, which should be built into all the international regimes which go to make up the international economic order.

8. OBSTACLES TO THIRD WORLD UNITY

The development of an effective alliance of the South is hampered by differences of ideology, culture, degree of industrialisation, interest in specific commodities and size. These differences are exacerbated by border disagreements and regional rivalries. Ideological differences have meant that attitudes to the New International Economic Order have varied considerably. For some radical 'socialist' states, these demands, while desirable, did not go far enough. On the other hand, for conservative capitalist less-developed countries some of the demands were seen as excessive. For example, at meetings on the issue of Third World debts, Mexico and Brazil decided to shun the demands for debt cancelling and relief for fear of losing their credit rating on the international capital markets. Several years later, in 1982–85, these two countries considered, but rejected, the idea of a 'debtors' cartel' suggested by Argentina. Once again, concern over credit ratings was a factor: more generally, Brazil and Mexico were interested in maintaining their links to developed capitalist states, including market access for their manufacturing exports and further inward direct investment by transnational corporations.

Radical countries believe that the post-war capitalist liberal international economic order is a major cause of both international inequality and the poverty of many people in the Third World. However, the governments of some newly-industrialising countries (for example, South Korea, Brazil and Mexico) actively pursued trade, through manufacturing exports, as a means to growth. Thus for some, the New International Economic Order was seen as a chance to gain a few marginal concessions within a basically acceptable order while for others it was seen as a platform for breaking up this order. Indeed, some of the most pro-capitalist less-developed countries (for example, Singapore) only paid sceptical lip-service to the New International Economic Order whose rationale and practicality was doubted.

The many obstacles to Third World unity have been strikingly evident in the largely unsuccessful record of attempts at regional economic cooperation and integration between less-developed countries. For example, the East African Economic Community which got off to a promising start at the end of the colonial era, collapsed in the 1970s after mounting strains appeared, going back to the 1960s. At independence, the Community (Uganda, Tanzania and Kenya) had a common airline, regional bank and regional free trade. Over time it emerged that most of the gains from regional trade in manufactures were going to Kenya. The member countries had started at different levels of development and the tendency was for these differences to widen. This may have been partly due to contrasting economic policies which were much more sympathetic to private enterprise and foreign investment in Kenya. By contrast, Tanzania pursued an 'African socialism' which involved a large degree of state regulation, and in the 'modern sector', public ownership. The Ugandan invasion of Tanzania in the 1970s also hastened the break-up of the Community. Other attempts at regional integration have not collapsed in this dramatic way, but difficulties have arisen in eliminating trade barriers, establishing joint projects, and adopting a unified set of rules on foreign investment. Such a unified position was attempted by the Andean Pact in the 1970s and, in principle, should have strengthened the bargaining position of these countries (Peru, Bolivia, Ecuador, Chile [until it pulled out] and Venezeula) in their dealings with transnational corporations. However, Chile left the Pact partly because of ideological disagreement with the foreign investment rules, and by the 1980s attempts at a consistent application of these rules had broken down.

The Association of South-East Asian Nations (ASEAN) – Thailand, Malaysia, Singapore, Indonesia, the Philippines and Brunei – has been more successful, but few of its regional projects have been carried through. Its members compete to attract foreign investment by means of tax concessions and export-processing zones. However, Malaysia and Indonesia provide examples of how some less-developed countries can exert leverage over developed capitalist states.[9] When Britain decided to impose more severe restrictions on Indonesia's textile exports the Indonesian government made it clear that British firms would not be allowed to win construction contracts and Britain backed down. Indonesia is a relatively large developing country with a population in excess of 150 million and large natural resources. By contrast, tiny less-developed countries have virtually no leverage.

However, small developing nations can gain some leverage if they work together as a group. The ASEAN has already shown how this can bring concessions in the case of Australian restrictions on imports of footwear and clothing from Malaysia and the Philippines in 1977. The Australians were threatened with joint retaliation by all members of ASEAN while Malaysia threatened to look for alternative sources of supply for its food imports from Australia. In the end, the Australian government made some concessions to the ASEAN countries despite the great political pressure exercised by Australian industrialists for a continuation of the import restrictions. It may be from such self-help efforts, rather than from ambitious attempts at changing international regimes, that less-developed countries can do most to improve their position within the global political economy. It should be noted that some Latin American countries have taken unilateral action on cargo entitlements for their national fleets while maintaining a low profile in UNCTAD debates on this issue. Asian and African countries have followed their example. However, shipping is one area where UNCTAD can claim a modest success, that is over the code of conduct affecting liner conferences which has facilitated a higher Third World share in this sector in contrast to the situation in bulk and tanker shipping. This success partly rested on divisions between Europe and America over liner shipping conferences (these conferences are a kind of cartel arrangement for particular shipping routes).[10]

9. COMMODITY AGREEMENTS AND REGIMES

Many commodity markets are highly 'politicised' in that governments intervene either individually or collectively to restrict or to encourage output and to raise or to lower prices. The type of intervention often reflects pressures from domestic interest groups, for example from farmers in the EEC in order to raise the prices of many foodstuffs; from urban, especially elite, people in many less-developed countries, in order to keep the price of food down (below the free-market level). If prices are to be persistently kept above free-market levels then producer interests need to be much stronger than consumer interests since, apart from the high price, consumers are likely to end up paying higher taxes. These taxes are required to finance stockpiles of surplus primary products since 'high' prices tend to lead to expanded supplies in excess of demand. Commodity agreements between countries face this surplus problem in so far as they keep the price above the free-market level. This surplus problem arose in the 1980s with the International Tin Agreement, which had been the longest-running and most successful of the few commodity agreements in existence. In the early 1980s the International Tin Council kept the price of tin at a level that resulted in massive stockpiles and the running-up of large debts by the Council. This provoked a closure of the London tin market in November 1985, and a collapse of the agreement.

However, commodity agreements may confine themselves to the more modest goal of stabilising primary product prices. The main method of achieving this is the buffer-stock scheme in which a commodity council (for example, the International Tin Council) holds both the commodity (contributed by the producing countries) and funds (contributed by the consuming countries). In such a scheme the consuming and producing countries need to agree on a price range defined in terms of a 'ceiling price' and a 'floor price'. The council then acts to prevent the price going through the 'ceiling' by selling off some of its commodity stock and to prevent the price falling through the 'floor' by buying up the commodity and adding it to its stockpile. Thus a commodity agreement of the buffer-stock type may fail because of either a disagreement between producing and consuming countries over the appropriate 'ceiling' and 'floor' prices or because of an unwillingness by some or all members of the agreement to make adequate contributions in funds and/or the commodity to the council. In the case of tin, cited above, members were unwilling to contribute the extra funds needed if the Council was to keep buying surplus tin and pay its bank debts. The tin agreement went beyond the buffer-stock principle in that it increasingly resorted to export restrictions (quotas) on producing countries in a way that was similar to that of a cartel. The main difference between a cartel and a commodity agreement is that the former includes only producers whereas the latter includes both producing and consuming countries. Thus resort to export quotas by the International Tin Council helped it to raise tin prices above the free-market level in a similar way to OPEC quotas raising the price of oil.

A buffer-stock scheme is only suited to commodities which are not perishable and which have relatively low storage costs. Thus many primary products exported by less-developed countries (for example, most tropical foodstuffs) do not lend themselves to commodity agreements except in so far as they use export quotas or take the form of a multilateral contract. This latter form involves a commitment by some consuming countries to import certain amounts at a given price and a commitment by some producing countries to supply the commodity at this price: for example the Sugar Agreement between the EEC and certain African and Caribbean countries. Some minerals which might lend themselves to buffer-stock schemes are mined and exported on a large scale by developed capitalist states, so that agreement between less-developed countries on production and pricing policies is not sufficient for an effective cartel. For example, Australia exports uranium and Canada nickel while South Africa (a nation which most less-developed countries would be ashamed to work with) is a major exporter of gold, platinum, vanadium, and other minerals.

Commodity agreements share with cartels one general problem: their membership may not include all the producers. Just as non-OPEC countries like Britain and Mexico expanded oil production after the oil price shocks of the 1970s, so China and Brazil expanded tin output from the late 1970s, that is at a time when the International Tin Council did not fully adjust its price-range in line with changes in market forces. The historically high price of tin in the early 1980s of between £8000 and £10,000 per tonne (as compared to below £1500 in the early 1970s) made it a very attractive commodity for non-members, as well as members, to produce. While the member producing countries were observing export quotas, the non-members were able to 'free ride' on the backs of the International Tin Council members. When the International Bauxite Association imposed a common export tax in the mid-1970s, this attempt to raise prices and tax revenues was undermined by increased production by non-members such as Australia, Guinea and Brazil.

The examples of tin and bauxite are striking because in many ways these two commodities meet more of the requirements of cartelisation than do most primary products. In both cases the developed capitalist states were highly dependent on imports from a small number of less-developed countries. In the case of tin, the great majority of tin exports are accounted for by Malaysia, Indonesia, Thailand and Bolivia. The first three of these countries have strong links with each other in the Association of South-East Asian Nations. In the case of bauxite, several leading producers (for example, Jamaica, Surinam and Guyana) have close Caribbean links. These links should have made cooperation easier. However, the breakdown of the International Tin Council in November 1985 can be partly attributed to a lack of agreement between Malaysia and Indonesia: a sharp drop in the tin price would make unprofitable far more Malaysian than Indonesian mines.

Another factor in the International Tin Council crisis was the lack of growth in demand for tin in the 1980s. While this was partly due to the world recession of the early 1980s, there were also longer-term trends towards substitutes for, and the technically more efficient use of, tin. The existence and development of substitutes is something that affects most primary products. In practice, different minerals exported by less-developed countries are sometimes substitutes for each other. In addition, research and development in the West and Japan is constantly developing new materials (for example, plastics) which can substitute for a growing number of minerals. Thus the outlook for commodity agreements and producer associations in the 1980s was poor. Even the survival of the few existing commodity agreements (rubber, coffee and sugar) was in doubt. As for the International Cocoa Agreement, this ran into difficulties in the 1980s 'because of the long-term expansion of production by certain producers (especially the Ivory Coast and Brazil)'.[11]

The International Coffee Agreement continued partly because of an unusual degree of American support, even though the agreement relied on a system of export quotas. The United States criticised other agreements (for example tin), for their use of quotas because restrictions on supply were seen as 'distorting' prices and 'interfering' with market forces. In the case of coffee the United States was concerned to provide economic support for some Latin American countries (such as Brazil and Colombia) which were leading coffee exporters. Such support, along with the more overt types of economic aid, may facilitate economic development in countries which are markets for American goods and hosts to American transnational corporations. It also may reduce the possibility of communist revolution: the establishment of both the International Coffee Agreement and the 'Alliance for Progress' came soon after the Cuban revolution and the emergence of Castro as a communist leader. The International Coffee Organisation has 75 members and has regulated the bulk of the US \$10 billion annual world trade in coffee under a United Nations treaty. However, there was a growing volume of trade outside its jurisdiction, notably cut-price sales by producers to non-members, at the same time as a growing number of producers failed to meet their official export quota (exports to member consumer countries). In October 1987 the Coffee Agreements showed renewed signs of life with a market-sharing deal. The consumer countries were afraid of debt defaults by coffee producers.

10. THE POLITICAL ECONOMY OF AID

The explanation and interpretation of aid flows to less-developed countries has resulted in an attack on aid from both Right and Left. Some Marxists and dependency writers have seen aid as 'imperialism' that is a means to sustaining world capitalism and the dependent position of less-developed countries. Right-wing neo-classical economists have criticised aid programmes on the grounds that they are bureaucratic, inefficient, biased in favour of the public sector and likely to sustain government intervention in the market mechanism. For example, food aid is said to reduce the pressure on the governments of less-developed countries to invest more in agriculture and allow food prices to rise, so giving farmers an incentive to produce more food. In between these two positions are reformist writers, concerned with equity as well as efficiency, who believe that public welfare provision on a national and international scale is necessary, given the shortcomings of the market mechanism.

Aid takes several forms. Bilateral aid is from one government to another. Multilateral aid is from an international institution such as the World Bank, the Asian Development Bank or the Inter-American Development Bank. Aid may be 'tied', that is the foreign exchange provided has to be spent on the goods and services of the donor country. This is often the case for bilateral aid. Aid may be geared to projects (for example, a dam), to programmes (such as secondary education provision), or it may be in commodity form as with food aid and tractors. Aid may be of a grant or a loan type, and the interest rate on the loan may be more or less 'concessional' (that is, below commercial rates). Aid flows grew during the 1950s and 1960s at a time of East–West competition for influence in the Third World and when the world economy was booming. Aid flows in real terms declined in the 1970s at a time when growth in developed countries slowed down, unemployment rose, and East–West tensions were eased during the period of détente. This real decline in aid flows may also have reflected growing criticisms of aid from left and right. Governments of the North seemed to have become more doubtful about the effectiveness of aid from a political viewpoint, that is in ensuring political stability and loyalty. The economic effectiveness of aid was also questioned since the record of African countries which received more aid per head than most less-developed countries was discouraging. In the 1970s the contrast between the economic success in industrialisation and growth of the newly-industrialising countries, especially those of the Far East, and the slow growth, stagnation and often outright decline of sub-Saharan Africa, became more glaring than it had been in the 1960s.

In 1983 the major aid donors were the leading capitalist countries, especially the United States, France, Japan and West Germany. The Soviet

Union has tended to give much more military aid than economic aid. However, it should be noted that economic aid may make it easier for Third World governments to switch their spending to arms.

Table 14.1 *The major aid donors, 1983*

	Volume of Overseas Development Assistance (in billions of US dollars)	Percentage of total Development Aid by Development Assistance Committee of the OECD
United States	7.95	28.9 (29.7)
France	3.915	14.2 (14.3)
Japan	3.761	13.7 (10.8)
West Germany	3.181	11.6 (11.3)
Britain	1.601	5.8 (6.4)

Note: Figures in brackets are for 1982.

Source: *Far Eastern Economic Review*, 13 June 1985, p. 86.

From a public choice perspective aid spending is seen as the result of the demand for, and supply of, aid policies. The capacity to supply aid is clearly related to the wealth and prosperity of a country. However, sometimes a relatively poor country may give aid for reasons of political prestige and international influence, for example China during the ascendancy of Mao. Public choice theory suggests that given the bureaucratic nature of the budgetary process in most countries, the level of aid in any one year will be constrained by the level in the previous year, that is budgetary politics tends to be 'incremental' in character. The capacity to supply aid may grow without a corresponding increase in aid due to a lack of growth in effective demand. The demand for aid is both internal and external to the donor country. Internal sources of demand stem from philanthropic concern, industrial interests who may see aid, especially 'tied' aid, as a means of boosting business, and from political concern by elite groups: those involved in foreign policy-making may be anxious to keep certain foreign governments in power. Given the relative weakness of pressure groups in this area, governments may have substantial scope for promoting their foreign policy objectives. For example, in the 1980s, United States foreign policy officials seem to have been concerned about the political stability of Mexico since they were quick to respond to Mexico's economic problems in 1982 and 1985 (after the earthquake). The timing of United States help in 1982 was influenced by the upsurge of the debt crisis which was a threat to a number of major American banks: thus it was in their interests to demand aid for Mexico.

Some writers have been interested in the question of whether aid is a 'public good' – that is, does aid confer benefits on countries other than the donor country? In so far as this is the case, small countries might be tempted to 'free ride' on the aid programmes of the large countries, and gain some extra exports without having to give aid. However, amongst developed capitalist states, the smaller countries (such as Sweden) are the most generous donors, in terms of aid as a percentage of GDP. The ideology and political culture of some of these countries may be conducive to a high demand for aid on philanthropic grounds. For example, Sweden is a highly developed social democratic welfare state in which ideas about the desirability of income redistribution are widely accepted, more so than in the United States with its ideological tradition of self-help and rugged individualism and suspicion of big government.

Empirical studies have related one country's per capita aid to that of other countries, in order to see if higher aid spending by others leads a country to give less aid. Bruno Frey finds that a country is more likely to increase its per capita aid if more is spent by other countries, particularly those of its 'reference group'. For example, Britain might compare its spending with that of other EEC countries.[12] This finding is evidence against 'free-riding' on aid. However, the interpretation of this finding is not clear-cut in that it could reflect rivalry between donors for influence (if one spends more, the others do) or it could reflect the greater ability of foreign aid agencies to get budget increases approved when they are able to point to large aid budgets in other donor countries, or some combination of these two interpretations. Paul Mosley suggests that

an important change in the aid-giving process in the last 20 years is that it has become, for the capitalist countries, less of an individualistic and more of a social process. A forum now exists, the Development Assistance Committee of OECD, in which each OECD donor's aid performance, measured not only by quantity but also by quality variables such as interest rates, proportion of aid given on grant terms, and proportion of aid given to 'least developed countries', is scrutinized annually by other members of the committee ... It is believed, for example, that Japan – a poor performer by many years by OECD standards on the criteria of ratio of aid to GNP and concessionality of its aid – was in the early 1970s persuaded to increase its overseas aid substantially purely as a result of pressures from other donors.[13]

The demand for and supply of multilateral aid is not so easy to explain from a realist/mercantilist perspective. The concept of inter-state rivalry would seem to imply bilateral 'tied' aid rather than multilateral aid, even though the latter can be seen as highly functional from a transnational capitalist viewpoint. This is because aid given by institutions such as the World Bank is conditioned by the pro-capitalist values which dominate this institution. The developed capitalist states have increasingly shown a common interest in promoting policies favourable to, and opportunities for, private enterprise and foreign investment in less-developed countries. While this is the case there is still the free-rider temptation for smaller and perhaps even medium-sized countries relative to America. The establishment of the World Bank took place at a time of unusual American economic ascendancy. The advantage of using multilateral as well as bilateral aid for all the developed capitalist states is that it is in some ways more acceptable to, and ultimately more able to influence the policies of less-developed countries. Also the World Bank operates with a consistent philosophy and is less subject to the short-term pressures of domestic politics.

With bilateral aid, political strings are often attached in a way that some Third World spokespeople have called 'neo-colonialist', that is it appears designed to keep them in a dependent relationship with the former colonial power. On the other hand, the World Bank can affect a certain professional neutrality and benevolence in its concentration on projects and economic policies. Bilateral aid giving is often related to concerns as to how countries vote at the United Nations, or perhaps whether they allow a foreign power to have a military base in their country. This does not mean the World Bank has been uninvolved in the domestic politics of less-developed countries. It has repeatedly tried to encourage the adoption of policies which give more scope to private enterprise and the market mechanism. Therefore, its advice has a consistent tendency to support what we have called 'transnational capitalism'. Further, the United States has sometimes used its influence within the World Bank to discourage loans to certain countries (for example, Allende's Chile). The World Bank may also be seen as part of the 'social process' of aid-giving, highlighted by Mosley.

The development of the World Bank as an influential institution which is increasingly involved in economic policy debates within less-developed countries (or at least more openly in the 1980s than earlier) is, perhaps, most easily explained by Robert Cox's concept of social forces, with its stress on the interaction between production relations (notably the rise of the transnational corporations), ideas (of a pro-market and private enterprise type) and institutions (for example, the Development Assistance Committee).[14] The rise of these pro-market ideas and the decline of welfarist and Keynesian ideas, was a striking feature of the early 1980s. The case for a New International Economic Order, involving the managed and 'authoritative' redistribution of resources was weakened in the 1980s, not only by changing material forces (for example, recession), but also by related changes in ideas, especially, though not only in the developed capitalist states. Thus the response of the major developed capitalist states, notably the United States, to the demands of the less-developed countries became even less sympathetic than was the case in the 1970s. In so far as the welfare state was coming under attack in some of the developed capitalist states, an extension of international welfarism (as advocated in the *Brandt Reports*) was unlikely. An instance of this was the failure of the United States to raise its contribution (in line with others) to financing the International Development Association (the 'soft loan' branch of the World Bank). With the Baker Plan, which we discussed in chapter 10, the United States came to favour an expanded role for the IBRD (the main branch of the World Bank group).

More generally, it can be argued that the volume and nature of aid has been influenced by the concern of leading capitalist countries to promote rather than weaken the position of transnational corporations. For example, the World Bank has a branch (the International Finance Corporation) which concentrates on projects that are joint ventures with private capital. The World Bank and other aid institutions consciously seek to avoid competing with private enterprise. Such avoidance is written into the statutes governing the distribution of United States aid and that of the World Bank Group as well as the African, Asian, Caribbean and Inter-American Development Banks. Bilateral aid may be given partly with a view to discouraging the nationalisation of the assets of foreign capital. Britain stopped aid to Tanzania in 1969 when it nationalised British banks in the country. However, some projects might be backed by Western donors (even if they compete with private capital) if the goal is to achieve political influence. Even here, such influence is often geared to the long-term promotion of pro-capitalist policies. Some of the most 'generous' aid (that is large-scale, and made on easy terms) has been given to states that have been staunchly anti-communist and welcoming to foreign business. For example, the United States gave vast amounts of economic aid (and also military aid) to Taiwan and South Korea in the 1950s and to South Vietnam in the 1960s and early 1970s.

11. CONCLUSIONS

The North–South divide reflects the unequal distribution of power resources in the global political economy. Its origins lie in the age of colonialism. This distribution limits the bargaining power of the Third World, but it also makes regime change based on United Nations institutions, where less-developed countries have a voting majority, especially appealing to these nations. At least this was the case in the 1970s, after the OPEC oil price rises of 1973–74. Since the 1970s, the 'South' has become more defensive relative to its richer, 'Northern' neighbours. As a consequence, calls for a New International Economic Order based on principles of 'authoritative' multilateral allocation, rather than on the market mechanism have resulted in few concessions of substance.

Less-developed countries differ greatly in size, culture, ideology, income and natural resource endowment. Their economic links to the North remain far stronger than those between themselves. Attempts at regional integration had little success. As for the commodity agreements so much discussed in the North–South dialogue, these were few in number, and by the late 1980s, were in danger of becoming still fewer. The newly-industrialising countries were faced with growing protectionism while the poorest less-developed countries (many of them African) comprised a 'Fourth World'. Their fate contrasted with that of some OPEC and Far Eastern countries. This complex picture is more in accord with the world systems perspective (with its semi-periphery category) than with the simpler (core–periphery) versions of dependency theory.

However, the stress of dependency theorists on the extreme and embedded inequalities within most less-developed countries and the economic and political links between Third World elites and those of developed capitalist states helps to explain the limited nature and success of the New International Economic Order: most less-developed countries are not anti-capitalist and the North–South rhetoric could serve as a 'soft option' to the elites and capitalists of many of these countries, when compared to policies promoting economic redistribution at home.

NOTES

1. World Bank, *Development Report, 1984* (Washington DC, International Bank for Reconstruction and Development, 1984), p. 11.
2. The Brandt Commission, *North–South: A Programme for Survival* (London, Pan Books, 1980); The Brandt Commission, *Common Crisis, North–South: Cooperation for Survival* (London, Pan Books, 1983).
3. Chris Edwards, *The Fragmented World* (London, Metheun, 1985) p. 284.
4. M. J. Gasiorowski, 'The Structure of Third World Economic Interdependence', *International Organization* (1985), Vol. 39, p. 337.
5. Stephen Krasner, *Structural Conflict* (Berkeley, Cal., University of California Press, 1985).
6. *The Economist*, 15 August 1987.
7. J. Bhagwati, 'Introduction', in J. Bhagwati (ed.), *The New International Economic Order* (Cambridge, Mass., MIT Press, 1977).
8. Robert L. Rothstein, 'Regime-Creation by a Coalition of the Weak: Lessons from the New International Economic Order and the Integrated Program for Commodities', *International Studies Quarterly* (1984), Vol. 28, pp. 307–28.
9. M. Shafaeddin, 'Import Capacity as a Bargaining Tool of Developing Countries', *Trade and Development: an UNCTAD Review*, (1984), No. 5, pp. 53–77.

10. Alan W. Cafruny, 'The Political Economy of International Shipping: Europe versus America', *International Organisation* (1985), Vol. 39, pp. 79–119. See also Alan W. Cafruny, *Who Rules the Waves? The Political Economy of International Shipping* (Berkeley, Cal., University of California Press, 1987).
11. J. Finlayson and M. Zacher, 'The Third World and the Management of International Commodity Trade: Accord and Discord', in W. Ladd Holist, and F. LaMond Tullis (eds), *The International Political Economy Yearbook* (Boulder, Col., Westview Press, 1985), pp. 199–222.
12. Bruno S. Frey, *International Political Economics* (Oxford, Basil Blackwell, 1984), pp. 99–100.
13. Paul Mosley, 'The Political Economy of Foreign Aid: A Model of the Market for a Public Good', *Economic Development and Cultural Change* (1985), Vol. 33, pp. 377–8.
14. For a categorisation of the views and 'policy networks' which were involved in the New International Economic Order debate in the 1970s, see Robert W. Cox, 'Ideologies and the New International Economic Order: Reflections on some Recent Literature', *International Organisation* (1979), Vol. 33, pp. 257–302.

FURTHER READING

R. Cassen et al., *Rich Country Interests and Third World Development* (London, Croom Helm, 1982).

G. M. Guess, *The Politics of United States Foreign Aid* (London, Croom Helm, 1987).

G. Kitching, *Development and Underdevelopment in Historical Perspective* (London, Methuen, 1982).

S. Lall and F. Stewart, *Theory and Reality in Development* (London, Macmillan, 1986).

C. T. Saunders (ed.), *East–West–South: Economic Interactions between Three Worlds* (London, Macmillan, 1982).

C. T. Saunders (ed.), *The Political Economy of New and Old Industrial Countries*, (London, Butterworth, 1984).

A. P. Thirlwall and J. Bergevin, 'Trends, Cycles and Asymmetries in the Terms of Trade of Primary Commodities from Developed and Less-Developed Countries', *World Development* (1985), Vol. 13, pp. 805–17.

T. G. Weiss, 'Alternatives for Multilateral Development Diplomacy: Some Suggestions', *World Development* (1985), Vol. 13, pp. 1187–209.

C. K. Wilber (ed.), *The Political Economy of Development and Underdevelopment* (New York, Random House, 1979).

15 Communist States and East–West Relations[1]

This chapter examines the origins and nature of the Soviet system, its limits and prospects, particularly since Gorbachev's accession to power; and the relations between the East and West, particularly with respect to trade, finance and technology transfer. We also examine developments in China since Mao Tse-Tung.

The Russian Revolutions of 1917 resulted in the world's first communist government, led by Lenin. The seizure of power by the Bolsheviks brought with it the creation of a new type of state, ideologically committed to the abolition of capitalism and the promotion of socialism and ultimately the communist society. Following the Soviet share in the spoils of victory in World War II, certain East European states were occupied by the Red Army and communist governments were established. The only East European communist states that did not depend for their creation on Soviet military might were Tito's Yugoslavia, and as it later emerged, Albania. In 1949, the world's most populous state, China, underwent a communist revolution, led by Mao Tse-Tung.

The Soviet state has risen remarkably in the inter-state system in a very short timespan. Whereas in 1917 Russia was a relatively weak and backward agrarian society, by the 1970s it had become qualitatively transformed: it was not only the second largest economy in the world (in terms of gross national product, GNP), but it had succeeded in promoting a military form of industrialisation which could match that of its major capitalist adversary, the United States. In so doing, the Soviet Communist Party (CPSU) had realised the dreams of Peter the Great. Whereas Russia was already the second largest nation in terms of military expenditures and GNP in 1913, it had only 11 per cent of the manufacturing capacity of that of the leading country, the United States, whereas Germany had 46 per cent and the UK 43 per cent, respectively. By 1983, the Soviet Union had 47 per cent of the leading country's (the United States) manufacturing output, compared to 29 per cent for Japan, and 17 per cent for West Germany, the next largest industrial economies.[2]

1. SOME QUESTIONS

The creation and rise of the Soviet Union and the spread of its dominance, particularly in Eastern Europe after World War II, have created a 'dilemma of interpretation' for political economy. There is considerable disagreement among experts and politicians over a range of questions. These include, is the Soviet Union, as it officially claims, a 'socialist' state? Or, is it a new type of society (neither capitalist nor socialist) or, more controversially, 'the highest stage of capitalism'?

Other key questions involve the relationships amongst the communist states, and between them and the capitalist states. These include whether the countries of the Council for Mutual Economic Assistance (CMEA) are dependent on what the world systems theorists call the 'capitalist world economy'. Also, what is the relationship between the Soviet Union and the other members of CMEA (East Germany, Czechoslovakia, Bulgaria, Poland, Romania, Hungary, Cuba, Mongolia, Vietnam)? Is it one of mutually beneficial interdependence, or one where the members are dependent on the Soviet Union? What is the relationship between the Soviet Union and China, the two major communist states?

With respect to the Soviet Union as a superpower, what limits are there to the continued growth of the Soviet Union as a hegemonic state (in the realist sense of the term), and to the Soviet system becoming the hegemonic (in a Gramscian sense) mode of production in the global political economy? What measures has the Soviet Union adopted in order to optimise its economy to meet the challenges of the 1980s and 1990s, in the so-called era of knowledge-based, high technology economic development? Is a more market-oriented form of socialism likely to be more effective in meeting these challenges?

2. THE SOVIET STATE: ITS ORIGINS, CHARACTERISTICS AND DEVELOPMENT

For Marx and Engels the creation of a socialist state presupposed a relatively advanced economy in which the abolition of the condition of scarcity was possible in the future communist society. However, the coming to power of the world's first communist-led government occurred in conditions almost totally at variance with the ones prescribed by Marx, although Marx noted in the 1882 preface to the Russian edition of the

Communist Manifesto that a revolution in Russia might serve as a signal for, and later a possible complement to, proletarian revolution in the West.

The Russian Revolution of 1917 occurred in a society in which the absolutist power of the Tsar had ruled. This feudal-agrarian society was backward, predominantly peasant-based, and with underdeveloped industry, although the Tsarist regime had been committed to rapid industrialisation, through a policy of 'catch-up mercantilism'. By the middle of the nineteenth century industrial production was only 15 per cent of Russian GNP, factory workers were only 1 per cent of the population, and only 7 per cent of the empire was urbanised.[3] By the time of the Russian Revolutions, only 2 per cent of the population could be described as 'urban proletarians'. Thus Russia in 1917 did not even approximate the preconditions for the type of socialist society which Marx had discussed.

The emergence of the Soviet state can be interpreted in terms of the pressures of the inter-state system, pressures which the Tsarist government was effectively unable to cope with. Robert Cox suggests that, following the analysis of Gramsci, the Russian Revolution was a successful 'war of movement', that is a seizure of control of a strong state by a determined, centralised revolutionary party, made possible by the Tsar's military defeats in World War I.[4] The Tsarist state had no firm base in the relatively underdeveloped civil society. It was not underpinned by what Gramsci called 'the fortresses and earthworks' of a strong civil society (which characterised the developed Western capitalist states), and because of this the Bolsheviks were not confronted by significantly powerful opposition after they consolidated rule following the civil war of 1917–21.

The Bolshevik one-party state was organised on the basis of Lenin's ideas concerning the primacy of politics in determining the possibility of socialism in the Soviet Union. The party was led by a vanguard group of intellectuals and members of the Red Army. It then proceeded to promote 'a revolution from above', in part to reverse what seemed to be a decline in the international position of Russia, and in part to promote the communist society. In order to do this the Bolsheviks removed all countervailing power centres associated with the old regime, developed and deployed a revolutionary ideology aimed at mobilising the masses and reshaping their attitudes, and took control of the major means of production to promote a highly military form of industrialisation. The internal structure of priorities and the pattern of growth were, for the Bolsheviks, fundamentally shaped by their perception of Russia's place in the inter-state system, and in particular by the belief that the new communist state was 'encircled' by belligerent capitalist states which would seek to undermine the revolution and restore the rule of capital. As a result the Bolshevik state moved towards monopolisation of power, and the suppression of opposition both within the civil society and the communist party itself.

However, at this time industrial production had fallen to about one-third of its 1914 level, and about half of the urban workers had either left the cities or died: thus the urban proletariat once again constituted 1 per cent of the Soviet population. In the face of an enormous crisis of social mobilisation, Lenin introduced the New Economic Policy in order to get 'a breathing space' for Russia. As a result, the New Economic Policy allowed for a limited amount of capitalism, including foreign direct investment. Foreign capitalists responded, and created joint enterprises as well as setting up their own subsidiaries under their control.

When Stalin came to power in the late 1920s, he pushed for rapid industrialisation, involving the use of coerced, but ostensibly 'free' labour, as well as forced labour camps, and also enforced a policy of collectivisation of agriculture, turning on the *kulaks* (the richer peasants) and crushing them. Stalin sought to extract a bigger share of the agricultural surplus from the peasants so as to help fund industrial growth, for example, through exporting food (while many peasants starved to death) to pay for imports of machinery and technology. In Marxist terminology, this is referred to as 'primitive accumulation'. This approach can be contrasted with one which attempts to give more incentives to peasants to increase the size of the agricultural surplus, that is the policy favoured by one of the leading Bolsheviks, Nikolai Bukharin, in the late 1920s. Recent agricultural policy in China in some ways reflects the strategy of Bukharin.

The first Soviet five year plan was launched in 1928. In 1930 there were 25 million private farms, and by 1934 some 250,000 collective farms had been created. It has been estimated that in the process approximately 10 million peasants died either through famine or slaughter. While the collectivisation of agriculture enabled the state to extract additional surplus, it led to a fall in agricultural productivity and output. (Agriculture in the contemporary Soviet Union is still highly inefficient when compared with that of its major capitalist rivals in the United States and the European Community, EC.) Between 1928 and 1937 the output of heavy industry rose three-fold, and electrical power supplies increased twenty-fold. Stalin also consolidated his own power within the Communist Party, destroying all elements regarded as a threat. In the late 1930s more than 7 million people were arrested, half of whom are said to have died in custody or were executed, including half of the Communist Party membership. These estimates of the human costs of the terror may be rather high, but are lower than some recent Soviet figures. The loss of life from collectivisation and purges in the 1930s has been put as high as 50 million.[5]

On the other hand, Stalinism created massive new opportunities for a generation of Russians, as the size of the state and the economy were enlarged. It was Stalin's policy to promote Party members who had risen from the peasantry and the growing industrial proletariat. There was a tremendous expansion of educational opportunities, allowing proletarians and peasants to forge new careers in the expanding bureaucracy and public enterprises. The system provided much more job security for the urban workers, as well as new social amenities. Although the regime came to rely on widespread use of terror, with massive and frequent purges of the Party (which also had the macabre effect of creating further opportunities for Stalin's supporters), it continued to gain support from many elements of Soviet society. Stalin was able to strengthen his appeal by drawing on traditions of Russian nationalism, and the cultural respect for strong leadership.

The Stalinist programme of 'socialism in one country' was not, however, a completely autarkic strategy of detachment from the world capitalist system. Timothy Luke has indicated that especially in this phase of Soviet development the import of foreign technologies was crucial, although many foreign experts had left the Soviet Union after 1933. Foreign technology was particularly important for sophisticated military goods and for the vehicle, electrical machinery and metal working industries. Indeed, the greatest annual growth rates occurred in industrial sectors importing high levels of Western technology. Luke suggests that Western technology was in fact the major causal element in Soviet economic growth for the period 1928–45. He adds that at the end of World War II the Soviet Union gained technology through the capture of industrial plants and equipment, particularly from Germany and Manchuria (that is Japanese technology), as well as the know-how of captured scientists. Entire factories were dismantled and taken to Russia.[6] The capture of scientists was probably crucial in helping the Soviet Union to develop its sophisticated weapons after the war.

However, Luke's analysis overstates the degree of Soviet dependence on foreign technology which existed in the 1930s. By consolidating and developing the relative internal and external autonomy of the Soviet state, the Stalinist regime was able to make substantial and effective use of foreign technology. This may have been particularly important in the period following World War II, but was less so in the 1930s. It would be unwise to overestimate the importance of foreign technology, and to, as a consequence, neglect the role of domestic capabilities and of Soviet economic strategy in this context. As Bruce Parrott makes clear, imports of foreign technology declined in the second five year plan (starting in 1933), and imported capital goods were only 2 per cent of gross investment.[7] This caused a number of problems, and forced Soviet technologists to switch to copying and 'reverse engineering'. Thus the conclusion to be made is that it was mainly Stalinist economic strategy, which involved some use of imported foreign technology, which pulled Russia into the twentieth century's first rank of military-industrial powers. The policies of his successors have sought to consolidate and extend this position within the global political economy, and to further Soviet hegemony within the world communist movement.

Soviet hegemony initially owed more to the supposedly shining example of socialism in the Soviet Union than to military and economic strength. Socialists in other countries saw the Soviet Union as the 'motherland' of socialism, whose survival and success was of overriding importance. Stalin was able to take advantage of this reservoir of idealism and goodwill in the world communist movement (organised in the Comintern) to recruit foreign agents and to penetrate both state and trade union bureaucracies in the West. Thus Stalin was able to use cultural hegemony to help promote the Soviet Union's material power position. After Stalin's death, this form of Soviet hegemony in the West gradually declined (as opposed to the cultural appeal of Marxist ideas, which may have increased in the 1960s and early 1970s). In the post-1945 period, Soviet hegemony within the world communist movement came to rely increasingly on military might, as the Red Army occupied and controlled much of Eastern Europe. In the less-developed countries, the appeal of the Soviet model came to be greater than in the West. For example, the combination of five year plans and a nationalist stress on self-sufficiency and independence was adopted by India after 1947, with the Soviet example in mind.

Soviet strategy prioritised military-industrial development at the expense of other aspects of the economy. After Hitler reneged on the Munich Pact of 1938, the Soviet Union allied with the United States and Britain against the Axis powers in World War II, and suffered heavy losses (estimated at 20 million people). By 1945 the Soviet Union was America's principal rival in the inter-state system. Thereafter, the Soviet relationship with the West became more hostile, particularly with the United States, and by 1947 the Cold War had set in. These developments intensified the Soviet state's drive to maintain its security, and to develop its military-industrial structure of production. By the late 1940s the Soviet economy had begun to grow, its military power had been reconstructed and the Soviet regime had been consolidated. Victory in the 'Great Patriotic War' deepened the legitimacy of the Communist Party.

The 'socialist' and 'democratic' character of the Soviet state was officially enshrined in the Stalinist Constitution of 1936. However, there is a gap between Soviet doctrine and the reality of the Soviet Union. Many, especially left-wing intellectuals, have contested the self-characterisation of the Soviet system as 'socialist'. (Many right-wing intellectuals are quite keen on the self-characterisation since it allows them to argue against socialism at home.) A variety of terms have, instead, been used.[8] The Soviet Union has been variously seen as being 'totalitarian', 'state capitalist', a 'bureaucratically deformed workers' state', a 'transitional state', 'neither capitalist nor socialist' and 'bureacratic collectivist': that is a new form of social formation which combines the political and economic domination of Soviet workers and peasants.

What seems centrally at issue in the debates over the nature of the Soviet system is the question whether the Soviet Union has inaugurated and developed an alternative social process of accumulation, or whether it merely represents 'the highest form of capitalist accumulation'. The latter term suggests that the system is organised as a massive transnational enterprise along centralised, hierarchical lines. The Soviet State 'exploits' the Soviet proletariat much more efficiently than capitalist firms who do not have such a monopoly of both economic and political power. Marxists (unlike world systems theorists) define capitalism in terms of free markets for labour as well as capital. For both perspectives the context is one of a system which guarantees private ownership and control of the major means of production. This includes the right of private individuals and firms to make profits, and to accumulate and transmit wealth. The Soviet system clearly has not manifested these characteristics (despite new laws enabling some limited private enterprise in service industries from 1987). The subordination of workers to management has some similarities to that of workers in capitalist countries, but job security has been greater. On the other hand, trade unions have lacked independence, being in some respects an arm of management. Moreover, the scope for labour mobility has been very restricted in the Soviet Union, both with respect to occupations and geographical location.

From realist as well as from certain world systems perspectives, Soviet policies are seen as a classic case of mercantilist strategy. This has been made possible by the vast reserves of energy and other raw materials in the Soviet Union (providing self-sufficiency in materials), as well as the development of a coercive state apparatus able to discipline labour and to mobilise the society for long-term goals, prioritising a military build-up, and the construction of an industrial infrastructure which could sustain this. Thus it has a military–industrial complex *par excellence*. Realists see Soviet imports of foreign technology as a carefully controlled means of accelerating Soviet development. The Soviet Union has a highly autonomous state able to pursue 'national interests' (defined by the CPSU) in a fairly straightforward way.[9]

Soviet theorists claim that the Soviet system in the post-war period has demonstrated its superiority to Western capitalism in a number of respects. First, it has promoted high rates of growth and productivity increase, and growth rates for industrial production in CMEA have consistently exceeded those for the EEC in the 1960s and 1970s (although these slowed considerably in the late 1970s and early 1980s). Second, there is considerably less waste (there is no planned obsolescence, mass advertising, and unsaleable surplus production, except where goods are defective). Certain forms of macro-inefficiency (for example, little or no unemployment) are largely absent in the centrally planned economies. Soviet claims for superior allocative and X-efficiency may, however, only hold for the earlier stages of industrialisation, rather than the later stages where dynamic efficiency (promoting innovation) may be more important for economic growth and productivity increases (on these concepts see chapter 12, section 5). Neo-Trotskyite critics in the West, have, however, argued that the Soviet economy is, in fact, characterised by its wastefulness.[10] One major source of inefficiency mentioned in this context is the incompetent, corrupt and self-seeking character of the Soviet bureaucracy.

Also, the Soviet Union's claim to superior efficiency rests partly on accepting the contestable assumption that the stress on developing the military–industrial base of the Soviet Union is necessary for the general welfare of the population. Both Soviet and American specialists generally agree that the United States and other major capitalist states have more efficient economies, and that the Soviet Union also wastes significant amounts of labour and material resources within the production process.[11]

Michael Ellman's systematic study of the CMEA states, concludes that these countries

do not differ fundamentally from the capitalist countries with respect to the labour process, the division of labour, and the social ownership of the means of production. In both groups of countries, most of the population is forced to engage in dreary labour in a stratified, unequal society in which the means of production are not in social ownership.[12]

Despite these criticisms, Ellman claims that the CMEA states have eliminated the enormous inequalities in ownership of the means of production in capitalism, and have much more equal distribution of incomes than many major developed capitalist states. However, what may be more important in the East is not simply the distribution of income, but the distribution of consumption, in that the provision of 'perks' and the access to higher quality goods and services is very unequal. This is because in these societies, the granting of consumption privileges is determined by political factors, and the distribution of political power is more unequal than in most Western countries. Further, there is little or no rotation of political elites in these states; virtually the whole of society is subordinated to an administrative hierarchy, and important political freedoms are notable by their absence.[13] Widespread self-management exists only in Yugoslavia (which is not a member of CMEA), but this still operates in the context of overall state planning.

None of the above should be taken as suggesting that East European societies are homogenous. There is, within the structure of each communist state, considerable variation not only in terms of markets and enterprise autonomy, but also with respect to the importance of civil society in each country. For example, most farms in Poland are privately owned and the Catholic Church is very influential and more autonomous than the Orthodox Church in Russia.

3. STATE SOCIALISM AND WORLD CAPITALISM

The debate over the relationship between the Soviet-centred state socialist system and the American-led world capitalist system can be related to the question concerning the limits to the rise of the Soviet Union in the global political economy, and to the issues concerning the prospects for socialism. Are there structural elements built into the state socialist system which effectively prevent them from either rising within the global political economy and/or achieving further socialist development? First, however, we shall briefly review the debate between world systems theory and the position of orthodox Marxists concerning the conceptualisation of the global political economy and the place of socialist states within it.

Peter Worsley contrasts the 'monistic' world view of Immanuel Wallerstein, that is, the idea that there is one 'world system', with the notion that there is not just 'one world', but 'three' or more. Worsley, whilst seeing the global political economy as an interlinked whole, abstracts the whole into two sets of major categories or polarities: that between developed and underdeveloped, and that between capitalist and communist states. World systems theory however, effectively categorises all states in terms of their level of development. Worsley sees the Soviet Union and the other state socialist societies as constituting 'a new World System'. This system comprises nationally-oriented forms of state directed, planned socialist economies, geared internally for popular mobilisation for economic development, and externally for the defence of the nation. Despite some limited degree of interdependence between capitalist and communist states, fundamental antagonisms exist between the two systems. Coexistence is primarily the outcome of military considerations.[14] World systems theorists argue on the other hand, that state socialist societies are effectively tied to the 'capitalist world-system', such that the pressures of inter-state rivalry and the world market are transmitted to the societies of the CMEA, forcing them to deviate from the path towards socialism.[15] The world systems perspective is usually criticised by Western

Marxists in that it prioritises exchange relations in defining and determining a mode of production. Consequently, it is argued that world systems theorists do not recognise the separate and distinct quality of the state socialist societies, which do not rest upon capitalist production relations. Orthodox Marxists usually argue that capitalist relations of exploitation are not significant in the state socialist societies:

Different relations of production determine different modes of production. These different modes may exist within the same social formation or society historically defined ... the fact that different modes and forms of production may exist within the same social formation does not mean, however, that they are unrelated to each other. Rather, one mode ... occupies a dominant position with a decisive influence on others ... to say that a mode dominates however does not mean that others do not exist ... [merely] ... that there are others that are dominated ... the lack of awareness of these points leads Wallerstein to underestimate dramatically the conflicts between different social systems, such as capitalism and socialism, as well as conflicts between classes in each social formation.[16]

The argument that state socialist societies are qualitatively different from capitalist societies is not necessarily incompatible with the argument that their economic development is increasingly bound up with the international division of labour and the world economy. Nor is it incompatible with the idea that some of the CMEA economies are in some ways dependent upon the West. World systems theorists and others have stressed several ways in which this relationship of dependence is manifested in the CMEA countries. Their arguments are, first, if they produce for profit on the world market their internal pricing systems will tend to reflect rewards for profitable export production. On the other hand, the monopolistic foreign trade organisations of the communist states act as a 'buffer' which diminishes this effect. Second, some Eastern European countries, notably Poland, have borrowed extensively from the West, and some (Romania, since 1972, and Hungary, since 1982) have joined the International Monetary Fund (IMF). The pressures exerted by foreign banks and financial institutions are reflected in the economic plans and priorities of the East. In order to pay for the increased costs of debt servicing, domestic consumption has been curtailed, as it was in the early 1980s. Third, recession in Western capitalist countries cuts the demand for Eastern exports, and makes debt servicing more difficult. Finally, the Western countries tend to increase their military expenditures in a recession, partly to offset lack of effective demand. This causes the Eastern countries to respond in kind, distorting economic priorities even further. Such factors, plus CMEA's need for high-technology, lead world systems theorists to conclude that CMEA is economically dependent on the West. This is reinforced by a systemic security interdependence with the West. The economic costs of military expenditure are higher for CMEA, than for NATO members.[17]

The argument concerning military expenditures in the West during recessions is a false generalisation: for the United States in the mid-1970s (the first post-war recession) the percentage of GNP devoted to military expenditures actually fell, and only rose substantially after 1978, a period coinciding with the second post-war recession, (1979–82) followed by significant American economic growth. It is true that any growth in the arsenals of either side, tends to be matched by the other, contributing to the East–West arms race, and tensions between the two sides. Hence military interdependence creates economic difficulties, perhaps more for the East than the West. It is important also to assess the degree to which East–West economic relations can be simply characterised as those akin to the relations between the advanced capitalist 'core' and other capitalist 'semi-peripheral' and 'peripheral' countries.

Orthodox Marxists, whilst noting that Western economic conditions and actions are important, particularly for certain Eastern European states, stress the self-sufficient nature of the CMEA economies taken as a whole, although they admit that, especially during the 1970s and 1980s their economies have become more integrated into the international division of labour. They stress, however, the crucial difference in the modes of production under 'socialism' and capitalism. Although world market conditions can have a severe impact on individual members of CMEA, this is less the case for CMEA as a whole. They stress that, albeit largely under Soviet control, the group is virtually self-sufficient in energy and crucial raw materials, and has a highly developed scientific and technological basis, which is particularly advanced in theoretical forms of knowledge. Eastern Marxists admit that Western corporations are much more successful in applying innovations, but argue that this is a temporary rather than a structural, long-term condition.[18]

A final criticism of the dependency argument is that, apart from indigenous resource endowments, Eastern European states, notably the Soviet Union, can take advantage of the structure of international markets and capitalist competition to obtain alternative sources of supply of various items. Good examples of this include the buying of Argentinian grain after the Carter embargo of 1980, and the divisions in Western ranks after President Reagan attempted to block the West Siberian pipeline deal in the early 1980s. This suggests that the world market provides both constraints and opportunities for communist states.

4. EAST–WEST TRADE AND FINANCE

The development of the Cold War after 1947 included a political campaign and an economic blockade against the state socialist countries, who reacted by forming CMEA in 1949. By the late 1950s, the Cold War had helped to motivate attempts to create a 'socialist division of labour', after an initial period in which each CMEA member pursued relatively autarkic policies. In the early years of the Cold War, CMEA was an instrument in helping to reconstruct the Soviet economy. Indeed, Soviet foreign economic policies towards CMEA in the early post-war period have been characterised as ruthlessly instrumental and coercive. These practices in part led to revolts in East Germany and helped to provoke the Hungarian uprising in 1956. By the early 1980s, a gradual 'liberalisation process' had emerged in the Soviet Union, and a slightly more relaxed attitude was taken towards the development of other models of state socialism.

From a low point in 1953, East-West trade grew rapidly through the 1960s. The Eastern European countries moved towards a reintegration into the world economy, including the development of co-production ventures with Western transnational corporations. In 1970 Eastern Europe accounted for around 19 per cent of world GNP (14 per cent of which was accounted for by the Soviet Union), whereas Western Europe generated 23 per cent, the United States 33 per cent and Japan 6 per cent. By 1970 the share of Eastern Europe in world exports was low, at around 9 per cent (4 per cent for the Soviet Union), whereas Western Europe's share was 43.5 per cent. This indicated a relatively low level of East European integration into the international division of labour at the start of the 1970s, and the potential for a substantial rise in East-West trade. Between 1971 and 1980, East European exports to the OECD rose from US $7.1 to $47.6 billion, and imports from the OECD rose from $7.0 to $46.6 billion, that is a seven-fold increase in trade. East-West trade increased slightly faster than world trade as a whole during the 1970s.[19] Thereafter trade fell in the early 1980s, and recovered slightly in 1984, with CMEA in surplus during the first half of the 1980s.

Food, fuels and semi-finished products made up 96 per cent of Soviet export earnings and 63 per cent of Eastern European exports to the OECD in 1983.[20] Some East European countries are more heavily involved in trade with the West, notably Yugoslavia, Romania, East Germany and, in absolute terms, the Soviet Union. Trade between the seven East European members of CMEA and the OECD was very low in 1970, amounting to only 2.3 per cent of total world trade, of which some 90 per cent was within Europe. Thus world systems arguments concerning trade dependency would seem, at best, only to relate to the period since 1970.

Advocates of increased East-West economic interdependence (such as some Western and Asian politicians, some Soviet leaders, and many heads of transnational corporations) argue that it can foster on both sides a vested interest in more stable political and military relations, as well as promoting a more advantageous international division of labour, with mutual gains from trade. During the period of détente, especially during the Nixon administration, American strategists (such as Henry Kissinger) hoped that this would result in increased Western structural influence over the Soviet Union and its allies, increasing the scope for issue-linkage. However, given the continuing relative self-sufficiency of the East, such influence was not likely to be significant. Further, the Soviet Union resisted 'linkage' between superpower détente and political competition in the Third World.

Estimates vary, but it is possible that more than 1000 transnational corporations have had some dealings with the CMEA countries since the 1960s. These dealings take various forms, only one of which, the 'joint venture', allows Western firms an equity stake. Other forms include technical collaboration and turnkey plants. As Samuel Pisar remarks, 'Churches, diplomats, intellectuals, armies – all have failed to obtain a foothold in the East. Only big business has managed to do so, and both East and West have benefitted from it.'[21]

Since 1945, the Soviet Union traditionally maintained full managerial control and ownership rights in its co-production ventures. However, in 1986 the state introduced a decree permitting 49 per cent foreign ownership in joint ventures, and facilities for repatriation of profits (this was previously prohibited under the Soviet Constitution). Some East European states (Hungary, Romania, Yugoslavia) and also China and more recently Vietnam, have become much more 'liberal' and have offered a wider and much more open door to foreign capital. The Soviet Union has its own transnational enterprises, operating a network of banks and trading companies worldwide, mainly geared to the promotion of Soviet exports of energy, raw materials and arms to the Third World. Western firms, engaging in deals with the Soviet Union, are often paid, not in hard currency, but in commodities such as minerals.

The substantial increase in East–West trade and finance since the 1960s, has brought costs, as well as benefits to the East European countries. The sizeable capital investments and technology imports in the East European economies in the 1970s and to a lesser extent in the 1980s, were designed to increase output and productivity across a range of fields. These were partly financed, during the 1970s by recycled OPEC surpluses and Western savings. Austerity measures, in some cases implemented under IMF pressure, were needed to generate the surplus to meet debt servicing requirements after global interest rates rose rapidly from 1979 onwards. These measures reflected the fact that most of the CMEA economies were more sensitive to changes in global economic conditions than was the case in the 1960s. Certain East European states borrowed heavily when rates were low, but began to repay when rates were higher. Their exports were being sold in stagnant markets where there was intensified competition from higher quality newly-industrialising states and other Western producers. At the same time, the terms of trade for primary and tertiary East European products was deteriorating. The debt situations of Poland and Romania became particularly acute.

5. TECHNOLOGY TRANSFER AND EAST-WEST RELATIONS

As was noted earlier, the Soviet Union has a long tradition of importing technology and capital from the West, stretching back to the reign of Peter the Great, when Western ideas and technology were used to build the glittering city of St Petersburg. Lenin's New Economic Policy involved substantial imports of capital and technology, although this declined with Stalin's relatively autarkic policies. Such imports increased substantially, particularly in the 1970s. Similar motives for importing technology apply today. Soviet planners are keen to raise productivity levels as well as the supply of consumer goods. In addition, the Soviet military needs certain types of foreign technology to improve its capabilities.

The Soviet Union is relatively starved of certain types of high-technology hardware: for example, in 1985, there were only about 30,000 mainframe and mini-computers in the Soviet Union compared with 620,000 in the United States.[22] On the other hand, in certain types of technology, notably concerning the commercial exploitation of space, the Soviet Union has a significant lead over all other nations, which reflects not only its scientific prowess, but also the capacity to centralise investment funds, and to plan over the long term in a very effective way. A good example of this was the Energia rocket system, successfully launched in May 1987. This, in concert with other systems under development, was intended to supply massive quantities of solar power to Soviet industry, cities and agriculture in the next century. This system will use giant mirrors to reflect the sun's rays into solar power stations which will beam down energy by laser. Western scientific experts conceded that Soviet plans were feasible, and were sufficiently advanced to give the Soviet Union a ten-year lead in the quest to exploit the highest frontiers of space. Displaying business acumen worthy of the most hard-nosed capitalists, the Soviet Union indicated that it was prepared to engage in joint ventures with Western countries which had fallen behind in the space race.[23]

The principal barriers to Soviet acquisition of Western technology lie within the Soviet Union's centrally planned economy. The Soviet Union has had great problems in both financing and absorbing imported technology. In this sense it is significant that the Soviet space energy programme noted above has been developed without significant use of Western technology. The problems of financing technology imports are related to Soviet earnings from energy exports (mainly to the West), gold and other commodity sales, and arms sales, as well as to the availability of cheap foreign credits. If Soviet terms of trade improve, as they did in the 1970s, its capacity to finance technology imports correspondingly increases, and vice versa. Thus the fall in world oil and gold prices in the 1980s had adverse effects on Soviet terms of trade. This has restricted the Soviet Union's ability to obtain the technology it required, as did a number of poor harvests which have made it necessary to import grain. The failure of the Soviet Union to produce many cheap and attractive consumer goods for export has limited its hard currency earnings.

On the other hand, the divisions over East–West relations and the competition between Western transnational corporations can be exploited by the Soviet Union to obtain cheaper foreign technology. The new Soviet leadership is very keen to involve transnational corporations in new joint ventures, but the main stumbling-block is insufficient Soviet hard currency earnings, plus the fact that the rouble is not convertible in the West. With this in mind, the Soviet Union has shown an interest in expanding trade, requested observer status for the Uruguay round of GATT negotiations, and paid close attention to Western efforts to stabilise the international monetary system during the 1980s.

According to Bornstein there is no systematic assessment of the Soviet Union's capacity to absorb and to diffuse Western technology available in non-classified publications.[24] However, he and others, such as Buchan,[25] have noted that the Soviet planning system militates against successful assimilation of foreign technology. As a result the overall impact on most of Soviet industry of such imports is probably quite small, although its impact may be greater in the more privileged and better organised military–industrial sector. None the less, technology-intensive products represented 57 per cent of OECD exports to the Soviet Union in 1982, compared to a peak of 73 per cent in 1970 and also in 1974. Foodstuffs now account for a quarter of Soviet imports from the OECD countries.[26]

The Soviet Union appears not only weaker than its Western counterparts in applying foreign technology outside its military sector, it is also less able to apply some of its own technologies than the West. Although basic research is good by world standards, it has been rarely fully translated into production. For example, scientists at Chelyabinsk Polytechnic invented a new 'world-beating' technique for rolling and drawing metals in 1966. Although this was then patented and used in 35 countries, a combination of design problems, bureaucratic wrangles, cash shortages and construction difficulties have meant that the Soviet Union ony began to use the process in the mid-1980s in Novosibirsk, Siberia. In 1985, the mill was still not working properly.[27]

On the other hand, the defence sector is different, since it has first call on investment funds and the cream of the labour force. Moreover, it has high quality control standards. In some military technologies the Sovet Union appeared to have cut the United States' lead (for example micro-electronics and computers) from 10 to 12 years in the mid-1960s to 3 to 5 years by the mid-1980s. The United States has traditionally sought to deny the communist countries access to certain types of technology, notably that which can be construed as having a military application. One way it has conducted economic welfare against the Soviet Union is through the CoCom. CoCom is the Western Coordinating Committee on Trade with Communist Nations, established by the United States and fourteen of its allies in 1949.[28] The United States has used this forum to pressurise its members (with varying degrees of success) to deny export licences for certain types of technology to the Soviet Union. Whilst intensifying attempts to prevent the Soviet Union from obtaining militarily useful technology, (for example, in CoCom and through the 1979 Export Administration Act) the United States retreated from an all-out trade embargo which looked possible after the 1979 invasion of Afghanistan (aimed at restoring Soviet control).

The main reason for this was the strength of domestic vested interests in the United States, rather than altruism on the part of the fiercely anti-communist President Reagan. The power of the American agribusiness lobby was demonstrated when President Carter instituted an embargo on grain exports to the Soviet Union in 1980, after the Soviet invasion of Afghanistan. Significant numbers of American grain exporters had come to depend on the Soviet market during the 1970s, and faced bankruptcy as a result of Carter's move. Their opposition contributed to a collapse in Carter's electoral position in the Mid-West, and to his defeat by Reagan in 1980. As President, Reagan made no move to resume the grain embargo, and instead concluded a long-term grain pact with the Soviet Union in 1983. This allowed West European members of NATO to point out the contradictions in United States policies whilst continuing their trade with the East, and simultaneously to promote some form of détente, even when anti-Soviet attitudes came to the fore in America. American trade and technology transfer policies with respect to the Soviet Union can be contrasted with those towards China in the 1980s. The United States took the lead in CoCom in pressing for procedural changes, mainly with the Chinese market in mind, following the shift in Chinese attitudes to trade and foreign investment after the eclipse of Maoism in the late 1970s.

In contrast to the United States, the Soviet state has less difficulty with organised domestic lobbies (although the strength of mainly urban consumer interests is reflected in both vast food subsidies, which create shortages and large-scale food imports). However, the Soviet Union can, because of its monopsony power over foreign trade negotiations, construct its trade strategy such a way as to divide its capitalist opponents and make more advantageous deals. This capacity was demonstrated in the early 1980s with respect to the supply of oil and gas to Western Europe. The divisions within the West, as well as Western Europe's need to diversify its energy resources, were skilfully exploited by the Soviet Union when it constructed the trans-Siberian oil and gas pipeline to supply both its own consumers and Western European states, notably West Germany and France. The Soviet Union in fact had the technology to build this pipeline itself, and one would have expected, at first sight, that it would have done so. Why did it choose to collaborate with the West in building the pipeline?

Soviet investment in energy was already running at 20–25 per cent of industrial investment, and the expensive exploitation of Siberian natural resources stretched Soviet investment potential to its limits. In the period of the second Cold War (1977–85), the Soviet Union also faced the necessity of increasing military expenditures in response to Western increases in arms spending. Thus the Soviet Union was probably concerned to finance Siberian investment with the help of foreign capital, at least in a way which avoided the necessity of reorganising its other investment programmes. Although this perhaps reflected the inflexibility of the Soviet planning system, the weakness of Soviet enterprises in applying new technology, and a desire to avoid depleting its reserves of hard currency, it has been argued that the pipeline represented part of a longer-term Soviet strategy of making key West European countries more dependent on its energy supplies. The Soviet Union's long-term aim was possibly to create a situation of asymmetrical interdependence with the West, as well as cultivating those vested interests in Western Europe which sought more constructive relations with the Soviet Union. This argument can also be linked to the suggestion that since many Western European producers have begun to lose their competitive edge *vis-à-vis* American and Japanese firms, they may be prepared to enter into more risky and perhaps less profitable deals with the Soviet Union. If the 'uneven development' of Western Europe in relation to East Asia and North America were to continue, and West European–East European links were to intensify, the Soviet dream of politically 'decoupling' Western Europe from the United States might begin to have some degree of substance in reality. On the other hand, most commentators believe that West European economic links with the East are unlikely to provide the Soviet Union and its allies with too much economic leverage over the West.[29]

The 'technology gap' which exists between the Soviet Union and the developed capitalist states for a wide range of activity is perhaps one of the reasons why the Soviet Union feared the United States Strategic Defence Initiative (SDI). Although the SDI may never achieve its military goals, it will serve to widen the gap across an enlarged, knowledge-intensive range of sectors, most of which will have a civilian as well as a military application.[30] The SDI is matched by a similar programme, although with a much more 'civilian focus', by the Japanese Ministry of International Trade and Industry, which has created a series of 'technopolis' cities which will bring together high-technology corporations in new greenfield sites. Each programme can be seen as the rival of the other in the race to develop the technologies of the future, and each involves massive amounts of government resources (although there is some limited Japanese cooperation with the United States in the SDI). These American and Japanese programmes have put pressure on all other states, not just the Soviet Union, to invest heavily in technological development to prevent a widening of the technology gap.

The Soviet state, with its developed planning system, and capacity to centralise investment programmes, has certain advantages with respect to this race, as is illustrated by its energy–space effort. Where the Soviet Union appears to have substantial difficulties is in translating innovations in military sectors into applications in other sectors of the economy, and using them for the production of consumer goods. Speeches made by Secretary Gorbachev after his coming to power in 1985 indicate that this problem was well appreciated by a majority in the Politburo, and this helps explain why the Soviet Union was intending to institute significant structural reforms in its economy between 1987 and 1991. These reforms include the introduction of private cooperatives, and, more fundamentally, the reintroduction of market incentives such that wholesale trade will determine supply and demand within most of the economy (the defence sector being largely exempted).

Finally, it is worth noting that the thaw in East–West relations since 1985 may mean that Soviet prospects for obtaining certain foreign technologies will improve. In early 1987 the United States Department of Commerce attempted to relax controls on high-technology exports, imposed in the 1970s and early 1980s because of Pentagon pressure. Proponents of liberalisation in America were able to cite a study carried out in 1987 by the American Academy of Sciences which showed that Pentagon controls had cost American corporations $9 billion in lost annual revenues during the 1980s. In 1984, the United States had made moves to dismantle certain controls for China trade. A more 'liberal' American attitude to Soviet trade in the 1990s is now to be expected, particularly since the Soviet Union has been successful in obtaining some of the technologies it required from Pacific Rim countries.[31]

6. SOVIET HEGEMONY AND EASTERN EUROPE

The economic relations between the Soviet Union and the other CMEA countries are seen by orthodox Marxists such as Syzmanski as qualitatively different from the relations between the developed capitalist states and the less-developed countries. These latter relations are characterised as forms of economic imperialism, whereas the Soviet–CMEA relationship is seen as based upon the Soviet Union's more cooperative policies of balanced growth. Whereas most capital-intensive industries are located in the major capitalist states and less-developed countries produce largely raw materials for the industries of the developed countries, the Soviet Union is the primary supplier of raw materials to Eastern Europe. On the other hand, the Soviet Union is politically hegemonic *vis-à-vis* its Eastern European economic partners, each of which is ruled by communist parties which are answerable, in the last analysis, to Moscow. The Soviet Union is also the second largest supplier of arms to less-developed countries, and, like other East European economies, has consistently had a substantial trade surplus with the world's poorer nations.

The economic relations between the Soviet Union and Eastern Europe are characterised by Syzmanski as highly interdependent, as well as being consciously coordinated and planned. On the other hand, all the CMEA members, with the exception of Romania, are highly dependent upon the Soviet Union for energy supplies. This dependence was dramatically illustrated after the 1973–74 oil price increases following the October War. Although the Soviet Union normally sells its oil and gas to CMEA at about 80 per cent of world market prices, it uses world prices as a basis for setting its oil prices. Thus, although the Soviet Union effectively subsidises Eastern European energy consumption, it has the capacity to charge higher prices if the necessity arises. This may also apply if world prices fall, as they did in the mid-1980s: the Soviet Union may not allow its prices to CMEA to fall proportionately. Moreover, the Soviet Union has constructed a series of nuclear power stations on its western borders to supply the CMEA countries. Thus, in having monopoly control over nuclear technology, the Soviet Union has a weapon of domination over its Eastern European customers. The nuclear accident in Chernobyl in 1986 also illustrated the dangers of these installations on a much wider scale.

A result of the change in the political economy of energy in the 1970s was to strengthen the Soviet terms of trade with its East European partners, making them more dependent on the Soviet Union. The realist and dependency interpretations of Soviet–East European relations stress that any concessions that the Soviet Union has made to its East European partners, have been 'tied' to a pattern of political relations which maintains the vulnerability and dependence of East European countries on the Soviet Union. Thus Soviet trade policies are seen as supplementing the military power of the Soviet Union in Eastern Europe, and helping to sustain Soviet dominance. This dominance, in the last analysis, ensures that the Soviet conception of foreign policy and of the road to communism prevails. Falling oil prices in the 1980s in some ways tended to weaken Soviet control over Eastern Europe, and as a result, it can be argued that, much more than the United States, it has an interest in high oil prices, or conversely in preventing the price of oil from falling too far.

Another way of looking at this examines not just the establishment and maintenance of Soviet dominance in the East, but also the costs of 'empire' and its implications for the future of Soviet policy in the region. This question became more central to the analysis of the future of Soviet dominance as the economic dynamism of the centrally-planned economies faltered in the 1970s and 1980s.

Although the East European countries were dependent on the Soviet Union, the costs of this relationship may be becoming increasingly high for the Soviet Union. Despite the fact that the Soviet Union gains significant security benefits from the status quo, the economic costs of maintaining the status quo have risen rapidly during the 1970s and 1980s. A recent analysis of the transformation of the Soviet bloc argues that whereas in certain respects (primarily in terms of security) the relations between the Soviet Union and the East European communist states can be seen as 'Soviet assets', they have been transformed, particularly in the last fifteen years into 'Soviet liabilities'.[32] Bunce argues that since 1945, apart from in the Stalinist phase, the relative contributions of the East European countries to Soviet national security, economic growth and domestic stability have declined. This is as a result of, first, the economic and political dependence of Eastern Europe on the Soviet Union: second, because of the costs to the Soviet Union of maintaining its East European monopoly of political and, to a lesser extent, economic power (the costs of the 'Soviet Empire'); and third, the costs which accompanied the bloc's reintegration with a global capitalism in crisis. Central to this argument is that the pressure of domestic, regional and global factors have increasingly meant declining Soviet returns in both the economic and security spheres. Thus, although the Soviet Union is the obvious regional hegemon, the maintenance of its dominance in fact contributes to its weakness as a national economy, relative to the developed capitalist states. In order to shore up the domestic legitimacy of a variety of East European regimes during the 1970s in particular, the Soviet Union was forced to bear increasing burdens, at precisely the time when its own economic performance was declining.

The economic performance of most of the East European states declined substantially in the 1970s, at the same time as East European workers had come increasingly to see the legitimacy of the system in terms of its capacity to produce increases in the standard of living. In order to attempt to maintain living standards, as well as to increase productivity by obtaining Western technology, these states turned to Western bankers and governments for loans, as well as to the Soviet Union for credits and indirect economic subsidies. The recessions in the West in the 1970s and 1980s meant that East European exports were badly hit, and also the cost of debt servicing rose with higher interest rates. Their attempts to increase productivity in the 1970s through the import of Western technology proved to be far from successful. Thus the Eastern European states came to be dependent on both the West and the Soviet Union for the maintenance of the structure of their political economies. The paradox of this is that Western capitalists and their states, in the case of Poland, helped to prop up the rule of the communist party elites. Thus it is argued by Bunce that the internal conflicts in the one-party states of Eastern Europe were partially resolved by Western help. Also, she suggests that the opening up to the West increased the pressure for domestic reforms as well as increasing the political and economic dependence of Eastern Europe on the Soviet Union.

Poland provides an extreme case. In order to meet its debts to the West a range of austerity measures were implemented. (Poland's debt stood at US $25 billion in 1982, that is $696 per capita, an amount equal to 648 per cent of its annual earnings from exports to the West.) Western bankers had been eager to extend loans in the early 1970s because of a surfeit of petrodollars, whereas by the 1980s they wanted a reassertion of state control which could ensure cuts in domestic consumption in order to repay loans. Thus, their 'interests' intersected with those of the Soviet Union and the Polish Communist Party leadership in their desire for a reassertion of order, and a restriction of the power of the independent trade union, Solidarity. As Valerie Bunce suggests:

The debt crisis had created what were from the perspective of global politics strange bedfellows, but from the perspective of global economics the alliance was not so much strange as it was familiar. It was ... a form of comprador collusion.[33]

The economic resources of all the states in the Soviet bloc declined relative to those of the West during the late 1970s: the debtor East European governments were themselves subjected to the 'power of capital', and more generally to market forces, in a similar way to the less-developed countries, and, in order to meet their debt obligations, had to impose similar austerity policies, which they maintained during the 1980s. At the same time, these states were also subjected to Soviet dominance, that is the political necessity of maintaining the Communist Party's monopoly of political power, in conditions where their leaders were necessarily identified with maintaining economic growth and an increasing standard of living.

The problems of state legitimacy in Eastern Europe would appear to be much more acute in a recession than they are in the West, simply because the party, by monopolising both economic and political power, is necessarily identified as being responsible for economic failure. Nevertheless, the concentration of political and economic power permitted the imposition of drastic austerity measures in the 1980s without provoking the emergence of a second 'Solidarity' outside of Poland: this seems to reinforce the point that Poland was a special case. On the other hand, the formal separation of state and economy in capitalism seems to enable some leaders of capitalist states (to a larger extent) to distance themselves from responsibility for economic crises. Thus, if it is true that the crisis in the East European economies in the 1980s did not become a crisis of legitimacy for communist party-ruled states, they have both Moscow and, to a much lesser extent, the capitalists of the West to thank. In particular, West Germany has given large credits to East Germany.

The relative decline of these states in the 1980s can be seen as indirectly a decline in Soviet power if, as a result of declining internal legitimacy and economic performance, these states became less able to contribute to the Soviet system of collective security and to maintain a 'socialist encirclement' of the Soviet Union. Thus, to the extent that this complex of factors can be seen as continuing in importance, this is likely to add to the prospect of a decline in a wider Soviet hegemony.

7. THE LIMITS TO THE RISE OF SOVIET POWER

The above discussion concerning the structural problems of the Soviet system with respect to technological innovation and diffusion (dynamic efficiency) suggests that internal structural limits have arisen, constraining the possibility of the Soviet Union moving to a position of primacy in the global political economy. Its hopes for improvement may require that the reforms proposed by Gorbachev and his colleagues are extremely successful. As Gorbachev has acknowledged, the very methods and factors which enabled the Soviet Union to rise rapidly within the global political economy since the 1930s, were themselves prohibitive of a further rise by the 1980s. Evidence for this is to be found in Soviet annual growth rates, which, according to Soviet statistical reports, fell from nearly 8 per cent in 1966, to 3.4 per cent in 1981, although there was a recovery to 4.9 per cent in 1986.[34] By mid-1987 Gorbachev was arguing that the Soviet economy had reached a 'pre-crisis situation', with structural reforms needed to prevent the emergence of a fundamental economic crisis.

In this section we consider first the factors which promoted the rise of the Soviet Union, and then assess its capacity both to maintain and develop its position in the global political economy. This is, in effect, the problem Gorbachev and his supporters were attempting to address.

The rise of the Soviet Union since the 1930s can be interpreted in terms of the capacity of the Stalinist state selectively to mobilise its resources to transform a backward agrarian society into a relatively modern industrial state, albeit using extremely coercive, sometimes terroristic means. This was possible because of the sheer size and resource endowment of the Soviet Union, which had plentiful supplies of coal, oil and iron. The central planning system, and the size of the economy enabled effective use of economies of scale. This took place under conditions where the planning system was highly appropriate for the coordination of the development of a set of military–industrial 'strategic' industries. As was noted above, the more complex an industrial system becomes, the more difficult it is to plan precisely and effectively. On the other hand, by maintaining a massive coercive apparatus, the Soviet state was able to propel the Soviet Union forwards into the twentieth century.

However, the borrowing of foreign ideas, allied to the stifling of certain forms of innnovation in the centralised Soviet system have had a long-term impact on certain Soviet capacities. Imagination and innovation become more and more necessary in complex economies which approach and extend the technological frontier. In other words, foreign technology is relatively easy for countries to obtain and to use in the early stages of their industrialisation (for example, the rise of Japan in the nineteenth century, and the Far Eastern newly-industrialising states in the 1960s), but much more difficult in the post-industrial phase of development.

The Soviet system's economic dynamism slowed in the 1970s and 1980s, and it seemed clear that a more rapid economic growth and technological innovation would only be possible if there were fundamental economic reforms, such as those introduced in Hungary, involving increased use of the market, and perhaps some decentralisation of political power, in the Soviet system.

This possibility faced substantial internal political obstacles. Economic changes, involving decentralisation of economic authority were seen as threatening the political position of some Soviet leaders, and what would be seen from a public choice perspective as entrenched 'vested interests'. Changes would affect upper cadres of the Communist Party and elements in the planning ministries, notably the Gosplan (state planning agency). Economic decentralisation, and the movement towards autonomous and self-financing Soviet enterprises might also undermine the privileges of the 750,000 middle-ranking bureaucrats, or *nomenklatura*.

Some have argued, therefore, that the necessary reforms might open, in political terms, a Soviet 'Pandora's Box', or at least political reaction from conservative elements, if the changes were not managed effectively. In this sense it was significant that the economic reforms introduced by the Central Committee of the CPSU in July 1987 followed a two-year period of cultural and political liberalisation and *glasnost* (which was generally popular with the intelligentsia), a purging of the conservative elements in the cadres, and a weakening of the place of the military within the Soviet political hierarchy. Thus much of the political ground had been prepared before the economic reforms took place. This gave considerable momentum to the reformers, as against the conservatives (in a contrast with the situation in China where the economist reforms took place when many of the old guard of the Maoist era still held positions of power in the ministries and in the Chinese Communist Party). Before the more fundamental structural reforms were decided on, simply through eliminating corrupt leadership elements and certain bureaucratic inefficiencies in the system, Gorbachev's policies made possible an improvement in Soviet economic performance between 1985–87.

The Soviet Union officially announced that it has postponed the achievement of the communist 'utopia', perhaps indefinitely, although it is by no means clear how market reform will bring full communism to the Soviet Union. The new party leadership claimed that the advance to communism may be 'inexorable', but the road to it was 'uneven, complex and controversial'. Gorbachev initially seemed to be more concerned with the lowering of expectations, improved planning, and some modest economic decentralisation and use of pay incentives. In the revised programme of the CPSU published on 25 October 1985, no allowance was made for the introduction of a market-oriented price system. This programme said that greater efforts would be made to stamp out drunkenness, and to get rid of 'bribery, pilfering, toadyism, fawning and wind-baggery', as a complement to other piecemeal reform efforts.[35] By 1987 it was realised that more wide-ranging structural reforms were needed, in order to unleash the creative potential of the Soviet people.

The domestic potential for the future rise of the Soviet Union within the global politcal economy therefore ultimately revolves around the possibility of reconciling the entrenched power of key political elements, notably those of the party elite, the military, and bureaucrats in the planning ministries, with the necessity of introducing market institutions which might promote the type of economic dynamism required to make the leap into a post-industrial high-technology economy, and to keep up with the West. If the new strategy fails, it may threaten, in the long term, both the economic position and the relative military power of the Soviet Union.

This problem for the Soviet Union may be intensified if the United

States maintains its commitment not just to the Strategic Defence Initiative, but to a wider arms race.[36] The desire to avoid this, in large part because of its economic costs, is reflected in the apparent willingness of the Soviets to make concessions over nuclear weapons reductions, for example in the signing of the intermediate nuclear forces treaty in December 1987, in order to get a more substantial arms reduction treaty with the United States in the late 1980s, and to rebuild political détente with its superpower adversary. The Soviet Union also conducted a successful campaign to win popular support for its disarmament proposals in the West.

These disarmament moves can be interpreted in terms of a wider Soviet international political offensive involving advocacy of the concepts of 'world society' and 'interdependence', thus demonstrating that the Soviet Union was prepared to reconcile its national with 'global interests'. Not only has Gorbachev launched domestic moves designed to revitalise the Soviet economy, he has also sought to rejuvenate the Soviet foreign policy apparatus, and to reshape Soviet policy, with judicious use of *realpolitik*. During the mid-1980s the Soviet Union began to rebuild its diplomatic links with non-communist countries in various parts of the globe (as well as with China). One area where Soviet influence has risen, as a consequence of a more imaginative foreign policy is the Middle East. In early 1987, the Soviet Union agreed to reduce its oil exports to the West (despite an estimated year-on loss of foreign currency of US $500 million) in order to cement relations with the Organisation of Petroleum-Exporting Countries (OPEC). It also moved to improve relations with fiercely anti-communist Saudi Arabia, the United Arab Emirates, Oman and Kuwait. It also put pressure on its traditional allies, Syria and Iraq, to help stabilise the region.

In this context it is important to note the convergence of interests between the superpowers in the region: both supported Iraq in its war with Iran, and both sought a *rapprochement* between Israel and the Arab states. Of particular significance was the Soviet Union's agreement to charter three tankers to Kuwait (with an implicit assurance of Soviet naval protection) in 1987, allowing the Soviet Union a legitimate presence in the Gulf, an objective it had sought for many years. These moves occurred in the context of growing anti-American sentiment among Arab states in the region.

The Soviet Union's hegemony, seen in more Gramscian terms, seems unlikely to rise significantly in the 1990s, although the 'new look' under Gorbachev has appealed to many intellectuals and commentators in the West, as well as to states which have perceived increasing common interests with the Soviet Union (such as Kuwait). However, ever since the 1950s, when the revelations about Stalin's atrocities became widely known in the West, the Soviet model has become less and less attractive to generations of Europeans and Asians (particularly after the Sino-Soviet split in 1960). The development of Euro-Communism in the 1960s and 1970s reflected a dissatisfaction in the Western communist movements with the USSR, and its model of development.

On the other hand, the Soviet system has been implanted in Eastern Europe for three generations, and thus although some elements of Eastern European youth tend to look to the West for cultural inspiration, most young people in Eastern Europe appear to be accustomed to working with and accepting the *status quo* in what is a largely materialistic culture. In recognition of this relative ambivalence amongst not only East European youth, but also the older generations, the Soviet Union was prepared, in the mid-1980s, to accept a cautious use of cultural and political liberalisation, and the gradual introduction of the market. Some political activity outside of the CPSU was tolerated (for example, in the new political clubs) provided that the communist state was accepted, in the last analysis, as politically unchallengeable. Some democratic reforms, and a clean-up of the legal system have also taken place since 1985.

The legitimacy of the Soviet system, which is fairly high in the Soviet Union, whilst lower elsewhere in the Soviet bloc, has probably tended to increase over time. If anything, Gorbachev's reforms are more likely to provoke protests from workers than the *nomenklatura*, since they involved an attack on slovenly behaviour and alcoholism at work, and, more crucially, the probability of price rises for foodstuffs and basic necessities. It seemed unlikely however, that Soviet workers would react as strongly to these moves as those of Poland did in the early 1980s. In addition, the Soviet leadership will not need to impose the kind of austerity measures introduced in Poland, since innovations in agriculture are likely to lead to more and better foodstuffs coming to market, and the legalisation of small-scale private enterprise in service industries will prove popular. The legalisation of such activity, previously part of the black economy, may lead to an improvement in services (such as hairdressing, shoe repair, television maintenance) and will provide useful tax revenue for the Soviet state. Much of this revenue will be used to subsidise low-income groups who will be affected by higher prices for basic commodities.

The combination of the factors mentioned above probably means that whilst the Soviet Union will still be strong, it will be more concerned with maintaining the *status quo* during the 1990s, than with promoting the 'class struggle' on a 'world scale'. That the Soviet Union is now a rather conservative power which effectively seeks to maintain its gains, and only cautiously to extend them, was vividly illustrated by the invasion and occupation of Afghanistan (where in 1987, 100,000 Soviet troops were still encamped), and earlier, by the delight shown by the Soviet leadership after the Helsinki accords of 1975, which effectively recognised the legitimacy of

Soviet domination over Eastern European CMEA states. This delight perhaps also reflected the fact that the cultural and political appeal of the Soviet system was still very weak, as evidenced in the strong nationalist and Islamic feelings in some Soviet republics, and in the enduring importance of Catholicism and nationalism in Eastern Europe.

8. CHINA SINCE MAO

The Chinese Revolution of 1949 took place in conditions vaguely akin to those in Russia in 1917: that is in a country where civil war followed on from foreign invasion in a backward, primarily agrarian society, with very little industry (virtually none when compared with pre-revolutionary Russia). Initially, the Communist Party of China allied with the Soviet Union, but this alliance came to an end in 1960, when the Soviet Union withdrew its technicians and economic aid. This break caused a challenge to Soviet ideological hegemony within the world communist movement. China accused the Soviet Union of exploitation ('hegemonism'), for example in the way the Soviet Union occupied Manchuria until 1955, and in the terms of the joint Sino-Soviet trading companies. The Chinese under Mao argued that the Soviet Union behaved in a 'social imperialist' way, seeking to dominate other socialist states.

Under Mao, the Chinese attempted to construct an alternative to the Soviet model, whilst none the less retaining large parts of it (such as state-owned industry and central planning, and a large measure of collective agriculture). In the Cultural Revolution (1965–68) a greater stress was given to moral as opposed to material incentives, and to the construction of an ideologically pure 'socialist man', often at the expense of economic efficiency. However, the Maoist era left China technologically backward, with low living standards, poorly equipped armed forces, and an underdeveloped, and even chaotic education infrastructure. Indeed, at one point Mao closed the universities and sent the students and professors to work in the countryside, because he argued that universities promoted elitism, reinforced the 'unhealthy' separation of mental and manual labour, and generated 'anti-socialist' consciousness. By the death of Mao in September 1976, public respect for the Communist Party had declined, cynicism was widespread, and 'socialist man' was far from being realised.

The post-Mao leadership, in which Deng Xiao-Ping was the dominant figure, sought to put 'production' before 'ideology', on the grounds that socialism presupposed a highly developed (but not necessarily capitalist) economy. Many of the reforms launched in 1978 by the 'Dengists', or pragmatists, were opposed by 'Reds' or leftists, who still defined the problem of communist development in generally Maoist terms. At the time of writing, the leftists appeared to have been outflanked by the Dengists. The outcome of this internal political battle is crucial for the future course of China in a similar way to that between 'reformers' and 'conservatives' in the Soviet Union.

The 'Dengists' put much greater stress on individual incentives and responsibility, especially in agriculture, where the state in effect leased land to the peasants. In both town and countryside, small-scale cooperatives and household enterprises sprang up in large numbers. (In 1987 the Soviet Union announced its intention of adopting certain aspects of this system, notably the reintroduction of family farms.) Whereas Mao stressed self-sufficiency and therefore had little place for trade (internal as well as international) in his strategy, and none at all for foreign investment, the Dengists sought to expand international contacts through trade, foreign investment, aid (as a recipient), tourism, cultural exchanges and sending students to study abroad. This shift reflected a concern to reduce the huge technology gap between China and the leading capitalist states.

In contrast to the 1960s, under Deng's leadership, China attempted to normalise its relationships with the Soviet Union (this was very much desired by the Soviet Union also), and refused to be a 'China card' for either of the superpowers. However, as has been noted, the modernisation programme was linked to an 'open door' policy towards foreign capital, and the capitalists from China's old enemy, Japan, moved swiftly to become the largest foreign presence in the growing Chinese economy. West German and American transnationals also built up a substantial stake during the 1980s, although the scale of their investments was less than was expected in the early phase of the 'Four Modernisations'. Like the Soviet Union, the Chinese were able to take advantage of the competition between foreign capitalists to make advantageous deals. In consequence of these economic, and other strategic developments, China developed much closer relations with the developed capitalist nations than with the Soviet Union. China created four 'special economic zones' and fourteen coastal cities plus Hainan Island, which were open to foreign capital. The negotiations with Britain over the reversion of Hong Kong in 1997, conducted under the slogan 'one nation, two systems', were remarkably successful, and may serve to maintain a vibrant capitalist pole in China (Hong Kong grew at an average annual rate of 9.6 per cent in 1978–82, and its GNP was US $26 billion in 1982). Hong Kong business people boasted of capitalising all of China, and at the very least their impact on the coast cities is likely to be significant.[37] Ironically, in the stock market crash of October 1987, the total collapse of the futures market on the Hong Kong stock exchange was only averted because of substantial financial support from the Bank of China.

The post-Mao leaders, in so far as they had ambitions to make China a superpower, both economically and militarily, put 'production' and 'efficiency' first, for international as well as domestic reasons. More prosperity, as a result of faster economic growth, can be seen as contributing to the domestic legitimacy of the Communist Party. The policies which have favoured increased foreign trade and investment and incentives for the Chinese would seem to have been adopted for pragmatic rather than ideological reasons. Since the technology gap facing China was significantly greater than that facing the Soviet Union, the Chinese had to devise bolder and perhaps riskier policies to 'catch up' the West and Japan, involving the widespread use of markets and material incentives, including the profit motive. These policies, according to China's own figures have led to a growth in production by 10 per cent per annum between 1978–87, in which period urban incomes have increased at least three-fold.[38]

Despite such impressive evidence of improving economic performance it is by no means certain that the 'Four Modernisations' will lead to the creation of a 'socialist' society, as many 'Reds' in the leadership were quick to point out. This issue was at the heart of continuing political divisions within the Chinese Communist Party.

In so far as China has been seen to succeed in its modernisation programme, it may have provided a significant catalyst for changes in the Soviet Union (especially in agriculture), as well as within the world communist movement and the Third World. (In 1987, Vietnam began to embark upon a significant modernisation programme along Chinese lines and opened the door to foreign investors.) In tandem with the new Soviet economic reforms, the Chinese path may also challenge the economic precepts of those socialist parties which favour centralised planning and widespread state ownership of the means of production. If the Chinese are to forge a link between their own cultural traditions and socialist values, it will probably be in the form of a 'Confucian socialism', that is with an emphasis on authority and upon leadership by a benevolent, well-educated, wise elite, and also through a reconstruction of the family as a basic unit of society (which Mao tried to minimise in importance in his 'socialist' vision). To this end, considerable attention should be paid by 'China watchers' to the developments in Chinese educational and social policies in the next decade, and the degree to which Confucian values are represented in party statements and debates.

NOTES

1. We would particularly like to thank Dr Neil Malcolm for his comments on this chapter.

2. Bruce Russett, 'The Mysterious Case of Vanishing Hegemony: Or, Is Mark Twain Really Dead?', *International Organisation* (1985), Vol. 39, Table 1, p. 212.

3. Timothy W. Luke, 'Technology and Soviet Foreign Trade: On the Political Economy of an Underdeveloped Superpower', *International Studies Quarterly* (1985), Vol. 25, p. 333.

4. Robert W. Cox, 'Gramsci, Hegemony, and International Relations: An Essay in Method', *Millenium* (1983), Vol. 12, pp. 162–75.

5. Stephen Cohen, *Bukharin and the Bolshevik Revolution* (New York, Vintage Books, 1975), pp. 339–41. The more recent Soviet estimates were reported in *The Sunday Times*, 17 April, 1988.

6. Luke, op. cit., pp. 340–3.

7. Bruce Parrott, *Politics and Technology in the Soviet Union* (Cambridge, Mass., MIT Press, 1983), p. 36.

8. Although they cannot be regarded as pure Realists, see Theda Skocpol, *States and Social Revolutions* (Cambridge University Press, 1979), pp. 206–35; Barrington Moore Jr, *Soviet Politics – The Dilemma of Power* (Harper and Row, New York, first published 1950, 1965 edition). For a world systems interpretation of the Soviet Union as a mercantilist state, see Walter L. Goldfrank, 'The Soviet Trajectory', in Christopher Chase-Dunn (ed.), *Socialist States in the World-System* (Sage, Beverly Hills, 1982), pp. 147–56.

9. For an overview of Marxist theories of the Soviet Union, see Paul Bellis, *Marxism and the USSR* (Macmillan, London, 1979), and for a specific interpretation see Albert Syzmanski, *Is the Red Flag Flying? The Political Economy of the Soviet Union Today* (London, Zed, 1979). The state capitalist thesis is found in Albert Bergesen, 'Rethinking the Role of Socialist States', in Chase-Dunn, op.cit., pp. 97–101. On totalitarianism, see Hannah Arendt, *The Origins of Totalitarianism* (New York, Meridian Books, 1951; 1960 edition). The industrial society thesis is developed by J. K. Galbraith, in *The New Industrial State* (Harmondsworth, Penguin, 1969). The 'deformed workers' state idea is in Leon Trotsky, 'The Revolution Betrayed', excerpt in C. Wright Mills, *The Marxists* (New York, Dell Publishing Co, 1962, 1966 edition), pp. 332–3. A good overview of perspectives is David Lane, *The Socialist Industrial State: Towards a Political Sociology of State Socialism* (London, Allen and Unwin, 1976).

   Recent interpretations which relate Soviet developments to the global political economy include: Erik P. Hoffman and Robbin F. Laird, *The Politics of Economic Modernisation in the USSR* (Ithaca NY, Cornell University Press, 1982); Karen Dawisha and Philip Hanson (eds), *Soviet–East European Dilemmas* (London, Heinemann, RIAA, 1981); C. Keeble (ed.), *The Soviet State: The Domestic Roots of Soviet Foreign Policy* (London, Gower, RIAA, 1985). A special edition of the journal, *International Organisation* (1986), Vol. 40, No. 2 was devoted to change in Eastern Europe and the Soviet Union.

10. See for example, the writings of Hillel Ticktin, in the early editions of the journal, *Critique*.

11. Michael Ellman, *Socialist Planning*, (Cambridge, Cambridge University Press, 1979), p. 256.

12. Ibid., p. 272.

13. Ibid., p. 273.

14. Peter Worsley, 'One World or Three? A Critique of the World-System Theory

of Immanuel Wallerstein', in Ralph Miliband and John Saville (eds), *The Socialist Register 1980* (London, Lawrence and Wishart, 1980), pp. 298–338.

15. Immanuel Wallerstein, *The Rise and Demise of the World Capitalist System: Concepts for Comparative Analysis* (Cambridge, Cambridge University Press, 1980).

16. Vicente Navarro, 'The Limits of World-Systems Theory', in Chase-Dunn, op.cit., pp. 89–90.

17. For an overview of world systems arguments see the editor's own essay, 'Socialist States in the Capitalist World-Economy, in Chase-Dunn, op.cit., pp. 21–56.

18. O. Bogomolov, 'Current Problems and Prospects of the World Economy in the Light of East–West Economic Relations', in Christopher T. Saunders (ed.), *East–West Trade and Finance in the World Economy* (London, Macmillan, 1985), pp. 43–60.

19. 'Comecon trade with West Falls', *Financial Times*, 14 November 1985.

20. F. Levcik and J. Stankowsky, 'East–West Economic Relations in the 1970s', in Saunders (ed.), op.cit., p. 88.

21. Samuel Pisar, in debate with Charles Levinson, *The Times*, 1 October 1974, quoted in Eleanor Brun and Jacques Hersh, 'Paradoxes in the Political Economy of Détente', *Theory and Society* (1978), Vol. 5, No. 3, p. 301.

22. J. Huxley and J. Bird, 'The Russian Bear Talks Shop', *The Sunday Times*, 15 December 1985.

23. Keith Hindley, 'Harvest of the Sun'. Part One: 'Russia's Giant Leap Through Space', Part Two, 'Reaching for the Stars', *The Times*, 10 and 11 August 1987.

24. M. Bornstein, 'West–East Technology Transfer: Impact on the USSR ...', *OECD Observer* (1986), Vol. 136, pp. 18–22.

25. David Buchan, *Western Security and Economic Strategy Towards the East* (London, Adelphi Papers/IISS, 1984).

26. Ibid.

27. Huxley and Bird, op.cit.

28. CoCom members are the US, Canada, Japan, Belgium, Denmark, France, Greece, Italy, Luxembourg, the Netherlands, Norway, Portugal, Turkey, the UK, and West Germany.

29. For example, Buchan, op.cit.

30. Konrad Seitz, 'SDI: The Technological Challenge for Europe', *The World Today* (1985), Vol. 41, pp. 154–7.

31. *Financial Times*, 2 February 1987.

32. Valerie Bunce, 'The Empire Strikes Back: The Evolution of the Eastern Bloc from a Soviet Asset to a Soviet Liability', *International Organisation* (1985), Vol. 39, No. 1, pp. 1–46.

33. Bunce, op.cit., p. 44.

34. Patrick Cockburn, 'Gorbachev and the Committee', *Financial Times*, 24 June 1987.

35. 'Soviet Utopia Postponed', *Financial Times*, editorial, 30 October 1985. See also 'It's a Long Way to Communism Under Gorbachev', *The Economist*, editorial, 2 November 1985, p. 61.

36. Patrick Cockburn, 'The High Price of Keeping up with Reagan', *Financial Times*, 7 November 1985.

37. Misashi Nishihara, *East Asian Security* (New York, Trilateral Commission, 1985), pp. 33–6.

38. Joseph Minter, 'The Economy', *The Observer*, 27 September 1987.

PART IV
PROSPECTS

16 American Hegemony and International Order

1. INTRODUCTION

A recurring theme in this book has been the hegemonic position of the United States and its impact in the global political economy. The nature, extent and significance of the decline in the relative, though not the absolute, material power resources of the United States is the subject of continuing debate. This chapter provides an appraisal of these debates, with some reference to recent developments and to the contribution and limitations of the various theoretical perspectives. In particular, it highlights the contribution of a Gramscian perspective in analysing the significance of the policies and rhetoric of the Reagan administration for the tendencies towards a United States-led transnational hegemony.

The debate about hegemony centres on the ability of the United States to exert control over outcomes. Such control can be seen in both positive and negative ways. Positive control of outcomes would be associated with the United States gaining acceptance for values, institutions and policies which embody an American world-view, for example, liberal democracy and open trade and investment (despite the rising pressure of 'protectionist' coalitions in the 1970s and 1980s). Specific examples of positive control would be if the United States managed to get other countries to adopt more expansionary macroeconomic policies, reduce trade barriers and participate in economic sanctions when it wishes them to do so.

Negative control of outcomes concerns the ability of the United States to prevent other countries from successfully implementing policies which are seen as (fundamentally) opposed to the American world-view, or to prevailing definitions of United States 'national interest', for example, the spread of autarkic communism, certain types of mercantilism in the capitalist world (e.g. the former British imperial preference system), a significant threat to American technological leadership, or perhaps its transnational corporations' control over the international oil industry.

There are two sets of empirical questions addressed in the literature, and each of these can be approached from different theoretical perspectives. One concerns the nature and extent of the decline of United States hegemony, and the related issue of at what point is it appropriate to talk of 'after hegemony'?[1] The other concerns the effects of such a decline, for example, on the stability of the liberal international economic order. Other issues relate to the theorisation and conceptualisation of power and hegemony itself, and to the question 'hegemony for whom?'. More normative issues concern the quality of hegemony, that is, as to whether it is 'benevolent' and/or 'coercive'.[2] From a neo-realist perspective, this issue would refer to the provision of 'public goods' (or 'evils') by the hegemon.

2. THEORIES OF HEGEMONIC DECLINE AND THE UNITED STATES

Hegemonic rise and fall is seen, by realists and world systems theorists, in terms of a cyclical view of history, in which the dynamism and power resources of a country propel it to hegemony. In the long term a combination of loss of the hegemon's economic primacy and the rise of new centres of economic and military power are inevitable. Hegemony is seen as a temporary, and increasingly short-term condition in the 'world system'.

Thus a range of such theorists, for example Robert Keohane, Immanuel Wallerstein, Christopher Chase-Dunn, as well as some Marxists like Fred Block, come to similar conclusions about United States hegemony.[3] For Wallerstein changes in the United States economy are evidence for American decline: for example, the decline in United States technological supremacy. This follows from his historicist argument that superiority in agriculture and industry leads to dominance in commerce and invisibles such as transport, communications and insurance. Commercial primacy leads to control in the financial sectors of banking and investment. These successive superiorities acquired by the hegemon are paralleled by a similar sequential process of loss of advantage, that is, from productive to commercial to financial.[4] The United States still has the leading position in international finance and banking, for example, New York is still the world's key financial centre, and the dollar the leading currency. Thus the logic of Wallerstein's argument is that United States hegemony, while in decline, is not yet 'over', since a major challenge to American financial dominance (for example, by Japan, which had seven of the world's ten largest banks in 1987) has yet fully to emerge. Such a challenge is, however, to be expected, particularly in the 1990s.

*Table 16.1 Annual real growth in gross national product per employed person,
1960-78*

| | Percentage change | |
	1960-73	1974-78
Japan	8.9	3.2
Italy	5.4	1.1
West Germany	4.7	3.0
France	4.5	3.0
United Kingdom	3.2	0.8
United States	1.8	0.1

Note: Between 1970 and 1979, the real median family income of Americans increased only
6.7 per cent. This compared to an increase of 37.6 per cent in the 1950s and 33.9 per cent in
the 1960s.
Source: John Agnew, *The United States in the World-Economy* (Cambridge, Cambridge
University Press, 1987), p. 131.

Robert Gilpin, from a neo-realist perspective, has suggested that at some
point in the evolution of United States hegemony, the costs of expanding
and maintaining American global power come to exceed the benefits.[5]
Gilpin cites a range of internal and external factors which contribute to the
erosion of United States hegemony. First, structural changes in the
hegemon's economy undermine its long-term capacity to finance its
military strength: its economy reaches a 'climacteric' and begins to stagnate
and lose its dynamism, whilst other 'later-comer economies' innovate and
grow more rapidly, partly because they are able to absorb technology
developed by the hegemon. The burden of military commitments links
with loss of economic growth to produce a fiscal crisis, wherein the
hegemon (the United States) begins to amass budget deficits and faces a
choice between investment, warfare and welfare. Underpinning this fiscal
crisis are a loss of technological dynamism and the fact that military
innovations become diffused so that the maintenance of military
supremacy requires increasing amounts of resources. A further internal
change, one that resembles the shifts in the structure of economic activity
noted by Wallerstein, is closely related to the preceding changes, that is,
there is a movement from agriculture through manufacture and into
services.[6]

Moreover, Gilpin, in a similar vein to Fred Hirsch's arguments in the
The Social Limits to Growth, stresses the 'corrupting influence of
affluence' (that is, the decay of certain values conducive to economic
growth).[7] Key external factors involve two related developments: 'the
increase in costs of political dominance and the loss of technological and
economic leadership'. Gilpin applies the theory of public goods to suggest
that hegemons are bedevilled by the 'free-rider problem' in the provision of

international security, although it can be argued that security is not necessarily a public good, since the concept of a public good implies non-excludability, and military alliances are designed to provide collective security for their members, not for non-members.

At any event, the costs of the provision of security come to outweigh the benefits. This is particularly the case when military expenditures are being financed when growth and productivity rates are in relative decline, as is indicated in the following tables. This is itself a symptom of the United States' declining international competitiveness (or at least that of some, but not necessarily all American producers) as well as, more fundamentally, its loss of productivity lead, especially in key (high-tech) sectors. Other countries are able to take advantage of military and economic innovations, despite attempts by the hegemon to prevent their diffusion. Gilpin sees substantial scope for technological leapfrogging by 'late-comers'.

Table 16.2 Gross domestic product per capita, as a percentage of American GDP per capita, 1960–79

	1960	1963	1970	1975	1979
Switzerland	57	66	70	118	139
Denmark	46	53	67	104	119
Sweden	67	75	86	118	115
West Germany	46	53	64	95	116
Belgium	44	47	55	90	107
Netherlands	47	55	58	90	101
France	47	55	58	90	100
Canada	79	72	81	101	91
Japan	16	22	41	63	82
United Kingdom	48	50	46	58	67

Source: Agnew, *The United States in the World-Economy*, p. 132, based on OECD statistics.

Table 16.3 Gross domestic product per capita, 1965–87 (in $US at current prices and exchange rates, figures rounded)

	1965	1975	1987 (est.)
Italy	1000	3800	11500
United Kingdom	2000	4200	11700
Canada	2800	7200	15500
France	3000	6400	15800
United States	3800	7000	17800
West Germany	3000	6600	19000
Japan	800	4400	19600

Source: *Financial Times*, 13 May 1987. Based on IMF and Eurostat statistics.

Table 16.4 Comparative productivity improvements for eleven capitalist countries, 1960–79

	1960–73	*1973–79*
Italy	6.6	2.4
United Kingdom	4.0	0.1
Canada	4.4	2.5
France	5.9	4.8
United States	2.8	0.9
West Germany	5.4	5.0
Japan	9.9	3.8
Netherlands	7.6	4.2
Belgium	7.0	4.9
Sweden	6.7	1.8
Denmark	7.2	4.1

Source: Agnew, *The United States in the World-Economy*, p. 139.

Thus the challenge from late developers is likely to undermine the hegemony of the United States, in much the same way as British hegemony was undermined by the 'catch-up mercantilisms' of Germany, the United States, France and Japan at the turn of the century. William Baumol finds that industrial productivity has tended to converge over the 1870–1970 period.[8] Gilpin argues that the United States and Russia still possess one element which may help to prolong their hegemonies relative to their spheres of influence: each is able to take advantage of, respectively, their western and eastern frontiers, that is, the 'sunbelt' states of the south and western United States, and the mineral riches of Siberia in the USSR. The USA can also exploit the mineral wealth of Alaska.

In terms of catching up technologically, however, it should be noted that the West European Ariane rocket is a rival to the rather ill-fated American space shuttle, while China has announced its intention of competing in the market for the launching of satellites. Moreover, the Japanese are currently developing a sizeable space programme which is bound to produce further competition to the United States. More pertinently, as was noted in the previous chapter, the USSR has a highly successful space programme, much of which makes American space planning look amateurish by comparison. Apart from the performance of hardware, the Soviet Union has a big lead in understanding the effects of long-term space travel, and has developed impressive expertise in space medicine and nutrition, even employing top French chefs to help cater for the gastronomic needs of its astronauts. Much of the American government's technological effort is restricted by its military–industrial character (which is also a problem for Soviet innovation). Many many commentators argue that this is far less likely to yield the kind of civilian spin-offs which accrued from such efforts in the 1950s.

Mark Rupert and David Rapkin have attempted to assess such decline and measured in terms of a range of variables, they argue that the United States' share of 'enabling capabilities' has been in steady decline since the early 1950s, with one or two exceptions.[9] For example, the USA has lost the effective monopoly of nuclear weapons which it held in 1950 and now confronts a world where the Soviet Union has effective parity, and where there has been a considerable nuclear proliferation; the share of American GNP as a percentage of world GNP fell from about one-third to less than a quarter, and the United States is no longer the world's workshop, since its share of world manufactures dropped from about 60 per cent to less than 30 per cent, by the early 1980s.[10] American relative decline has occurred at the same time as the United States political economy has become more internationalised, that is, the United States is now much more interdependent with the rest of the world. At the same time, the American share in world trade by value has fallen from over 16 per cent in the mid-1960s to 12 per cent in the mid-1980s.[11] This theme of American internationalisation and the constraints of interdependence is at the heart of probably the most influential American book written in the field of international political economy during the 1970s, namely *Power and Interdependence*, by Robert Keohane and Joseph Nye.

In consequence of such evidence, as well as because of a loss of confidence in American military power after the Vietnam war, a consensus amongst many American theorists emerged in the 1970s and early 1980s that American hegemony was more or less over. (Some European writers, such as Susan Strange, have been sceptical about the loss of US hegemonic power: they continue to emphasise the vast, absolute size of American power resources, and the extraordinary weight this carries in the global political economy.) The critical acclaim given to Keohane's most recent book, *After Hegemony*, reflects the widespread nature of this consensus amongst American academics. This concern took on a wider aspect during the 1980s, when a national debate was launched over the decline in American competitiveness, reflecting worries over the challenge to American economic pre-eminence from the producers of the Pacific Rim, especially Japan.

As has been noted, many writers (notably Gilpin and Keohane) have stressed the special importance of high-technology industries in any evaluation of the 'hegemonic' character of power resources. The relative loss of American shares in the exports of manufactures appears to be rather wide-ranging, and extends to high-technology products, as is shown in Table 16.5. In addition, the United States is now more likely to import innovative technologies (measured in terms of patents) from its major capitalist competitors in West Germany and in Japan than vice versa. This is in contrast to the situation which prevailed relative to West Germany until the mid-1960s, and to Japan until the mid-1970s.[12] The US balance in high-technology trade, which had shown a record surplus of $26.6 billion as recently as 1980, showed a deficit, for the first time since World War II in 1986, after three years where the surplus was being progressively reduced. Trade in electronics and communications equipment, which was in surplus until 1982, was in deficit in 1986 by 18.3 billion dollars. Indeed, American imports of high-technology products have grown six times faster than exports in the 1980s. Much of the deficit in high-technology trade can be explained by the practices of American transnational corporations, particularly in the electronics industry, which has increasingly used off-shore production in efforts to remain competitive in high-volume products such as personal computers.[13]

To counter these trends, the United States government was, by 1987, considering the establishment of a Federal Department of Science and Technology, an institutional innovation suggested by the Presidential Commission on Competitiveness in 1985. Some, like Robert Reich of Harvard University, have argued that as much as one-third of the Pentagon's vast research budget could be diverted to such a department without damaging US national security, whereas others such as former Admiral Bobby Inman (Deputy Director of the Central Intelligence Agency during the first Reagan Administration), favour redefining the Pentagon's role to give it special responsibility for the development of commercial high-technology. As Guy de Jonquieres and Anatole Kaletsky note, Inman and others within the military establishment are in fact

Table 16.5 American shares in industrial country exports to world market

High-technology product groups	1970	1980
Aircraft	71%	62%
Computers and office machines	42	36
Scientific, medical and control equipment	32	29
Telecommunications equipment	19	13
Medical and pharmaceutical products	18	16
Selected other product groups		
Agricultural machinery, tractors	32	31
Heating and cooling equipment	24	22
Machine tools	17	13
Pumps and compressors	29	21
Construction and mining machinery	39	39

Sources: United States Department of Labor, *Trends in Technology-Intensive Trade* (1980); OECD, *Foreign Trade*, Series C. Cited in L. A. Fox and S. Cooney, 'Protectionism Returns', *Foreign Policy* (1983–4), No. 53, p. 83.

arguing for a return to the immediate post-war role of the Pentagon, when it was charged with consciously attempting to build American strength in emergent technologies. In addition, to counter the problem of waste in military production, the Pentagon moved, during the 1980s, to a more competitive system of tendering, with impressive cost savings in some areas.

Against the adverse trends for the USA, it is worth remembering that the United States is still massively outspending all other countries in research and development, with expenditures rising from just over $60 billion in 1980 to a total estimated at more than $120 billion in 1987 by the National Science Foundation. What is crucial is how this expenditure is used, since the Pentagon accounted for about one-third of the American total by 1987. Much of Pentagon sponsorship of research and development programmes has been very narrowly focused on meeting specific procurement needs. What should be emphasised, therefore, is that a reorientation of American military–industrial strategy, given the gigantic sums of Federal funds involved, could produce impressive commercial gains for the United States economy. American automobile producers have also shown that through reconstructing their managerial and productions systems, building a 'world car' and rationalising their global production, they can still compete with Japanese and South Korean producers. American capitalists are now more willing to learn management and production techniques from their Japanese counterparts, and where necessary to forge alliances with them, and other foreign firms.[14]

When compared with all other developed capitalist countries, the United States is much more self-sufficient in energy and raw materials (and contrasts dramatically with the highly vulnerable position of the Japanese economy). In the 1970s energy policy, notably in oil, was used to improve the relative competitiveness of American industries (see chapter 13). It also has a vast internal market which has proven crucial for developing scale economies in production and distribution.

Finally, especially since the late 1970s, the United States has attracted vast amounts of foreign capital. This will help to revitalise the US economy during the 1990s, perhaps in a similar way to the impact of American investment in Western Europe after World War II. In this respect, American relative material decline might be halted, particularly compared with that of Western Europe, where a number of writers have seen evidence of what has been called 'Euro-sclerosis'. The United States has much more flexible labour markets than those which prevail in Western Europe (where unions are much stronger). America also benefits from inflows of both highly skilled and unskilled labour, thus expanding the size of its internal market and productive base. In some industries, giant American firms are at the cutting-edge of technological developments, notable in telecommunications and informatics, where fifth generation computers are being developed (Japan is America's key rival in these fields). Information technology is probably the most important and dynamic part of the Western industrial structure, and it has been argued that it has hardly begun to attain a fraction of its technical possibilities, or even to penetrate very many of its potential markets. With respect to information technology, one commentator concludes:

Japan seems to be going from strength to strength; the United States has lost ground but maintains a basic strength and resilience and is responding to the Japanese challenge; Europe lags a long way behind and shows signs of making some appropriate changes, but on too small a scale.[15]

However, one politically significant aspect to the debate concerning American economic performance concerns the long-term effects on the standard of living of ordinary Americans, which, as will be noted from Tables 16.2 and 16.3, has also declined significantly in relative terms. At the same time Americans are comparatively less well insulated against the effects of illness and unemployment since the American welfare system is very underdeveloped when compared with its counterparts in Europe. This is a major reason why the calls for increased American productivity and growth have embraced both labour and capital, as well as the Democratic and Republican Parties in the United States. In America both major political parties sought to redress the relative decline in standards of living not by redistributive policies (favoured by left-wing parties in Western Europe) but by attempting to regenerate American economic growth, notably through large reductions in income taxes.

3. AMERICAN STRATEGIC OPTIONS

In the face of such evidence how do world systems theorists envisage the development of United States strategy to cope with hegemonic decline, and to maintain the liberal international economic order? Chase-Dunn argues that the United States will rationally seek to organise a 'core-wide' approach to the management of the world economy in order to maintain its political and economic centrality. This means the United States would have to accept a 'collective capitalist' approach (similar to the one advocated by the influential Trilateral Commission) to world order and avoid unilateral policies: in other words, it will necessarily have to adopt a more cooperative strategy, particularly *vis-à-vis* its major capitalist rivals. A go-it-alone policy would swim against the tide of history. This 'collective capitalist' perspective is similar to the Kautskian notion of ultra-imperialism.[16] Others, such as Robert Keohane, have argued for a similar strategy, developing game theory and rational choice arguments to highlight the gains to be made from 'rational', self-interested cooperation.

Realists like Inman, and many in the Pentagon, argue for a strategy based upon the refurbishment of America's strategic industries. Many Democrats stress the necessity of protectionism, and measures which punish countries (especially Japan) which run up consistent trade surpluses with the United States, effectively repudiating the traditional post-war American commitment to an open trading system. The two strategies can be related, on the one hand, to the liberal internationalism of a 'multinational bloc' (such as that discussed in chapter 9), and, on the other, to a realist-mercantilist or nationalist bloc, stressing the concept of strategic industries. Liberals are apt to stress the primary importance of intensifying the interdependence between the United States and Japan, as well as with Western European and other countries. In practice the options do not offer simple either/or choices. The political debate in the United States in the late 1980s has concerned the appropriate balance between the two.

Interpretation of the implications of changes in the distribution of material power resources is more complex than is suggested by some of the writers mentioned above. This complexity involves not only the distribution of material capacities, but also political aspects such as alliances, security and other structures, combinations of unilateralism, bilateralism and multilateralism in United States policy (which we call a 'mixed strategy'), and to other cultural and social resources, especially as they affect the mobilisation of material resources. Moreover, in an era of transnational capitalism, it is erroneous to limit the conception of hegemony by defining it simply in terms of the power of one state relative to other states.

Following our discussion of the two concepts of hegemony (see chapter 6), we suggest that any analysis must also take account of the class nature of hegemony, and the way this relates to the development of historic blocs. As will be noted from our previous arguments (and from our chapters outlining two major themes of the book), in the American case there may be a tension between the strategies espoused by a realist-mercantilist bloc, embedded in the United States military–industrial complex and in certain industries demanding protection, and that of a 'liberal internationalist', transnational, or 'multinational bloc'. These two blocs are linked to particular conceptions of interest and identity, and to forms of consciousness which interact with institutional and material forces at the national and global levels.

4. HEGEMONIC DECLINE AND MATERIAL POWER RESOURCES: A CRITIQUE

In this section we focus on material power resources, alliances, and on examining elements of the practice of American strategy. We discuss other aspects of American power in subsequent sections.

A decline in United States relative power resources may be mitigated by some relative improvement in the resources of its allies. The example of North Atlantic Treaty Organisation (NATO) is a case in point, in that the West European countries had faster growth than the United States during the long post-war boom, and Japan has gradually (though somewhat reluctantly) built up its armed forces to the point where the post-war barrier of a maximum of 1 per cent of GNP for military expenditures was broken in 1986. This expansion has occurred in ways which have been carefully encouraged by, and coordinated with, the United States government. Despite increased military expenditures by other NATO countries and Japan, the United States retains the central position within its alliance structures. The European members of NATO have been slow to develop, on their own initiative, either a 'West European' (that is, including France) defence perspective and identity, or widespread cooperation in armaments-related production. Moreover, the United States has increased its imports of European military equipment, enlarging the mutual stakes in the prevailing alliance arrangements.

On the other hand, the USSR lost not only its key Middle Eastern ally Egypt in the early 1970s, but more crucially its leading communist ally, China, in the 1960s, and has felt obliged to spend huge sums on building its Siberian and Far Eastern defences. As Bruce Russett has argued, this 'loss' more than cancels out the 'gains' that the USSR made in Cuba, Angola, Ethiopia and Mozambique. Despite the quantity of the Soviet build-up in some regions, there is reason to believe that this may have been substantially offset by the qualitative superiority of NATO weapons, for example, fighter aircraft and anti-tank missiles. The continuing special position of the United States in the world security structure takes on added significance if the United States' continuing centrality in other less fundamental structures, for example, money, production/knowledge and trade, is taken into account.[17]

It may be the case that the continuing centrality of the United States in these other structures is bound up with its primacy in the security structure. Another example which indicates the fallacy of gauging changes in power and hegemony in a crudely quantitative and aggregative way, is the role of the United States in the monetary regime. The United States' share of votes in the International Monetary Fund (IMF) has declined, reflecting its falling share of world gross national product, but it remains sufficiently large to block any significant change in policy. The United States remains the only country with this veto power, that is, it has, in this case, negative control over outcomes in an institution constructed on the basis of principles favoured by the United States. (The EEC countries only have veto power if they act as a group.) In this sense, the United States combines some positive, with a high degree of negative control. Some Marxist writers have shown a strong awareness of the continuing economic centrality of the United States, and its crucial importance as a market for Western Europe, and especially Japan, as well as for Third World exports.[18]

Although the United States has been associated with the creation of multilateral regimes (unlike Britain in the nineteenth century), in practice its foreign policies are a mixture of unilateralism and bilateralism, as well as multilateralism. Examples of unilateral 'leadership' include the Nixon shocks of August 1971, and in the early 1980s, the imposition of sanctions on supplies for the Siberian pipeline. American policies in Central and South America have been generally unilateralist (relative to American allies) ever since the Monroe Doctrine. The centrality of the United States in its military alliances is linked to a network of bilateral relationships, notably with West Germany, Japan and Britain, but also with Canada, France, Israel and Mexico, amongst others. Some of these bilateral 'special relationships' have been used to obtain support in Europe and Japan for the Strategic Defense Initiative. The forging of free trade links with Israel under the 1984 Trade Act, contrasts with the multilateral approach to trade liberalisation of the General Agreement on Tariffs and Trade (GATT).

It should be noted that the United States was the driving force behind calls for the Uruguay trade round in the mid-1980s. The possibility of further American bilateral trade initiatives was one source of leverage used by the American government to induce other countries to widen the GATT agenda, to include consideration of changes in agricultural trade, and in services, areas in which America has a comparative advantage. In addition, the resort to voluntary export restraints and the surge of protectionist bills in the United States Congress, served notice that access to the American market was not to be taken for granted. It also induced a surge of inward direct investment, bolstering the share of the United States in world manufacturing output.

This type of strategy and use of the coercive possibilities implied in having the world's biggest market, contrasts with the policy of imperial, free-trade Britain in the late nineteenth and early twentieth centuries. Britain did not use such economic leverage, and clung to free trade even when all its major rivals only paid lip-service to such policies. Also, Britain retreated into the 'soft option' of exploiting its empire markets, one sign, perhaps, of a growing complacency. One explanation for Britain's policies during this period is offered by both world systems and public choice writers, that is, that 'internationalist' interests became ascendant in the UK (for example, the financial interests of the City of London, most exporters, and many sections of labour who benefited from cheap imports of food). This coalition of interests effectively shaped Britain's foreign economic policy.

The influence of such 'internationalist' interests in the United States in the 1980s and 1990s may serve to limit the ability of the American government to pursue a strategy which involves too much use, or threat of protectionism. The over-valuation of the dollar in the early to mid-1980s tended to weaken America's manufacturing base, and was exactly the kind of outcome which world systems writers' analysis of interests would lead one to expect. A similar analysis is often made for Britain in the 1920s, when a high and overvalued pound was associated with high interest rates. In the American case, interests associated with the military–industrial complex also contributed to the overvaluation of the dollar, in that they influenced and supported Reagan's rapid increase in military spending, which in turn fuelled the massive budget deficit of the mid-1980s. It was only after 1985 that the rate of increase of this deficit began to decline, and the dollar's exchange rate fell substantially. American strategy in 1985–87 appeared to reflect a loss of influence by the realist-mercantilist forces, relative to those of 'internationalists'. The Baker Initiatives and progress on nuclear arms talks were evidence of this. On the other hand, protectionist pressures continued, and reached new heights in the Congress.

5. HEGEMONY, CULTURE AND MOBILISATION

However, the above interpretation begs the question, 'which types of American power resource have declined and what are their effects?' Elsewhere in this book we have referred to the importance of broader social capacities and political culture within particular nation-states. Realists and world systems theorists, as well as some Marxists, tend to underestimate the mobilising role of certain aspects of the United States political culture. Realists in particular tended to pay much more attention to the distribution of power resources than to their mobilisation, that is, they concentrated on what Keohane has called 'basic force' rather than 'force activation' models.[19] This was perhaps linked to the assumptions held by Realists, that is, that states act coherently as units, and that (autonomous) states are the only important units in international relations.[20]

In this section we seek to help remedy a deficiency in much political economy writing, that is, where cultural and social factors are relatively ignored and/or not theorised. Often (at best) they are subordinated to the economic and military forces which lie at the heart of materialist concepts of political economy, and the abstractions which this entails. One advantage of the Gramscian perspective is that it draws attention to the role of ideas and institutions within national cultures and also at the international level. We use this perspective to highlight some of the strengths as well as weaknesses of the United States political system, the political culture and American capitalism, relative to its rivals, particularly in Western Europe and Japan. This perspective can also be applied to analyse the relative cultural power of the United States and Soviet systems.

The explanation and appraisal of the policies of the Reagan administration can vary significantly, depending on whether the cultural, as well as material dimension is integrated into the analysis. For example, an orthodox Marxist approach, such as that used by Mike Davis, focuses on changes in the structure of production, the circulation of capital and the distribution of income and wealth.[21]

Davis argues that the 1980s have been characterised by a 'crisis of American hegemony' in so far as it denotes a decline in the internal coherence of the American system. This is seen as involving domestic restructuring and political realignments, and a change in the relationship between the American and world economies. Domestically, a turning-point was reached by 1984–85 and the United States became a split-level economy in which the service sector was ever more important, and the general shift in the growth dynamic from North-East to South-West was intensified. This generated increased social inequality in America, accompanied by an erosion of welfarist political coalitions.[22]

Moreover, Davis argues that the upturn in the United States economy in the 1980s 'dramatically speeded up the transformation of American hegemony away from a "Fordist" or mass-accumulation pattern'. He notes three trends which were important. First, there was a shift in profit distribution towards interest incomes which strengthened a 'neo-rentier bloc reminiscent of the speculative capitalism of the 1920s'. Second, American industrial corporations began to shift away from consumer durables towards 'volatile high-profit sectors like military production and financial services'. Third, there was a shift in dominant trade relations and capital flows 'as the locus of accumulation in new technologies has been displaced from Atlantic to Pacific circuits of capital'.[23]

This view of a 'crisis of hegemony' may have implied that the transformation was taking place under politically unstable conditions. It perhaps tended to overlook aspects of the American culture which may have acted as both a 'glue' and a 'lubricant' for the changes in question, aspects which were central to the symbolism and cultural meaning of the

Reagan administration. Ronald Reagan's rhetoric was not merely a populist appeal engineered for the purposes of electoral success, it was also geared towards an attempt to recreate a sense of national purpose, self-confidence and reassertiveness, particularly in the wake of President Carter's recriminations about an American 'crisis of confidence' in the 1970s. Also, and perhaps most fundamentally, the virtues of the market, of rugged individualism and the capacity of Americans to use their skills and vitality to reach and to expand the 'highest frontiers' of technological development, were all stressed in the Reagan speeches. Reagan thus contributed to attempts to reconstruct belief in 'American exceptionalism', a belief which Daniel Bell claimed had come to an end in the mid-1970s.[24] Typical of the mood which Reagan sought to create, with its stress on American nationalism (the 'American breed'), the Enlightenment ideas of progress, practical knowledge, and the promise of the future, was the following extract from his 1980 acceptance speech:

There are no words to express the extraordinary strength and character of this breed of people we call Americans. . . . They are the kinds of men and women Tom Paine had in mind when he wrote during the darkest days of the American Revolution, 'we have it in our power to begin the world over again'. Nearly 150 years after Tom Paine wrote these words, an American President told the generation of the Great Depression that it had a 'rendezvous with destiny'. I believe that this generation of Americans today also has a rendezvous with destiny. Tonight, let us dedicate ourselves to renewing the American Compact. I ask you not simply to 'trust me' but to trust your values – our values . . . to trust that American spirit which knows no ethnic, religious, social, political, regional or economic boundaries; the spirit which burned with zeal in the hearts of millions of immigrants from every corner of the earth who came here in search of freedom.[25]

Reagan, who was the most popular post-war President (despite a temporary loss of popularity during the 1986–87 Irangate scandal), can thus be seen as central to the attempted remobilisation of powerful elements within the American political culture, and contributing to the internal reconstruction of American hegemony in a Gramscian sense. Reagan's ideas had a peculiar potency in a society where the threat of violence and crime were endemic: on the one hand, these ideas helped to motivate Americans to strive harder to put themselves out of reach of the violent ghetto, whilst on the other hand, in a society so attuned to the myths of the media, they offered the promise of a better tomorrow. This potency may thus in fact have been increased by the widening of income inequalities noted by Davis. The implications of this for American power and for the relations between the United States and its key capitalist allies are discussed below.

The notion of hegemony within a country is more than a notion concerned with social integration and political order, in that the integrative ideas, values, institutions and material forces may combine and interact systematically to create the conditions for the primacy of a class or a fraction of a class within the society. In the American case, it seems clear that these social forces structurally underpinned the 'power of capital', and the hegemony of the United States' most efficient capitalists. The inequalities stressed by Davis may not have the significance that he implies: namely that such inequality may contribute to an internal loss of legitimacy and coherence within the American political economy. Rather, they highlight the nature and dynamics of the hegemonic culture in the United States, and the way in which substantial change was possible without either threatening the legitimacy of the state or altering the fundamental orientations of Americans towards the capitalist system. In some circumstances a recession (such as that between 1979–82) may thus actually facilitate a reconsolidation of such values, attitudes and principles. This need not always be the case: in some countries, with different political cultures and different party systems, social movements, etc. recession has contributed to significant changes in hegemony, for example, Germany in the 1930s. What seems crucial is the degree to which there is a hegemonic congruence between the key social forces, and a substantial anchorage within political and cultural traditions.

Thus Britain and America in the 1930s avoided the fundamental 'crisis of representation' and the 'crisis of hegemony' experienced in the Weimar Republic, although it might be argued that logically the 'socialist revolution' ought to have come, if anywhere, in Britain in the 1930s: Britain was the first industrial nation, it had a working class which was several generations old, it had a large workers' party, many large trade unions, and the Great Depression of the 1930s came after a decade of high unemployment, which was very severe in some sectors. Although the structural weakness of the UK economy was striking, the strength of the British state remained largely intact. This strength was the product of a long process of political evolution, in which the state had become deeply embedded in civil society.

Moreover, the United States had no strong socialist movement to challenge capitalist hegemony and in this sense American capitalism, in the 1980s, was perhaps more stable and domestically 'hegemonic' than its West European and Japanese counterparts. Although Japan had a sizeable Socialist Party and a smaller, but still significant Communist Party, its challenge was not so strong as that of the left-wing parties in Europe. In this respect, Japan may be closer to the United States than the West European countries. Having said this, it is true to say that the left was on the defensive in the 1980s, on a world-wide basis.

If the arguments we have made concerning the remobilisation of aspects of the American political culture (and economy) are also related to the ideological offensive of the 'new Cold War' and increased military expenditures, American 'domestic' mobilisation took on an international significance, particularly when the West Europeans and the Japanese were less willing and able to mobilise extra resources for military expenditures (although America's allies did increase their military expenditures, this was less then the proportionate increase in the United States). This reinforced the United States position at the apex of the security structure, despite the fact that American military expenditures have been accompanied by significant waste and may have deleterious long-term economic effects. The security structure is the most crucial for the maintenance of international hegemony.

The Reagan rhetoric about the virtues of private enterprise and the 'magic' of the market-place, may have been primarily designed with an American audience in mind, but it also had an international significance. At the Cancun Conference in 1981, Reagan lectured the Third World representatives on the need to liberalise their economies. Such a liberalisation would fit in with the interests of American (and other) transnational corporations and with the 'fight against (centrally planned) communism'. The ideological appeal of the United States is strengthened in so far as market values and perhaps (to a lesser extent) some ideas favouring the extension of liberal democracy become more influential in other countries. Thus the 'capitalist road' of Deng's China (to say nothing of the liberalisation of the highly mercantilist Japanese economy in the 1970s and 1980s) had a wider international significance. The former case contrasts with the time when Maoist ideas drawn from the period of the Cultural Revolution influenced some Western youth, particularly students in the late 1960s.

The development of capitalist democracy in Japan and Western Europe since 1945, as well as their growing interpenetration of capital and production, has made them 'organic' rather than 'tactical' allies of the United States. The 'democratisation' of Western Europe continued into the 1980s, although the United States has not always encouraged this process, for example, in Greece and Spain. Nevertheless such developments are congruent with the Cold War rhetoric of the need to extend the 'free world' and to 'roll back' the 'threat' of communism. In this context it was significant that, at a time of rising Western and Japanese military expenditures after 1979, following years of publicly saying little on this issue, some Japanese leaders increasingly began to portray the issues of international security in Cold War terms, aligning Japan more closely with American positions. In contrast, many West European leaders, worried about the demise of détente, adopted a more cautious tone. Since 1985, such rhetoric has given way to a less belligerent tone, as the Soviet Union has moved to make concessions in arms negotiations, and as American corporations have shown more interest in penetrating the vast Soviet market.

The spread of American ideas and values has been associated with, and facilitated by, the emergence of English (or 'American') as the international language, which capitalised on the effects of an earlier British cultural imperialism. This development was promoted by the United States in various ways, for example, by the setting-up of American schools and universities in other countries, by the sponsorship of important foreign university programmes and research of certain think-tanks abroad by the United States government, and more pervasively by American 'philanthropic' foundations. This promoted study and research which was congruent with the American vision of a 'liberal' world order. Moreover, such activities were sometimes linked to key aspects of the operation of American transnational corporations, which may be explained partly by Helge Hveem's notion of 'technocapital'.[26] Transnational corporations are able to take full advantage of advances in communications and transportation, and indeed their attempts to gain market dominance and to extend the power of the market on an international scale are bound up with communications power, embodied partly in the pervasive use of advertising to spread the corporate message world-wide. The American government has also built up a network of electronic media throughout the world, much of it directed at winning a propaganda war with the USSR. Indeed the 'politicisation' of Voice of America by Reagan (that is, he staffed it with right-wing free-marketeers) caused widespread indignation and many resignations from the United States International Communications Agency. This propaganda drive may reach a new level if and when television satellites come to be used as actively as radio.

The international use of English may go with a kind of 'cultural bilateralism'. Japanese businessmen in Europe usually know only one foreign language well – English. Indeed, perhaps, this is linked to the tendency of Japanese firms investing in Europe to locate in Britain in the 1980s. More dramatically, China has promoted the learning of English on a large, nationwide scale. Cultural exchanges between China and Western countries have grown, but English-speaking countries, notably the United States, are the ones which are likely to be most intensively involved. The United States may well have reason to hope that increased contacts with and the spread of English in China will facilitate a cultural shift (counter-revolution?) in a capitalist direction. This point is reinforced by the fact that the United States' two main competitors in the race to be involved in China's future development have been Japan and Germany, and the latter is particularly noted for its mastery of English. Perhaps more important in the long term, with respect to the Far East, a more pervasive Anglo-Saxonism may serve to prevent the emergence of a stronger form of

'Confucian' identification between China, Japan and other regional states.

For most of Europe, and for many parts of the Third World, the primary foreign language learned is also English. Thus there may be a certain congruence between this 'cultural bilateralism' and the web of bilateral relationships which exist in the foreign policies of a large number of states with the United States. Since 1945, each of the major West European countries has defined its foreign policy positions, even the question of an integrated Europe, primarily in terms of the effects such policies might have on its relations with the United States. Indeed, it can be said that the foreign relations of these states have been stronger with the United States than with any of their European 'partners', with the partial exception of the emerging Franco-German axis. In time, it may well be possible to suggest that such a congruence between international alignments and a more pervasive 'Americanism' may result in shifts in identity as well as inter-state interests.

An example from antiquity may serve to illustrate the links between 'political' and 'cultural' bilateralism, forged partly in the face of a threatening outside power. Ancient Rome built up an 'Italian Alliance' by means of bilateral treaties with dozens of Italian states, without the terms being too burdensome on the allies. A sense of Italian solidarity was gradually developed to the point where most allies stayed loyal to Rome. Indeed, many made considerable sacrifices, for example, at the time of Hannibal's invasion, which lasted well over a decade. The extension of Roman citizenship, first within, and then beyond Italy, facilitated the extension and consolidation of a huge empire which lasted for centuries (the final collapse of its eastern, 'Byzantine', half was not until 1453). This example can be used to show how an underlying 'inevitability thesis' concerning the decline of hegemony is to be found in both realist and world systems writing. Both perspectives assume that identity and interests are constructed on a relatively fixed, primarily national basis, and as such any hegemon is likely to be met with the inevitable challenge of rival national interests and identities, which, in the long term, serve to erode the hegemon's position. As a result of this assumption, these perspectives often ignore the possibility of changes in identification and interest in ways that might extend the power resources of the hegemon, facilitate cooperation, and mitigate certain conflicts. (This shortcoming may also be seen to apply to much Marxist writing.)

As we have seen, since 1945 the United States forged a range of 'special' bilateral relationships. We hope that our analysis has shown how these links may be cumulative in the long term, in that ideas, institutions and material forces gradually may become more congruent with the United States and its continuing centrality, and they may interact in a synergistic, positive-sum way. As such, if this process develops, American power resources are effectively extended, although the material aggregates of American power may indicate that the contrary appears to be the case, that is, if the ultimate test we use to measure American power is in terms of its influence over international outcomes. Of course, in some cases this can cut both ways for the United States, for example, the 'Jewish lobby' can be seen as an effective constraint on United States policy in the Middle East, although this may be a special case.

While other countries can, and to some extent have, attempted to forge links in a way that could be seen to involve such cultural imperialism (for example, France and the Soviet Union), the United States is uniquely well placed to expand its cultural resources and influence on a global basis. One reason for this is that the United States has been, and continues to be, able to absorb people (often with high skill levels, for example doctors and scientists from India during the 1970s and 1980s) from many parts of the world. The cultural/ethnic pluralism of the United States has been underpinned by a remarkable degree of conformism and agreement about the basic principles of the American way of life. This has given the United States a tremendous power to communicate with other nations, whilst having little to fear from its interaction with other cultures. This contrasts with the United States' key economic and military rivals, that is, Japan and the USSR. Japanese society is exceptionally insular and xenophobic: almost all Japanese continue to have great difficulty in establishing close personal relationships with foreigners, and indeed there is little indication that most Japanese would regard this as desirable. It is no accident that immigation into Japan has been negligible, nor that the largest group of immigrants, the Koreans, are treated as racially and socially inferior, treatment rooted in the days of Imperial Japan. Indeed there is considerable fear and mistrust of the Japanese in much of Asia, not least in China. Thus, although the Japanese mixture of Shinto, Confucianism and capitalism has proven a formidable rival to the United States, Japan may face significant cultural limits to its future capacity to fully transnationalise its economy, or at least to become the model for other nations to emulate.

Although the Soviet Union is a multi-national and multi-ethnic state, it has been less well placed than the United States to utilise what cultural pluralism it has on an international scale. Instead, the USSR, at least until the coming to power of Gorbachev in 1985, has restricted the international displays of its culture to state-approved films and 'art', and the carefully managed foreign tours of the Bolshoi Ballet and the wizardry of its chess grandmasters, provided that the secret police, the KGB, can ensure that none of their virtuosos defect to the West. This reflects the tremendously tight controls which have been imposed by the Soviet state on contacts with foreigners, controls which applied also to the interaction of the Soviet nationalities themselves. This official xenophobia contrasts with the cultural universalism of the United States, as does the fact that the Soviet state has still not achieved full 'Russification' of language and culture. The political doctrine of the Soviet Union is centralist, monolithic and atheist, and has implied very little autonomy for the forces of civil society, and in particular little scope for diversity of belief, faith or lifestyle. Thus, the growth in the proportion of the population with Islamic traditions has been seen as more of a long-term problem than an opportunity. This contrasts with the assimilation of Hispanics in the United States, that is, the latest large immigrant group to enter America's 'melting pot'. This means that the cultural appeal of the United States is much greater than that of the Soviet Union, not least because the American system provides high levels of consumption and political liberty, when compared with the less economically dynamic, and more statist USSR.

Such cultural appeal contrasts with the early attraction of the Soviet model, particularly in the depressed conditions of the 1930s, when, it seemed to many in the West, the USSR had solved the problems of unemployment and rapid industrialisation. This model was influential in the Third World, for example, in post-independence India and in China after the 1949 revolution, but its influence may be on the wane. Marxist-Leninist ideas still have a following in many less-developed countries, but the economic performance of Ethiopia, Mozambique and even Cuba compares poorly with some capitalist newly-industrialising countries. Indeed, the economic success of countries like South Korea and Taiwan has been one influence on China's new economic policies. In the West, the left has come to seem more on the defensive in recent years, at the same time as it has become more critical of the USSR. Thus what was once an almost romantic attachment to Russia on the left (which enabled the USSR to set up spying networks and to cultivate policies sympathetic to its interests) has been replaced by disaffection with 'the God that failed'.

6. UNITED STATES LEADERSHIP AND TRANSNATIONAL HEGEMONY

Using a Gramscian approach, some writers have argued that a 'transnational' hegemony may be emerging in which a transnational capitalist class predominates, leading a hegemonic bloc of mainly transnational capital, and 'incorporated' labour. As has been noted in chapter 7, we would suggest that at the geographical centre of such a potential 'transnational' hegemony would be a group of capitalist countries led by the United States. At the political level, the leadership of such a transnational bloc would involve more of the cooperation and collective management that has been developed in institutions like the IMF and which was exemplified in the 1985 and 1987 Baker initiatives, and the activities of the Group of Five capitalist countries, such as in the Louvre Agreement on money and managed exchange rates of February 1987. The success in reducing the exchange rate for the dollar in the latter part of 1985 required policy measures on interest rates in Japan and West Germany, as well as the United States. The continuation of such cooperation in the longer-term requires more international awareness and sensitivity on the part of the United States, such as through measures to further reduce its budget deficit. Given such awareness, and an ability of the United States government to resist many, if not all interest group pressures, then a United States-led transnational historic bloc becomes possible and likely. However, this interest group requirement may not be met given the nature of what Theodore Lowi has called 'interest group liberalism' in the United States, which militates against the coherence of policy.[27] In addition, the division of powers within the constitutional structure of the United States may impede some types of international cooperation. For example, President and Congress may fail to work effectively together, as has been shown in the stalemate over the budget deficit in the 1980s. Admittedly, Reagan did not veto the 1985 Gramm–Rudman Bill, which in principle required the United States budget to be balanced within five years. Continuing differences between President and Congress meant that, though declining slowly, the budget deficit was still very high in 1987. This political failure was a major factor in the stock market crash of October of that year. Incoherence, incompetence and myopia in American policy-making were widely perceived to exist at this time, provoking a crisis of confidence in United States economic management. The degree to which the United States government responds to pressures from the global financial and capital markets, by raising taxes and cutting spending will determine whether it can restore confidence and improve the business climate. This could be a condition for a further sustained and large inflow of finance capital into the American economy.

At the same time as foreign investment has been growing in the United States, American transnational corporations have continued to expand abroad. American transnational firms have come closer to maintaining their share in world markets, than the American economy has to maintaining its share in world GNP. None the less, non-American transnational corporations have grown in size, strength and numbers, relative to American ones, notably with the upsurge of Japanese foreign direct investment in the late 1970s and 1980s, much of it in the United States. One consequence of these trends has been an increase in the number of alliances between Japanese, American and West European transnational corporations and banks.

The fact that non-American transnational corporations have increased their strength relative to American companies, does not significantly alter the ability of the United States government to achieve certain of its desired outcomes, such as liberal economic policies, including an open door to foreign direct investment. Indeed, one could argue that the growth of transnational corporations in other developed capitalist countries is making for an increased congruence between, and influence of, the internationalist interests in these countries. These trends are linked to the increasing importance of foreign direct investment within the United States itself, as foreign based transnational corporations have come to see access to the United States market as increasingly crucial. These transnational corporations have thus become more dependent upon the United States market at the same time as American manufacturing capital has shifted its assets either abroad or, within the United States, towards high-profit sectors like energy reserves, financial services, real-estate, emergent technology and defence. This can be interpreted as having the effect of generally strengthening a possible transnational historic bloc, as well as through the impact of high world-wide interest rates, privatisation, and market liberalisation, strengthening the structural power of internationally-mobile (finance) capital.

7. CONCLUSIONS

American's decline in the global political economy, and its effects have been exaggerated. America's relative material power resources compare very favourably with those of Britain 100 years ago, especially when the strength of its alliances and the centrality of its place in key international regimes is considered. America's strategy can limit the pace of the relative material decline of the United States, and perhaps even halt and reverse it. The capacities of the United States are still formidable and, in overall terms, significantly greater than Western Europe and Japan. However, Japan poses a substantial technological challenge to the United States, a challenge partly offset by the growing interdependence of the two nations' economic structures.

The cultural aspects of the United States give it a certain advantage compared to Japan and the USSR, in that it can exploit the possibilities of ethnic pluralism in a way that they cannot. It also has the advantage that English/American is the international language. Such cultural factors help to underpin the range and strength of the bilateral relations forged by the United States. This permits an American cultural imperialism.

The centrality of the United States and the regimes it has created can be seen as facilitating an emerging transnational historic bloc, in which the leadership of the more dynamic transnational corporations has come increasingly to the fore. These developments are associated with the growing mobility of capital, the revival and spread of market forces, and the ideological hegemony of associated liberal 'frameworks of thought'. They are also associated with an increase in the structural 'power of capital' relative to labour and to certain states.

In consequence, fears that a decline in American dominance will lead to a breakdown in the liberal international economic order are largely misplaced, especially when the importance of economic interdependence among the major capitalist states, and the open door to foreign direct investment are recognised.

The other apparently paradoxical implication of our analysis is that, in so far as American hegemony becomes more transnational in character, it will become less 'all-American'.

NOTES

1. Robert O. Keohane, *After Hegemony: Cooperation and Discord in the World Political Economy* (Princeton NJ, Princeton University Press, 1984).
2. Duncan Snidal, 'The Limits of Hegemonic Stability Theory', *International Organisation* (1985), Vol. 39, pp. 579–614.
3. Keohane, op. cit.; Fred Block, *The Origins of International Economic Disorder* (Berkeley, Cal., University of California Press, 1977); Immanuel Wallerstein, *The Modern World System II* (New York, Academic Press, 1980); and 'The Three Instances of Hegemony in the History of the Capitalist World Economy' (Paper read at the Conference of Europeanists, 29 April–1 May 1982, Washington DC); Christopher Chase-Dunn, 'International Economic Policy in a Declining Core State', in William P. Avery and David P. Rapkin, *America in a Changing World Political Economy* (London, Longman, 1982, pp. 77–96.
4. Wallerstein, *The Modern World System II*, pp. 38–9, cited in Mark E. Rupert and David P. Rapkin, 'The Erosion of US Leadership Capabilities', in P. M. Johnson and William R. Thompson (eds), *Rhythms in Politics and Economics* (New York, Praeger, 1985).
5. Robert Gilpin, *War and Change in World Politics* (Cambridge, Cambridge University Press, 1981), p. 156.
6. Wallerstein, *The Modern World System*, op. cit.
7. Fred Hirsch, *The Social Limits to Growth* (London, Routledge and Kegan Paul/Twentieth Century Fund, 1976).
8. W. J. Baumol, 'Productivity Growth, Convergence and Welfare: What the Long-Run Data Show', *American Economic Review* (1986), Vol. 76, pp. 1072–85.
9. Rupert and Rapkin, op. cit., p.177.
10. Nobuhiko Ushiba et al., *Sharing International Responsibilities* (New York, Trilateral Commission, 1981), p. 8.
11. John Agnew, *The United States in the World-Economy* (Cambridge, Cambridge University Press, 1987), p. 139.

12. Guy de Jonquieres and Anatole Kaletsky, 'The Enemy Within', *Financial Times*, 11 May 1987. Based on IMF statistics.
13. Guy de Jonquieres and Anatole Kaletsky, 'We are hoist with our own petard', *Financial Times*, 20 May 1987.
14. Guy de Jonquieres and Anatole Kaletsky, 'Beware the simple solution', *Financial Times*, 18 May 1987.
15. Rod Coombs, 'Rising in the east, setting in the west', *Times Higher Education Supplement*, 6 February 1987. Coombs reviews Erik Arnold, *Parallel Convergence: national strategies in information technology* (London, Pinter, 1987); Paul Jowett and Margaret Rothwell, *The Economics of Information Technology* (London, Macmillan, 1987); Ian Mackintosh, *Sunrise Europe: the dynamics of information technology* (Oxford, Basil Blackwell, 1987).
16. Chase-Dunn, 'International Economic Policy in a Declining Core State', in Avery and Rapkin, op. cit.
17. This discussion builds upon Susan Strange's argument that there is a hierarchy of structures in the global political economy with the military structure being the most fundamental.
18. James Petras and Robert Rhodes, 'The Reconsolidation of US Hegemony', *New Left Review* (1976), No. 97, pp. 37–53.
19. Keohane, *After Hegemony*, pp. 34–5.
20. Robert O. Keohane and Joseph S. Nye, *Power and Interdependence* (Boston, Mass., Little, Brown, 1977), p. 25.
21. Mike Davis, 'The Political Economy of Late-Imperial America', *New Left Review* (1984), No. 143, pp. 6–38; and his 'Reaganomics' Magical Mystery Tour', *New Left Review* (1985), No. 149, pp. 45–65.
22. Davis, 'The Political Economy of Late Imperial America', op. cit.
23. Davis, 'Reaganomics Magical Mystery Tour', op. cit., p. 47.
24. Daniel Bell, 'The End of American Exceptionalism', *The Public Interest* (1975), No. 41, pp. 193–224.
25. Cited in David McKay, 'The Decline and Rise of American Exceptionalism', Paper, American Politics Group, British Political Studies Association, Exeter, 3–5 January 1984, p. 11.
26. Helge Hveem, 'The Global Dominance System: Notes on a Theory of Global Political Economy', *Journal of Peace Research* (1973), Vol. 4, pp. 319–40.
27. Theodore Lowi, *The End of Liberalism: The Second Republic of the United States* (New York, W. W. Norton, 1979).
    Note: some of the ideas in this chapter were first developed in Stephen Gill, 'American Hegemony: its Limits and Prospects in the Reagan Era', *Millenium* (1986), Vol. 15, pp. 311–35.

17 Contradictions, Problems and Prospects

1. INTRODUCTION

In this chapter various future scenarios and trends are examined with a view to a consideration of the major issues which we think should be on the agenda of study in international relations in the 1990s and beyond. In the first half of the chapter, we discuss the limits to, and contradictions between, transnationalisation and militarisation in the global political economy. In the second half we widen the focus to address the relationship between these trends, some of the forces behind them, as well as ecological problems.

2. SCENARIOS AND MODELS

Various writers have suggested scenarios, or what Robert Gilpin called 'models of the future'. Gilpin has suggested three models: the sovereignty-at-bay, the *dependencia* and the mercantilist.[1] The first two of these stress the role of transnational corporations. The first, liberal interpretation, sees the transnational corporations in 'benign' terms, as promoting growth from which all can gain. The second, *dependencia*, interpretation stresses the hierarchical and exploitive character of transnational firms: growth may be achieved but only at the cost of international, North–South and internal inequalities combined with dependence on the financial headquarters of the world. By contrast, the mercantilist model stresses the power of states to regulate trade and transnationals, and for Gilpin is associated with a tendency towards what he calls 'loose regional blocs' centred in the rapidly-growing Pacific Basin, in the expanded European Economic Community (with some links to the Middle East and Africa), and in the Americas.[2] The latter go with reduced global economic growth and decreased interdependence. Clearly for Gilpin, different models are associated with different perspectives: liberal, dependency/Marxist and realist. The same is true for Robert Cox, who places more stress upon the class interests which are represented in each model or scenario. Cox also gives more attention to the prospects for a 'hegemonic' or 'non-hegemonic' world order in the 1990s and beyond.[3]

Cox also discusses three possibilities. First, there might be a broadening of American hegemony and international economic leadership along the lines advocated by the Trilateral Commission, that is to encompass Western Europe and Japan. Such a hegemony would reflect the interests of transnational capital and associated skilled and professional labour. It would require the internationalisation of the state, and the spread of liberal frameworks of thought. A second possibility is a world fragmented into regional economic spheres. This world would be non-hegemonic. A third possibility is of a Third World-based counter-hegemony which succeeds in establishing some form of a New International Economic Order. Our discussion of North–South relations in chapter 14 concluded that the Third World was too varied, weak and divided to seriously challenge the leading capitalist states, and undermine or significantly change the hegemonic arrangements in the global political economy. However, such counter-hegemonic ideas might limit the extension of the type of hegemony advocated by the Trilateralists. Indeed Cox claims, 'In the world-hegemonic model, hegemony is more intense and consistent at the core, and more laden with contradictions at the periphery.'[4]

In the rest of this chapter we shall speculate on and consider several scenarios of which the transnational one is given most attention, since in some respects it appears to be the most likely. This is akin to that described by Cox as the Trilateral one, but it does not correspond to the idea of the end of the nation-state or the optimistic representation of the sovereignty-at-bay model. Rather, as was pointed out in chapters 7, 10 and 11, the structural power of transnational corporations is bound up with the existence of a world divided into separate nation-states. The other scenarios we consider are the mercantilist/regional one mentioned by both Gilpin and Cox and also two far more pessimistic scenarios: that of a further escalation in the militarisation of the planet and of space, and secondly, that of ecological breakdown. These scenarios will now be examined in more detail, and, where appropriate, the tensions and contradictions they entail will be addressed.

3. TOWARDS A TRANSNATIONAL HEGEMONY?

Certain developments in the 1980s can be interpreted as increasing the likelihood of transnational hegemony. At the same time, there are difficulties which can be identified in these developments. In this section we identify contradictions in, critiques of, and some practical limits to, the realisation of the transnational hegemony scenario.

The recession of the early 1980s was the most severe since that of the 1930s. However the highly mercantilist tendencies associated with the response to the slump of the 1930s have been much more muted in the 1980s: the world economy appears still to be moving, broadly defined, in a more liberal direction. This is despite consistent talk of trade wars, and various forms of sectoral protectionism which Gilpin sees as a major feature of the contemporary international economy.[5]

In the early 1980s a number of power relations were altered: between capital and labour; between transnational capital and national capital; between North and South, and, more specifically between oil-importers and oil-exporters. The severe recession of 1979–82 promoted these shifts partly through creating rising unemployment and a glut of primary products. By contrast, capital became scarce. This was indicated by high real interest rates which particularly hit indebted developing nations. Governments anxious to obtain foreign exchange came under pressure to modify their policies so as to appease the International Monetary Fund (IMF) and to attract investment and finance from transnational firms. Even developed countries, such as France, had to alter their policies in a more monetarist direction.

The importance of the recession stemmed not so much from its immediate effects as from the way it contributed to a cumulative process in which the social forces associated with transnationalisation gained in strength and credibility. This development can be highlighted if we compare the prevailing social forces and frameworks of thought which governed state–economy relations throughout the Organisation for Economic Cooperation and Development (OECD) countries during the period from the 1950s up to the early 1970s. These forces centred on coalitions between mainly national capital and labour, with the state steering the mixed economy. This was practised through various national mixtures of welfarism, Keynesianism and corporatism. During the 1970s the hegemony of these arrangements was challenged. Inflation and unemployment soared, growth rates declined, and worries about resource scarcity and the broader governability of the world economy preoccupied the leaders of the largest capitalist economies. These worries even involved doubts about the appropriateness and viability of liberal democracy.

In the early 1980s, monetarist and pro-market ideas came to prevail in policy. Governments were increasingly reluctant to let budget deficits rise during recession. The more general promotion of a pro-market approach was associated with the Reagan administration, although ironically, in its readiness to let the United States budget deficit and borrowing soar, it differed from most of the members of the OECD. More generally, slower growth meant that it was much more difficult for states simultaneously to finance welfare and military expenditures, as well as sectoral support schemes, without provoking a fiscal crisis. The notion of the fiscal crisis of the state was first developed in the early 1970s by James O'Connor with the major capitalist states in mind.[6]

Since O'Connor wrote, many of the capitalist states have succeeded in lowering popular expectations of increased living standards and welfare provision without provoking a legitimation crisis, while slowing the growth or even reducing the share of the budget deficit as a percentage of gross national product (GNP). However, other types of budgetary crisis deepened, such as that for the European Economic Community. The latter case was a legacy of the national-Keynesian phase of post-war growth, since the Common Agricultural Policy was both highly interventionist and protective of national capital. Fiscal crisis was most evident in the Third World where tax revenue was adversely affected by lower commodity prices, while the burden of government spending was raised through higher interest rates on foreign debts. Such countries were driven to cut government expenditure plans and sell off public sector assets (privatisation). In Latin America this was happening in the late 1980s as a result of efforts to mitigate the debt crisis by means of debt-for-equity deals. This type of structural fiscal crisis can be contrasted with that in the United States in the 1980s, which was, in effect, a product of huge cuts in taxes and a large military build-up, without substantial corrective action to reduce other government expenditures.

Privatisation can, in some senses, be seen as one response to the fiscal crisis of the state. However, it can be seen at a deeper level, as extending the power of markets, and the power of capital relative to that of the state. Since the early 1980s, privatisation has been increasing in developed countries, notably in Britain, which has been a trend-setter in this regard. Indeed, the United Kingdom's policies have consistently promoted transnational hegemony. A crucial aspect of British policy was to encourage the growth of 'property-owning democracy', by widening popular share ownership to levels approaching those in the United States, and thereby to increase the political support for capitalism. (This is the other side of the coin to Prime Minister Thatcher's stated aim of eradicating socialism in Britain.) In addition, the selling off of publicly-owned companies by stock market flotation has extended the degree of foreign ownership of UK-based companies. In the United States case, privatisation may come to be seen as one way of easing the process of domestic adjustment associated with reducing the Federal deficit. Proposals for privatisation in America have included the selling of Federal land and resources, prisons, and even the contracting-out of welfare administration. Thus despite slow growth, the fiscal crisis and the methods used in its resolution, may have served to increase, rather than to reduce, capitalist hegemony. In this process, labour has become increasingly marginalised in economic policy matters in the major capitalist nations: higher unemployment and industrial restructuring have helped to give capital the upper hand.

Despite an increase in the use of certain trade barriers, there has been a striking liberalisation of capital and exchange markets during the past two decades. The result has been a huge increase in capital flows and in financial interdependence. Increased global economic integration was promoted by the rise in foreign investment. However, a rise in capital flows can create problems for the realisation of the transnational hegemony scenario. The size and volatility of these flows in the 1980s made for exchange rate instability which in turn fuelled demands for protection. Such instability contrasts with the heyday of the Bretton Woods system in the 1950s and 1960s. Now the capitalist world economy is both more integrated and more unstable than in the era of the post-war boom.

These developments highlighted the way in which bank lending may have gone beyond the bounds of prudence: that is, to the point where the stability of the international financial system was put at risk. In less-developed countries such as Brazil, inequitable growth has led to heightened class conflict and political instability. If such tendencies spread, transnational capital may find an increasing number of such countries politically unattractive for their foreign investments. The smaller the proportion of the world that is open and attractive to transnationals, the more limited is their structural power.

In response to widespread concern about global economic stability, many writers have noted that there is a need for the major capitalist nations to coordinate their macroeconomic policies (broadly defined) and aid programmes in order to ensure consistent growth in the world economy. However, for most of the 1970s and 1980s the consistency goal generally eluded them. Differing priorities and concerns for national autonomy, as well as the temptations to free ride were frequently cited as causes for this. Another cause, often cited by realists and others, was the decline in the hegemonic power of the United States, and a shift in American orientations towards the rest of the world. This shift, it is argued, involved a repudiation of the universalist concerns of the founders of the Bretton Woods system, to a more self-regarding nationalist perspective, placing American interests before those of global economic management. What was needed, according to many theorists, was a collective international authority which had the power to create the political conditions for effective coordination and policy consistency.[7]

In effect, this debate perceived a growing lack of congruence between the 'world economy', with its tendencies to promote ever-greater levels of economic integration, and an 'international political system' composed of many rival states. For liberals, the question is how can a political system be made to operate so as to realise the global welfare gains from interdependence? For realists, the question is how can global interdependence be managed so as to allow for national welfare and autonomy?

Both of these positions are, however, ultimately premissed on the idea of an *international* system, that is one in which the major actors are states. However, as our discussion of transnationalisation suggests, states are by no means the only important actors. Indeed, the very operation of transnational firms creates the need to rethink some basic concepts of political economy, such as comparative advantage, power and authority. We have already seen, in chapter 7, how the phenomenon of transnationalisation goes with a range of social forces, and creates what we called the *internationalisation of authority*. We have also seen how the links between the elites who steer such enterprises and their counterparts in government and international organisations, are developing and intensifying. As the handling of the debt crisis has illustrated, such tendencies towards the further internationalisation of authority can involve commercial banks and international organisations, as well as the representatives of national governments. What has changed, however, is that organised labour is increasingly excluded from these political processes and discussions.

In consequence it may be possible to speak of a proto-international state. By this we do not simply mean the idea of a collective state apparatus, since our concept relates to what might be termed the 'extended state', that is one in which the forces of state and civil society are fused. In this construct, the internationalisation of the state would correspond to the internationalisation of some aspects of civil society, and the emergence of some type of nascent global culture. As any student of liberal democratic politics will know, there are conflicts and divisions within civil society, and these are frequently reflected and represented in the political arena. We do not wish to suggest that the social forces which are represented in the formal and informal political arenas which might constitute this proto-state are in complete harmony or agreement. Nor do we wish to suggest that they merely reflect domestic civil societies. In a global political economy beset by conflicts and contradictions, there is no simple or smooth solution to international problems. However, in so far as the political perspectives associated with transnational capital gain the dominant voice in such forums, we might argue that what is emerging is not simply an internationalised state, but a 'transnationalised' one.

Even if transnational interests were to predominate in such processes, in practice there are divisions within the ranks of the transnational corporations. For example, there are differences between firms in finance, and production and extraction (although vertically-integrated companies in extractive industries may be involved in both production and extraction). Corporations in the latter categories have more reason to take a long-term view than transnational banks which are heavily involved in short-term loans and deposits. Freedom of capital flows, which is associated with volatile exchange rates, may suit international banks more than transnational corporations in manufacturing. However, even the latter may be forced to take a short-term view because of fears of takeovers (for example, through the widespread use of 'junk bonds' in the United States in the 1980s). The struggles within the ranks of transnational capital take place both within and between nations. It is resolved in different ways, in some cases promoting conglomeration, or even a fusion of financial and industrial capital. Each of these struggles and alliances is premissed on the need to survive in the international marketplace, where competition is often intense. Such divisions would militate against a coherent political coalition of transnational capital, even if one fraction became temporarily dominant. Further, many transnational firms retain, in varying degrees, a special relationship with, and sometimes, loyalty to, their parent state. This has been traditionally the case for Japanese companies, and very few transnationals are likely, at least in the next decade, to become truly cosmopolitan and global in nature.

Let us now discuss two important critiques of the transnational hegemony scenario. These critiques may serve to rally political opposition to further transnationalisation and to limit a movement towards an increase in the structural power of internationally-mobile capital.

The apparent excesses and even irrationality of unrestrained markets may lead to doubts about the wisdom of following pro-market policies. Thus what might re-emerge is a statist-mercantilist critique of the rationality of the international market and the dominance of a strict financial orthodoxy akin to that which Karl Polanyi discussed as a part of the 'Great Transformation' of the 1930s. (Elements of this type of critique are also taken up by left-wing writers.) Just as the floating rates of the 1930s came to be seen as chaotic, so might the floating rates of the 1980s. In addition, the effects of monetarist and IMF-sponsored policies may be seen as divisive and inequitable. Severe austerity programmes may not just provoke a reaction to the dominant monetarist and pro-market ideas, they may also trigger off extreme political instability in a range of countries.

The above critique can be seen as double-sided in that, on the one hand, global markets are seen as chaotic, and on the other, they are seen as threatening national sovereignty and cultural integrity. Nationalists also object to the transfer of formal political authority to international organisations, and resent the often shadowy coordination of the financial policies of the major capitalist nations.

A second kind of critique of markets would concern the inequitable outcomes they produce. Competition by governments to attract capital may raise the share of capital, and reduce the share of labour in national income. Further, the tax and other concessions to transnational corporations may reinforce rather than reduce the capital-intensive and labour-saving bias which is often attributed to these firms. As a result of these tendencies transnational companies may seem better for creating output growth than employment. The intensive, rather than extensive, patterns of growth which have been associated with the trans-nationalisation process can be criticised by those who prioritise high employment as a welfare goal.

4. THE NATIONAL-MERCANTILIST SCENARIO

Mercantilists justify their arguments against the extension of economic interdependence favoured by most transnational corporations mainly on the grounds of national security, but also for other cultural and political reasons. In order to assure security such states may attempt to restrict the operations of transnational firms and, more generally, trade and capital flows. Labour flows may be curtailed for reasons of cultural xenophobia and political stability. A preference for nationally-owned production will be especially strong for 'strategic' industries. Here very strict controls may be applied, effectively preventing transnationalisation. However, the economies of scale in research and development in arms and other forms of 'strategic' production are often so great as to make international collaboration increasingly necessary. Even so military–industrial complex can be seen as at the centre of a national-capitalist coalition to rival that of internationally-mobile capital, in a given nation.

As we saw in chapter 8, there are forces making for growing militarisation in a world with many states. What this implies is there may be a significant contradiction between the transnationalisation trend and that of militarisation. The spread of arms increases the risk of economic disruption as well as decreasing the size of the market for other forms of transnational production.

More generally, a source of instability threatening to transnational firms arises from tensions between states which lead to war and the threat of war. On the one hand, transnationals benefit from being able to play off one government against another and from the competition by governments to attract foreign investment. On the other hand, they want this competition to remain peaceful unless perhaps they are major arms producers. Thus apart from tensions between industrial and financial capital, there are conflicts of interest between transnationals engaged in arms production and their 'civilian' counterparts.

The problem of political instability for transnationals is compounded by the fact that, in black Africa for example, a fundamental problem is the relatively underdeveloped or even unattainable condition of national and social integration. Civil wars and tribal rivalries are evidence of this. This lack of national cohesion is also a problem for transnational hegemony because order and relatively efficient government are necessary conditions for the security of their long-term investment. As a result, certain parts of Africa are becoming marginal to the interests of much transnational capital and indeed, to the strategic interests of the major powers.

Despite these contradictions, the sum of the transnational pressures we have discussed in this book implies that substantial regionalisation of the global political economy is unlikely. The financial, technological and foreign investment links between Japan, Europe and North America are stronger than ever before. In the 1980s Japan became much more transnational as its firms reacted to the rise in the yen and its financial institutions sent surplus Japanese savings abroad. In the regionalisation scenario Latin America is often seen as in the United States economic sphere-of-interest. However, the European and Japanese direct investment stake was, by the mid-1980s, rising faster than that of America in this region. Japanese banks were major lenders to the Mexican government. Cross-investments of this type were also to be found in Africa (often seen as in the European sphere of influence) and Asia and the Far East (often viewed as in Japan's sphere). Perhaps the major gap to be filled was Western investment in Japan. This was growing during the 1980s, despite bureaucratic and nationalist obstruction. The pressures of capital accumulation for most transnational companies are such that they need to be active in all major areas of the world. For example, if European firms were limited to the region of Europe and Africa, they would generally be unable to fully realise economies of scale, especially in research and development. In other words, with the exception of the disintegrative forces associated with a range of security complexes and nationalist blocs, the major and dominant trend is towards a more integrated global economy. This is still the case despite evidence of attempts, for example, to organise Euro-mercantilist responses to the Japanese and American technological challenge in the 1980s.

5. MILITARISATION AND CATASTROPHE

The growing number of weapons and their availability, including nuclear weapons in some developing nations, raises the spectre of nuclear and chemical, as well as conventional war. Indeed mustard gas was used in the Iran–Iraq War of the 1980s for the first time since the Great War of 1914–18. The very length and duration of this war is a terrible testimony to the shared interests of many countries in supplying both sides with arms. For example, in 1987 China supplied long-range missiles to Iran which enabled it to attack shipping in the Persian Gulf despite a massive United States naval presence.

At the superpower level, the possibility of a more destabilised nuclear balance has been raised with respect to the Strategic Defence Initiative, as well as technical improvements in other nuclear weapons systems which have reduced reaction time and thus increased the temptation of one side to consider taking first-strike action against the other. Even if the superpowers succeed in bringing this instability under greater political control through arms agreements, the risk of nuclear war will continue. This is particularly the case in the Third World, where the risks will increase if further proliferation takes place. Even if nuclear exchanges were confined to a few countries, it would almost certainly adversely affect other countries through environmental degradation and nuclear fall-out. The notion of a nuclear desert is the ultimate example of this.

If it could be safely assumed that leaders had full information about the costs and benefits of war, and that they would therefore make rational decisions about whether to fight, this horrifying scenario would be much less likely. However, in the light of the perverse expectations at the outbreak of World War I (that the war would end quickly), the megalomaniacal dreams of a Hitler, the ambitions of a Shah of Iran or a Saddam Hussein (the Iraqi leader who started the Iran–Iraq war), it would be optimistic to regard these assumptions as plausible. Rather, given that there have been more than 160 wars since 1945, recent history would suggest that a pessimistic scenario is all too likely, at least in the Third World. Indeed, as was noted in chapter 8, there seems to be little prospect of war taking place between the leading states, in contrast to the strong probability of repeated outbreaks of war in the Third World. Such wars however, might trigger an escalation of conflict between the superpowers, and have a range of dangerous side-effects for the developed countries.

A verdict on the likelihood of global and regional wars that relies only on established perspectives may err on the side of optimism. The current versions of neo-realism, public choice and much Marxist writing usually contain some notion of the rational actor, that is a micro- as opposed to a macro-rationality. For Marxists, the capitalist system as a whole is beset by contradictions, or a macro-irrationality, even though many agents such as firms are assumed to be rationally pursuing their interests at the micro-level. For neo-realists like Waltz, each state in the anarchic inter-state system acts much like a firm in a market structure. Overall, however, the system is beyond rational control. Even apart from limits to systemic rationality there may be irrationality at the level of state, group or individual actors. In particular, 'rational action' may be impossible because of limited knowledge or short time-horizons, such that it almost inevitably ignores some long-term effects.

On a slightly more optimistic note, certain limits to the spread of militarisation were noted in chapter 8, notably cultural and economic ones. In a range of countries, driven by concern over the effects of high military expenditures on economic performance, there appear to be the stirrings of attempts to cut back on armaments and armed forces: China has cut its army by over one million, and the post-Brezhnev leadership in the Soviet Union seems to have favoured attempts at negotiating arms agreements so as to curtail the growth of military spending. Also, in so far as the United States' military build-up is associated with low productivity growth, high interest rates and a huge trade deficit, a range of interests in and outside of the America are pressing for cuts in United States military expenditures. On the other hand, if substantial cuts in domestic military expenditures are made, the superpowers may bolster attempts to export arms to the Third World, in order to maintain their economies of scale in certain types of military production.

6. ECOLOGICAL CRISIS

Whereas military crises are likely to be sudden and dramatic, environmental crises are apt to build up slowly over decades, although sudden dangers to the environment can occur as a result of nuclear accidents, chemical spillage and other catastrophes. Other threats stem from the long-term effects of nuclear testing above and below ground, despite international conventions purporting to control such experiments.

The relentless process of deforestation, the burning of fossil fuels, and the proliferation of aerosol cans which progressively serve to reduce the earth's ozone layer threaten to produce major climactic changes some time in the next century. For peasants desperate for fuel, for firms anxious to make swift profits, and for governments intent on re-election within a few years, these long-term environmental dangers seem remote. The problem can be seen as one of insufficiently long time-horizons. It can also be seen as an example of the free-rider problem with governments tempted to leave action on acid rain and deforestation to others.

Deforestation and the spread of deserts can be seen as hingeing on the extreme inequalities of power and wealth in the Third World. Peasants cannot afford to buy fuel and thus cut down trees. This allows the desert to spread. Some transnational firms contribute to the deforestation problem in their race to exploit natural resources, such as those in Amazonia. The Brazilian government, intent on rapid industrialisation, has cooperated with such firms, and has itself cleared out the indigenous Amazonians to prepare the way for the companies.

In the Brazilian and Indian cases discussed in chapters 11 and 14, the thirst for industrialisation was linked to the realist-mercantilist concept of strategic industries. These are in turn related to each nation's quest for regional power status. On this basis the next Chernobyl might well be in the Third World. It could even be at holy Varanasi (Benares) on the river Ganges where the nuclear plant has acquired the status of a sacred cow. Indian engineers have admitted that it is never likely to make a profit, and will probably need indefinite state subsidies. Ironically, many religious Indians believe that the Ganges can soak up and purify any amount of material and spiritual pollution. Further, nuclear accidents do not simply arise from power stations. This was illustrated in a tragic case in Brazil in 1987. Radioactive canisters from a closed-down medical centre became the deadly playthings of children.

In developed countries there are various interests, some of them transnational, which oppose policies which protect the environment. For example, producers of artificial fertilisers and pesticides do not wish to see a shift towards an organic (as opposed to inorganic) agriculture. However, it is now well known that the products of these firms have been poisoning the soil, reducing humus content and polluting rivers and lakes. In addition, the kind of intensive inorganic agriculture promoted by these firms is resulting in dramatic soil erosion in developed countries such as the United States, as well as in some developing nations.

As Jon Bennett points out, the quest for short-run profits in agriculture has self-defeating long-term consquences. Intensive agriculture, based upon continual planting of cash crops and the heavy use of chemical fertilisers may maximise short-term output but it reduces the long-term fertility of the soil. In addition, there is a tendency, particularly in the United States, to use what is called called crop monoculture, in effect growing acre upon acre of the same product. The new agriculture is based upon one or two seed strains, thus narrowing the genetic base of American crops. The new seed varieties, whilst productive in the short term, are less resistant to disease. All of this leads to disturbances in the local plant and wildlife ecosystem, and creates the need for chemical pesticides. Also Bennett observes, 'genetically uniform harvests cannot be replanted the next year ... [creating] ... greater dependence on seed companies.' Apart from being capital-intensive, this form of agriculture absorbs large amounts of energy, mainly in the form of petroleum. Bennett notes, 'The energy required to feed one person in the USA is more than 310 gallons of petroleum a year.'[8] Hence a variety of firms, many of them transnational, have a vested interest in the continuation of intensive agriculture. These interests cover a range of industries: food marketing, seed companies, chemical firms and oil corporations.

Another example of the power of vested interests is that of power stations and utilities, chemical firms and heavy industry, whose costs would be increased if they were forced to cut emissions which contribute to pollution and acid rain. On the other hand, some firms, including transnational corporations in manufacturing, could easily adjust to environmental measures, even producing the equipment for reducing pollution. Firms engaged in mineral extraction are after profits this century rather than ensuring mineral supplies well into the next century. An example of this is in the exploitation and development of North Sea oil and gas, where the firms involved have favoured rapid extraction of reserves, at least when oil prices have been high.

Perhaps the most short-term profit orientation is that linked to speculative finance, such as that which helped to generate the financial conditions for the debt crisis of the early 1980s. In this context, countries which need to finance their debts are under severe pressure to obtain foreign exchange by the swiftest means possibile. This may mean, as in the Brazilian case, an acceleration in the wholesale destruction of the ecology of large areas, as in Amazonia, to obtain the needed finance.

None the less, political pressures on environmental issues, while minimal in developing countries, are building up in the industrialised countries. Green Parties and environmentalist networks have sprouted, and the literature on ecological issues has begun to flourish. Some ecological organisations operate internationally, such as Greenpeace and Friends of the Earth.

Tighter environmental regulations, such as bans on leaded petrol, are being adopted. The United States Congress passed a Bill in 1987 requiring all aid projects to which America contributes to be monitored for environmental effects. If damaging effects are found then American funds must be withheld. This applies not just to bilateral United States aid but to the World Bank in which the USA has a 20 per cent stake. In 1987 the World Bank announced its intention to set up an environmental department and to employ more specialists in this area. Hopefully a similar initiative will also arise within the European Community. West Germany has taken unilateral action in making payments to East European countries, especially East Germany, on condition that they reduce the emissions which result in acid rain. It is rational for suffering countries to pay the offenders so long as the payments are less than the value placed on the environmental effects which are to be eliminated.

This type of solution will encounter the free-rider problem when a given group of countries are victims of developments in some other country or group of countries. For example the destruction of the Amazon forest is likely to have (climactic) repercussions on countries in the Northern Hemisphere. The organising of payments on a collective basis, and agreement over the respective contributions of each party will be difficult. In general, the lead will have to come from the richer developed countries given the lack of financial resources in developing nations and their obsession with industrialisation. Indeed, some developing countries have welcomed foreign investment in polluting industries so that they are not likely to take environmental measures without 'environmental aid' from developed countries. This might be facilitated by an extension of the United Nations' activity in this direction.

The process of depletion of resources may well affect the balance of power between countries in the next century. Already some developing nations have become increasingly dependent on food imports from North America. The United States has been able to exert influence on countries like Egypt and Mozambique because of their need for food aid. Both of these countries once had strong links to the Soviet Union which, of course has to import grain from North America. However, the potential for food as an American political weapon in the next century could be jeopardised by soil erosion, and climactic change, even if other countries fail to overcome their food deficits by increasing their own production. Soil erosion in the United States is now so developed that 'By 1985, it was estimated that the country had irrevocably lost a third of its valuable topsoil, primarily through the cutting of hedgerows and natural woodland borders.'[9] Some parts of the Soviet Union are also badly affected by such erosion.

The implication of this is that environmentally sound policies now may have a political pay-off in the next country. Unfortunately, social and political time-horizons tend to be much too short for this point to carry much weight. One of the reasons for this relates to a wider and more insidious influence which pervades modern capitalism. This influence, what can be called that of the commoditisation of culture, is promoted, with significant impact in the Third World, by transnational corporations. Commoditisation is linked to the widespread adoption of values which favour consumption now rather than later. In so far as such values shape social consciousness and the political agenda, politicians will be inclined to prefer measures which maintain or boost consumption of goods, services and hence the environmental inputs upon which they depend. This depletion of the environment can be related to a cultural contradiction of capitalism first identified by Fred Hirsch. He argued, in *The Social Limits to Growth*, that the competitive, individualistic and short-term outlook typical of modern capitalist societies, allied to the encouragement to consume today and pay later tends to undermine the very cultural and social resources which are needed for capitalism to succeed in the long term. These resources of the work ethic, the need to save and conserve for the future, and a sense of social obligation as in the provision of public goods all constitute conditions of existence for the capitalist system. Hirsch suggested that capitalism, in its early stages, was able to benefit from the moral legacy of feudalism and Christianity with their systems of rights and obligations. Consumerism and the breaking of traditional bonds meant that this moral legacy, like the environment, was in danger of rapidly becoming depleted.[10]

7. ETHICAL ISSUES AND THE GLOBAL POLITICAL ECONOMY

The choice between alternative scenarios partly involves a choice between different values. Both the transnational and mercantilist scenarios prioritise material strength and affluence. The mercantilist tradition, *à la* List, also stresses the need for the cultural integrity of a country to be protected and developed, in part because this will have a long-term material payoff in terms of more advanced productive forces and heightened national control over economic development.[11]

The rationale for transnational hegemony is centred on a particular concept of economic efficiency, and an associated concept of political order. Such order is seen as a necessary underpinning for profitable capital accumulation. This is presumed to serve the material interests of consumers, and to provide them with a means of self-actualisation and creation of personal identity through consumption. Consumption is also seen in this perspective as an expression of achievement, that is making money. Reference to efficiency is commonplace in the context of competition in international trade. It is also central in, for example, International Monetary Fund diagnoses and policy recommendations which tend to identify the attainment of efficiency with reliance on the market mechanism.

Such references to efficiency tend to gloss over the question of 'efficiency for whom?' Productive efficiency may be achieved but the appropriateness of the products may be questionable. For example, the successful promotion of cigarettes in the Third World by the tobacco transnationals has led to a massive increase in lung cancer. Even where the products (such as of cattle ranching in the Amazon) are considered appropriate their production may have adverse environmental implications which are overlooked (such as deforestation and soil exhaustion in Amazonia). Thus the concept of efficiency requires specifying the relevant time-horizon, as well as who benefits and who loses from its application. Allocative efficiency presupposes a given distribution of income which sets the pattern of demand. Reliance on market forces may 'efficiently' produce goods and services which are very unequally distributed. Further, the achievement of productive efficiency may serve to maintain and generate extreme inequalities of income and wealth.

The mercantilist perspective, stressing national autonomy, independence and power may be associated with pride in the national culture. For example, in China critics of the Communist Party's open door policies have expressed a fear of 'spiritual pollution'. This fear, whilst also reflecting the vested interests of Party bureaucrats, is part of a wider nationalist reaction to transnational corporations and foreign influence. These have been widely interpreted as undermining the cultural integrity of nations, and/or preventing the formation of a coherent common culture and national identity in emerging nations. In addition they are often seen as undermining the possibility of national control over economic development and national security. However, the stress on the nation may overshadow the concern for equity both within and beyond the nation, as well as for the welfare of other nations whom their actions may affect. It may lend itself to militarisation in an atavistic form, inimical to democracy and cultural pluralism. Indeed, it might be asserted that both the transnational and mercantilist perspectives place democracy and popular participation low on their list of priorities.

The transnational and mercantilist perspectives are the dominant ones in today's global political economy, and each is vying for hegemony. What are the prospects for a counter-hegemony based in an alternative set of concepts and concerns? Such an alternative, to be successful, must identify and deal with perceived problems such as militarisation and the excesses and inequity of the market-place. It must have a material basis and institutional expression which are able to go beyond purely national contexts. There are prototypes for such transnational, counter-hegemonic networks. Organisations like Amnesty International, Greenpeace, European Nuclear Disarmament and the other peace movements, Intermediate Technology, Oxfam, and the more informal Live Aid come to mind in this respect. However, they are often too specialised (an exception to this would be the Transnational Institute), too small or too temporary and lacking in resources. Moreover, they tend to have weak links with potential allies in the trades unions and socialist parties.[12]

For a counter-hegemony based upon ethical, democratic and ecological values to have a chance of being successful, it would require more material and institutional power. This might, for example, be partly provided through an institution which is embedded in the civil society of many states such as the Catholic Church or the more decentralised Islamic faith. In each case, however, significant changes in organisation and practice would be necessary for these institutions to challenge the dominant or hegemonic forces in the global political economy. In addition, counter-hegemonic groups and institutions would probably have to create a grand, transnational coalition in order to synergise their potential. Given that religion can divide as well as unite, the growth of inter-faith groups, such as the World Council of Churches, may be a condition for the realisation of such a coalition, as would links to elements in the established political parties of the centre and the left.

Essential to the realisation of this potential would be success in education, as well as in publicity and use of the media. The success of the Live Aid initiative of 1985–87 suggests considerable potential here. However, this type of popular, transnational educational appeal would have to be continued on a more regular and systematic basis, stressing the long-term and global nature of poverty and hunger. As some critics of the Live Aid programme pointed out, malnutrition does not simply exist in Ethiopia and the Sudan, it is also a serious problem in some wealthy countries, such as the United States. In the US case, malnutrition is mainly caused by the over-consumption of unhealthy junk foods, as well as there being evidence of starvation.

Technological developments, while in many ways bolstering trans-national hegemony, have sometimes opened up other possibilities, for example community radio stations and the expansion in the number of television channels, catering for different viewer constituencies. The above-mentioned groups and organisations might come together to have their own satellite broadcasting channels. The major problem for this form of counter-hegemony would be raising enough capital to launch their programmes. A second would be to gain the involvement of workers' organisations in their projects. Workers' organisations are usually narrowly materialistic, with short-term time-horizons focused on increasing wages. What would need to be cultivated is a wider concern with democratic procedures, the local community and the international environment, as well as an educational forum premissed upon a critique of the wider consumer culture. This would of course be opposed by the transnational corporations who are actively attempting to modify educational and mass media institutions for their own ends.

An alternative hegemony would need a foothold in productive enterprises, as well as control over research capacities. For example, if the cooperative movement could be transnationalised, and build links with organisations like Intermediate Technology then this requirement would be partly met. It would also require making links with those established political parties ready to pay serious attention to counter-hegemonic concerns, without simply trying to coopt them for obvious political gain. In practice some attention to environmental concerns has begun in large established parties in Western Europe and North America. A counter-hegemony is unlikely to succeed unless it can make major inroads into some large established organisations. Relying only on a series of small, recently created bodies is not enough.

8. AN AGENDA FOR STUDY

Our comments in the previous sections are somewhat speculative. A lack of political economy research on ethical and ecological issues is one reason why this is the case. While we think that political economy research needs to pay more attention to global linkages, some linkages have received more attention than others. Links between trade and money have gained more attention since the emergence of the debt crisis. The rise of OPEC and the oil price increases of the 1970s led to an examination of linkages between energy and security, energy and North–South relations and the beginnings of some consideration of long-term resource questions. However, it is noteworthy that such research was in response to a threat to the established interests of the wealthy and powerful groups, classes and nations. However, many of the latter studies, for example the Club of Rome-sponsored, *The Limits to Growth*, were conspicuous by their lack of an integrated political economy approach to resource questions.[13] None the less, also in this period there was a growth in research on transnational corporations often linked to questions of international inequality and the autonomy of national policies. Our suggestion is that such topics need to be connected with the burgeoning literature on militarisation, and ecological problems.

In sum we feel that the central issues concerning the development of the global political economy in the coming decades will relate to the complex interaction between the forces making for transnationalisation, militarisation and ecological crisis. What in large part will determine the resolution of the contradictions implied in these processes will be a series of political responses at a range of levels, and the synthesis which emerges between them. New research will thus need to reconceptualise the global political economy with these dynamics in mind.

With respect to these substantive questions, we would refer the reader back to some of the issues raised in the Preface and first chapter of this book. These concerned the development and use of the abstractions of 'political' and 'economic', 'international' and 'global' political economy. Liberal conceptions of the 'political' and the 'economic' are often related to notions of economic efficiency: that which is political is often defined in terms of its interference with the operation of the free market. As we pointed out in our Preface, the concept of efficiency, itself built upon a specific concept of economic freedom, is a highly contestable one.[14] The important political issues relate to the questions: 'efficient for whom?'; 'efficient with respect to the use of which resources?', and 'over what time-horizons are the issues understood? A focus on short-term profit maximisation tends to ignore or undervalue the use of, or access to, long-term natural resources. A focus on material aspects of political economy may mean neglect of the effects on different cultures and societies of different types of economic system, and vice versa. This is the crux of the argument in Hirsch's discussion of the 'social limits' to growth.[15]

What is argued, therefore, is the need, not only for a new research agenda, but also for a conceptual retooling. This may also require a paradigm shift, in that the perspectives which are extant were mostly developed before or during the stage of 'national capitalism'. In addition, some of the perspectives understand historical development as a repetitive and cyclical process. Our argument is that in fundamental ways, the global political economy has reached an unprecedented stage of development. The present is not like the past. Today, the security, trade, money, direct investment, communications and cultural dimensions of global interdependence, are such that there is now an integrated *global political economy*, whereas in the past, there was a less complex *international political economy* (and before 1500 a series of regional political economies).

By the same token, the future is unlikely simply to reproduce the tendencies of the present. None the less, in new research, longer time-horizons will need to be incorporated. One kind of concern for the long-term future is embodied in the literature on international regimes. Here the possibilities of future cooperation tend to be examined in a rather managerial and even elitist way. We suggest that more research and theorisation is needed with regard to cooperation not just amongst governments and international elites, but also at intermediate, and at the lower, grass-roots levels. Indeed, these levels are reinforcing, in so far as the agendas of what might be called the international establishments may be changed by popular mobilisation. For example, in West Germany, the political agenda has changed because of the growing influence of the ecological movement. Without such mobilisation, involving groups within and across nations, some environmental issues will not be tackled, or else will be tackled too late.

The changing of the time-horizons of politically dominant groups can go with changes in their conceptions of interest and identity. For example, a growing sense of belonging to 'planet earth' may mean that different peoples identify more strongly with each other and come to see a shared interest in cooperating to generate ecologically sound policies. At the same time a reduced emphasis on consumption as the summation of the definition of self is necessary if time-horizons are to be extended. Crucial to the development of longer time horizons is a reduction in the fear and possibility of war, drought and famine, particularly in Third World contexts. Planning for a future which might never exist appears futile.

The need to cater and plan for a long-term future raises the question: what types of institutions and institutional forms are likely to promote a longer-term view and associated policies? At the level of international institutions, some useful cooperation has been promoted by the World Council of Churches, and also by the United Nations, especially the Children's Fund (UNICEF). One topic of research which might well bring these organisations together might be collaboration in formulating a policy to help African countries to overcome their agricultural problems in the 1990s. In fact the Trilateral Commission, which is largely representative of dominant, though relatively enlightened transnational interests, began to discuss this idea at its 1986 plenary meetings. Such a project would also interest grass-roots organisations such as Oxfam and Live Aid, and could win the participation of ecologically conscious groups such as Friends of the Earth and the Green parties if the approach taken to solve the agricultural crisis were based on organic and sensitive methods.

What this suggests is more research is needed into the ways in which different ideological and political groups can cooperate, and under what conditions, to create broader-based transnational coalitions of interest, premissed on longer time-horizons. Having said this, the hegemonic orientation is still towards the short term and is almost exclusively materialist. This is the case in communist as well as capitalist countries. Little is known or is understood in the West about how far such changes are possible in Eastern Europe, although there is some evidence that peace groups have formed (often under state supervision) and new political clubs are being permitted in the Soviet Union. How far will these developments open up the possibility of a greater stress on human needs as opposed to military production, and on an environmentally-sensitive form of agricultural and industrial development?

As we have explained earlier, the feasibility of an alternative approach may depend on the development of a more comprehensive intellectual apparatus, and the development of research technology to back this up. It will also require more popular control over the direction of research so that the market power of large firms or the political power of the military-industrial complexes does not restrict and distort the agenda. Most of the current research operates within the orientations dictated by these powerful sets of interests. Our hope is that this book can make a small contribution to the redefinition of the research agenda, and to a wider consideration of the problems and prospects which link together the inhabitants of the earth.

NOTES

1. Robert Gilpin, 'Three Models of the Future', in G. Modelski (ed.), *Transnational Corporations and World Order* (San Francisco, W. H. Freeman, 1979), pp. 353–72.
2. Robert Gilpin, *The Political Economy of International Relations* (Princeton NJ, Princeton University Press, 1987), pp. 397–401.
3. Robert W. Cox, 'Gramsci, Hegemony and International Relations: An Essay in Method', *Millennium* (1983), Vol. 12, No. 2, pp. 162–75.
4. Cox, op. cit., p. 171.
5. Gilpin, *The Political Economy of International Relations*, pp. 401–7.
6. James O'Connor, *The Fiscal Crisis of the State* (New York, St Martin's Press, 1973).
7. Benjamin Cohen, *Organising the World's Money: the Political Economy of International Monetary Relations* (London, Macmillan, 1978).
8. Jon Bennett, with Susan George, *The Hunger Machine* (Oxford, Polity Press/Basil Blackwell, 1987), pp. 182–3.
9. Bennett, op. cit., pp. 181–2.
10. Fred Hirsch, *The Social Limits to Growth* (London, Routledge/Twentieth Century Fund, 1976).
11. Friedrich List, *The National System of Political Economy* (New York, Kelley, 1966).
12. American counterparts to these international groups include the so-called RESULTS groups. On these see Bennett, op. cit., pp. 191–216, 223.
13. Donella L. Meadows et al., *The Limits to Growth: a report for the Club of Rome's project on the predicament of mankind* (London, Pan Books, 1974).
14. On essential contestability see William R. Connally, *The Terms of Political Discourse* (London, Macmillan, 1983) 2nd edition.
15. Hirsch, op. cit.

Index